BIOGRAPHIES AND AUTOBIOGRAPHIES IN MODERN ITALY
A FESTSCHRIFT FOR JOHN WOODHOUSE

LEGENDA

LEGENDA, founded in 1995 by the European Humanities Research Centre of the University of Oxford, is now a joint imprint of the Modern Humanities Research Association and Maney Publishing. Titles range from medieval texts to contemporary cinema and form a widely comparative view of the modern humanities, including works on Arabic, Catalan, English, French, German, Greek, Italian, Portuguese, Russian, Spanish, and Yiddish literature. An Editorial Board of distinguished academic specialists works in collaboration with leading scholarly bodies such as the Society for French Studies and the British Comparative Literature Association.

MHRA

The Modern Humanities Research Association (MHRA) encourages and promotes advanced study and research in the field of the modern humanities, especially modern European languages and literature, including English, and also cinema. It also aims to break down the barriers between scholars working in different disciplines and to maintain the unity of humanistic scholarship in the face of increasing specialization. The Association fulfils this purpose primarily through the publication of journals, bibliographies, monographs and other aids to research.

Maney Publishing is one of the few remaining independent British academic publishers. Founded in 1900 the company has offices both in the UK, in Leeds and London, and in North America, in Boston. Since 1945 Maney Publishing has worked closely with learned societies, their editors, authors, and members, in publishing academic books and journals to the highest traditional standards of materials and production.

EDITORIAL BOARD

Chairman
Professor Martin McLaughlin, Magdalen College, Oxford

Professor John Batchelor, University of Newcastle (English)
Professor Malcolm Cook, University of Exeter (French)
Professor Colin Davis, Royal Holloway University of London
(Modern Literature, Film and Theory)
Professor Robin Fiddian, Wadham College, Oxford (Spanish)
Professor Paul Garner, University of Leeds (Spanish)
Professor Marian Hobson Jeanneret,
Queen Mary University of London (French)
Professor Catriona Kelly, New College, Oxford (Russian)
Professor Martin Maiden, Trinity College, Oxford (Linguistics)
Professor Peter Matthews, St John's College, Cambridge (Linguistics)
Dr Stephen Parkinson, Linacre College, Oxford (Portuguese)
Professor Ritchie Robertson, St John's College, Oxford (German)
Professor Lesley Sharpe, University of Exeter (German)
Professor David Shepherd, University of Sheffield (Russian)
Professor Alison Sinclair, Clare College, Cambridge (Spanish)
Professor David Treece, King's College London (Portuguese)
Professor Diego Zancani, Balliol College, Oxford (Italian)

Managing Editor
Dr Graham Nelson
41 Wellington Square, Oxford OX1 2JF, UK

legenda@mhra.org.uk
www.legenda.mhra.org.uk

John Woodhouse, Oxford, 1990
(Photograph: Paul Lowe)

Biographies and Autobiographies in Modern Italy

A Festschrift for John Woodhouse

Edited by Peter Hainsworth and Martin McLaughlin

LEGENDA

Modern Humanities Research Association and Maney Publishing
2007

Published by the
Modern Humanities Research Association and Maney Publishing
1 Carlton House Terrace
London SW1Y 5DB
United Kingdom

LEGENDA is an imprint of the
Modern Humanities Research Association and Maney Publishing

Maney Publishing is the trading name of W. S. Maney & Son Ltd,
whose registered office is at Suite 1C, Joseph's Well, Hanover Walk, Leeds LS3 1AB

ISBN 978-1-905981-07-6

First published 2007

All rights reserved. No part of this publication may be reproduced or disseminated or transmitted in any form or by any means, electronic, mechanical, photocopying, recording or otherwise, or stored in any retrieval system, or otherwise used in any manner whatsoever without the express permission of the copyright owner

© *Modern Humanities Research Association and W. S. Maney & Son Ltd 2007*

Printed in Great Britain

Cover: 875 Design

Copy-Editor: Dr Avery T. Willis

CONTENTS

	Acknowledgements	ix
	Notes on the Contributors	x
	Tabula Gratulatoria	xii
1	Introduction PETER HAINSWORTH AND MARTIN MCLAUGHLIN	1

PART I: GENERAL ISSUES AND SIGNAL CASES

2	The Public and the Private in Modern Italian Literature: The Case of Montale PETER HAINSWORTH	8
3	The Battle of the Biographers: Primo Levi and 'Life-Writing' ROBERT S. C. GORDON	23

PART II: D'ANNUNZIO AND OTHER *FIN DE SIÈCLE* FIGURES

4	Enrico Nencioni: An Italian Victorian GUILIANA PIERI	38
5	Pescara and the Abruzzo in the Imagination of Gabriele D'Annunzio GIANNI OLIVA	55
6	British Material for the Biography of a Tuscan: Llewelyn Lloyd (1879–1949) T. GWYNFOR GRIFFITH	79
7	Italo Svevo: Journalism and the Life of a Writer ANTONELLA BRAIDA	97

PART III: SELF-IMAGES IN FASCIST CULTURE

8	Intellectual (Auto-)Biography in Bontempelli JON USHER	114
9	Italian War-Correspondents and The Spanish Civil War: Propaganda and Autobiography CHARLES BURDETT	133

PART IV: AUTOBIOGRAPHICAL STRAINS IN CONTEMPORARY ITALIAN WRITING

10 Concessions to Autobiography in Calvino 148
    MARTIN MCLAUGHLIN

11 Umberto Eco: Autobiography into Romance 168
    JANE E. EVERSON

12 The Dummy Interlocutor and Oriana Fallaci's Self-Projection in
    La rabbia e l'orgoglio 188
    JOHN GATT-RUTTER

    Bibliography of Publications by John Woodhouse 205
    Index 211

ACKNOWLEDGEMENTS

The editors are grateful to the Faculty of Medieval and Modern Languages of the University of Oxford for a grant for the translation of Gianni Oliva's essay by Francesca Southerden.

Paul Diffley was initially one of the editors and contributed enormously to planning the volume and getting it moving. We are grateful to him for all his work in those early stages.

Our warm thanks too to Graham Nelson at Legenda, who carried through the final production with remarkable speed, good humour and efficiency.

P.H. & M.M.

NOTES ON THE CONTRIBUTORS

Antonella Braida was Lecturer in Italian at the University of Durham and now teaches Italian at the Université de Franche-Comté. She is particularly interested in the reception of Dante in Britain and is the author of *Dante and the Romantics* (Palgrave, 2004). She co-edited with Giuliana Pieri *Image and Word: Reflections of Art and Literature from the Middle Ages to the Present* (Legenda, 2003).

Charles Burdett is Senior Lecturer in Italian Studies at the University of Bristol. His main research interest is in travel writing and the wider historical and cultural questions that it raises. His *Journeys through Fascism: Italian Travel-Writing between the Wars* (Berghahn) will appear in 2007. He is the editor with Claire Gorrara and Helmut Peitsch, of *European Memories of the Second World War* (Berghahn, 1999) and with Derek Duncan, of *Cultural Encounters: European Travel Writing of the 1930s* (Berghahn, 2002).

Jane Everson is Professor of Italian literature at Royal Holloway, University of London. She is the author of a number of studies on Renaissance narrative poetry including *The Italian Romance epic in the age of Humanism* (OUP, 2001). Her research interests include the history of printing in Italy and adaptations of medieval and Renaissance themes in contemporary Italian literature. She is currently preparing an edition of *Il Mambriano* by Francesco Cieco da Ferrara, and leading a research project on the Italian Academies.

John Gatt-Rutter is Vaccari Professor in Italian Studies at La Trobe University in Melbourne. He has published mainly on twentieth-century Italian writers, including a biography of Italo Svevo (OUP, 1988) and a literary study of Oriana Fallaci (Berg, 1996). Currently his main interest is in biographies and autobiographies of Italian Australians.

Robert S. C. Gordon is Reader in Modern Italian Culture at the University of Cambridge and Fellow of Gonville and Caius College. His recent publications include *Primo Levi's Ordinary Virtues: From Testimony to Ethics* (Oxford, 2001), *Introduction to 20th-Century Italian Literature: A Difficult Modernity* (Duckworth, 2005) and (co-edited with Guido Bonsaver) *Culture, Censorship and the State in 20th-Century Italy* (Legenda, 2005).

T. Gwynfor Griffith is Emeritus Professor of Italian Language and Literature, University of Manchester. His principal research interests are the history of Italian Language, Italian Renaissance Literature, especially Bandello and Trissino, and Italo-Welsh relations. His latest book is *O Hendrefigillt i Livorno* (Gomer, 2000).

Peter Hainsworth is Emeritus Fellow of Lady Margaret Hall, Oxford. His research interests are principally in Petrarch and early Italian poetry and in modern poetry and fiction, with an emphasis on the relationship between literature and Fascism. He co-edited with David Robey the *Oxford Companion to Italian Literature* (OUP, 2002).

Martin McLaughlin is Fiat-Serena Professor of Italian Studies and Fellow of Magdalen College, Oxford. His publications include *Literary Imitation in the Italian Renaissance* (OUP, 1995), *Italo Calvino* (Edinburgh UP, 1998), and he has edited a volume of essays, *Britain and Italy from Romanticism to Modernism* (Legenda, 2000). He has also translated two works by Italo Calvino, *Why Read the Classics?* (Cape, 1999), and *Hermit in Paris* (Cape, 2003), as well as Umberto Eco's essays *On Literature* (Secker and Warburg, 2005).

Gianni Oliva holds the Chair of Italian Literature at the University of Chieti where he heads the Literature and Philology section of the Department of Medieval and Modern Studies. He has worked on D'Annunzio, Verga, Capuana, 'realismo provinciale', Florentine Aestheticism, and, currently, the Rossetti family. He has recently edited the complete works of D'Annunzio.

Giuliana Pieri is Senior Lecturer in the Italian department of Royal Holloway, University of London. Her research interests focus on D'Annunzio, Anglo-Italian cultural and artistic relations, and on Italian crime fiction. She co-edited with Antonella Braida *Image and Word: Reflections of Art and Literature from the Middle Ages to the Present* (Legenda, 2003). She is currently working on representations of Mussolini in Italian sculpture and painting and on the correspondence between the Italian painter and patriot Nino Costa and George Howard, 9th Earl of Carlisle.

Jon Usher is professor of Italian at Edinburgh University. His principal field of research is the re-use of classical authors in fourteenth-century Italy, with a particular focus on Boccaccio and Petrarch. He has also research interests in computers and literature, combinatorial fiction and, most recently, the Italian culture of Walter Savage Landor. For his publications see http://www.casaboccaccio.it/
.

TABULA GRATULATORIA

Richard Andrews, University of Leeds
Zygmunt G. Barański, New Hall, Cambridge
John C. Barnes, University College, Dublin
Guido Bonsaver, Pembroke College, Oxford
Steven Botterill, University of California, Berkeley
Antonella Braida, Besançon
Peter Brand, Edinburgh
Italian Dept, University of Bristol
Bojan Bujic, Magdalen College, Oxford
Charles Burdett, University of Bristol
Nadia Cannata, Università per Stranieri, Siena
Luisa Carrer, Faculty of Medieval and Modern Languages, Oxford
Malcolm Cook, Exeter
Gisela Cooper, TOIA, Oxford
Richard Cooper, Brasenose College, Oxford
Nicholas and Pamela Coote, TOIA, Oxford
Sabrina Damiani, Christ Church, Oxford
Vilma de Gasperin, Jesus College, Oxford
Paul Diffley, Department of Italian, University of Exeter
Marco Dorigatti, St Peter's College, Oxford
Jane Everson, Royal Holloway
Conor Fahy, Ely
Nicola Gardini, St Cross College, Oxford
John Gatt Rutter, La Trobe University, Melbourne
Robert Gordon, Gonville and Caius College, Cambridge
Manuele Gragnolati, Somerville College, Oxford
Gwyn and Paola Griffith, Alderley Edge
Peter Hainsworth, Lady Margaret Hall, Oxford
Robert Hastings, Manchester
Geoffrey Hinton, TOIA, Oxford
Philip Horne, Oxford
Italian Cultural Institute, London
Elizabeth Jeffreys, Exeter College, Oxford
Giulio Lepschy, University College, London
Laura Lepschy, University College, London
John Lindon, University College, London
Valerio Lucchesi, Corpus Christi College, Oxford
Magdalen College Library, Oxford
Martin Maiden, Trinity College, Oxford
Nicholas Mann, University of London
Martin McLaughlin, Magdalen College, Oxford

Eileen A. Millar, Glasgow
Patricia Milner, TOIA, Oxford
Anne Mullen, St Anne's College, Oxford
Graham Nelson, St Anne's College, Oxford
Gianni Oliva, Università di Chieti
Stephen Parkinson, Linacre College
Emilio Pasquini, Università di Bologna
Franca Pellegrini, Christ Church, Oxford
Pembroke College Library, Oxford
Lino Pertile, Dept of Romance Languages and Literatures, Harvard University
School of Languages and European Studies, University of Reading
Giuliana Pieri, Royal Holloway
Jim Reed, Queen's College, Oxford
Denis Reidy, British Library
Brian Richardson, Dept of Italian, University of Leeds
Christina Roaf, Oxford
Ritchie Robertson, St John's College, Oxford
David Robey, University of Reading
Corinna Salvadori Lonergan, Trinity College, Dublin
Michael Sheringham, All Souls, Oxford
Nicoletta Simborowski, Hertford College, Oxford
G. S. Smith, New College, Oxford
Francesca Southerden, Hertford College, Oxford
Eric Southworth, St Peter's College, Oxford
Giuseppe Stellardi, St Hugh's College, Oxford
Emmanuela Tandello, Christ Church, Oxford
Taylor Institution Library, Oxford
John Took, University College, London
Jon Usher, University of Edinburgh
Giancarla Vanoli, Faculty of Medieval and Modern Languages, Oxford
Giles Walker, Oriel College, Oxford
Caroline Waring, St John's College, Oxford
Chris Wells, St Edmund Hall, Oxford
David Wells, Birkbeck College, London
Michelangelo Zaccarello, Università degli Studi di Verona
Diego Zancani, Balliol College, Oxford

CHAPTER 1

Introduction

Peter Hainsworth and Martin McLaughlin

Biography and autobiography are flourishing as never before. Biography in particular is a genre that sells, especially in the UK, and one which supports professional practitioners and which offers academics in the humanities the relatively unusual prospect of producing work that is widely read. At the same time the status of these and other forms of what is now often called life-writing is often felt to be uncertain.[1] Practising biographers plead for academics to take their work seriously. Most theoretical reflection, of which there has been a vast amount since the 1960s, highlights problems inherent in standard practice — the risk of making an individual's life follow the narrative patterns of fiction, the inevitable omission of whole swathes of lived experience, and all the distortions imposed (even in the most honest seeming autobiography) by the retrospective, distanced eye. Not that the questions have impeded the practice. In many cases they have been incorporated into the specific biography or autobiography, so much so that some measure of representation of the biographer or autobiographer engaged in the actual process of writing is now almost routine (see in particular chapters 2 and 3 below).

At least that is broadly speaking the state of affairs in the English-speaking world and in Northern Europe as a whole. Italy is somewhat different. Autobiography and biography have not enjoyed the same widespread success within Italian literary culture or given rise to such theoretical questioning. There are only a few classics of Italian autobiography — those by Cellini, Vico and Alfieri spring to mind — and, compared to England and America, relatively few new ones have been written during the last hundred years or so that have been highly regarded or even widely read. There have been more biographies of Italians of course, and the *Dizionario biografico degli italiani* is comparable in scope and detail with the *Dictionary of National Biography*, but it is still unfinished, and in any case the most read and admired biographies inside and outside the country have tended to be by foreigners, mostly American and English scholars, ranging from E. H. Wilkins on Petrarch to Denis Mack Smith on Mussolini.[2] John Woodhouse's D'Annunzio is the outstanding recent example of work in this tradition, to which should be added his work on Gabriele Rossetti and his recently published biography of General Santi Ceccherini.[3]

It is a tradition which is characteristically pragmatic in approach and liberal in outlook, and which, while being alert to the risks of fictionalisation, tends to shy away from theoretical debate. Its continuing vitality and the force of John Woodhouse's example is evident in this collection of essays by friends, former colleagues and pupils dedicated to a range of figures from Italian culture from the immediate post-Unification years to the present. Most of these figures are creative writers, though not all; most are well-known, though not all. Some have written autobiographically, though none has produced a full-scale autobiography. Several essays concern themselves with filling out these partial autobiographies, or, in other instances, with teasing out concealed autobiographical sub-texts. Rather than attempting psychological analysis and reconstruction of the individual in isolation, the essays prefer to concentrate on how their subjects respond to and are affected by the wider social and political history of the country, and at times play significant roles within it. This too fits well enough with the tradition. Where the volume goes beyond it to a moderate degree is in giving a definite emphasis to general questions of the sort we mentioned initially, though always in relation to the specific context of Italy and specific individuals.

Such general and theoretical questions are raised most prominently in the first section of this quadripartite collection, a section which offers case studies of two of the most well-known twentieth-century Italian writers. In the first chapter Peter Hainsworth focuses on some of the features that distinguish Italian biography and autobiography. He argues that the constructed public self has tended strongly to predominate over the private, individual self throughout the history of Italian literature, although from Dante onwards it has been normal for the literary work to suggest that the private experiences are essential to its very existence. In the twentieth century political and social pressures have strengthened this tendency, though demands for more information to be disclosed are gradually having an effect. Hainsworth proposes as an emblematic and signally important instance the case of Italy's major poet of the century, Eugenio Montale, who himself actively continued the Italian tradition of self-representation in many ways and whose public image has been largely constructed within its terms.

The second case study here concerns Primo Levi. Levi is one of the few Italian prose writers of the post-war years with a worldwide reputation. Two large-scale biographies of him were published in English within weeks of each other in 2002. Robert Gordon examines the contrasting approaches of the two biographers, each working with the conventions of a different narrative genre, and sets them in the developing, self-aware practice of modern biography. He then shows how their narrative choices and the obstacles and risks they find themselves facing are anticipated in various ways in Levi's own autobiographical writings, not least in their self-consciousness and in moments of subsequent self-commentary. Levi, like other writers examined later in the volume, was all too aware of the prominence of biography (writing about others' lives) in his own work, and the problems surrounding such writing, from questions of privacy and potentially artificial narrative shape, to those of causality and ultimate meaning.

The four studies that follow in the Part II are concerned with the late nineteenth and early twentieth centuries, the period of disorientation for the freshly unified country in which decadence and modernisation, patriotic fervour and social unrest seemed to come together all at once, most flamboyantly in the mesmerising figure of Gabriele D'Annunzio. Drawing on unpublished papers and correspondence, Giuliana Pieri reassesses the critic and essayist Enrico Nencioni, D'Annunzio's mentor, who has often been dismissed as a lightweight late romantic. Pieri sees him as taking advantage of the changing cultural possibilities offered to the intellectual in Umbertine Italy to create a distinctive form of artistic and literary essay. It is one that is studiedly aestheticising after the contemporary English manner and which freely incorporates biographical and autobiographical motifs in an attempt to capture the inner spiritual life of its subject. The results may be bizarre by modern standards, but they exerted a significant influence on D'Annunzio, who developed his representations of female beauty in his novels from Nencioni's pseudo-autobiographical reworking of Pre-Raphaelite typologies. Pieri moves beyond Nencioni's biographers' hyperboles to uncover a writer who found in the genre of biography a medium that blended his own aesthetic and ethical ideals.

D'Annunzio himself comes to the fore in Gianni Oliva's exploration of the mythicized and timeless form that his native Abruzzo, whether past or present, assumes in his work, offering regularly both a point of departure and longed-for goal for himself and for his protagonists. Oliva finds a particular importance in the convent of S. Maria del Gesù hear Francavilla, which was acquired by the painter Francesco Paolo Michetti as a refuge for young writers and artists. Here D'Annunzio created some of his impressive evocations of the Abruzzese landscape, although perhaps the most powerful ones (to be found in *Il trionfo della morte*) stem from a summer spent with his mistress, Barbara Leoni, at some distance from Francavilla. Oliva documents the way D'Annunzio's travels in and observations of the Abruzzo landscape and customs are reworked in key episodes of his fiction.

Another figure who emerges from the mixture of Italian and British culture in the early twentieth century is Llewelyn Lloyd. Lloyd was an Italian post-*macchiaiolo* painter of Welsh extraction, the quality of whose work has been increasingly acknowledged by art historians in recent decades. T. Gwynfor Griffith investigates aspects of his life and his antecedents which have remained obscure, beginning with his name. Griffith explores a family history which may be unusual but which is by no means freakish, since it was conditioned by economic and political factors that affected the lives of whole populations in different ways. Writing as a scholarly biographer-detective, he reconstructs piece by piece the fortunes of the family in Wales and the factors lying behind their gradual establishment in Livorno, which began in the second decade of the nineteenth century, before Lloyd's father arrived there in 1859 and a loosening of ties with Wales followed in the next generation.

The cross-cultural theme and this movement between the worlds of commerce and art are continued in Antonella Braida's study of the earlier part of Italo Svevo's career, which she shows is much more coherent and self-constructed than the accepted image of the 'amateur writer' suggests. Opting to review for the Triestine newspaper, *L'Indipendente*, was a deliberate choice in favour of an irredentist organ with an Italian orientation, but one that was also open to English and other European writing which literary journalism in Italy itself largely ignored. Svevo seized the chances he was offered to develop his interest in scientific writers such as

Darwin and in literary Naturalists like Zola, writers ignored by the contemporary Decadent movement. This crucial phase of Svevo's career allowed the writer to develop also his ideas about the need for truthfulness as a basic criterion in fiction in opposition to the aestheticism of D'Annunzio. Braida shows that these early articles and reviews form a crucial stage in his self-construction as a writer.

The two essays that follow and make up the third Part of the volume are concerned with two different forms of autobiographical writing under Fascism. D'Annunzio remains a strong presence in Jon Usher's examination of Massimo Bontempelli's forging of his self-image as a writer in the 1930s. Part of the process was a polemical assault, at some personal risk, on D'Annunzio's status and significance at a time when Fascism had made him into one of its major cultural icons. For Bontempelli and his generation D'Annunzio was a figure who belonged to their youth and had been superseded by Marinetti's Futurism. But by the 1930s Bontempelli had rejected Futurism as well, just as he claimed to have rejected all his past selves in his search to find a new self and a new culture that would be appropriate to the changing times. Bontempelli deploys parodistic strategies to construct an autobiographical commentary on his conversion from the D'Annunzian and Futurist modes as well as on broader shifts in Italian culture.

The second essay in Part III turns from literary individualism to cultural conformism. One of the episodes that was a prelude to Italy's disastrous misfortunes in World War II was its intervention on the Fascist side in the Spanish Civil War. Charles Burdett examines the responses of some reporters for major newspapers to the events they witnessed. Most of these were highly rated at the time, though only the future novelist Guido Piovene is at all well known today. Their despatches show them conforming, enthusiastically it seems, to the regime's propaganda needs, even though one or another might write at some moment about recognising tragically that a dead Communist had also been a human being. Burdett points out that they were almost certainly sincerely committed to the Fascist cause and had the approval of most of their readers. Nor does it seem that many seriously changed their minds later. Certainly after the war only Piovene claimed that he felt compromised by what he had written about Spain. Burdett's account illustrates how nuances of autobiographical introspection can be discerned in what was primarily a propagandistic genre of writing.

The final three chapters, which form Part IV, consider three major recent authors, each quite different from the others, but all raising or engaging with problems of writing about the self in the context of the modern world. Italo Calvino holds personal experience at a distance in most of his many-sided oeuvre and was generally ambivalent about revealing information about himself. Martin McLaughlin looks at those stories (written mostly at moments of personal crisis) in which he does undertake a disguised recreation and reassessment of his past, especially of his formative years and the complex feelings surrounding his memories of his mother and father. In these stories and in the few that he wrote about his partisan experiences, Calvino's quite distinctive emphasis falls on the processes of remembering and forgetting rather than on precise recollection, in other words, on the past as it lives on in the present self, and, in the case of the partisan stories, of the significance of shared historical experience when the world seems to have moved on.

Jane Everson explores autobiographical traces in an author who was born just too late to be part of the partisan war. She examines Umberto Eco's second novel, *Foucault's Pendulum*, one of only two of his fictions to be set in our own times, and shows how its protagonists are embodiments of the author at different phases of his life, especially in terms of his experience of Italy and of the country's political history from the 1960s to the 1980s. She also demonstrates how the intellectual and linguistic interests which Eco explores in the almost contemporary lectures that make up *In Search of a Perfect Language*, resurface in the novel. However, if the playfulness is still evident, there is also a greater sense of the serious dangers that arise when the pursuit of absolute order is not just linguistic but social and political. The combination of the three ingredients of fictional elements, scholarly interests and the author's own lived experience, combine only in this, Eco's darkest novel, dealing as it does with the violent years in Italy between the late 1960s and the mid 1980s, the 'anni di piombo'.

The political sphere comes back with a vengeance in Oriana Fallaci's denunciation of Islam in all its forms in her controversial *La rabbia e l'orgoglio*, written soon after the attack on New York in September 2001. John Gatt-Rutter shows how the adoption of a speaking voice which proclaims itself as that of the author hectoring an ill-defined 'you' (at different moments Fallaci's editor, figures within Islam, the Pope, Western intellectuals and so on), leads not to sincerity but to a kind of monologic theatre. The actual reader and addressee is a spectator, though one the rhetoric of the text aims to convert and incite, whilst those addressed actually have no voice with which to reply. Here first-person writing is anything but a game or literary conundrum; Gatt-Rutter observes that *La rabbia e l'orgoglio* along with all of Fallaci's other works constitutes one enormous autobiographical macrotext, and although here the autobiographical persona exists in exile and in silence, Fallaci's pamphlet is autobiography in the service of invective. Gatt-Rutter concludes with a statement of the need to undertake in reality the kind of dialogue which Fallaci effectively disallows.

This volume offers perspectives on the inflections of biography and autobiography in Italian culture from the late nineteenth century until the dawn of the twenty-first century. It is not, of course, intended to represent a comprehensive survey of the period but it does chart the modulations of life-writing in some of the major literary figures of the time, from D'Annunzio, Svevo and Montale to Primo Levi, Calvino and Umberto Eco. At the same time it shows how biography and the construction of a 'bella (auto-) biografia'[4] remain key concerns in less canonical figures such as Nencioni and Bontempelli, as well as in writers who stand between journalism and literature such as Piovene and Fallaci.

These essays are dedicated to John Woodhouse as a mark of warm friendship and esteem. Not all of them keep to the pragmatic parameters of his own work, flexible though these are, but they all share his deep conviction that the life and work of an author are mutually illuminating and that the literary work is impoverished by being seen solely within terms of a textual universe. John held firmly to that belief at a time when many of his colleagues, especially those a few years younger, thought that the opposite was self-evident. As a dedicated individualist, he may be surprised — we hope pleasurably so — to find that in his pioneering work on D'Annunzio and Calvino, as well as in his work on Renaissance culture, he has pointed the way for much current research in Italian studies.

Notes to Chapter 1

1. For just one instance of the use of the term and its scope, see *Encyclopedia of Life Writing*, ed. by Margaretta Jolly, 2 vols (London: Fitzroy Dearborn, 2001).
2. Ernest Hatch Wilkins, *Life of Petrarch* (Chicago: Chicago University Press, 1961); Denis Mack Smith, *Mussolini* (London: Weidenfeld & Nicholson, 1981).
3. John Woodhouse, *Gabriele D'Annunzio. Defiant Archangel* (Oxford: Clarendon Press, 1998); *Il generale e il comandante. Ceccherini e D'Annunzio a Fiume* (Bologna: Gedit, 2004).
4. Ungaretti's phrase — 'L'autore non ha altra ambizione [...] se non quella di lasciare una sua bella biografia' [the author has no other ambition (...) than to leave behind a fine biography] — is to be found in the preface to *L'allegria*, now in his *Vita d'un uomo. Tutte le poesie*, ed. by Leone Piccioni (Milan: Mondadori, 1992), p. 528.

PART I

General Issues and Signal Cases

CHAPTER 2

The Public and the Private in Modern Italian Literature: The Case of Montale

Peter Hainsworth

It is common in Western European culture (and probably elsewhere) for a writer's public and private selves to enjoy an uneasy, often unstable relationship with each other. Though efforts may be made to bring the two into harmony or to proclaim their fundamental identity, they keep on sliding apart or alternatively clashing with each other, it normally being felt that the private is the more genuine self, the public one a face that has been assumed for one reason or another. When, by accident or design, a hitherto hidden side of a well-known individual is displayed, it is easy to feel that we have seen through the image to the real person, even if we are aware that the ostensibly private can be artificially created and that, in the modern media world, the spontaneous gesture, whether manufactured or not, is immediately taken up and incorporated into the public image. In the case of literary figures, the public face is a complex one, which regularly includes ostensibly private elements. The literary work may indeed be valued precisely because it does appear to express (in public) personal feelings or experiences of a kind which are commonly concealed or repressed, or which simply fail to find expression elsewhere for one reason or another. At the same time it is quite possible to feel that, however great the work may be, however achieved the expression, it is somehow incomplete, and that we will understand and appreciate it more fully if we can bring to bear further knowledge of what constituted the lived experience behind it. We may well feel in fact that we will understand the author (especially a great author) all the more, the more we know about his or her life from autobiographical writings (including diaries, letters, notes etc) and biographical accounts, from formal literary biographies to partial accounts and passing observations from contemporaries. Of course if we change the focus to the history of literary culture, then these para-literary writings will assume enhanced importance, since it is likely to be the conditions and occasions of literary production that concern us rather than purely literary interpretation. Something similar happens if it is the figure of the author which fascinates us rather than the literary works for which he or she is famous.

In practice biography and autobiography cannot be so neatly and abstractly pigeon-holed. Writing about one's own or another person's life seems inevitably to involve irreconcilable tensions between confession and repression, disclosure and concealment, fabrication and veracity, the general modern consensus being that a life-story will always be partial. Indeed the idea of a full and objective account of any phenomenon, let alone something so multifaceted as an individual's life, seems now to be chimerical. But even if the more radical forms of post-modern scepticism are pushed aside, biography and autobiography seem particularly subject to forces that get in the way of their ostensible aspiration to truth-telling and which often lead academic historians and critics to have doubts about their validity. Internally there is the perspective of the teller, who not only takes a particular slant on the subject and events in his or her life, but is under pressure to produce a readable narrative with at least some of the features of realist fiction — such as character, psychological analysis, turning-points. Then there are external pressures: individuals are almost always concerned with the image that they give or are made to give to the world, families and friends have investments in that image too and, in the case of the great and the good (or the enormously bad), a whole society may have an interest in seeing a specific individual in a particular light. In America and the UK a major motive-force behind the flood of biographies that appear each year and at least a portion of the similar flood of autobiographies is the promise of new revelations — that is, the disclosure of information which will cast the life of the subject and the events he or she lived through in a different, ostensibly more truthful light. In the case of contemporaries there is often the commercial assumption that the more radical the revision of the individual's image and the more holes which are filled in about his or her private life, the better, though the many biographies of the famous and not so famous dead that are bought and read may have little or no scandalous intent.

A cursory glance round any bookshop suggests that the Italian reading-public has nothing like the appetite for autobiography and biography of the British and Americans, at least as regards their co-nationals, though translations from other languages are fairly common. Autobiographies by Italians are sparse; though there is more biography, it still does not compare to what is to be found in English. A few figures are much in evidence — the Pope, Mussolini, current sports and media personalities, for instance — but, though you will find something, you will be hard put to find much on the lives of many prominent twentieth-century politicians, intellectuals and writers, and even less on figures from earlier centuries. Nor are libraries all that much richer. Academic biographies are few, often not very revealing and sometimes downright puzzling. Arguably the most important and certainly the most influential and controversial study of Fascism to have been written is Renzo De Felice's monumental life of Mussolini,[1] but Mussolini's personal life, feelings, relationships and even his day-to-day life are lost in the impressive but overwhelmingly detailed reconstruction of the larger picture, so much so that, especially to a foreigner, it barely seems a biography at all. With other figures, there are usually significant omissions regarding the subject's personal life. It is not just information that might be considered scandalous or compromising that is omitted but accounts in any detail of friendships, adventures and misfortunes. To cite just one striking example, there is the startling event of Giuseppe Ungaretti's return to Italy from Brazil in 1942, recorded in biographies as baldly as I have recorded it here, almost as if what must have been a long, dangerous journey over enemy-dominated seas were no different from catching the train from Rome to Bologna.[2] What is more, if the figure in question is considered explicitly or implicitly among the great and the good of the country, or of a particular region, it is common for the writing to adopt an admiring, celebratory tone which is in stark contrast to common British and American practice. Very often biographies of Italians which create readable, informed narrative and are willing to consider the more problematic sides of the individual in question, are written by foreigners. John Woodhouse's life of D'Annunzio is the outstanding recent example.[3] Like others before it, it has subsequently appeared in an Italian version.[4]

It does not follow that Italians are less interested than the British and Americans in finding out about the lives of their famous men and women, including their writers, only that the rules for what can be said in public about the private sphere are quite different. They are rules with a long history and have remained surprisingly consistent, though there are signs that they are finally changing. They stem of course from deeply entrenched cultural practices, which extend far beyond the narrowly literary sphere, but which, all the same, have been shaped in important ways by literature. As with so much else, it is Dante, Petrarch and Boccaccio who establish the basic patterns for autobiography and biography in Italy. Dante and Petrarch foreground their personal experience at a time when the norm in vernacular literature was to discount it — witness Jean de Meung, Chrétien de Troyes or Chaucer — or to assimilate it to general patterns — witness the love-lyric. Neither produces an autobiography as such, but each constructs in his writing a complex multi-faceted self, with befores and afters, which has an aura of reality but which offers to the reader only a factually sparse and often contradictory narrative. Subsequent commentaries and critical discussions have completed the life-stories in often widely dissimilar ways over the centuries and have found no solutions to enigmas such as the historical relations between the writers and the women they call Beatrice and Laura, or between the writers and the women who were actually their wives or mistresses, let alone unearthing firm information regarding relations with mothers, fathers, patrons and creditors. In other words each writer makes the autobiographical essential to his literary project, but only on the basis of a high degree of indeterminacy.[5] In Leopardian fashion *avant la lettre*, the scant detail seems to act as a stimulus to the imagination of the reader, enhancing poetic effect rather than detracting from it. At the same time the ostensible grounding of the work in autobiography acts as a guarantee of authenticity.

Boccaccio interweaves a similar more or less fictional narrative of his life into his poems and stories, but he is more important in this context for his practice as a biographer. As the first author of lives of both his predecessors, he derives his informational content largely from their writings, with minimal additions that are often factually unreliable. More importantly he absorbs humanist and classical practice in Latin. In what will then become standard practice during the Renaissance,[6] generalities and abstraction predominate over concrete detail, anecdote and narrative coherence in what are primarily celebrations of the aesthetic, literary and moral values identifiable in the works, which are now metonymically extended to the life of the man. Specific experiences that do not conform with the acceptable public image are perceived as irrelevant. It is the personal in the public or the public in the personal that the biographer is concerned with.

Highly selective and allusive autobiography and celebratory humanist biography will remain the norm over the subsequent centuries. In biography the results are indeed sometimes informative as well as celebratory, Vasari's *Vite* being the outstanding Renaissance instance. But writing about the self seems to remain close to the point where Dante and Petrarch had left it. In the Renaissance Machiavelli, Aretino, and Ariosto, and then subsequently Foscolo and Leopardi all make reference to personal experience a founding feature of their work. None tell the story of their lives as such. Though Leopardi did begin to assemble fragments of a prose autobiography, in verse he writes 'Le ricordanze' rather than an Italian *Prelude*. Nor did any of them keep diaries in the manner of a Pepys or a Boswell, or produce a correspondence comparable to that of Keats. Those famous examples of explicit autobiography that do exist in Italian seem to confirm the rule: Cellini, Vico and Alfieri almost challengingly construct their self-images and edit their experiences. In that respect they will be followed by memorialists and diarists of the Risorgimento period, such as Silvio Pellico, Luigi Settembrini and Giulio Cesare Abba. The *Noterelle* of the last of these, which are cast as a diary of his experiences as a volunteer with Garibaldi's Thousand, are in fact artfully elaborated decades after the event, any residual immediacy being a calculated illusion.[7] Exceptions of note are to be found in the 18th century, in the memoirs of Casanova and Goldoni; here the process of self-construction has a more relaxed and intimate air and there is a new wealth of circumstantial detail and anecdote. But in a way these also confirm the rule: they are written in French and entry into another language really does mean entry into another system. As for biography, the humanist model continues to make itself felt even when positivism brings about a new concern with factuality. The perceived need to celebrate models and heroes of the new Italy if anything acts as a reinforcement. All the same a new willingness to present a mass of documented information in concerted narrative form and to explore (sympathetically) at least some of psychological complexities and material problems of the author in question becomes the norm. The positive consequences are evident in such biographies as Piero Nardi's of Fogazzaro[8] and Tom Antongini's of D'Annunzio.[9] Celebratory biography might continue, and with Fascism will devolve into propaganda, but, by and large, much biography of the first half of the twentieth-century in Italy seems comparable with what was being produced in other modern European countries.

Within literary production itself traditional practice had remained strong in spite of the propulsion towards objectivity and submersion of the lyric self promoted by positivism and realism. And in the mid-twentieth century it seems to re-affirm itself with a vengeance, as fragmented, allusive autobiography returns as a dominating feature of the works of canonical authors, such as Montale, Ungaretti and Gadda. I shall examine Montale's case in more detail below. But Ungaretti is particularly striking for proposing that his collected poems and prose form somehow the *Vita di un uomo*, though there is no autobiographical narrative as such and the life in question may be freely interpreted as representative, individual or somehow both.

Carlo Emilio Gadda's baroque prose might seem a long way from Ungaretti's minimalism. But they have much in common, not least in their highly selective approach to their earlier lives. Gadda returns repeatedly to core experiences — the First World, War, his imprisonment after Caporetto, the death of his brother, his relationship with his mother — but his accounts veer away disconcertingly from these apparent centres, or overlay them, or dissolve, leaving certain issues that, in the work of a writer who makes so much of self-obsession, might seem of legitimate concern (his sexuality, for instance) completely untouched. This strong embracing of certain aspects of traditional practice is characteristic of Italian literary modernism in the 1920s and 30s: the aim, made explicit in hermetic thinking about poetry but valid far beyond hermeticism, is to achieve an essential literariness or poeticness as against the inertness of familiar prose, including the prose of workaday narrative fiction. Within this perspective the personal may be a starting- or end-point but only in severely edited or reshaped form. Even neo-realist fiction will feel the compulsion to recast the factual in the name of the poetic, at best in a heroic attempt to bring the poetic and the real together and ideally to make them coincide. Vittorini's *Uomini e no* (1946) and Pavese's *La casa in collina* (1947), for instance, both present highly literary transfigurations of war-time experiences while still strongly implying their deeply personal nature.

Overall one is left with a strong impression of discretion or reticence, as if there are things that cannot or should not be openly written about, especially as regards personal relations. Italian writers of the mid-twentieth century may in reality have been rebels or individualists at various times; on the whole they prefer to present themselves as social conformists, if and when they choose to talk directly about their personal lives at all. The impression tends to be confirmed rather than modified when one turns to critics and biographers. The important writers of the 1920s and '30s were part of a close-knit literary society, centred on Florence and Rome, in which everyone knew everyone else, for good and ill. An enormous amount has written about the poetry, fiction, criticism and other forms of journalism of the time, much of it by the protagonists themselves, but the focus has been overall literary production itself, and the (laudable) efforts to maintain its autonomy in the face of an increasingly threatening totalitarian regime. Such collections of letters as have so far appeared are mostly unrevealing, and no diaries or significant memoirs by major participants have yet been published. So far we have no synthetic accounts by biographers and literary historians, which probe the evolving emotional and social relationships of the major participants. The contrast with the situation regarding the Bloomsbury group is remarkable.

The discretion (if that is what it is) is so widely shared as to be almost a norm and cannot be accounted for solely on the long-standing literary grounds that I have so far discussed. The literary conventions seem in fact to re-enact patterns of behaviour that are equally deeply ingrained in Italian society as a whole. In particular there is the closed nature of the Italian family, with its often well-founded suspicions of a larger civil society which traditionally has been rich in rhetoric and poor in the actual safeguards that it offers to the individual and the family unit. Public conformism in such a society is a form of self-protection, a way of not exposing the self to potential depredations by others and of confirming one's status in one's own eyes. Since others are in the same position, there is usually a group interest in maintaining such fictional versions of the self in public, though private knowledge may be a quite different matter and may itself be shared while never being publicly voiced. To the Northern European these are attitudes that may smack of hypocrisy or worse, with roots in the Counter-Reformation and the Inquisition.

But modern Italy also has had to deal with a specific problem of Fascism. Everyone who lived through some or all of the years between the March on Rome and the end of the Second World War has had to come to terms with the fact that for twenty years Italy was ruled by a dictator, who for much of the time enjoyed great popular support, but who then led the country to defeat, destruction and civil war or something approaching it. Except for those few individuals who could legitimately say that they were active anti-Fascists before Mussolini's fall in 1943 (such as the members of the *Giustizia e Libertà* group in Turin), most Italians have found it difficult to make sense of their experiences in those years, let alone put forward a convincing case for their behaviour being morally and politically acceptable, collectively and as individuals, in large part because for decades after the war the only publicly acceptable position was one of open anti-Fascism. In this situation a strategy that had the tacit agreement of the majority was that of silence, and, though there were moments when individuals were forced to speak out to condemn or defend themselves, on the whole it worked. Writers were no exception. Though some may have had more or less serious troubles with the authorities from time to time, none was actively involved in anti-Fascist activity until the late 1930s at the earliest and some (like Ungaretti and Gadda) were active supporters of the regime for at least a time. Especially if works that they wrote during the Fascist years were proclaimed as classics of modern literature (such as Ungaretti's *Sentimento del tempo*, Gadda's *Adalgisa*, or for that matter Montale's *Ossi di seppia* and *Le occasioni*), they found it impossible to retrace in print their concrete experiences of Fascism, preferring instead to say nothing (as is the case with Ungaretti), or to suggest that basically they disapproved of the regime, which is the strategy followed by Gadda.[10] Partial exceptions are to be found in Vittorini and Pratolini who saw their post-war communism as fundamentally coherent with the revolutionary Fascism they had preached as young enthusiasts in the 1930s, although even they preferred to discuss generalities or to present fictionalised versions of what happened. Not that embarrassment is the whole story; the restraint and discretion mentioned earlier are also involved. Vittorini, Pratolini and various other writers were active in the Resistance from 1943 onwards. None of them published anything but the most elliptical resumés of their experiences.

As members of the same literary culture, writers of biographies of modern authors — partial or wholescale, literary or historical, popular or academic — naturally shared the same attitudes, complexes and taboos as the writers they were writing about. Very often they were friends, though, in the traditional manner of Italian biographers, they tended to adopt an admiring, rather deferential tone, which accorded with the elevated status of the author in question. In such a climate, investigative or critical biographies were unthinkable, the biographer gliding smoothly over potentially embarrassing episodes for the most part, and, on those few occasions when the need to be explicit arose, firmly defending his subject against personal criticisms from others.

Over the last three decades, however, there have been some significant changes. Traditional practice is still strong in biographical writing as it is in so many other areas of Italian culture, but modernity in one form or another has gradually extended the limits of what can and what cannot be written about a canonical author. Authors born in the late nineteenth and early twentieth centuries are now almost all dead. What can be said about them can no longer affect them as individuals and has a decreasing importance for their descendants, though it may affect contemporary Italy's view of the culture of the past and hence its own self-image. The first book of memoirs of literary life in 1930s Florence to present an ambiguous and nuanced picture of various writers' relationships with the Fascist regime is Silvio Guarnieri's significantly titled *L'ultimo testimone* of 1989.[11] Guarnieri makes it plain that even at this distance from Fascism, it took resolve and an awareness that the truth was likely to be lost for ever to cast doubt on what had become orthodox pieties. More has been published since then, though there is still much more to be said on Fascism and literature, as there is on various authors' personal lives. That is not to imply that there are necessarily hidden scandals waiting to be uncovered, only that there are large gaps in the information currently publicly available and that it is still possible to paint an all too rosy picture of literary activity in the Fascist period.

The information available is almost certain to grow immensely over the next few decades. Archives of authors' manuscripts, personal libraries and notes have a long history in Italy, going back to Petrarch, though these have often revealed little about the reality of their personal lives. The twentieth century saw a new scholarly interest in documentation that was omnivorous and all-embracing and one that writers everywhere seem to have been happy to support with gifts and bequests from their personal archives. So far as modern Italian literature is concerned, the main (though not the sole) documentary centre has become the *Fondo di manoscritti di autori contemporanei*, founded in Pavia in 1969 by Maria Corti, which, as well as manuscripts of literary works, has amassed a vast body of letters, diaries and other personal papers covering most of the principal twentieth-century authors, given either by the authors themselves or by their heirs.[12] In other words, within the literary and scholarly world itself, no doubt in part as a result of a fetishization of all relics relating to the figure of the Author, the seeds have been laid for more detailed and extensive biographical investigation than has been possible hitherto. Caution rules still and the constraints on what can or cannot be published are fierce. So far little has been released which touches on aspects of writers' lives which might be seen as scandalous or controversial, or simply too personal. Just how touchy the issue might be was shown by the family's reaction to the publication in the summer of 2004 of some of Calvino's still embargoed letters to Elsa de' Giorgi of the mid-1950s (in the Pavia archive).[13] But time-limits have been set. Over the next few decades much more will be published that will throw light on the lives of Montale, Ungaretti, Gadda and a host of other authors. No doubt some of what will be published will be controversial, and perhaps make for headlines in the

Italian media. But it may also be that the release of new information will lead to a better understanding of the literary culture of which they were part and away from summary judgements, positive or negative, of their lives and work.

The tensions and contradictions which I have been discussing are particularly in evidence in the case of Montale, partly because of the exceptional stature he now enjoys as Italy's greatest twentieth-century poet. In the 1950s and 60s Montale, Ungaretti and Quasimodo were often rather unconvincingly put together as yet another *tre corone* of Italian poetry. Rightly or wrongly, Montale now overshadows the other two and has become an emblematic figure in a way that is not true of any other writer of his time. His work is generally felt to maintain its literary importance throughout its whole course, even though the first three books are normally held up as his greatest achievement. For many critics it is also representative of the progress and survival of the best of Italian culture through one of its most tormented centuries.[14] With the fading of left-wing ideology, which led critics such as Pasolini and Fortini to have reservations about the man and his political position, even when they felt forced to admire the poetry,[15] there has been an increased readiness to make him an icon not just of poetic but also of moral value. The 'decenza quotidiana', which he admires in his friend Sergio Fadin in the 'Visita a Fadin' of *La bufera e altro*, has been taken as one which Montale himself modestly but almost heroically adhered to and which encapsulates a viable mode of moral conduct in the face of the various threats posed by totalitarianism, war and mass culture in the twentieth century. Montale was ironically self-deprecating in his public comments on his life, but that seems only to have encouraged the tendency to cite him as a moral and a literary exemplar.

Montale is also an outstanding case of autobiographical writing in the traditional Italian mould, as I have outlined it. Throughout its course his poetry contains references, direct and indirect, to real people and places, to public and private events that actually occurred, and evoke a self who is identifiable as the historical Eugenio Montale, with, of course, elements of fictionalisation. In an interview with Giansiro Ferrata of 1961, he identified 'un filo autobiografico, certamente romanzesco' running through his first three collections of poems.[16] It is a comment which characteristically points simultaneously in two directions. All the same, taken in sequence, the collections suggest the passage through life of a specific individual, who evolves, with some moments of abrupt change, as a poet and simultaneously in the way he thinks and feels more generally, though it is also a poetry which wishes to reach out beyond the single life.[17] The contradiction is perhaps inevitable, if the poetry is not to tip into the impenetrably private. Since the poems first appeared, however, even sophisticated readers who were personally close to Montale, have found the sense of many of them hard to interpret, even if they were convinced of the poetic value of what they read. The difficulties are not just linguistic and stylistic in a narrow sense but, especially in *Le occasioni* (1939) and *La bufera e altro* (1956), stem from a highly elliptic and allusive approach to meaning and to lived experience.[18] Only in the later collections will reference to private experience become more open and direct, although the difference is one of degree. In fact it is only the reader who has become immersed in the earlier, more obviously difficult poems who will feel an easy familiarity with the names and back-references. In other words the reader of Montale, much like the reader of Petrarch and Dante, is drawn into a life-story which is tantalisingly incomplete, which seems to demand deciphering and supplementation and which the author himself seems to use as a shaping force within his work as a whole.

In spite of the interest in Montale's life and his perceived role as a great poet, so far there is still only one book-length biography in existence. Written, it seems with Montale's full co-operation, by the journalist Giulio Nascimbeni, it first appeared in 1969, in a Longanesi series called *Gente famosa*.[19] Subjects of other volumes included Sofia Loren, Maria Callas, Padre Pio, Richard Nixon, members of the exiled Italian Royal family and Haile Selasse. Montale was the first writer. At this stage he seemed to be a grand old man of poetry. He had been made *senatore a vita* in 1967 and had published no book-length collection since *La bufera e altro* of 1956, which many critics felt rounded off his poetic career. If he was often in the public eye, it was as much for his often pugnacious cultural journalism as for his poetry. All the same he had just released the first series of 'Xenia' poems, which Nascimbeni was able to discuss. This first form of the biography then dated rapidly, with the award of the Nobel prize in 1975 and the publication of *Satura* (1971) and subsequent volumes which cast Montale's life and career in a whole new light. These new developments were then covered in a second edition — principally by addition rather than rewriting — which appeared in 1986, five years after Montale's death, and which is still available.

Nascimbeni's readable and in many ways informative account has been enormously influential. It presents an image of Montale's personality and of events in his life which is admiring but which has a convincing aura of authenticity, largely because of the deft use of quotations from Montale's writings and from Nascimbeni's interviews with him. A sense also emerges of how the encounters with Montale in his flat in via Bigli in Milan took on a familiar, almost relaxed air, which allowed Montale's personality to come through strongly for Nascimbeni and subsequently for the reader. So we get a sense of the self-deflating tenor, the ironic humorist and conversationalist, the self-aware slightly bumbling figure who is also a great poet who was punished for his unwillingness to conform to Fascist diktat. All this emerges in the course of charting the various phases in Montale's life — Genoa and the Cinque Terre, World War I, Florence and the directorship of the Gabinetto Vieusseux until his dismissal for political reasons in 1938, the definitive move to Milan and the bourgeoning of his journalistic activity after the war. That there was at least initially a polemical edge to the picture is suggested in the first edition only in a brief reference to negative comments on the limitations of his liberal antifascism that had appeared in *Belfagor*.[20]

Nascimbeni had either dealt summarily with a large number of issues, not all of them controversial by any means, that might reasonably be felt to be of interest to the reader of Montale, or not dealt with them at all. Information about some of these has gradually trickled out, or been teased out by the patient and persistent research. Aside from Contorbia's *Immagini di una vita*, the contribution of which is primarily photographic, there have been two general surveys since Nascimbeni.[21] These are the *Cronologia* that first appeared in Giorgio Zampa's 1984 Meridiano edition of the collected poems and which then reappears in each of the various volumes of the *Opere* of Montale in the same series and Giuseppe Marcenaro's Eugenio Montale, published in the Bruno Mondadori 'Biblioteca degli Scrittori' series in 1999.[22] The Meridiano *Cronologia* is substantially in accordance with the pattern of the series as a whole, being more than twenty pages long, and it is factually more precise and informative than Nascimbeni's account, though it largely supplements rather than revises what he had written. It is also rich in quotations from letters to and from Montale, most going back to the pre-war years, and many still not published elsewhere. Taken together they fill out the image of Montale as suffering from an often paralysing depression during the 1930s, in part for personal reasons but also it is strongly suggested because of his horror at the apparently unstoppable success of the Fascist regime. The image of Montale as a victim of Fascist abuse of power is then reinforced by the quotation almost in its entirety of the resolution of the Consiglio d'Amministrazione del Gabinetto Vieusseux of 1 December 1938 to dismiss Montale from his post as Director. No other document is quoted in this way.

What the *Cronologia* also provides is some information about the female figures who had barely been mentioned in Nascimbeni and left largely unidentified. Admittedly the information is clipped and oblique. But Irma Brandeis, the Clizia of *Le occasioni* and *La bufera*, is identified as having had a complicated relationship with Montale from 1933 to 1939 and the main stages in the Montale's relationship with his eventual wife, Drusilla Tanzi, the Mosca of the poems, are plainly charted, with the clear implication that Montale was torn between the two until 1939, when he finally renounced the idea of going to live with Clizia in America. Other figures also make fleeting appearances — Anna Degli Uberti, Gerti Tolazzi, Maria Luisa Spaziani (not identified as the Volpe of certain poems of *La bufera*, however) and a mysterious G.B.H., an Italian woman whom Montale knew in London in 1948–49.

By the mid-1990s the gallery of Montale's muses (to use the title of a 1996 book of pictures and quotations)[23] was much fuller. Esterina Rossi, Paola Nicoli, Liuba Blumenthal, Dora Markus, Lucia Rodocanachi from the pre-war years had all acquired faces (largely through Contorbia's *Immagini di una vita*) and greater or lesser definition as individuals, though Dora Markus has remained limited to Bobi Bazlen's now famous photo of a pair of legs. Similarly the women who figure, generally more fleetingly, in the later poems, have also been identified — Carla Fracci, Laura Papi and others, culminating in Annalisa Cima, the moving spirit and the repository of the *Diario postumo*, though G.B.H. remains as enigmatic as ever.

Much of this work of identification was carried out by scholars working directly on the interpretation of the poems, Dante Isella, Luciano Rebay, Gianfranco Contini and Giorgio Zampa in particular. What they left in shadow was the actual relationship between Montale and the person in question. So the reader is left to guess, sometimes with innuendoes enticing in one direction or another, whether the relationship was one of friendship, whether it had an erotic element, whether it was fleeting, let alone what the other person made of it or how it affected other people. A few snippets from Mosca's letters (mostly about Montale's new-found enthusiasm for painting in the 1950s) are quoted in Zampa's *Cronologia*. A recent significant development was the publication in 2006 of Montale's letters to Irma Brandeis, which she had deposited at the Gabinetto Vieusseux and which became available to scholarly scrutiny in 2003.[24] Gossipy, at times comic, the letters have at their core the disastrous progression of a love-affair, which at one point seemed as if it might lead to his transference to the USA but which eventually succumbed ignominiously to devastating emotional blackmail from Mosca. Montale, it seems, could indeed be as inadequate in the management of his personal affairs as he sometimes said he was. At the same time the letters heighten the suspicion suggested by certain poems that Montale the poet needed his muse to be distant and unattainable, as if he were under some obligation to follow the historic pattern of Italian love poetry (and to some extent of love-poetry generally). That need for distance goes with a certain conventional silence on the part of the beloved which would perhaps change the reception of the poems if it were breached. Of Irma herself only one letter to Montale has survived and some somewhat enigmatic diary notes. So far it seems that Clizia, like Mosca and Volpe, must not speak of her relationship with Montale, even if Irma Brandeis can write fiction and criticism in her own name and even translate some of the poems addressed to her.[25] In this respect, as in some others, the figures of Beatrice and Laura continue to stretch their ghostly fingers into modern poetry.

Then, too, the *Lettere a Clizia* are personal, even sometimes embarrassingly revealing, in a way that traditional Italian practice would not easily have sanctioned. Marcenaro had already given signs in 1999 that the agenda of biography and autobiography was no longer rigidly fixed. His short study is directed at the modern student. It consists of a sober, factual account of Montale's life and career, with appropriate prose and poetry quotations, followed by an alphabetical 'dizionario', filling out what has been said about people, books and events in the narrative of the first part. Two features stand out. Firstly the 'heroic' aspect of Montale's position in the 1930s is muted. He is now, by implication, much more an everyman who has to adapt to very difficult circumstances. The second is that, though Marcenaro does not have the advantage of drawing on the letters to Irma Brandeis, the love-affairs can be recounted in more or less neutral fashion. The deaths of the protagonists and changes in expectations regarding sexual mores mean that elements of scandal or prurience have largely been eliminated.

Other aspects of Montale's life have had some measure of light cast on them. Various collections of letters to and from friends have been published in the years since Montale's death. As published, they are remarkably unrevealing in what they say explicitly, being often concerned with meetings, publishing questions,[26] holidays and travel arrangements and with only smatterings of literary gossip. Certainly none of them, severally or together, constitute a body of letters comparable to those of some famous writers ranging from Leopardi to Elizabeth Bishop. But what they do suggest is the complexity of Montale's personality. At times he is the now almost mythic Eusebio playing arch verbal games with Gianfranco Contini (who becomes Trabucco in the letters)[27] and Sandro Penna (who becomes Piuma and then Merlo and even 'blackbird')[28] in a way that he seems first to have tried out rather exaggeratedly in his letters to Bianca Messina (addressed as Tapioca), the wife of the sculptor Francesco Messina. But he could be more serious even in letters to friends; it is plain from his letters to his comrade-in-arms Francesco Meriano[29] that as a young officer he was far more enthusiastic and committed as a young officer in the last stages of World War I than 'Valmorbia' in *Ossi di seppia* might suggest, though, according to Francesco Messina, he was already making fun of his front-line experiences soon after the war ended. From the correspondence with Penna two things become plain, first that, to an extent we might not expect from the apparently passive image of himself that Montale generally preferred to project, especially in the poems and imaginative prose, he played an active part in literary manoeuvrings in Florence in the early 1930s, particularly in connection with the first *Premio dell'Antico Fattore*. He was apparently doing everything he could to make sure the prize went to Penna, but, to his embarrassment, ended up winning the prize himself with 'La casa dei doganieri'. He then worked hard to get a collection of Penna's poems published in spite of the obstacle created by their overt homosexual content. Behind this episode lies a short period of closeness to Penna, the nature of which is not clear.[30]

Overall the letters as published do not give much away and generally reinforce or elaborate the established (Nascimbeni) image of Montale. In particular there remains the problem of the difficult issue of Montale's relations with the Fascist regime. It is not necessary to be a cynic or to wish to criticize Montale for his conduct to suspect that losing his post as the director of the Vieusseux was not the whole story. Montale had signed Croce's manifesto against Fascism and remained privately critical of the regime throughout its course. At the same time, though not a party member, he had no more difficulty finding work as a reviewer than any other *letterato* of the time. By the mid-1930s Italian critics, whether they were committed Fascists or not, were acknowledging him as one of the most important poets of the time; for some he was already more important than any of his contemporaries. On these grounds alone it seems exaggerated to speak of him as an anti-Fascist in the 1930s, given that the term suggests someone who was a good deal more active than Montale ever was in the pre-war years. He concluded his 1946 'Intenzioni' as follows: 'Ho vissuto il mio tempo col minimum di vigliaccheria ch'era consentito alle mie deboli forze, ma c'è chi ha fatto di più, molto di più, anche se non ha pubblicato libri' [I have lived my time with the minimum amount of cowardice that was granted to my feeble resources, but there are people who did more, much more, even though they did not publish books].[31] In all probability, like many others who fundamentally disapproved of the regime, he found himself making compromises or negotiating a way through what became an increasingly dangerous minefield. Some hints of what these might have been are given by Silvio Guarnieri. More recently Mirella Serri's study of Giaime Pintor includes the correspondence relating to the Weimar Conference of the Nazi European Writers Union in 1942 which Montale was pressed to attend as a member of the Italian delegation but managed to avoid on health grounds.[32] Rather than explore the very human and in their way admirable implications of Montale's conduct during that episode (which involved various Italian writers and remained a tabu area up to the publication of Serri's book), commentators have preferred to highlight traces of anti-Fascism in Montale's wartime poetry. *Finisterre*, containing 15 poems later to be included in *La bufera e altro*, but which had mostly already appeared in Bottai's *Primato* and elsewhere, was published in Switzerland in an edition of 150 copies in mid-1943.[33] It was a late and small gesture, especially given the oblique character of the poems. The anti-Fascism is more explicit in 'Primavera hitleriana', which was provoked by Hitler's visit to Florence in 1938. It was first published in 1946 in *Inventario* and then in an *Antologia poetica della resistenza italiana*, though so far as is known it had no underground circulation during the war-years.[34]

It is not surprising that, behind the scenes at conferences or in private conversations, professional *montalisti* with access to unpublished papers and former acquaintances (*amici*) of Montale regularly depict a quite different individual (or a series of quite different individuals), often with less edifying features, as the reality behind the public image. To a degree that is to be expected; the Montale of gossip and speculation, the various personae who inhabit the published poems and the prose, the Montale of public occasions, the Montale of other people's memoirs, the Montale of records and letters — all these alternately overlap, merge and diverge, and are, in principle, no more and no less contradictory or irreconcilable than will be the case with any human being whose life and work has had a public dimension, with documentation extending over something like six decades, and at its centre a complex body of direct and indirect self-commentary. But it is not all just a question of point of view. There are significant questions regarding Montale's life to which there should be factual answers though the implications of those answers may be highly problematical.

The list that includes Montale, Gadda and Ungaretti could be easily extended and would include post-war writers as well as writers who lived through the Fascist period. It has become easier to discuss in public the trajectory of a writer's political activities and allegiances, and some writers and their biographers have found it possible to talk and write about personal life to a degree that would have been unthinkable fifty years ago. In part this seems to have happened because of a new sense that the domestic and the everyday have value as literary topics and that it is in those arenas that people actually confront the grand issues of their time. That it has become possible to write about such things in Italy without tipping over into the scandalous or the self-indulgent seems to be demonstrated by autobiographical writers such as Natalia Ginzburg and Primo Levi and by biographies such as the recent one of Cristina Campo by Cristina De Stefano.[35] Boundaries are still maintained, but they are being pushed further back. Though there are inevitable risks, it must be the case that in a modern European culture discussing more (not necessarily all) of what has been private in Italy and moderating the tendency to preserve a monolithic public image can only be a sign of cultural health and buoyancy.

Notes to Chapter 2

1. Renzo de Felice, *Mussolini*, 4 vols (Turin: Einaudi, 1965–1990).
2. See Leone Piccioni, *Vita di un poeta. Giuseppe Ungaretti* (Milan: Rizzoli, 1970), pp.149–50 and Walter Mauro, *Vita di Giuseppe Ungaretti* (Milan: Camunia, 1990), pp.119–20.

3. John Woodhouse, *Gabriele D'Annunzio. Defiant Archangel* (Oxford: Oxford University Press, 1998).
4. John Woodhouse, *Gabriele D'Annunzio. Arcangelo ribelle* (Rome: Carocci, 1999).
5. See Peter Hainsworth, 'Rhetorics of Autobiography in Dante, Petrarch and Boccaccio', *Journal of the Institute of Romance Studies*, 3 (1995), 53–63.
6. For a full survey see Martin McLaughlin, 'Biography and autobiography in the Italian Renaissance' in *Mapping Lives. The Uses of Biography*, ed. by Peter France and William St. Clair (Oxford: Oxford University Press, 2002), pp. 37–65.
7. See Luigi Russo, 'Abba e la letteratura garibaldina', *Scrittori-poeti e scrittori-letterati* (Bari: Laterza, 1945), pp. 203–41.
8. Piero Nardi, *Antonio Fogazzaro* (Milan: Mondadori, 1938).
9. Tom Antongini, *Vita segreta di D'Annunzio* (Milan: Mondadori, 1939).
10. See Peter Hainsworth 'Fascism and Anti-fascism in Gadda', in *Carlo Emilio Gadda: Contemporary Perspectives*, ed. by Manuela Bertone and Robert Dombroski (Toronto: University of Toronto Press, 1997), pp. 221–41.
11. Silvio Guarnieri, *L'ultimo testimone: storia di una società letteraria* (Milan: Mondadori, 1989).
12. See Corti's own extremely diplomatic account of the founding and growth of the archive in *Ombre dal fondo* (Turin: Einaudi, 1997).
13. In August 2004 the journalist Stefano Paolo published a series of articles in the *Corriere della sera* in which he quoted from some of Calvino's letters to Elsa de' Giorgi, including some which were supposed to have remained embargoed for twenty-five years. An Italian court found in favour of Calvino's widow that the newspaper did not have the right to quote from the letters, and publication then stopped.
14. See for example the tributes paid on Montale's death assembled in Armida Marasco, *Per Eugenio Montale. Gli interventi della stampa quotidiana* (Lecce: Congedo Editore, 1982).
15. See for example Pasolini's 1957 review of *La bufera e altro*, subsequently included in *Passione e ideologia* (1960), and now in Pier Paolo Pasolini, *Saggi sulla letteratura e sull'arte*, ed. by Walter Siti and Silvia De Laude, 2 vols (Milan: Mondadori, 1999), I, 1027–31; and Franco Fortini, 'La poesia del Novecento', in *Letteratura Italiana Laterza*, 9.2 (1976), 359–72.
16. 'Biografie al microfono' [Intervista di Giansiro Ferrata, 1961], now in Eugenio Montale, *Il secondo mestiere. Arte, musica, società*, ed. by Giorgio Zampa (Milan: Mondadori, 1996), pp.1611–21 (p. 1615).
17. 'Il bisogno di un poeta è la ricerca di una verità puntuale, non di una verità generale. Una verità del poeta-soggetto che non rinneghi quella dell'uomo-soggetto empirico' [A poet needs to seek a precise truth, not a generic one: a truth that belongs to the poet as subject but which at the same time does not deny the truth of man as empirical subject]. See 'Intenzioni (Intervista immaginaria)' in *Il secondo mestiere,* pp. 1475–84 (p. 1479).
18. 'Non pensai a una lirica pura nel senso ch'essa poi ebbe anche da noi, a un giuoco di suggestioni sonore; ma piuttosto a un frutto che dovesse contenere i suoi motivi senza rivelarli, o meglio senza spiattellarli' [I did not think of a pure lyric in the sense that the term subsequently came to have in Italy too, a game of evocations based on sounds; but rather as a fruit that had to contain its themes without revealing them, or rather without making them obvious]. See 'Intenzioni', p. 1481.
19. G. Nascimbeni, *Montale. Biografia di un poeta* (Milan: Longanesi, 1969; expanded and revised edition 1986).
20. Nascimbeni, *Montale. Biografia di un poeta*, p.173. The article in question was Umberto Carpi 'Montale dopo il fascismo: i primi anni di collaborazione al *Corriere della sera*', *Belfagor*, 23 (1968), 197–230, later incorporated into his book *Montale dopo il fascismo dalla 'Bufera' a 'Satura'* (Padua: Liviana, 1971). Carpi stated much more forcefully than Pasolini and Fortini that Montale was fundamentally a political reactionary.
21. Franco Contorbia, *Eugenio Montale. Immagini di una vita* (Milan: Librex, 1985).
22. Eugenio Montale, *Tutte le poesie*, ed. by Giorgio Zampa (Milan: Mondadori, 1984), pp. LVII-LXXIX and Giuseppe Marcenaro, *Eugenio Montale* (Milan: Edizioni Bruno Mondadori, 1999).
23. Giusi Baldissone (ed.), *Le muse di Montale. Galleria di occasioni femminili nella poesia montaliana* (Novara: Interlinea, 1996).

24. Eugenio Montale, *Lettere a Clizia,* ed. by Rosanna Bettarini, Gloria Manghetti and Franco Zabagli (Milan: Mondadori, 2006).
25. Paolo De Caro has published *Journey to Irma. Una approssimazione all'ispiratrice americana di Eugenio Montale. Parte prima, Irma, un 'romanzo'*, (Foggia: Matteo De Meo Stampatore 1999) and *Irma politica. L'ispiratrice di Eugenio Montale dall'americanismo all' antifascismo* (Foggia: Renzulli, 2001).
26. On Montale's relations with Einaudi see *Il Carteggio Montale-Einaudi per 'Le occasioni"* (Turin: Einaudi, 1988).
27. See *Eusebio e Trabucco. Carteggio di Eugenio Montale 1923–1925,* ed. by Laura Barile (Milan: Scheiwiller, 1995); *Eusebio e Trabucco. Carteggio di Eugenio Montale e Gianfranco Contini,* ed. by Dante Isella (Milan: Adelphi, 1997).
28. *Eugenio Montale, Sandro Penna*. Introduzione di Elio Pecora; testo, apparato critico e postfazione di Roberto Deidier (Milan: Archinto, 1995).
29. These are included in *Arte e vita. Francesco Meriano,* ed. by Gloria Manghetti, Carlo Ernesto Meriano and Vanni Scheiwiller (Milan: Scheiwiller, 1982), pp. 141ff. They date to 1918–22.
30. On Montale and Penna, see Cesare Garboli, *Montale, Penna e il desiderio* (Milan: Mondadori, 1996).
31. 'Intenzioni', p.1481.
32. Mirella Serri, *Il breve viaggio. Giaime Pintor nella Weimar nazista* (Venice: Marsilio, 2002). For the text of Montale's letter of refusal, see pp. 228–29.
33. The edition is reproduced in *Tutte le poesie,* pp. 923–98.
34. See *Tutte le poesie,* pp.1090 and 1096.
35. Cristina De Stefano, *Belinda e il mostro. Vita segreta di Cristina Campo* (Milan: Adelphi, 2002).

CHAPTER 3

❖

The Battle of the Biographers: Primo Levi and 'Life-Writing'

Robert S. C. Gordon

In late March 2002 — almost exactly fifteen years after his suicide on 11 April 1987 — two massive biographies of Primo Levi appeared in Britain, to much critical acclaim and attention: Carole Angier's *The Double Bond. Primo Levi. A Biography*, and Ian Thomson's *Primo Levi*.[1] The response to their all but simultaneous publication — after eight and eleven years of work, respectively[2] — confirmed, if confirmation were needed, Levi's position as one of the pre-eminent Italian writers of his generation and perhaps *the* pre-eminent Holocaust survivor-writer for the English-speaking world. All the major broadsheet newspapers and serious cultural magazines ran reviews, calling in major generalist reviewers.[3] Many could not resist measuring the books' significance in a manner quite peculiar to modern English biography — by crude page count (Angier came in at over 900 pages; Thomson at an 'economical' 600). One reviewer wearily wondered, 'what would Levi, famous for his own concision and restraint, have made of these 1,522 pages? Does his entire oeuvre even add up to as much?'[4] Another, in a state of some exasperation, resorted to weighing Angier (hardback edition): 'Hilary Spurling [...] attests "she could hardly put it down". I could hardly pick it up: it weighs 2 kilos'.[5] The sarcasm — and the none-too-subtle hint that the reviewer had not turned every last page — only served to underscore the cultural 'weight' of the subject in hand. Here was a writer fully integrated into the ideal library of the 'cultured' Anglophone reader, a writer whose biography was an object to behold and to own, if not necessarily to read.

There is, however, more to be gleaned from the brief flurry of interest in Levi in Spring 2002 than insight into the merry-go-round of book reviewing amongst London *literati*. The two tomes offer important examples of radically different practices of biography itself. Further, they operate in complex relation to the distinct role played by biographical writing in Levi's testimonial and literary *oeuvre* which underpins them. This essay aims to position the two biographies and responses to them in relation to trends in biography and to Levi's work, and in so doing to raise fundamental questions about the practices of autobiography, biography and testimony, all 'truth-telling', 'life-writing' genres of a kind, and all closely bound up with crucial questions of history and representation.

The Biographer as Chronicler, Researcher, Detective

Ian Thomson's biography declares itself from the outset as committed to a model of enquiry and writing based on research and sober sequence. In both structure and style, it lays its emphasis on information, and eschews interpretation and engagement. If we look first of all for structural evidence, there are several striking pointers to his approach. The title of the book — *Primo Levi*, with no qualifier or subtitle of any kind, not even 'A Biography' — is declarative in its simplicity. All but one of the 30 chapter titles are similarly open and descriptive, quickly decodeable as sequential stages in a largely typical, ordinary (middle-class, mid-twentieth-century) lived life. They move through such archetypal terms (with only one qualifier at most) as 'Childhood', 'Adolescence', 'University', 'Wartime', 'Captivity', 'Homecoming', 'Responsibilities', 'Acclaim', 'Retirement', 'Recognition', 'Last Six Days' (T, vii-viii).[6] Furthermore, graphically aligned to the right on the Contents page, as if to underscore the regularity of the sequence, we find every chapter (except the first and last but one, for which see below) has a subtitle of strictly sequential dates. This is biography written, in structure at least, as linear chronicle.

Within each chapter — in a manner which evokes Levi's own narrative style — Thomson subdivides the sequence into discrete units, divided by simple numbering and also, on a smaller scale still, by extra line spaces, allowing him to build up a patchwork of different items of relevant research and information. This militates against an elaborate, evolving grand interpretation of data, against a biography *à thèse*, and in favour of a form of gap-filling exercise: each micro unit increases our knowledge around Levi, moving towards a mosaic portrait of the man.[7]

A final element of structure to note, an exception which proves the rule, is the framing of the biography by chapters on Levi's suicide: chapter 1, '11 April 1987' (T, 1–5) and the penultimate chapter, 'April 1987: The Last Six Days' (T, 534–40).[8] To some degree, this negates the resistance to interpretation noted above and sets the biography up as an enquiry into the central mystery of Levi's death.[9] But the manner in which Thomson writes his opening and closing affirms even more starkly than the rest of the book his role as detached gatherer of information or evidence: here his chronicle is that of the police or even pathologist's report, as the opening of chapter 1 illustrates:

> Some time between 10:00 am and 10:15am on the morning of 11 April 1987 the commissariat at 73 Via Massena in Turin received a phone call. It had been relayed form the police emergency number 113: there had been an accident. An ambulance accompanied by the police flying-squad proceeded to 75 Corso Re Umberto. [...] In their first report to the Public Prosecutor's Office, dated that same Saturday 11 April, the police noted: '... Corpse found in vicinity of life ... Identified as Primo Levi.' The body had fallen fifteen metres head-first down the stairwell of the building and struck the marble floor at the foot of the lift shaft. Death was instantaneous. (T, 1)

The genre of the detective story, or, even more specifically, the 'police procedural' is stamped all over this 'sad chronicle', as Thomson calls it (T, 5).[10] The chapter continues, again in familiar detective genre fashion, keeping the opening focus studiedly away from Levi himself and on a minor and soon forgotten 'character' in the drama, Jolanda Gasperi, the concierge who discovered the body. The focus on those surrounding Levi, rather than on Levi itself — taken to an extreme here — will return in the chapter on the death at the end of the book (T, 534–40). There, the narrative follows Levi's final days, but looks through the events as seen and heard of by secondary figures shortly before and shortly after his death: Gaia Servadio, Giulio Einaudi, Piero Fassino,[11] Nuto Revelli and others. Again, it should be noted that this echoes neatly Levi's own narrative technique, since even his most autobiographical works speak relatively little of himself and include a wide variety of cameos and character sketches of those milling around him and encountered by him (see the final section in this chapter, below, on Levi's Life Writing).

The sequences on Levi's death crystallize in simple form the evidence-driven facet of Thomson's work which holds throughout. In the early chapter on the suicide of Levi's paternal grandfather, Michele Levi, Thomson is struck more than anything by the documentary coincidence of the pathologist's report: '*precipitazione dall'alto* [...] exactly the same words would appear on Primo Levi's autopsy ninety-nine years later' (T, 10). On the literary side of things, although Thomson will not delve into Levi's own texts (see below), he gathers a fascinating range of Levi's readings (especially in youth) and his literary influences. For *Se questo è un uomo* (*If This is a Man*, 1947) alone, in the thorough chapter dealing with its composition in 1946–47 (T, 228–50), Thomson suggests connections to: Homer, Tibullus, Manzoni, Gide, Dante, Jean Henri Fabre, Huxley, Saba, Luciana Nissim, Darwin, Jack London, Dostoevsky, Nietzsche, H.G. Wells, Julien Benda, Conrad,[12] Coleridge, Cocteau.

The short 'Preface' to the book (T, xi-xiv) and the apparatus of Acknowledgements, Notes and Bibliography at the end (T, 545–604) provide further indications of Thomson's biographical method. In particular, two aspects are worth noting, on the primacy of research and on the contiguous, complementary relation of the biography to Levi's own texts. On the former, Preface and apparatus both give a strong impression of the range and sheer effort involved in Thomson's 'sleuth'-work (T, xiii). In his 11 years of research, he spoke to over 300 people, he travelled across continents following up leads 'obsessively' (T, xi) and in the strangest directions. Once again, we are offered an image of the biographer as detective, as researcher, interested in unearthing the scrap of information or serendipitous fact.

The final and perhaps most striking declaration of biographical intent, made on the first page of the 'Preface', is the promise to use information gleaned through research above and beyond, indeed *to the exclusion of* Levi's own published words:

> From the start, I was determined to construct a life of Primo Levi not found in his books. It seemed to me dishonest, as well as dangerous, to recast Levi's printed words in a biography. (T, xi)[13]

And indeed, Thomson only very rarely dips into, let alone uses Levi's own words, not because they are not important, but precisely because they are the single reason for writing the biography, they should be left to stand alone, not reduced to (often flawed or elaborated) evidence.

For Thomson, then, the biographer works on the micro-scale, looking far and wide for as great a mass of fragmentary details on as many levels as possible. A final

Levian analogy works here, since this method — combining research, sleuthing, reportage or chronicle at the level of minute detail — tacks close to Levi's own practice and literary use of chemistry (and indeed his epistemology), in essays and in works such as *Il sistema periodico* (*The Periodic Table*, 1975). Or perhaps we are even closer to a tool in Levi's office life at the SIVA paint factory, which is also a method of research (one amongst many activities and literary proclivities Levi shared with Georges Perec): the index card (T, 257).[14]

The Biographer as Psychoanalyst and Subject

If we turn to Carole Angier's book, it is immediately apparent that we are dealing with a method radically opposed to Thomson's. This is not to say that she does not share with Thomson the 'obsessive' and exhaustive thirst for research, for interviews and for the unearthing of new documents.[15] Angier's encounters with interviewees, however, and her use of documents point towards a desire for matrices of interpretation, for psychological and textual complexity, and for intimate and intellectual engagement with her material which could hardly be more alien to Thomson's mindset.

As with *Primo Levi*, the structure of *The Double Bond* is eloquent in itself. The main title itself already contains, in metaphorical synthesis, both the central interpretative thesis of the book and perhaps its single most significant documentary discovery. 'The Double Bond' — *Il doppio legame* — was the title of the book left unfinished by Levi at his death, made up of letters to a lady on organic chemistry, of which Angier uncovered three previously unknown chapters to add to the three Levi had shown to his editors at Einaudi. 'The Double Bond' or 'double bind' further captures Angier's contention that Levi's life was conditioned and indeed imprisoned by his unresolved, repressed, contradictory relationship with sexuality and women (especially his wife and mother); with his very physicality. His ultimately fatal depression — although in large part, for Angier as for Thomson, an endogenous, cyclical medical condition rather than an exogenous response to events in his life — expressed itself and was exacerbated by this 'double bind'. The image and the thesis behind it run declaredly throughout the book, much to the annoyance of several reviewers, who see it as taking on a tendentious life of its own beyond the available evidence.[16] What is certain is that both the idiom of the title and the nature of the thesis itself (a problem, bound up with sexuality, founded in childhood and early relationships, read 'between the lines' of later statements) declare Angier's biographical project as psychoanalytical in shape: if Thomson writes at times like the pathologist in the morgue, Angier wants to be the psychopathologist of Levi's everyday life.

Chapter structure and titles extend this interpretative, metaphorical tendency. With the exception of the middle of the three Parts of the book — dealing with the years immediately before, during and after Auschwitz, where she adopts temporarily a chronicler's mode ('Milan: July 1942 — 8 September 1943', 'Auschwitz: 22 February 1944 — 27 January 1945', etc.) — Angier's titles are imaged and not explicatory: 'Paradiso', 'Botticelli Angels', 'Primo Levi Primo', 'Levi Uomo', 'Centaur', and so on. There is chronological sequence here, but the sequence is interrupted by an alternating series of embedded short chapters written from the present tense of the biographer, with mostly one-word titles set in italics (e.g., *'Burning'*, *'Gabriella'*, *'Dancing'*, *'Lilith'*).[17]

The metaphorical titles and the embedded structure speak of a refractive eye behind this biography, turning gathered material towards an axis of interpretation, of (literary and psycho-) analysis. The 'Preface' elaborates on this in an intense and risky declaration of intent. In a move redolent of the heuristic pattern of Freudian psychoanalysis at its most cunning, Angier bases her work in paradoxes of silence, obstacle, denial: precisely because Levi, his family, Turin, its bourgeoisie and its Jews, the anonymous sources and the dead are all bound by silence, that of which they do not speak must not be allowed to remain silent. This means reading Levi's reserve as 'his armour but also the gap in it' (A, xvii). It means upturning the cause and effect of the silence, and reading in a desire not to speak a repressed desire to speak: and this allows Angier to claim she is doing what Levi would have done if he had been able: '*because he wanted to be released from [his prisons] too*' (A, xx; italics in the original).

Three important consequences flow from this. First, a transcending of the nature of evidence in the positivist biographical method: to break the barriers of silence you have to come at this world and this man obliquely. Hence, Angier admits into evidence, indeed puts at the heart of her evidence, 'secret witnesses'(A, xviii-xix), unnamed or pseudonymous (Gisella, Lilith); speculation (re-imagining character and event, speculating on Lucia's role and attitude); and even fiction, especially two minor novels by a friend and a family member, which apparently used Levi's parents for source material.[18] Most of this material is separated out into the interpolated chapters, which Angier calls the 'less stable' or 'irrational' chapters (A, xvii), thinner with evidence, but to her more 'true' than the 'stable' or 'rationally tested, known or knowable' parts of the book and of Levi (ibid). The stretching of the bounds of admissible evidence also takes in the immense and often densely subtle use Angier makes of Levi's entire corpus of literary work as source of fact and reflection, of strikingly distorted fact, of displaced workings-through of fear and desires, of telling displacements and silences. On this Angier and Thomson are diametrically opposed.

Following on from this change in the nature of evidence is a change in the ways of writing biography: 'Where I can, I tell Primo Levi's story straight. Where I cannot — because I cannot betray my sources, or because I have felt and imagined the past from a story, or from an encounter — I simply give you the story, or the encounter' (ibid). The biographer here becomes much more of a writer of narrative, and thus much closer to her subject, than the conventionally modest portraitist of 'great men'. Her achievement relies much more on the narrative, 'literary' power of the 'character' at the heart of the biography than on the demonstrable concreteness of her knowledge about him. And indeed, Angier's biography is incomparably more writerly, more stylistically elegant, fluent, varied and charged than Thomson's (for good or ill).[19]

Finally, but perhaps most significantly of all, Angier herself becomes a key voice and subject of her biography. This occurs in a number of ways. She is personal, opinionated when she intervenes with impassioned, at times moving declarations of Levi's genius ('If one day there is a new Holocaust, and we can save only one chapter of one book from the twentieth century, it should be this one: chapter 11 of *If This is a Man*', A, 330). In the 'irrational' chapters, her drama parallels Levi's: her search for Levi is staged in *her* encounters with Alberto Salmoni (with whom she has a flirtatious frisson), with Gisella and Lilith (with whom she jousts for understanding and extra insight), with Lucia Levi (who refuses to deal with her, but whom she addresses anyway, as she imagines her burning Levi's papers or as paranoid as Pirandello's infamous wife). And Angier, in a classic, complex process of psychoanalytical transference, writes at times like another of Levi's women confidantes, at others as though identifying with Levi himself.[20]

The 'New "New Biography"'

Angier's method, and Thomson's apparent resistance to it, do not come out of nowhere. Modern literary biography in English has its distinctive history as a genre, one which has run parallel in many respects to the history of the novel. Standard accounts move from the 18th century (Boswell, Johnson) through the monumental Victorian project of the *DNB* to the modernist interest in a 'new biography' epitomized by Woolf's 1927 essay of that name and Strachey's *Eminent Victorians* (1918). All these lines have fed into the remarkable contemporary success of the genre, including its more innovative manifestations.[21] Two aspects related to these recent trends are pertinent here.

First, biography has tended to be subsumed within a larger field of so-called 'Life-Writing', containing all the myriad ways and forms in which the experience of an individual life is recorded.[22] These would include both biography and autobiography, but also diaries, letters and wills, oral histories and testimonies, sociological and historiographical data and documents, collective histories, visual records and so on. These have been especially important in a 'political' process of recovering the non-literary histories of hidden or excluded individuals or groups, from women and children to slaves, from the colonized to the ethnically oppressed, from the insane to the criminal. But perhaps before these, and catalyst to these, came the turn to life-writing by and about the non-heroic, the non-exceptional, ordinary men and women, living in contact with the larger, determining movements of history (especially through the experience of modern warfare). Levi's own life — and the biographical accounts of it — intersect this first aspect in at least three ways. First, as a Jew in Fascist and Nazi-Fascist Italy and then in Auschwitz, he lived through the most extreme manifestation in the modern era of the crushing, oppressive sweep of history over the individual. Secondly, Holocaust testimony as a genre, to the history of which Levi makes such a fundamental contribution, has been one of the key stages in the surge in life-writing in the modern era. Finally, and perhaps most significantly of all, in the very mode of his writing, in his implicit ethics, and in his character as evinced by both Thomson and Angier, Levi represents one of the most subtle and resilient embodiments of the 'ordinary' in modern literature.[23]

Secondly, recent practice in biography has also responded to formal and epistemological problems implicit in the genre. Knowledge about an individual is no longer perceived as simply and transparently available to one narrow genre, as the fluidity of the 'life-writing' label already suggests. Category borders are stretched in a manner that has a touch of the post-modern about it (with all due caution in using the term). And a post-modern epistemological scepticism also lies behind a tendency to acknowledge within biographies biography's failure, its provisional, contingent, limited claims to knowledge and its status as an act of shaped narrative, seen through the necessarily partial and subjective filter of the subject, the biographer's 'I'. Clearly, Angier's work stands four-square within this new trend.

In some instances, this provisional and partial take on life-writing emerges as a direct consequence of the formal and legal institutions surrounding literature. Problems of copyright, ownership, questions of privacy and literary legacy dog the biographical researcher and have led to inventive circumnavigations: Ian Hamilton's *In Search of J.D. Salinger* turned the impossibility of gaining access to the reclusive Salinger into the main subject of his quasi-biography; Peter Ackroyd notably wrote a life of T.S. Eliot without permission to quote any of his work.[24] Similarly, if to a lesser degree, the biographers of Levi had to contend with the non-cooperation of Levi's wife (also his literary executor) and hence both must acknowledge the lacunae in their work at the level of document and at the level of the personal history of Levi's family.

Beyond institutional obstacles, however, there have also been 'internal' forces pushing biography away from the chiselled certainties of conventional 'lives'. Perhaps the most compelling practical illustration of this is Richard Holmes' 1985 collection of auto/biographical essays, *Footsteps*.[25] The essays in *Footsteps* do not amount to a *theory* of biography; they rather trace the birth of this newly sensitized form of biographer in Holmes himself. He lets us in on his journeys in pursuit of Robert Louis Stevenson, Mary Wollstonecraft, Gérard de Nerval, and Shelley and his contemporaries, and thus Holmes' own journey in becoming a certain kind of biographer.

For Holmes, biography is 'a tracking of the physical trail of someone's path through the past, a following of footsteps' (p.27), and the writing of the biography is the writing of that pursuit: 'you would never quite catch them. But maybe, if you were lucky, you might write about the pursuit of that fleeting figure in such a way as to bring it alive in the present' (ibid). Beyond the gathering of factual materials, biography requires what he calls 'a fictional or imaginary relationship between the biographer and his subject; not merely a "point of view" or an "interpretation", but a continuous living dialogue between the two as they move over the same historical ground, the same trail of events' (p.66). This open relationship between biographer and subject starts in identification, even a form of love (ibid), but moves on from that, through a necessary disillusionment. To follow his /her elusive trail, the biographer must open out to new possible forms, even irrational forms of writing, when the subject demands it:

> Here at last began for me too the overflowing of the irrational into normal forms of biography. All the logical and traditional structures that I had

> learned so painstakingly — the chronology, the developments of character, the structure of friendships, the sense of trust and the subject's inner identity — began to twist and dissolve. It was becoming more and more difficult to tell, or to account for Nerval's life in the ordinary narrative, linear way. (p.249)

At the same time, even the most extraordinary life must be written with sensitivity to the ordinary, so often excluded from the documentary record: 'The re-creation of the daily, ordinary texture of an individual life — full of the mundane, trivial, funny and humdrum goings-on of a single loving relationship — in a word, the re-creation of *intimacy* — is almost the hardest thing in biography; and when achieved, the most triumphant.' (p.120)

The lines of connection between all this and Angier's biography are not hard to draw. Angier's 'Preface' is eloquent on the necessarily flawed and provisional status of any single biography, rational or irrational:

> I have been suggesting that only the second, unstable biography [within *The Double Bond*] is a failure, but of course both are. [...] All biographies are like archaeology, constructing whole civilizations on a few shards of pottery. [...] there will be many more books about Primo Levi [...] sometimes suddenly [...] you realize you were completely wrong, some vital piece of evidence was missing, and you never knew them at all. Getting to know someone from his biography is as provisional and unpredictable as that. But no more than that. (A, xviii)

Her general conception of the role of the 'irrational' chapters in her work chimes with Holmes' conception of biography as always existing in the pursuit of its elusive subject; and with his confession of a baffled need for new forms of biographical discourse in the face of certain, perplexing subjects (Nerval for him; Levi for Angier). Angier's work turns on her 'relationship' with Levi, despite/ because of what Holmes calls its 'fictional or imaginary' basis. More than one reviewer accused Angier of being 'in love' with Levi — a necessary stage for Holmes — and signs of her equally necessary 'disillusionment' are there in her dogged pursuit of his human flaws, of how he was, as she puts it, 'bad at life' (A, xx). At one of the most intensely emotional, fictional and irrational moments of her book — when she describes her fear that Lucia Levi will burn Levi's papers — Angier evokes the work of another key figure in modern biography, Michael Holroyd, and his essay on the uncanny recurrence of book burning by authors and their executors, 'Smoke with Fire. On the Ethics of Biography'.[26] Holroyd ends his essay by using Tom Stoppard's time-shifting play *Arcadia* as a model of the biographical pursuit, one in which the biographer reaches out to the past, through fragments and inevitable misconceptions to make contact across time:

> I believe the literary biographer can stretch out a hand to his subject and invite him, invite her, to write one more work, posthumously and in collaboration. [...] Though it still has its uses as a reference work, biography is no longer a mere inventory of facts suspended between a chronology and some sources. We know the value of dreams and fantasies, the shadow of the life that isn't lived but lingers within people, and the lies we tell are part of the truth we live. (p.19)

Angier's strange merging of her own work with Levi's — noted earlier — has its sources in this conception of the biographer's ethics.

Traditional biography has far from been eclipsed by these new forms and sensitivities in biography, of course, and Thomson could be seen as powerful evidence of this. But it is worth noting, finally, that even his account of Levi's life is not without either its own sense of limit and contingency, or its own clues to the biographer's presence. Thomson starts out from the premise that it is 'fantastically difficult' to make 'narrative' from an 'inchoate life' (T, xi); and his 'index-card' style, eschewing interpretation and preferring description and data, precisely seems to acknowledge the frailty of the single truth about another person. Indeed, Angier is paradoxically happier than Thomson to push a single, all-encompassing interpretation of her subject — the double bond/ bind theory — because she knows and declares hers as only one solution of many (although at times, she seems rather to present it as straightforwardly true). And if Thomson most often relegates talk of himself to paratextual sites — Preface, notes etc — he is in those places keen to emphasize *his* energetic pursuit of his subject; and *his own* encounter with Levi, evoked in the chapter 'In London. 1986' (T, 488–507), perhaps the key origin of the biography. Thomson's work is, in other words, alive to many of the same issues and obstacles which push Angier in more radical, self-evidently experimental directions.

Levi's 'Life-Writing'

The battle of the Levi biographies represents a fascinating case study of the state of biography in the English-speaking world. But it becomes more interesting and more resonant still if we recognise that there is a complex interplay between many of the issues raised there, and several fundamental questions about aspects of Levi's own work.

Already, in the discussion of the two biographies above, the shifting of terms from biography to 'life-writing' inserted the problems of biography into a wider sphere including autobiography and testimony.[27] Levi's work is clearly rooted in these first-person fields of life-writing, in his Holocaust work and beyond. At the same time, however, his is a strikingly extrovert autobiographical voice, revealing relatively little about himself and instead filling his writing canvas with a rich array of portraits of individuals encountered, of moments, groups, systems and the people within them.[28] For our purposes, then, we can reformulate the nature of Levi's life-writing by saying that he bends autobiographical and testimonial writing as far as he can towards the biographical (in the broadest sense of writing about and giving a sense of other people's lives); and in doing so, he encounters, in modified form, many of the same problems and obstacles — to do with method and the ethics of writing — that we have come across in our discussion of his biographers and of biography in general.

Besides those touched on already in passing above, we can note briefly four large issues shared between biography and the biographical aspect to Levi's 'life-writing': privacy, narrative and truth, causality, and meaning.

Reticence or discretion was a central trait of Levi's character (a Turinese facet, as both Thomson and Angier point out), but he also built it into his testimonial accounts of those close to him. One instance in *Se questo è un uomo* (*If This Is a Man*) can stand for many others: at the moment of deportation from Fossoli to Auschwitz, the prisoners step beyond the bounds of the living, each reacting to imminent death in their own way, as Levi comments, 'Molte cose furono allora fra noi dette e fatte: ma di queste è bene che non resti memoria' [Many things were said and done at that time between us; but of these it is right that no memory remain; I, 10]. Days later, as the train journey nears its end, Levi marks another moment of discretion:

> Accanto a me, serrata come me fra corpo e corpo, era stata per tutto il viaggio una donna. Ci conoscevamo da molti anni e la sventura ci aveva colti insieme, ma poco sapevamo l'uno dell'altra. Ci dicemmo allora, nell'ora della decisione, cose che non si dicono fra i vivi. (I, 13)
>
> [Next to me, pressed like me between body upon body, there had been for the whole journey a woman. We had known each other for many years and misfortune had surprised us together, but we knew little one of the other. In that moment of truth, we said to each other things that are not said by living people.][29]

Marking out certain areas of deepest trauma and humiliation as properly beyond even the witness's gaze shores up the dignity of other people's lives and protects the private sphere from the intrusions of representation. For similar reasons, when asked why he spoke and wrote so little of his family, his reply was that he preferred not to write of the living,[30] showing himself alert not only to the recurrent problem of modern biography — the invasion of privacy — but also to the effect on this question of *when* one is writing about others, as well as what or how.

It is worth noting also that Levi was not immune to the countervailing pleasures of learning the intimate secrets of others' lives: indeed, he describes himself as someone who seems naturally to attract such secrets: 'Mi vennero raccontate moltissime storie [...], spesso intricate e sempre intime [...]: io sono uno a cui molte cose vengono raccontate' [Many many stories were told to me [...] often intricate and always intimate stories [...]: I am a person to whom many things are told] (*Il sistema periodico*, I, 798). And in a piece in the collection *Racconti e saggi* [*Stories and Essays*], he recalls an old plan of his to write a book on gossip, perhaps the most basic root of all for biography ('Del pettegolezzo', II, 982–85).[31]

In his reticence about writing about the living, Levi is not only concerned about betraying the confidence and denting the already weakened dignity of others, but also about the risks of turning lives into stories, about the distortions that narrative inevitably brings. Levi was a careful shaper of stories, even when working in 'truth-telling' genres (as most life-writing does); indeed he invested a great deal in his own role as storyteller, as one who listens to others' stories and then retells their stories in turn to us. A paradigmatic example for this is the title story of the collection *Lilít* ('Lilít', II, 18–23), in which Levi meditates elegiacally on the mystery of the passing on of stories:

È inesplicabile che il destino abbia scelto un epicureo per ripetere questa favola pia ed empia, intessuta di poesia, di ignoranza, di acutezza temeraria, e della tristezza non medicabile che cresce sulle rovine delle civiltà perdute. (II, 23)

[It is inexplicable that destiny chose an epicurean to relate this pious and impious fable, interwoven with poetry, ignorance, rash subtlety, and that incurable sadness that grows on the ruins of lost civilizations.]

Both biographers detail the changes in fact made by Levi to many of his stories for the sake of narrative form, and of a form of wisdom captured by the shaped story. Indeed, this is a key reason why Thomson eschews use of the texts themselves as biographical evidence. Levi clearly set store by this form of wisdom or other truth, proudly claiming that he was no historian (II, 1005), but nor had he invented anything in his testimony (I, 6). Even at the level of narrative arc of time, Levi's biographical impulse contrasts with biography *per se* since it aims to capture character or encounter in moments, in single, metonymic portraits rather than in arcs of development. He did, however, come to worry about the distortions made upon other people's real lives and characters by the demands and perspectives of testimonial-biographical narrative. He says as much in a 1981 interview: when asked how people react to being transformed into 'characters', he confesses himself guilty of what he calls 'this minor violation' and talks of friends' 'unease' at the process.[32] Levi, like Philip Roth in *The Counterlife* or Woody Allen in *Deconstructing Harry*, even integrates these meta-biographical/meta-narrative problems of turning real people into characters into his works, at several points in *Il sistema periodico* (*The Periodic Table*) and *La chiave a stella* (*The Wrench*, 1978), in the Pirandellian stories 'Lavoro creativo' and 'Nel parco' (I, 651–60; 671–80), and others.

A third area where Levi's biographical-testimonial interests overlap with those of modern biography is that of the nature of causality in human lives. The Holocaust sets into particularly sharp relief the balance between individual self-determination (reduced to a minimum in the de-individualized macrocosm of the *Lager*), external historical cause and luck or chance (maximized even to the absurd in the *Lager*); and all three are keys axes of biographical causality, of what determines the course of any individual life and/or life-story.[33] Levi's most eloquent essay on the issue of luck and destiny — one that obsessed him from the opening words of his first book, 'Per mia fortuna, sono stato deportato ad Auschwitz solo nel 1944' [It was my good fortune to have been deported to Auschwitz only in 1944] (I, 5) — is the 1985 piece, 'Pipetta da guerra' (*Racconti e saggi*, II, 886–89) where he narrates how a chain of chance was the difference between life and death for Primo and his friend Alberto. Shortly before evacuation, Levi and Alberto came into contact with scarlet-fever — Levi fell almost fatally ill, but Albert had had the disease as a child and was immune, and so died on the death-march out of Auschwitz whilst Levi was left behind. Levi survived, 'Alberto fu vittima della piccola causa, della scarlattina da cui era guarito bambino' [Alberto fell victim to a minor cause, to the scarlet-fever that I had been cured of as a boy] (II, 889). The logic and scale of cause and effect was all skewed, chance and the movements of history determined life and death with a force overwhelmingly beyond the capacity of individual self-determination.

Levi was also interested in other forms of overarching determinants of individual lives, such as the past, language, nationality, evinced in his chronicle of the history and language of his own ancestors in 'Argon' in *Il sistema periodico* (*The Periodic Table*) (I, 741–56), or in his extended reflections on the national character of the Germans, the Russians and (briefly) the Americans, in *La tregua* (*The Truce*, 1963), *Se non ora, quando?* (*If Not Now, When?*, 1982) and elsewhere. In this, as in many other things, Levi demonstrates a fluid movement between a focus on the individual and his/her life-story as an end in itself, on the one hand, and the reading of that life as standing for a given moment or type, on the other. In a manner reminiscent of older traditions of life-writing, Levi's biographical mode often presents the individual as emblematic — whether it is the intensely moving story of Hurbinek, in the early pages of *La tregua*, who dies without speaking, without a name, and becomes an emblem of the devastation of both the Final Solution and the bind of survival (I, 215–16); or Chaim Rumkowski, a man whose life embodies the problems of the 'grey zone' in *I sommersi e i salvati* (*The Drowned and The Saved*, 1986; II, 1043); or, with a lighter touch, the myriad encounters with people as emblems of their work, their trades in *L'altrui mestiere* (*Other People's Trades*, 1985) (or his own work in *Il sistema periodico*). This final aspect of Levi's life-writing is perhaps the most telling of all: a way in which he writes other people's lives in an almost pre-modern mode (rooted in early Italian traditions of chronicles and exempla), returning to a sense of the life as both individual and archetypal, forging exempla out of the encounter with the ordinary lived life. In this, perhaps more than in any other way, his own collage of written lives coincides in his own particular fashion with the concerns of 'life-writing' and contrasts with other, monumental conceptions of biography.

Notes to Chapter 3

1. Carole Angier, *The Double Bond. Primo Levi. A Biography* (London: Viking, Penguin, 2002); Ian Thomson, *Primo Levi* (London: Hutchinson, 2002). Future references to the two biographies will be in the form A plus page number for Angier's work, T plus page number for Thomson's. Neither of them was the first biography of Levi to appear in English. See the much weaker Myriam Anissimov, *Primo Levi. The Tragedy of an Optimist* (London: Aurum Press, 1998; first published in French in 1996). References to Levi's work will be in the form I, 99, and refer to Primo Levi, *Opere*, ed. by Marco Belpoliti, 2 vols (Turin: Einaudi, 1997).
2. Thomson has hinted that knowing about Angier's work pushed him to finish ('A Race to the Bookshop', *The Guardian*, 1 March 2003). One reviewer reflected on the general phenomenon of multiple biographies (of Austen, Beckett, Greene, Trollope etc.) (David Sexton, 'Battle of the biographers', *Evening Standard*, 26 March 2002); but as another noted, 'It must be unprecedented for a European writer to attract two British biographers barely a decade after his death' (Blake Morrison, 'A Prisoner Outside the Gates', *The Guardian*, 23 March 2002).
3. Several reviews are gathered at the following website: http://members.tripod.com/arlindo_correia/angier.html.
4. Lavinia Greenlaw, 'The Agonised Self', *New Statesman*, 1 April 2002.
5. Peter Conrad, 'Levi: No Stone Unturned', *The Observer*, 24 March 2002. And cf. Clive James who describes them as two books 'which weigh on the spirit almost as much as they do on the muscles'('The Unmysterious Suicide', *Times Literary Supplement*, 21 June 2002).
6. The last chapter before the 'Epilogue', 'April 1987: The Last Six Days' (T, 534–40) echoes the final chapter of *Se questo è un uomo*, 'Storia di dieci giorni' (I, 147–60). Angier uses this model more directly still, structuring her own account of Levi's last ten days in Auschwitz before liberation in diary form ('Ten Days', A, 355–67).

7. This also explains a weakness of Thomson's style, in several rather clichéd overviews of historical context (e.g. 'There was much rain that Spring of 1943', T, 125; 'The 1940s gave way to the 1950s', T, 261), or awkward grand statements on Levi's larger significance ('he was loved by a multitude', T, xiv).
8. Both Thomson and Angier have no doubt that it was suicide. They both also make reference to the few who have doggedly questioned this certainty (see, e.g., Diego Gambetta, 'Primo Levi's Last Moments', *Boston Review*, Summer 1999, pp.25–29).
9. It is remarkable how many reviews (or editors' titles for reviews) couch biography in terms of a mystery to be solved, the search for a single key to unlocking the life: Joan Acocella, 'A Hard Case', *The New Yorker*, 19 June 2002; Carole Angier, 'The Secret Life of Primo Levi', *The Guardian*, 9 March 2002 [a pre-publication article on her book]; Anon., 'Il mistero di Primo Levi', *La repubblica*, 10 March 2002; Anon, 'The Riddle of Turin', *The Economist*, 11 April 2002; Giorgio Di Rienzo, 'Il mistero di Primo Levi', *Corriere della sera*, 13 March 2002; Alberto Papuzzi, 'Primo Levi. Il volto segreto', *La stampa*, 27 March 2002; A. Stille, 'Secrets of Primo Levi', *NYRB*, 15 August 2002; and cf. against all these, Clive James, 'The Unmysterious Suicide', *Times Literary Supplement*, 21 June 2002. See also the dust jacket to Angier, where Hilary Spurling compares the book to a 'thriller' and Michael Holroyd talks of 'solv[ing] the almost intractable problems', but tellingly he means not of Levi's life but of the task of the modern biographer.
10. Thomson — a literary journalist and travel writer — has a direct link to the genre of the 'giallo' as a translator of Leonardo Sciascia (*Death of an Inquisitor and Other Stories*, London: Harvill, 1984).
11. The cameo appearance of Fassino in Levi's last days is interesting, as Fassino is today leader of the PDS, the successor party to the PCI (a fact Thomson, however, does not note, nor is Fassino's name even in the book's patchy index). Angier makes no mention of him. In general, as several reviewers pointed out, Thomson is better on the Italian literary and political context of post-war Italy (not necessarily on earlier literature), although claims that he is also better on the history of the War are perhaps overstated (Clive James notes at least one gaffe on the Normandy landings; another would be bracketing Croce with Giovanni Gentile as 'the regime's prominent ideologues', T, 65; labelling Manzoni as 'secular', T, 246; talking of a television personality in 1948, T, 255); and both are very thorough on the Resistance in North Western Italy.
12. There is an interesting divergence between the biographers here. Angier says Levi was recommending Conrad to friends at the age of 16 (A, 71). Thomson says he read him for the first time only in 1947 (T, 250). Conrad was a crucial influence for Levi's and others of his generation: see, e.g., Martin McLaughlin and Arianna Scicutella, 'Calvino e Conrad: dalla tesi di laurea alle *Lezioni americane*', *Italian Studies*, 57 (2002), 113–32.
13. Thomson (whether he has Angier or Anissimov in mind here specifically) is responding to a common general assumption that there is nothing to say about Levi as he said it all so eloquently himself (e.g. Peter Preston, who notes, 'nobody could say it better [than Levi's work itself]; nobody can approach its emotional truth', 'You Wait for 10 Years for One Biography of Primo Levi ...', *The Observer*, 7 April 2002.
14. See David Bellos, *Georges Perec. A Life in Words* (London, Harvill, 1993), pp. 51–63, 398–403; A. Cavaglion 'Asimmetrie' in *Primo Levi*, special issue of *Riga*, 13 (1997), 222–29 (p.228).
15. Indeed, at certain moments she is more in line with the positivist biographical method than he: e.g., her notes are voluminous and far more detailed and variably sourced that his (A, 733–863; ie., roughly three-times the length of his) ; she, not he, includes an extended family tree (A, 2–3).
16. This seems to have been one root cause of the extreme hostility Angier's book proved capable of stirring in certain reviewers: see, e.g., Thomas Laqueur, 'Travelling in the Classic Style', *London Review of Books*, 5 September 2002, p. 12.
17. Again, Part Two, in and around Auschwitz, is treated somewhat differently: there is only one interpolated chapter, *'Gabriella'* (A, 224–29).
18. Luisa Accati, *Il matrimonio di Raffaele Albanese* (Turin: Anabasi, 1994); Paolo Levi, *Il filo della memoria* (Milan: Rizzoli, 1984); and see A, 59–67, 520–23.
19. One simple contrast, of the hundreds possible, to mark Angier's more narrative-driven style, is with Thomson's 'police procedural' account of the suicide. Angier does not open with this, and

when she reaches it in her final pages, it is with great melodrama ('And then it happened. [...]', A, 719) and empathetic, fictional imagination: 'I think he looked for Lucia to stop him. He leaned and looked, but she wasn't there; and he let go' (A, 731).

20. The Preface has several moments and turns of phrase where Angier and Levi share terms and sensibilities and seem almost to merge: 'I have taken over his own title ['The Double Bond'], like a torch from a previous runner [...] Despite all my own double binds, I knew I had to [...] make it the heart of the book [...] the best solution he ever found to [his double bind] was writing. It seems the best solution to me too' (A, xvii, xix, xxi).
21. A brief 'potted' history is to be found in the 'Biography' entry in the *Oxford Companion to English Literature*, ed. by Margaret Drabble, 6th edn (Oxford: Oxford University Press, 2000). Also useful is David Ellis, *Literary Lives. Biography and the Search for Understanding* (Edinburgh: Edinburgh University Press, 2000). Whilst writing this essay, I was fortunate enough also to read Catherine Galloway's 'Close Reading: Translation, Re-writing, and Re-visiting in Anna Banti and Virginia Woolf' (unpublished doctoral thesis, University of Cambridge, 2003), which has much of interest to say on the nature of modern biography.
22. See the monumental *Encyclopedia of Life Writing*, ed. by Margaretta Jolly, 2 vols (London: Fitzroy Dearborn, 2001).
23. On the ordinariness of modern biography's interest in daily life, which 'has something of the feminine' about it, see Michael Holroyd, *Works on Paper. The Craft of Biography and Autobiography* (London: Little, Brown, 2002), p.22. On Levi's 'ordinariness', see Robert S. C. Gordon, *Primo Levi's Ordinary Virtues* (Oxford: Oxford University Press, 2001).
24. Ian Hamilton, *In Search of J.D. Salinger* (London: Heinemann, 1988); Peter Ackroyd, *T.S. Eliot* (London: Hamish Hamilton, 1984).
25. Richard Holmes, *Footsteps. Adventures of a Romantic Biographer* (London: Harper Collins, 1996).
26. In Michael Holroyd, *Works on Paper*, pp. 10–19 (and see A, 198–91).
27. See Massimo Lollini, *Il vuoto della forma. Scrittura, testimonianza, verità* (Genoa: Marietti, 2001).
28. Mirna Cicioni uses the term 'autography' to capture this aspect of Levi's work: see M. Cicioni, '"Different Springs and Different Airs": Primo Levi's Multiple Autography', *Menorah*, 3.2 (December 1989), 20–31.
29. Here and throughout, Angier needs to ignore Levi's impulse to discretion, since for her this reticence is all about her core theme, and from this derives the hostility of certain reviewers. Her dramatic account of Fossoli and Levi's female companion referred to here contains extraordinary revelations (A, 262–81). For more on discretion, see Gordon, *Primo Levi's Ordinary Virtues*, pp. 73–88.
30. See Primo Levi, *The Voice of Memory. Interviews 1961–1987*, ed. by Marco Belpoliti and Robert Gordon (Cambridge: Polity Press, 2001), pp. 82, 148–51.
31. On biography's origin in gossip, see Ellis, *Literary Lives*, pp.18–19.
32. See Levi, *The Voice of Memory*, p.150.
33. See Ellis, 'History, Chance and Self-Determination' in *Literary Lives*, pp.117–36, where he discusses, among other things, suicide and its impact on these larger issues. Note also a recent trend in life-writing studies to read illness narrative as a specific form of life-writing (into which depression might be inserted): see Anne Hunsaker Hawkins, *Reconstructing Illness. Studies in Pathography*, 2nd edn (West Lafayette, Indiana: Purdue University Press, 1999); and the reviewer of Angier in *The Economist* ('The Riddle of Turin', 11 April 2002), who labelled her work a 'traumatography'.

PART II

❖

D'Annunzio and Other *Fin de siècle* Figures

CHAPTER 4

❖

Enrico Nencioni: An Italian Victorian

Giuliana Pieri

Enrico Nencioni (1837–1896) was probably the single most important cultural mediator of Umbertine Italy. He was a poet, critic, journalist, writer and, from 1883, lecturer in Italian at the Istituto Superiore di Magistero, in Florence, and at the prestigious Collegio della SS. Annunziata at Poggio Imperiale. He was considered the authority in Italy on contemporary English literature, writing articles on the Brownings, Thomas Carlyle, Mary Shelley, Alfred Tennyson, A. C. Swinburne, D. G. Rossetti and Walter Pater. He corresponded with the most eminent Italian writers of his time — Capuana, Fogazzaro, De Amicis, Serao, D'Annunzio, Carducci — and contributed to all the major literary journals of his time — *Fanfulla della Domenica*, *Italia Nuova*, *Nuova Antologia*, *Domenica Letteraria*, *Cronaca Bizantina*. Yet by the time of his death, he was already a half-forgotten figure and, as D'Annunzio perceptively wrote, a misunderstood one:

> Enrico Nencioni non era per i piú se non un commentatore elegante e sentimentale di poeti nordici, un malinconico sognatore dotato di morbidezza quasi feminea [sic], inclinato verso le forme squisite e gracili dell'arte: insomma un artefice di medaglioni scolpiti a mezzo rilievo e miniati su avorio per donne vereconde. Il carattere essenziale del suo spirito è invece l'amore della forza possente e della passione dominatrice.[1]
>
> [For most people Enrico Nencioni was but an elegant and sentimental commentator of Northern poets, a melancholy dreamer endowed with an almost feminine softness, inclined towards exquisite, slender forms of art: in short, a creator of miniature portraits carved in low relief and painted on ivory for modest women. In reality the fundamental essence of his spirit was a love of mighty strength and ruling passion.]

In the decades immediately after Nencioni's death (1896), opinions on him varied. For his former friends and those who had been in close contact with him, the Florentine possessed an 'ingegno così candido e puro così misto e complesso' [mind so innocent and yet so mixed and complex];[2] he was 'l'amico, il compagno, il fratello di ogni artista e di ogni poeta' [the friend, the companion, the brother of every artist and every poet];[3] and 'uno dei piú grandi maestri del tempo nostro, uno dei piú grandi *coltivatori d'anime* che possa vantare l'Italia' [one of the greatest masters of our time, one of the greatest cultivators of souls that Italy can boast of].[4] A similar appreciation was shared, in the late nineteenth century, by

English commentators who praised his activity as literary critic: 'he is the Sainte-Beuve of Italy [...]. For the Italian public, he is the discoverer of Browning, of Tennyson, and of Swinburne';[5] and recognized his role in the spreading of a knowledge of English literature in Italy describing him as 'a high authority upon English literature'.[6]

However, in the early years of the twentieth century, those critics who belonged to the new generation of intellectuals, who had not met Nencioni, distanced themselves from the laudatory tone that characterized his friends. In 1910, asking what was left of Nencioni's legacy, Borgese's peremptory answer was:

> Ben poco [...] in generale egli [...] manca di prospettiva e di punto di vista. La sua anima era troppo esclusivamente occupata dalle letterature inglese, francese e tedesca piú che dall'italiana [...] il torto degli amici [di Nencioni] consiste nell'aver confuso il valore grandissimo della persona viva — amico, fratello, consigliere, ispiratore — col mediocre significato dello scrittore morto.

> [Very little (...) in general he (...) lacked perspective and judgement. His mind was too exclusively concerned with English, French and German literature rather than with Italian writers. (...) His friends' mistake was to confuse the very great value of the living person — friend, brother, adviser, inspirer — with the mediocre significance of the dead writer.][7]

This judgement sums up the point of view of the new generation of writers and intellectuals in the years that led up to World War 1. The new nationalist streak of Italian letters saw Nencioni by and large as irrelevant and did not understand or approve of his passion for foreign literatures. Croce was less critical but equally unenthusiastic. For the Neapolitan critic, Nencioni exemplified the *anima artistica* without actually being an artist. He placed Nencioni in the category of those 'spiriti delicati e aristocratici' [delicate and aristocratic spirits] who 'preferiscono leggere e rileggere, guardare e riguardare, e comporsi nel libro della memoria la loro bella opera d'arte' [prefer to read and re-read, look and look again, and compose their beautiful work of art in the pages of their memory].[8] In the post-war period, scholars have paid indirect attention to Nencioni through the publication of his correspondence with D'Annunzio.[9] Mario Praz highlighted Nencioni's relevance in the context of his analysis of Anglo-Italian cultural relations: his study of the influence of Swinburne on Nencioni's *Rapsodia Lirica* is to this day the only critical study of Nencioni's poetry.[10] Significantly, the volumes published by Marzorati on the history of Italian literature relegated Nencioni to the section on late-romantic critics, reinforcing the idea of the Florentine as an old-fashioned man, who, in late nineteenth-century Italy, firmly belonged to an earlier generation, though his ability as a literary critic was acknowledged: 'un interprete raffinato e polemico della civiltà letteraria tardo-romantica' [a refined and polemical interpreter of late-Romantic literary culture].[11]

Overall, biographical and critical studies are very limited. They are still mostly connected with the posthumous editions of Nencioni's works and consist mainly of brief notes confined to the introductions or appendices of these volumes.[12] The most recent study to discuss, albeit tangentially, Nencioni's role as a cultural *trait d'union* in *fin-de-siècle* Italy is Strowel's 1994 article on the Florentine socialite and dilettante Carlo Placci.[13] The Biblioteca Marucelliana, which houses the bulk of Nencioni's archive, has also recently completed the cataloguing of Nencioni's private papers.[14] What is still missing is an analysis of Nencioni's writings and their relevance in the context of Nencioni's life, and the influence they exercised on contemporary Italian writers. All the studies mentioned above have concentrated on his life, letters and his critical output, albeit in an unsystematic way, and have left aside his creative works: his *Medaglioni*, short biographical sketches of *donne illustri*, and his 'roundabout papers' — he borrowed the idea from Thackeray[15] — which were highly praised by his contemporaries.[16] This general lack of critical attention has its origin in a widespread misconception about Nencioni. Nardi, in the only extensive post-war study on the Florentine critic, exemplifies this negative view by describing him as an 'aristocratico lettore di testi poco noti o rari, maestro di dilettanti raffinati' [aristocratic reader of lesser known and rare texts, master of sophisticated dilettanti], and 'una figura emblematica — nella sua normalità — della scelte e delle aspirazioni contraddittorie della classe media, intellettual-borghese, cui egli fedelmente appartenne' [an emblematic figure — in his ordinariness — of the contradictory choices and aspirations of the educated bourgeois middle-class, to which he faithfully belonged].[17]

The aim of the present study is two-fold. It is a first step towards a reassessment of Nencioni's creative output, and at the same time an analysis of the changing literary and cultural climate of *fin-de-siècle* Italy. A brief biographical note will be followed by the analysis of the impact of Nencioni as a mentor and writer in Umbertine Italy. This will allow me to focus on the changes to the role of intellectuals and men of letters in Italy in the last decades of the nineteenth century. I shall then look at Nencioni's creative works and analyse his interest in biography and autobiography focusing in particular on his representation of women. Ultimately, this chapter aims at challenging the negative perception of the essentially bourgeois character of Nencioni and of the culture he so clearly represented.

Bruno Cicognani, remembering his mentor after his death, described him thus: 'Alto e magro, le lenti d'oro, i capelli ondulati, la "mosca" al mento come i vecchi contadini' [tall and thin, with gold-rimmed glasses, wavy hair, with a goatee like that of an old farmer].[18] He is depicted as an old-fashioned gentleman 'vestito all'inglese, quasi sempre in grigio' [dressed in the English way, almost always in grey].[19] However, all his friends recalled the charm of the man — 'dalla magra ed esile persona, da quegli occhi quasi velati, dalla voce, dal gesto nervoso, irrequieto, emanava un fascino strano, onde sentivi di esser dinanzi a un uomo diverso dagli altri' [his thin and slender figure, those almost misty eyes, his voice, his nervous, restless gestures, all exuded a strange charm, so that you felt you were in the presence of a man quite different from everybody else][20] — and his vibrant conversation, having, as he did, a — 'vera indole di improvvisatore, che si rivela soprattutto nella sorpresa scoppiettante della conversazione' [a real improviser's disposition, which revealed itself above all in the sparkling surprise of his conversation].[21]

Nencioni's passion for and involvement in education, and in particular that of young women, was certainly nurtured from an early age. His mother was in fact the founder of a girls' school, the Istituto Nencioni, in Via delle Oche in Florence.

The young Nencioni studied at the prestigious Scuole Pie where among his school friends were Giosuè Carducci, Ferdinando Martini and Giuseppe Chiarini. These friends were the core group of the so-called *amici pedanti*, who found their inspiration in Greek and Roman literature and the Renaissance, and were staunchly anti-Romantic. Nencioni, despite what critics have claimed, was never one of them: 'gli *amici pedanti* [...] eran tutti legati a me di sincera amicizia. E il vedermi sempre in loro compagnia fece passare anche me per un *amico pedante*' [the *pedantic friends* were all bound to me by sincere friendship. Seeing me always in their company made me appear a *pedantic friend* as well].[22] Despite his close friendship with this group and with Carducci in particular — 'potrei empire un grosso volume di aneddoti sulla vita domestica e scolastica del Carducci' [I could fill a large volume with anecdotes of the domestic and academic life of Carducci][23] — Nencioni's ideals were always very different: he was the Romantic amidst a group of strongly Classical young men. Nencioni was indeed an enthusiast of foreign literature, at a time when in Italy there was a general lack of knowledge of contemporary foreign writers, and above all of English authors: 'de' Francesi e degli Inglesi leggeva tutto quanto potesse. Anche i libri che nessuno leggeva' [of French and English authors he used to read everything he could, even those books that nobody read].[24]

Nencioni's first job, befitting a young middle-class well-educated man with no private means, was as a private tutor in the household of Count Augusto De Gori Pannilini at Siena. He was in the Gori household between 1859 and 1870. In 1875 he moved to Naples for five years working for Princess Caramanico dei Conti d'Aquino. His breakthrough in the publishing world came in 1879, when his friend Martini founded, in Rome, the literary journal *Fanfulla della Domenica*. At the time Nencioni's career in literary criticism was limited to an article on Browning in the *Nuova Antologia* published in 1867.[25] Nencioni accepted the offer to contribute to Martini's new journal and moved to Rome with his Florentine wife, Talía Amerighi.

The Roman years (1879–83) were very happy ones for Nencioni. The frenzy of critical activity during this period is well documented in his letters: 'Sono sommerso dal lavoro: ho qui un pacco di lettere da rispondere [sic], masse di manoscritti da leggere, e ho da finire l'articolo su Edgardo Poe' [I am swamped with work: I have here a volume of letters to reply to, masses of manuscripts to read, and I have to finish the article on Edgar Poe].[26] At this time he frequented the salons of Martini and of Count Giuseppe Primoli, whose palazzo in the Via dell'Orso was one of the most active cultural and social centres in fin-de-siècle Rome.[27] He also frequently visited with Carducci and Serao. In addition, these were the years of the intense relationship with the young D'Annunzio, who dedicated to his mentor the *Elegie Romane* (1892), a tribute to their friendship during these early Roman years. Nencioni also contributed to other Roman literary papers — *Domenica Letteraria*, *Domenica del Fracassa*, *Cronaca Bizantina* — and published his only volume of verses, *Poesie*, in 1880.

In 1883, Nencioni moved back to Florence to take up a post at the Istituto di Magistero. Later he also became a teacher at the Collegio of the SS. Annunziata at Poggio Imperiale, the most prestigious girls' school in Italy. These posts gave him the financial security he needed for his family but left him with an intense nostalgia for Rome, its beauty, climate and vibrant cultural and intellectual milieu. He kept contributing to the Roman papers, and in particular to *Nuova Antologia*, as well as forming a reputation, in Florence, as a public speaker with his lectures at the Circolo Filologico and Palazzo Ginori.

Among those who paid tribute to Nencioni in a special issue of the *Marzocco*, in 1900 — he had died in 1896 of a heart condition — were Carducci, D'Annunzio, Martini, Serao, Pasquale Villari, Guido Biagi and Isidoro Del Lungo. These tributes, from the most influential writers and critics in Italy at the time, naturally have a eulogistic tone. D'Annunzio called him 'eloquentissimo pedagogo' [a highly eloquent pedagogue] and compared his friendship with Nencioni to the those found in the intellectual atmosphere of Plato's dialogues.[28] Even allowing for a degree of biographers' hyperbole, Nencioni really does appear from the memories and tributes of his contemporaries as the Socrates for a generation of young Italian writers and critics. His influence was exercised mainly in private, but also, in the 1880s and 1890s, in the many lectures that he gave in Florence. Cicognani remembered Nencioni's ability as a public speaker — 'l'ascoltare una delle sue conferenze era per me un diletto quale non ò [sic] mai piú provato. Non ò mai piú sentito leggere com'egli leggeva' [to listen to one of his lectures was for me a delight that I have never felt again since. I have never since heard reading like he used to read][29] — and Placci proclaimed him 'uno dei piú svaganti conferenzieri d'Italia' [one of the most entertaining lecturers in Italy].[30]

Ermengarda Caramelli, one of his former pupils, interestingly remembered the typical audience at Nencioni's lectures; a mix of literati, high society ladies and theatrical people: 'le piú spiccate personalità della scuola e delle lettere, le piú note dame dell'aristocrazia, i nomi piú cari all'arte drammatica, quali Eleonora Duse e Tommaso Salvini, si facevano un dovere di accorrere a sentirlo' [the most illustrious figures from academia and literature, the most famous ladies of the aristocracy, the loftiest names from the theatre, like Eleonora Duse and Tommaso Salvini, felt duty bound to rush to listen to him].[31] Yet, Nencioni's relationship with Roman and Florentine high society, his acquaintance with both the literati and glitterati of his time, and his close friendship with Italy's most distinguished dilettanti — Count Primoli and Placci are the best example — have been misunderstood by twentieth-century critics. This, despite the fact that the late-nineteenth century saw, in Italy and Europe, the triumph of the dilettante, who acted as a *trait-d'union* between Paris, London and, in Italy, Rome and Florence, and was socially a product of the high-life of the Belle Epoque. Croce, in his eulogy of the culture of newly Unified Italy, described the new cosmopolitan cultural climate that called for the figure of the dilettante. Focussing on the cultural exchanges between Italy and Europe, he portrays the new Italy inhabited by Nencioni and his friends:

> Era come una grande conversazione, che si era accesa da un capo all'altro d'Italia, nella quale si apprendeva quanto giornalmente accadeva nel paese e fuori e si assisteva a scontri e dibattiti d'idee, e si ascoltavano proposte, e il sapere e l'esperienza si allargavano, e le menti si facevano esperte e acute [...]. E ritrovi piú eletti avevano luogo nei salotti [...] dove passavano illustri forestieri

> visitatori dell'Italia e si discorreva del presente e dell'avvenire, con piena informazione delle cose italiane e straniere, con elegante dottrina, elevatezza e serenità d'animo.[32]
>
> [It was like a huge conversation, which had sparked off from one end of Italy to the other, in which one could learn what was happening in the country and abroad on a daily basis, and one could witness clashes and debates over ideas, and listen to proposals, and knowledge and experience were broadening, and minds were becoming sharper and acute (...). More exclusive gatherings took place in the salons (...) through which famous foreign visitors passed and people discussed the present and the future, with full knowledge of Italian and foreign affairs, with elegant erudition, nobility and serenity of mind.]

As Nardi has rightly pointed out, between Nencioni and his disciple-friends there was a powerful cultural osmosis. In particular, Placci and Primoli were instrumental in keeping Nencioni up to date with the latest literary news.[33] However, the influence of Placci on Nencioni has been dismissed by twentieth-century scholars who have preferred the more obvious view of Nencioni's influence on him. Placci's critical dilettantism, did not prevent Nencioni from seeking his friend's advice on literary matters, especially when writing on English literature, and there are several instances of mutual intellectual exchanges in their correspondence.[34] Besides, Nencioni always thought highly of Placci's articles.[35]

Nencioni's friendship with Primoli, albeit also showing examples of mutual cultural exchange, followed the more traditional relationship between the maestro and his aristocratic pupil/patron. His letters to Primoli, whilst his hopes for a teaching post in Rome were still high, are exemplary of the relationship between the Florentine *borghese* and his Society friends. They are also the perfect standpoint from which to examine the changing social position of Italian intellectuals in the post-Risorgimento period: writing articles for literary journals was, together with a position in the public sector, the sole means of guaranteeing one's financial security, in the absence of private and state patronage of any substance. Nencioni's correspondence with Primoli in 1883–84 is full of an intense longing for Rome as well as frequent requests for help in securing a teaching post in the capital, as in this letter:

> Credo però che se il Ministro avesse voluto avrebbe potuto darmi una delle cattedre di letteratura francese o inglese in quell'istituto superiore fem. — o un posto all'Università [...] pur di farmi tornare a Roma. [...] Ma *non dispero* — e conto su lei, caro Primoli, più che sopra qualunque altro amico. [...] Se nò, finisce che rinuncio all'ufficio e torno a viver della mia penna — pur di stare a Roma. Io soffro di una crescente e incurabile *nostalgia romana*.[36]
>
> [I think that if the Minister had wanted to, he could have given me one of the posts in French or English literature at that girls' private school or a chair at the University (...) just to get me back to Rome. (...) However, *I don't despair* and I rely on you, my dear Primoli, more than on any other friend. (...) Otherwise I'll end up giving up my post and going back to making a living out of my pen just so that I can stay in Rome. I am suffering from an increasing and incurable *nostalgia for Rome*.]

Another letter shows the difficulty of obtaining an academic post, in Italy, in the 1880s, given the country's long-standing surplus of graduates in search of a public post, a problem that was aggravated in the post-Unification period:

> Io la pregavo di parlare a quegli amici del Baccelli e tentare di farmi nominare Professore straordinario (o anche incaricato) di letterature moderne comparate all'Università di Roma. Ora so che è vacante la Cattedra di *Storia* nell'Ist. Sup. fem. di Roma. Non potrebbero fare il baratto? Dare a me quello e dare a, e mandar altri a quella che ho io di letteratura nell'Ist. Sup. fem di Firenze? — Lo stipendio è lo stesso. *Ho scritto ieri* anche *al Martini* e al *Carducci*. Lo dica lei alla sign. Bla De Renzis. Io mi impegno fin d'ora di far lezione alla sua brava figlia.[37]

> [Do please talk to those friends of Baccelli and try to get me appointed as *professore straordinario* (or even visiting professor) of modern comparative literature at the university of Rome. I know that at the moment the chair of History at the Istituto Superiore for girls in Rome is vacant. Could they not swap? Give me that one and send somebody else to the chair I have at the Istituto Superiore for girls in Florence? The salary is the same. I also wrote to Martini and Carducci yesterday. Please tell Mrs Bla de Renzis. I promise to start teaching her good daughter now.]

Yet Nencioni, unlike his disciple D'Annunzio, did not embrace the other financial opportunity open to critics and writers in Umbertine Italy: the new lucrative publishing market. Italy, in the 1880s, saw a growing commercialisation of literature. Whilst D'Annunzio was ready to embrace it and profit as much as possible from it, Nencioni does show in this respect his lack of modernity. He never published any collections of his essays and articles in volume form — except for an early collection of *Medaglioni*, in 1883. Rather, he seems to have favoured the art of elegant, intellectual conversation, with the occasional offering of public lectures. The reason may well be in the peculiar character (or lack of it) of the Italian bourgeoisie in the post-Unification period, which Martin Clark sums up thus: 'Over most of Italy, the upper and middles classes were not "modern", not educated or travelled or enlightened [...] In short, they were not "middle class" at all, but aristocrats manqué.'[38] This form of aristocratic dilettantism brings Nencioni closer than other commentators have admitted to his dilettante friends in Florence and Rome, whilst showing the contradictions inherent in the new social and intellectual hierarchy in Italy: aristocrats, cultural dandies, writers and critics are still mixing socially but the financial gap between them is widening.

Nardi has argued that Nencioni's relationship with Italy's intellectual and social elite was influenced by Mazzinian ideals: 'Nencioni si rivolge a questi giovani blasé e disincantati con una fiducia ancora tutta mazziniana nella volontà e nell'azione' [Nencioni addressed those blasé and disenchanted young men with a still fully Mazzinian confidence in will and action].[39] The conviction and passion of his arguments were certainly always remarked upon by his contemporaries. However, it seems to me, that other elements are more important, and that the reason for Nencioni's appeal for his contemporaries can be found in the aesthetic and moral dimension of his writings.

Nencioni's aesthetic preoccupations and his guiding principle, beauty, made him a crucial point of reference for Italy's young *esteti* and Aesthetic dilettanti.[40] He was influenced by contemporary Aestheticism and in particular by the work of Pater which Nencioni helped to introduce into Italy. The notion of the impression created upon the critic by his object of analysis and the free play of associations that this impression generates are fundamental for understanding Nencioni's writings on literature and help to explain the autobiographical undercurrent of most of his works. Literary and personal memories are constantly woven into the fabric of Nencioni's prose. His 'roundabout papers', as Cicognani noted, 'sono leggeri tessuti di impressioni e di rimembranze; trame sottili di immaginazioni poetiche; capricciosi divagamenti con passaggi dal narrativo all'evocazione o alla lirica; armoniosi impasti di toni diversi' [are light weavings of impressions and remembrances; fine webs of poetic imaginings; whimsical digressions with shifts from narrative to evocation to lyricism; harmonious mixtures of different tones].[41] Biagi also drew attention to the digressive style of Nencioni: 'Si può dire che le digressioni, le apparenti divagazioni, sieno quasi la sostanza di quei lavori, e che tutto il resto non sia che un mezzo per condurre piano piano il lettore a cotesti punti essenziali del discorso' [One could say that the digressions, the apparent deviations, are almost the substance of those works, and that everything else is but a means by which to lead the reader slowly but surely to those essential parts of the argument].[42] Nencioni's 'roundabout papers' are very carefully constructed: he moves effortlessly from the main topic to personal memories, lyrical passages, philosophical considerations, moral statements, reflections on the human condition, and references to poets and writers. What he achieves is a mixture of erudition and *bello stile* that would have appealed to his educated public, a public that liked to be instructed and entertained by beautiful prose. Nencioni's style was naturally elegant and retained a degree of spontaneity typical of the spoken language. His stylistic *sprezzatura* is not easily found in Italian critics and prose writers of the late nineteenth century. Again it was D'Annunzio who best captured the essence of Nencioni's style, praising it 'per una specie di grazia negletta e volubile, per certe sprezzature efficaci e per certe deliziose delicatezze che vi s'incontrano all'improvviso, per certe accensioni subitanee del colorito, per certi movimenti rapidi e fieri del ritmo, per un pullular frequente di vivacità umoristica' [for a sort of unkempt, volatile grace, for certain delightful delicate touches that take us by surprise, for the sudden flaring up of colour, for some rapid, confident movements of rhythm, for the frequent bursts of humorous vivacity].[43]

Nencioni, however, was not only a master of style. The moral dimension in his writings is equally, if not more, important. Nardi suggested that this feature may have been influenced by Mazzini.[44] A close scrutiny of Nencioni's private papers, however, shows that the lesson of Thomas Carlyle was also very influential. In an unpublished paper, Nencioni claimed that Carlyle's *On Heroes and Hero-Worship* summed up his own creed.[45] The influence of Carlyle seems to have informed Nencioni's interest in biography and autobiography; his main focus is always the man behind the writer: 'L'uomo è lo studio piú importante per l'uomo. Quindi, nessun libro piú interessante, piú umanamante utile e dilettevole, di una buona biografia. Essa è scienza, e dramma ad un tempo' [Man is the most important study for man.

Hence, there is no book more interesting, more humanly useful and pleasant than a good biography. It is both science and theatre at the same time].[46] In the preface to the first translation into Italian of Carlyle's *On Hero and Hero Worship*, Nencioni commented on Carlyle's vision of history as a series of biographies of heroes and praised his ability to 'comunicare con lo spirito dello storico-personaggio: la cosa vera, importante, essenziale, è per lui il sentimento interiore degli uomini che han vissuto' [to communicate with the spirit of the historical figure: the true, important and essential thing for him is the internal sentiment of people who have lived].[47] Nencioni also used this introduction to attack contemporary Realism which, according to him, had destroyed any sense of the ideal and heroic in literature with the ultimate consequence of separating art from its moral dimension and consequently equating it with the activity of a dilettante: 'dal naturalismo al materialismo, al pessimismo, al fatalismo, all'indifferentismo — e, in Arte, al dilettantismo!' [from naturalism, to materialism, to pessimism, to fatalism, to indifferentism, and, in Art, to dilettantism!].[48] Nencioni saw a direct link between the portrayal of the vilest aspects of human nature and the moral illnesses of his time: 'Il materialismo larvato coi nomi di positivismo e di naturalismo ha ridotto la letteratura di questi ultimi venti anni a una trascrizione di ambienti, a uno studio puramente fisiologico di piccole cause, di impulsi ereditari, che fanno la creatura umana incapace di reazione e di resistenza individuale' [materialism concealed under the name of positivism and naturalism has reduced the literature of the past twenty years to a mere transcription of settings, to a purely physiological study of trivial causes, hereditary impulses, which render the human creature incapable of any reaction or personal resistance].[49] This had reduced life to insignificance: 'una vana e faticosa e snervante *rêverie* — o in una caccia affannosa ai diletti sensuali, raffinati fino al delirio, fino alla crudeltà' [a pointless, tiring and debilitating reverie or a frantic hunt for sensual pleasures, refined to the point of delirium, and even of cruelty].[50] His judgement on Naturalism shows his misunderstanding of the tenets of the movement but must be viewed in the context of a general critique of the excesses of all fin-de-siècle 'isms': 'Naturalisti, veristi, *parnassiens*, estetici, simbolisti, impressionisti, decadenti, vibristi, tutti gli *ismi* e gli *isti* delle nuove scuole, dai programmi così presuntuosi, non hanno dato un solo vero e grande poeta' [naturalists, *veristi*, parnassiens, aesthetes, symbolists, impressionists, decadents, sensationists, all the *isms* and *ists* of the new schools, with their pretentious programmes, have not produced a single truly great poet].[51]

This critical stance has been attacked by twentieth-century critics and has resulted in the widespread notion of Nencioni being an old-fashioned, late-Romantic commentator whose bourgeois tastes did not stretch to the most challenging aesthetic ideas of his time. Nardi, in particular, is highly critical of Nencioni's alleged misinterpretation of Decadent suggestions in contemporary English literature; she claims that 'l'ingenua mentalità borghese di Nencioni, incentrata sul "buon gusto", finisce, peraltro, per neutralizzare il materiale piú scabroso ed inquietante attinto dalla letteratura anglo-americana contemporanea' [the naïve bourgeois mentality of Nencioni, centred upon 'good taste', ends, in some respects, by neutralising the most sordid and disturbing material drawn from contemporary Anglo-American literature].⁵² This view follows an interpretative line that started with Praz's study of Nencioni's Decadent imagery in the *Rapsodia Lirica*, a poem published in 1896 in the Roman journal *Convito* (libro VIII). This poem, as Praz noted, is a 'libero intreccio di passi swimburniani' [free interlacing of Swinburnian passages].⁵³ Praz highlighted Nencioni's fundamental misunderstanding of Swinburne's feminine imagery: 'L'ingenuo italiano tratta borghesemente la scabrosa poesia del Swinburne, e nell'inborghesirla le toglie virulenza, e trasforma la sintesi lussuriosa in una provinciale galleria di ritratti di famose peccatrici, come averebbe fatto un buon secentista' [the naïve Italian treats in a bourgeois manner Swinburne's scabrous poetry and in this bourgeoisification he takes away its virulence and transforms the English poet's luxuriant synthesis into a provincial gallery of portraits of famous loose women, as a good seventeenth-century writer would have done].⁵⁴ However, both critics here betray what Forgacs has perceptively called the Romantic (and Crocean) notion of 'the intellectual as initiator or as anti-conformist outsider'.⁵⁵ There is no doubt that Nencioni, both in his writings on literature and his own creative work, is not an innovator *à la* D'Annunzio in terms of language and style, but an analysis of his feminine imagery betrays his convergence with, rather than misinterpretation of, fin-de-siècle culture.

As I have argued elsewhere, Nencioni's article on Dante Gabriel Rossetti of 1884 was of great importance not only for introducing his Italian readers to the English Pre-Raphaelite movement and the art and poetry of D.G. Rossetti, but also because it contained two portrayals of what he considered to be Rossetti's typically ambivalent view of female beauty: the virginal beauty exemplified by *Beata Beatrix*, and the femme fatale, *Lady Lilith*.⁵⁶ In the absence of any direct knowledge of Pre-Raphaelite paintings at the time in Italy, Nencioni's ekphrastic creatures came to embody a new type of Pre-Raphaelite beauty and had a major influence on D'Annunzio.

Nencioni's roundabout paper 'Resurrezioni fiorentine' (1884), a nostalgic piece on the Florence of his youth, contains two similarly opposing ideals of feminine beauty, the virginal and the sensuous woman. The first type is represented by the description of his first love, a woman he saw and never forgot in the church of the Annunziata:

> Una testina ideale che bisognerebbe veder dipinta sopra un fondo d'oro pallido, come usavano i vecchi maestri di Firenze e di Perugia [...] Un collo svelto ed esile come quello delle Madonne del Botticelli. I belli occhi indulgenti e profondi, erano dolcemente luminosi [...] i capelli castagni, lisci, e bipartiti verginalmente sulla fronte [...] Vestiva quel giorno un abito di mussolina chiara a mille righe, e aveva sul petto una giunchiglia, il primo profumo dell'anno.⁵⁷

> [A small, ideal head which one ought to see painted on a background of pale gold as the old masters of Florence and Perugia used to do (...) A slim and slender neck like those of the Madonnas of Botticelli. Her beautiful eyes, forgiving and deep, were gently luminous (...) her smooth brown hair was virginally parted in the middle of her forehead [(...) That day she wore a dress of pale pinstriped muslin, and on her chest she had a jonquil, the first fragrance of the year.]

The muslin-clad woman shows a close resemblance to D'Annunzio's Roman Pre-Raphaelite beauties, which from 1885 populated the 'Cronache' in the Roman weekly *La Tribuna*, and might indicate Nencioni's influence on his younger friend. D'Annunzio at that time eagerly read Nencioni's articles, as he told him in numerous letters.[58] The long thick hair of the second Florentine 'resurrection' from his past points towards a different type of beauty:

> Quell'altra figura di donna, appena intravista in una sala della Galleria Pitti, idolatrata per cinque settimane, e ricordata per venticinque anni! Di che colore sarà oggi quella massa di solido oro, quel volume magnifico di biondi capelli che ammirai sul tuo collo, mentre tu guardavi, inchinata sul quadro, una marina rossastra di Rysdael?[59]
>
> [That other female figure, barely glimpsed in a room in the Pitti gallery, idolized for five weeks and remembered for twenty five years! What colour will that mass of solid gold be today, that magnificent volume of blonde hair which I admired on your neck whilst you were contemplating a reddish seascape by Rysdael, bending over the painting?]

It is a sensual and seductive woman with her distinctive physical attributes; most notably the long thick loose hair.[60] The final quarter of the nineteenth century saw an increasing preoccupation with this opposing view of femininity.[61]

Other instances of this dual conception of feminine beauty can be found in the *Medaglioni*, Nencioni's biographies of 'belle e virtuose adultere' [beautiful and virtuous adulteresses].[62] They are stories of doomed love, women's self-sacrifice and self-effacement, and always end with the death of the heroine. They show Nencioni's fascination for tragic romantic love stories, as well as pointing towards the late nineteenth-century interest in fallen women. The virginal beauty of 'Enriqueta' — 'era bella d'una bellezza spirituale ed eterea' [she was beautiful, with a spiritual and ethereal beauty] — shows how seductive this type of woman can be: 'I magnifici capelli biondi, quando li scioglieva [...] pareva che le pesassero, e davano al delicato viso un'attitudine di molle *abbandono*' [Her wonderful blonde hair, when she untied it [...] looked as if it weighed her down, and gave her delicate face an air of soft *abandon*].[63] The long thick flowing hair and her languorous expression are part of the late nineteenth-century vocabulary of seduction and show how the virgin and the *femme fatale* have become entwined. In the same *Medaglione*, Enriqueta's rival is presented as the epitome of feminine evil and yet her description focuses on the very same elements as her angelic counterpart, namely her hair and her seductive enticement: 'Quella tenebrosa figura di donna coi capelli neri che le piovevano come serpenti; folti e indomabili [...] con quel sorriso di invito e di *abbandono* [...] sorriso di sirena e di sfinge' [That dark figure of a woman with black hair clustering round her like snakes; thick and untameable [...] with that smile of invitation and abandonment [...] the smile of a siren and a sphinx.][64]

Another instance of *fin-de-siècle* and Decadent imagery is the association of female beauty with death.[65] Proserpina is a muslin-clad woman with long fair hair, whose beauty reaches its climax in the image of her dead body:

> *Proserpina* è un nome di donna che ricorda la *bellezza*, i *fiori* e la *morte*. E io le misi nome Proserpina e lei sorrideva a sentirsi chiamare così, il primo giorno che la vidi in un giardino fiorito, di maggio, in una villa fiorentina sui poggi d'Arcetri. Era vestita di mussolina bianca, e accesa in viso dal moto e dal sole.

> Aveva fiori in seno, fiori sulle chiome, e due grandi mazzi sciolti in mano, e vi posava il bel volto, e, socchiusi i belli occhi, ne aspirava l'odore con voluttà. [...] Un mese dopo, era morta. La rividi una sera distesa a terra su dei cuscini, fra quattro ceri, ravvolta nel manto d'oro dei suoi capelli, come Teodolinda o Ginevra.[66]

> [*Proserpina* is a female name which reminds one of *beauty*, *flowers* and *death*. I gave her the name Proserpina and she smiled to hear herself called in that way the first day I saw her in a garden full of flowers, in May, in a Florentine villa on the hills of Arcetri. She wore white muslin, and her face had the glow of exertion and the sun. She had flowers on her breast, in her hair and two great loose bunches in her arms, and resting her fair face in them, with half-closed eyes, she breathed in their scent with delight (...) A month later she was dead. I saw her again one evening lying on the floor on some cushions, surrounded by four candles, enveloped in the golden mantle of her hair like Theodolinda or Guinevere].

The same image reappears in another 'roundabout paper', 'Consule Planco',[67] and again in the *Medaglione* written on the death of one of his pupils at the SS. Annunziata, a young woman called Leila, who died at the age of seventeen: 'Ho qui dinanzi due ritratti di Leila — la viva e la morta. La morta è anche piú bella. Il dolce sorriso è diventato piú etereo, piú ineffabile e celestiale' [I have in front of me two portraits of Leila: dead and living. In death, she is even more beautiful. The sweet smile has become more ethereal, ineffable and celestial].[68] Incidentally, the portrait of the dead Leila made a strong impression on Fogazzaro, whose later novel *Leila* seems to have been inspired by the photograph of the young woman that he saw at Nencioni's house.[69] D'Annunzio's novel *Trionfo della Morte* (1894), gave Italy and Europe one of the most striking representations of this morbid fantasy of extreme female passivity.

Nencioni's creative writings with their emphasis on a dual conception of femininity confirm stereotypes of masculinity and femininity which were widely accepted in nineteenth-century European art, literature and culture. There is no misunderstanding on Nencioni's part, but rather an acceptance in common with other writers and artists of the fixed roles that nineteenth-century European society envisaged for men and women. The main argument for Nencioni's petit-bourgeois 'misunderstanding' of the challenges brought to these stereotypes by Decadent writers and artists, is in itself a misinterpretation of the way in which the increasingly eroticised and demonic images of women did not actually challenge but simply reinforced those bourgeois values of proper femininity, by presenting female perversion as a sign of male desire and control over women's sexuality and behaviour.[70]

Nencioni translated, and perhaps simplified, for his public more complex images of femininity, in which sexuality and perversion were becoming increasingly important. These images were being developed in contemporary English and French literature and art, and were becoming the hallmark of the work of D'Annunzio. Nencioni's translations may be ingenuous versions of more compelling and disturbing feminine icons, but they still reinforce the dualism between the male and female spheres which characterised late nineteenth-century European culture.

As I have suggested above, the cult or myth of the exceptional individual, of the writer and intellectual as innovator, both in terms of form and ideology, has overshadowed a host of Italian writers who were active in Italy in the decades after Unification. Nencioni is an example of this bias. His role as a mentor for a generation of Italian writers and intellectuals, and educator of young women, most of whom were destined for the teaching profession, gives him an important place in the development of Italian culture and letters in the last decades of the nineteenth century. Nencioni was an intellectual 'broker',[71] translating, publicising and criticising foreign and Italian authors. He was not a trendsetter, but a maestro to both his pupils and friends, as well as an avid reader of foreign texts which he did not 'misunderstand' because of his petit-bourgeois taste.

This introductory analysis of Nencioni's roundabout papers and *Medaglioni* and the representation of feminine beauty and exemplary womanhood in these texts, shows how Nencioni shared the ideology of his time, permeated as it was by a strong current of misogyny. His feminine beauties may be less complex, sexualised and troubling than their full-blown Decadent counterparts, whom Nencioni admired so much, but they nevertheless stemmed from the same late nineteenth-century prescriptive view of femininity and masculinity. Nencioni's writings are certainly less innovative than those of the English and Italian Decadents he so much admired, yet they feed on the same European *fin-de-siècle* female imagery, showing Nencioni's important place in the passage between late-Romantic and Decadent Italian culture. It is however in Nencioni's sustained interest in biography that one should see the most innovative element of his work. Carlyle and Thackeray are undoubtedly important models for Nencioni. The latter's digressive model suited Nencioni perfectly and resulted in a stylistic and linguistic lightness and fluidity rare in Italian writers of the time. Ultimately, both his writings on literature and his creative output seem to stem from the same belief that 'la storia — quella che merita questo nome; non quella cattedratica a gergo metafisico o quella d'archivio a filze di date e di nomi — la storia è una sintesi biografica' [History — that which deserves this name, not academic History clad in metaphysical jargon or the History of archives made up of strings of dates and names — History is a synthesis made from biography].[72]

Notes to Chapter 4

1. Gabriele D'Annunzio, 'Per la morte di un poeta', in Enrico Nencioni, *Saggi critici di letteratura italiana* (Florence: Le Monnier, 1898), pp. v–xxii (xiii). The article was published originally in *La Tribuna* (1 September 1896). It can also be found in Gabriele D'Annunzio, 'Elogio di Enrico Nencioni', in D'Annunzio, *Prose Scelte. Antologia d'Autore (1906)*, ed. by Pietro Gibellini (Milan: Giunti, 1995), pp. 56–65.
2. Giosuè Carducci, 'Prefazione', in Enrico Nencioni, *Saggi critici di letteratura inglese* (Florence: Le Monnier, 1897), p. v.
3. *Le più belle pagine di Enrico Nencioni*, ed. by Bruno Cicognani (Milan: Garzanti, 1943), p. 363.
4. *Le più belle pagine*, p. 367.
5. George Arthur Greene, *Italian Lyrists of Today* (London: Macmillan, 1893), p. 173.
6. Richard Garnett, *A History of Italian Literature* (London: William Heinemann, 1898), p. 411.
7. Giuseppe Antonio Borgese, in *Le più belle pagine*, pp. 374–75; originally in G.A. Borgese, *La vita e il libro* (Milan: Bocca, 1910).

8. Benedetto Croce, in *Le piú belle pagine*, p. 317; originally published in *La Critica*, 1 (1906).
9. Renato Forcella, 'Lettere ad Enrico Nencioni (1880–189)', *Nuova Antologia*, 18 (1939), 3–30; Giuseppe Fatini, 'D'Annunzio e Nencioni', *Quaderni dannunziani*, 18–19 (1960), 645–70; Augusta Brettoni, 'Nove lettere inedite di G. D'Annunzio a E. Nencioni (1889–95)', *Studi e problemi di critica testuale*, 21 (1980), 195–207.
10. Mario Praz, '*La belle dame sans merci*', in *La carne, la morte e il diavolo nella letteratura romantica* (Milan-Rome: Società editrice "La Cultura", 1930; repr. Milan: Sansoni, 1992), pp. 221–25. See also Mario Praz, 'Enrico Nencioni', in *Il patto col serpente* (Milan: Mondadori, 1972; repr. 1995), pp. 336–40.
11. Marziano Guglielminetti, 'Enrico Nencioni', in *Letteratura Italiana. I Critici*, 5 vols (Milan: Marzorati, 1969), II, 1117–36. Nencioni's taste is described as belonging to 'la piú estenuata tradizione del romanticismo europeo' [the most worn-out tradition of European Romanticism] (p. 1119). See also in the same volume Luigi Russo, 'Nencioni scrittore europeizzante', 1136–39.
12. See in chronological order: Francesco Pera, *Biografia di Enrico Nencioni* (Livorno: Meucci, 1896); Ermengarda Caramelli, 'Enrico Nencioni', in *Figure d'altri tempi* (Florence: Le Monnier, 1931), pp. 79–113; Bruno Cicognani, 'Introduction', in *Le piú belle pagine*, pp. 1–22. For a complete bibliography see Monica Maria Angeli, 'Enrico Nencioni', *Accademie e Biblioteche d'Italia* (January-March 1997), 33–41.
13. Marie-Pierre Strowel, 'Carlo Placci between Italy and Britain in the 1880s: his friends, his essays and the role of Enrico Nencioni', *MLR*, 89 (1994), 71–87.
14. *Le carte di Enrico Nencioni*, ed. by Monica Maria Angeli (Florence: Manent, 1999).
15. Nencioni had reviewed Thackeray's volume *Roundabout Papers* in 1871: Enrico Nencioni, 'Rassegna letteraria. L'ultimo libro di Thackeray, *Roundabout Papers*', *L'Italia Nuova*, 103–04 (2–3 January 1871), 1; continued in 105 (4 January 1871), 1. A selection of Nencioni's roundabout papers was published after his death, in *Impressioni e rimembranze*, ed. by Isidoro Del Lungo (Florence: Le Monnier, 1923).
16. Enrico Nencioni, *Medaglioni* (Rome: Sommaruga, 1883; repr. Florence: Bemporad & figlio, 1897); this was the second and only other volume of Nencioni's works to be published during his lifetime; the first being Enrico Nencioni, *Poesie* (Bologna: Zanichelli, 1880). All the others are posthumous collections: *Nuovi Medaglioni* (Bologna: Zanichelli, 1922); *Impressioni e rimembranze*, ed. by Del Lungo (1923). A selection of his poems and creative writings is also in *Le piú belle pagine*. Nencioni's other published works include in chronological order: *Saggi critici di letteratura inglese* (Florence: Le Monnier, 1897); *Saggi critici di letteratura italiana* (Florence: Le Monnier, 1898); *Nuovi saggi critici di letterature straniere ed altri scritti* (Florence: Le Monnier, 1909).
17. Isabella Nardi, *Un critico vittoriano: Enrico Nencioni* (Perugia: Edizioni Scientifiche Italiane, 1985), pp. 56, 41.
18. *Le piú belle pagine*, p. 13.
19. Ibid., p. 325.
20. Guido Biagi, *Il Marzocco* 19 (1900), special issue, unpaginated, also in *Impressioni e rimembranze*, p. 224.
21. Carlo Placci, in *Le piú belle pagine*, p. 355.
22. Enrico Nencioni, 'Consule Planco', in *Impressioni e rimembranze*, p. 73. Originally published in April 1882, this 'roundabout paper' is full of Nencioni's memories of his youth, his friendship with Martini and Carducci and the atmosphere and culture of Florence before the revolution of 1848.
23. Ibid. 66.
24. Ferdinando Martini, *Confessioni e ricordi*, ed. by Mauro Vannini (Florence: Ponte alle Grazie, 1990), pp. 140–41.
25. E. Nencioni, 'Robert Browning', in *Saggi critici di letteratura inglese*, pp. 1–18; originally published in *Nuova Antologia*, 5 (July 1867). See also Dominic Bisignano, 'Enrico Nencioni and Robert Browning', *English Miscellany*, 14 (1962), 195–210.
26. Nencioni to Primoli, Rome, 12 September 1881, in Marcello Spaziani, *Con Gégé Primoli nella Roma Bizantina* (Rome: Edizioni di Storia e Letteratura, 1962), p. 89.
27. On Primoli see also Joseph-Napoléon Primoli, *Pages Inédites*, ed. by Marcello Spaziani (Rome:

Edizioni di Storia e Letteratura, 1959); and Lamberto Vitali, *Un fotografo fin de siècle. Il conte Primoli* (Turin: Einaudi, 1981).
28. D'Annunzio, 'Per la morte di un poeta', p. VIII.
29. *Le più belle pagine*, p. 2.
30. Ibid. p. 355.
31. Caramelli, *Figure d'altri tempi*, p. 117.
32. Benedetto Croce, *Storia d'Italia dal 1871 al 1915* (Bari: Laterza, 1928), pp. 66–67.
33. 'Placci e Primoli, con le loro amicizie cosmopolite, i loro viaggi intercontinentali e le loro letture plurilingui mettono in contatto Nencioni, chiuso nel giro dei suoi impegni didattici e angustiato dalla mancanza di mezzi, con le novità librarie anglo-francesi, con gli intellettuali europei più noti e con i mecenati più in vista' [Placci and Primoli with their cosmopolitan friendships, their intercontinental travels and their multilingual readings put Nencioni, stuck in his round of teaching commitments and worried about his lack of means, in touch with the latest Anglo-French publications, as well as with the most famous European intellectuals and the most prominent patrons]. See Nardi, *Un critico vittoriano*, p. 47.
34. Nencioni to Placci, May 1889: 'Per il 1° giugno darò l'articolo su Il Piacere [...]. Perciò ti son grato se mi scrivi tue impressioni' [On 1st of June I shall hand in the article on Il Piacere (...). I would therefore be grateful if you could send me your impressions], in Nardi, *Un critico vittoriano*, p. 138. See also Nencioni to Placci, 20 July 1889, 'Ho bisogno di consultarti per la prossima *Rassegna Inglese*' [I need to consult you for the next *Rassegna Inglese*], ibid., pp. 138–39. See also an unpublished letter of Placci to Nencioni in which he discusses an article by Swinburne on Hugo's *La Fin de Satan*: 'Ho sott'occhi un articolo pazzo del Swinburne a questo proposito. In un mare di cavalloni di superlativi e di burrascosi complimenti nuota qualche idea critica, giusta e sobria. Questa per esempio. Dice che Hugo ha in comune con Dante "that unique effect achieved by alternation or combination of the very homeliest with the very sublimest images or comparisons". Come è giusto. Del resto per il S. questa *Fine di Satana* "has done for the 19th century what was done for the 13th by the *Divina Commedia* and for the 17th by *Paradise Lost*"' [I am looking at a crazy article by Swinburne concerning this. Amidst a tempestuous sea of superlatives and stormy compliments there swims some critical judgement which is fair and restrained. This one for instance: he says that Hugo has in common with Dante 'that unique effect achieved by alternation or combination of the very homeliest with the very sublimest images or comparisons'. This is right. Besides for Swinburne this *End of Satan* 'has done for the 19th century what was done for the 13th by the *Divina Commedia* and for the 17th by *Paradise Lost*']: Biblioteca Marucelliana, Firenze, carteggio Nencioni, C Ne 255 1–13, letter no. 503,957.
35. 'Caro Charly, *crescit eundo* [...] ho letto e ammirato *Bagni di Lucca*: uno dei più belli e artistici, certo il meglio scritto, dei tuoi articoli' [Dear Charly, *crescit eundo* (...) I have read with admiration *Bagni di Lucca*: one of the finest and most artistic, certainly the best written, of your articles], August 1885, in Nardi, *Un critico vittoriano*, p. 131.
36. Nencioni to Primoli, Florence, undated, Archivio dei Conti di Campello, Fondazione Primoli, Rome, scat. VII, no. 3337, unpublished.
37. Nencioni to Primoli, Florence, undated, Archivio dei Conti di Campello, Fondazione Primoli, Rome, scat. VII, no. 3340, unpublished.
38. Martin Clark, *Modern Italy 1871–1995* (London and New York: Longman, 1996), p. 29.
39. Nardi, *Un critico vittoriano*, p. 71.
40. An unwritten chapter of Italy's cultural history in the early twentieth century still needs to analyze the intellectual and cultural background to the 'riviste estetizzanti' in Florence — *La Vita Nuova* and *Il Marzocco* — and the young writers and critics that centred around them, in order to reposition figures such as Nencioni among the fathers of Italian *estetismo*. On the riviste see Gianni Oliva, *I nobili spiriti: Pascoli, D'Annunzio e le riviste dell'estetismo fiorentino* (Florence: Minerva Italica, 1979; repr. Venice: Marsilio, 2002).
41. *Le più belle pagine*, p. 331. Cicognani also thought that they could be considered a precedent for the Italian literary/journalistic genre, the 'elzeviro nelle terze pagine dei quotidiani' [literary article in the cultural pages of daily papers] (p. 17).
42. Ibid., p. 369.

43. D'Annunzio, 'Per la morte di un poeta', p. XVI.
44. 'La lezione mazziniana garantisce [...] a Nencioni una rigorosa linea operativa che lo rende immune dal "vaporoso" clima nostalgico-medievaleggiante instauratosi ormai anche in Italia' [The lesson of Mazzini guaranteed Nencioni a rigorous working approach which made him immune to the 'hazy' nostalgic mediaevalising climate which by that time had been established in Italy too]. See Nardi, *Un critico vittoriano*, p. 27.
45. Florence, Biblioteca Marucelliana, G.3.1–7, cc. 8–9, unpublished papers.
46. Nencioni, 'Rassegna di letteratura inglese', in *Saggi critici di letteratura inglese*, p. 370.
47. Tommaso Carlyle, *Gli eroi*, ed. and trans. by Maria Pezzè Pascolato, with a preface by Nencioni (Florence: Barbera, 1896), p. XI. Nencioni had already translated some passages from Carlyle in 'Le "Letture su gli eroi"', in *Saggi critici di letteratura inglese*, pp. 154–83; originally published in *Nuova Antologia*, in December 1886.
48. *Saggi critici di letteratura inglese*, p. XXV.
49. Nencioni, 'Rassegna di letteratura inglese', in *Saggi critici di letteratura inglese*, p. 325; originally published in *Nuova Antologia*, June 1887.
50. Ibid., p. 326.
51. Nencioni, 'Una nuova poetessa americana', in *Saggi critici di letteratura inglese*, p. 231; originally published in *Nuova Antologia*, February 1892.
52. Nardi, *Un critico vittoriano*, p. 39.
53. Praz, *La carne, la morte e il diavolo*, p. 221.
54. Ibid.
55. David Forgacs, *Italian Culture in the Industrial Era 1880–1980. Cultural Industries, Politics and the Public* (Manchester and New York: Manchester University Press, 1990), p. 8.
56. Nencioni, 'Le poesie e le pitture di Dante Gabriele Rossetti', *Fanfulla della Domenica* (17 February 1884) (unpaginated). See also Nencioni, 'Poeti inglesi moderni — Nuovi canti di Mary Robinson', *Nuova Antologia*, 87 (16 June 1886), 605–20, containing a short history of the Pre-Raphaelite movement. For Nencioni's role in the diffusion of Pre-Raphaelitism in Italy in the 1880s see Giuliana Pieri, 'The Critical Reception of Pre-Raphaelitism in Italy 1878–1910', *MLR*, 99 (2004), 364–81.
57. Nencioni, 'Resurrezioni Fiorentine' (6 July 1884), in *Impressioni e rimembranze*, p. 131.
58. There are several letters which show D'Annunzio's interest in Nencioni's articles especially those written between 1881 and 1885. See Forcella, 'Lettere ad Enrico Nencioni', letters no. III, X, XI, and XII. For D'Annunzio's journalistic works see: Gabriele D'Annunzio, *Scritti giornalistici 1882–1888*, ed. by Annamaria Andreoli (Milan: A. Mondadori, 1996). On D'Annunzio's Pre-Raphaelite feminine beauties in his journalistic pieces see also Giuliana Pieri, 'D'Annunzio and Alma-Tadema: between Pre-Raphaelitism and Aestheticism', *MLR*, 96 (2001), 361–69.
59. Nencioni, 'Resurrezioni fiorentine', pp. 131–32.
60. For the fascination for women's hair see L. De Girolami Cheney, 'Locks, Tresses, and Manes in Pre-Raphaelite Painting', in *Pre-Raphaelitism and Medievalism in the Arts* (Lewiston, Queenston, Lampeter: The Edwin Mellen Press, 1992), pp. 159–93.
61. Nina Auerbach, *Woman and the Demon, the Life of a Victorian Myth* (Cambridge, Mass: Harvard University Press, 1982). On the ideological construction of the demonic woman see also Sally Shuttleworth, 'Demonic mothers: ideologies of bourgeois motherhood in the mid-Victorian era', in *Rewriting the Victorians*, ed. by Linda M. Shires (New York and London: Routledge, 1992), pp. 31–51. See also Kimberley Reynolds and Nicola Humble, *Victorian Heroines. Representation of Femininity in Nineteenth-century Literature and Art* (New York and London: Harvester Wheatsheaf, 1993).
62. Nencioni, 'Proserpina' (23 May 1886), in *Impressioni e rimembranze*, ed. by Del Lungo, p. 186.
63. Nencioni, 'Enriqueta', in *Nuovi medaglioni*, pp. 4–5 (my emphasis).
64. Ibid., p. 8 (my emphasis).
65. See Elisabeth Bronfer, *Over her Dead Body: Death, Femininity and the Aesthetic* (Manchester: Manchester University Press, 1992).
66. Nencioni, 'Proserpina', pp. 174 –75.
67. 'Era distesa a terra, su due cuscini, fra quattro ceri accesi [...] bianco-vestita, le mani incrociate sul petto, circondata da un magnifica ghirlanda di fiori, pareva dormire, sorridendo a qualche

divino sogno [...] quel che mi colpì più di tutto, fu il manto d'oro dei suoi capelli [...] il flutto d'oro dei suoi capelli le scendeva in doppio rivo fino ai piedi' [she was lying on the floor, on two cushions, amid four burning candles (...) dressed in white, her arms crossed over her breast, surrounded by a wonderful garland of flowers, she looked as if she was asleep, smiling at some divine dream (...) what impressed me most was the golden mantle of her hair (...) the billowing gold of her hair descended in a double stream down to her feet]. E. Nencioni, 'Consule Planco', in *Impressioni e rimembranze*, pp. 69–70.
68. Nencioni, 'Leila', in *Nuovi Medaglioni*, p. 131.
69. Nardi, p. 164. Correspondence between Nencioni and Fogazzaro is at the Biblioteca Marucelliana, Florence, in the Carteggio Nencioni.
70. See in particular Bram Dijkstra, *Idols of Perversity. Fantasies of Feminine Evil in fin-de-siècle Culture* (Oxford: Oxford University Press, 1986). Dijstrka's iconographic analysis shows how women, in the second half of the nineteenth century, when depicted as evil, tended to mirror male sexual desire. This, in his view, stems from a deep-set misogyny which is part of a wider discourse on sexuality and race in the late nineteenth and early twentieth century.
71. Forgacs, *Italian Culture in the Industrial Era*, p. 5.
72. Nencioni, 'Rassegna di letteratura inglese',in *Saggi critici di letteratura inglese*, p. 370.

CHAPTER 5

❖

Pescara and the Abruzzo in the Imagination of Gabriele D'Annunzio

Gianni Oliva

For JOHN WOODHOUSE 'abruzzese'

Pescara: A Site of Memory

> Taluno ha detto che ogni opera d'arte ha la sua cuna terrestre e che v'è una certa predestinazione, segreta o manifesta, nella figura de' luoghi ov'ella incomincia a vivere.
>
> [It has been said that every work of art has its cradle in the earth and that there is a kind of hidden or visible predestination in the character of the places where it comes to life.][1]

This passage is vital for an understanding of how a poetics of space comes to play an important role within D'Annunzio's work, surfacing as a constant factor, a point of eternal return and a permanent unifying element though it undergoes obvious metamorphoses. If it is true that D'Annunzio's work, which is essentially antinarrative, implies a dissolution of time, space functions to give it a fixed character. Place is a geographical entity, but also a linguistic and cultural one, and thus the land of the Abruzzi ends up by becoming, amongst the other poles of D'Annunzio's geography, the one with the most functional character precisely because it is lived, studied and documented in visceral fashion, even if it often undergoes an instinctive process of transfiguration.[2]

'I am the Abruzzo' the poet is said to have exclaimed on one occasion, as though wanting to articulate a deep and indissoluble identity, an ethnicity nurtured within himself as part of his upbringing and culture. It is no coincidence that he would write, again in the *Libro segreto* [*Private Book*]: 'Porto la terra d'Abruzzi, porto il limo della mia foce alle suola delle mie scarpe, al tacco de' miei stivali. Quando mi ritrovo fra gente estranea dissociato, diverso, ostilmente selvatico, io mi seggo e ponendo una coscia su l'altra accavallata, agito leggermente il piede che mi sembra quasi appesantirsi di quella terra, di quel poco di gleba, di quell'umido sabbione' [I carry the land of the Abruzzo, the silt of its estuary on the sole of my shoes, on the heels of my boots. Whenever I find myself in the company of strangers, cut off, set apart, belligerently antisocial, I sit myself down and placing one thigh on top of the other with my legs crossed, I lightly shake my foot which seems almost to grow heavy with the weight of that soil, that little clod of earth, that damp lump of sand].³ All this means that, despite the countless stratifications or hybrid layers built up and worn down over time during D'Annunzio's experiences as a man and as a writer, there remains in him a constant bedrock which can resurface at any given moment to make him exclusively and consciously *different*. The ancient stock to which he belongs is a weighty heritage, and one which he never completely shakes off: 'I miei padri erano anacoreti nella Maiella. Si flagellavano a sangue, masticavano la neve onde s'empievan le pugna, strozzavano i lupi, spennavano le aquile, intagliavano la sigla nei massi con un chiodo della Croce raccolto da Elena' [My forefathers were hermits who lived in the Maiella. They whipped themselves until they bled, chewed fistfuls of snow, strangled wolves, plucked the feathers of eagles, carved their initials into the rocks with a nail from the Cross found by St Helena]. (ibid.)

D'Annunzio travels through his geographical reality to breathe new life into places, emotions and civilizations which become the raw materials which his poetics and his personality reshape again and again. We find an Abruzzo which first emerges as a *virginal* and primitive space gradually transformed into a mythical and fabled entity, the point of convergence of a series of ancestral rites: in the end it becomes a site of memory. This locus enables D'Annunzio to relate ideal places to real ones, establishing important points of reference inside and outside the self. In other words, space embodies a poetics of knowledge that extends from geographical places to the heart itself, and Abruzzo becomes the reference point for this writing from the soul, the land to research for man's origins, his species, and his abode.

Within this process, Pescara assumes a key role: it is the starting point for the adventure, in some ways the very centre of this world. The gaze of both the naturalistic observer and the ironic reporter is directed towards this microcosm of a city, in the same way that, years later, it will become the focus of the melancholic writer of memoirs. It was also the bedrock for a book never written, an ambitious narrative undertaking planned as a follow-on from his experience of short story writing, as he wrote to Enrico Nencioni on 6 September 1884:

> Incomincerò subito un romanzo di cui ho già tutto l'organismo vivente nel cervello. Voglio fare un romanzo, dirò così, omerico, epico, in cui molti personaggi operino e grandi masse di uomini si muovano; un romanzo con moltissimi fatti e con poca analisi, un romanzo a sfondo storico. L'azione si svolgerà a Pescara, tra il '50 e il '75. Ho qui una meravigliosa miniera di documenti.
>
> [I'll immediately begin writing a novel whose entire living organism I already have in my head. I want to write a novel which I would call Homeric, epic, in which many characters act and in which great masses of people move about; a novel full of action and with only minimal reflection, a novel with a historical backdrop. The action will take place in Pescara, between '50 and '75. I have here with me a wonderful mine of documents.]⁴

Although the attraction of the Naturalist method led him to conceive of an experiment *à la* Zola, which with its solid, intricate structure, did not suit his own character as a writer, nevertheless his native city would provide him with the starting point for the narration of a world which he knew in detail: a world which at any rate seems to have already been sketched out in his early short stories, with its river and sea and its *figurines* taken from real life. The future poet, at that time a 'curly-haired' youth in one of the stories, meets in Corso Manthoné a depressed and haunted figure whom others call Cincinnato and asks him, almost as though questioning himself, 'Di che paese sei?' [Where are you from?], whilst, 'più in là, sul fiume, s'allungava il ponte di ferro tagliando il cielo a piccoli quadri; in fondo, sotto il ponte, il verde degli alberi s'era oscurato. Dalle caserme veniva un rumorìo confuso di gridi, di risa e di squilli' [Further over, on the river, the iron bridge stretched into the distance, cutting the sky into little squares; on the far side, underneath the bridge, the green of the trees had grown dark. From the barracks came the confused sound of cries, laughter and music].[5] This is the essence of Pescara stirring within him. These are the sounds that he will never forget. Those *figurines* file past as though on a stage, coarsely dressed, from Anna the Virgin to Orsola the Virgin, from Don Giovanni Ussorio to Cincinnato himself and Mungià, whilst observations full of local colour and relating to social mores abound:

> Fuori, era la novena di Natale, la bella festività de' vecchi e de' fanciulli. Erano certi vespri chiari e rigidi, sotto cui tutto il paese di Pescara si popolava di marinari e si empiva dei suoni delle zampogne. L'odore acuto delle zuppe di pesce si propagava nell'aria dalle cantine aperte. Lentamente alle finestre, alle porte, nelle vie i lumi apparivano. Il sole indugiava roseo su i terrazzi di pietra della casa di Farina, su i comignoli della casa di Memma, sul campanile di S.Giacomo.

> [Outside, it was the Christmas novena, the joyous celebration for the old and the young. It consisted of clear crisp evenings, during which the whole town of Pescara became populated with sailors and was filled with the sound of bagpipes. The pungent smell of fish soup spread through the air from the open cellars. Slowly, lights appeared at the windows and doors, and in the streets. The pinkish sun lingered on the stone terraces of Farina's house, on the chimneypots of Memma's house, on the bell-tower of S. Giacomo.][6]

The pages of his short stories conjure up a picture of a down-trodden people, but still alive and kicking, and often addicted to gaming ('Pescara città di gioco' [Pescara, Gambling City]), to the extent that it is conceivable that even the behaviour of the future 'adventurer' of *Il venturiero senza ventura* [*The Hapless Adventurer*] derives from that same matrix:

> Io ho sempre vissuto contro tutto e contro tutti [...] affermando e confermando ed esaltando me medesimo; ho giocato col destino, ho giocato con gli eventi, con le sorti, con le sfingi e con le chimere [...] io serbo nella memoria certi volti di giocatori veri, senza guadagno, senza alcuna cupidigia di oro [...] voglio ancora svelare me a me stesso, voglio dire come l'impronta della mia città natale sia stampata in me, e nel meglio di me, fieramente [...].

> [I have always lived in opposition to everything and everyone (...) asserting, proving and feeling proud of myself; I have played with fate, I have played with events, with destinies, with sphinxes and chimeras (...) I remember certain faces of real gamblers who winning nothing, had not an ounce of greed for gold (...) I still want to reveal something of myself to myself, I want to explain how the imprint of my native city has proudly made its mark on me, on the better side of me (...).][7]

Some of the images of places in Pescara will be immortalized in the author's first poetic compositions, delicate watercolours from the 'Studi a guazzo' [Studies in Gouache] series, such as 'Vespro d'agosto' ['August Vespers'] below, subtitled 'Ricordi di Pescara' ['Memories of Pescara'], a veritable picture postcard from Abruzzo in colour, with its sea and river:

> Rientran lente da le liete pèsche
> sette vele latine,
> e portan seco delle ondate fresche
> di fragranze marine.
> Son bianche, rosse, gialle e su ci raggia
> l'occhiata ultima il sole;
> s'allunga a l'aura una canzon selvaggia
> d'amore e di viole.
>
> Ne 'l ciel di perla le rondini brune
> ricaman voli a sghembo;
> non si vede de 'l mar là tra le dune
> che un cinereo lembo.
> Il fiume è pieno di riflessi; a schiera
> le sette vele stanche
> vengono innanzi insieme con la sera:
> son gialle, rosse, e bianche.

[They return slowly from their happy fishing trips/ seven lateen sails,/ and bring with them cool waves/ of perfume from the sea.
   They are white, red, yellow and on them/ the sun radiates its final look;/ at dawn a wild song/ of love and violets sounds out.
   In the pearly sky the brown swallows/ embroider oblique flights;/ all one sees of the sea there amongst the dunes/ is an ashen strip.
   The river is full of reflections; en masse/ the seven tired sails/ advance with the evening:/ they are yellow, red and white.][8]

This is just one example of the young D'Annunzio's pictorial talents: influenced by his painter friend Michetti, he develops into an author of hazy and delicate landscapes which take the Adriatic Abruzzo as their subject, sometimes greenish and foaming, surrounded by gentle hills — 'i colli in cerchia gradanti al mare' [a circle of hills sloping down to the sea][9] — at others calm and silvery in the summer heat. This is the period when the poet expresses the abundant vigour of his youth, when quoting Keats' *Endymion*, he would have liked to remain young forever: 'I shall be young again, be young!'

Pescara's sea is thus the dominant theme and if, beneath the freshness of the poet's school-time memories, it is readily transformed and becomes interchangeable now and again with the Greek sea of antiquity; it cannot but retain its natural properties precisely because it is the product of a visual experience undertaken by a shrewd observer. Often his poetic instinct manipulates the landscape and at those moments his imagination has the power to transform the waves into 'truppe/ d'alligatori in fregola' [troops/ of alligators on heat] or to see in the water 'cumuli d'alighe/ riarse, fracidi rottami, sugheri/ carogne brulicanti/ di mosconi e di vermini' [piles of dry seaweed, sodden wrecks, corks/ carcasses swarming/ with blowflies and worms][10] which, as symbols of death, are clear projections of his melancholic disposition. It is evident that from this point onwards the young poet never misses an opportunity to identify totally with nature, upon which he projects his particular state of mind, sometimes happy, sometimes uneasy.

There is more besides just the sea, however. Amongst the *Ricordi di Pescara* of the author's debut collection we also find included the October countryside or a flash of moonlight on the river, the river being another undisputed presence which, in his maturity, will provide him with the title for his collection of short stories:

> Era già adulto ottobre. Ne 'l cupo cobalto de 'l cielo
> su su da la marina sorgeva la luna, sì come
> un viso di pacchiana, tra biondi vapori, ne 'l fiume
> diafano una striscia rossastra gittando.

> [It was already late October. In the dark cobalt blue of the sky/ up up from the shore the moon rose, just like/ a garish face, amongst blonde vapours,/ casting a reddish stripe on the transparent river].[11]

Elsewhere, his gaze captures the image of three young girls whose features foreshadow the delightful sculptures by Costantino Barbella:

> Scendon lente le scale con anfore larghe di rame
> su 'l capo tre fanciulle formose cantando stornelli
> [...] Scendono: l'acque tranquille de 'l fiume
> scorron verdi tra 'l verde, e le nuvole sparse de 'l vespro
> vi treman entro in vaghi riflessi di minio e di giallo;
> da l'altra riva un uomo sta immobil pescando con l'amo.

> [They descend the steps slowly with broad copper amphoras/ on their heads, three shapely young girls singing ditties/ (...) they descend: the calm waters of the river/ flow green between the greenery, and the sparse clouds of the evening/ shimmer in it in beautiful reflections of bright red and yellow;/ on the other bank a man stands motionless, fishing with a hook.][12]

Meanwhile, looking out of the window in Corso Manthoné, he pauses to savour the September sun which 'batte su' tetti bruni' [beats down on the brown roofs] and on the 'vecchi mattoni scrostati/ de la torretta' [old dilapidated bricks/ of the turret], listening to the 'vivaci colombi' [lively doves], watching the cat who 'sonnecchia' [dozes] and Ninetta who sits embroidering in the courtyard, identifying herself with the caged goldfinch who 'gitta un capriccio di trilli a l'azzurro/ lontano' [sends out a capriccio of trills onto/ the distant sky].[13]

The youth who is so keen to escape everyday life does not yet know the extent to which those images and feelings will remain etched on his memory, together with the figures of his hard-working mother and sisters. And when, like a new Ulysses, hardened to the ways of the world, he will face the dangers of his voyage, he will be gripped like that Greek hero by a nostalgia for his stony Ithaca, by thoughts of his 'madre lontana' [distant mother], his 'dolci sorelle' [sweet sisters], the 'focolare' [hearth], his native river and his father's tomb:

> E m'apparve il bel fiume ove nato
> fui di stirpe sabella,
> Aterno di rossa corrente
> cui cavalca il ponte construtto

> di carene di travi
> d'ormeggi, spalmato di pece,
> in vista al monte nevoso
> che ha forma d'ubero pieno.
>
> E la tomba m'apparve sul poggio
> chiomante di pini, ove il padre
> riposa le sue grandi ossa
> ond'io m'ebbi tempra sì dura.

[And there appeared to me the beautiful river where I was born/ from Sabellian stock,/ the red-watered Aterno/ spanned by the bridge made/ from keels of ships,/ from moorings, smeared with tar,/ in sight of the snowy mountain/ in the shape of a full udder.

And the tomb appeared to me on the hillock/ bristling with pines, where my father/ rests his great bones/ who gave me such a steely temper.][14]

But time which passes cannot be regained and man, sucked into the vortex of a seemingly more and more 'inimitable' life, is destined to change his character, to identify himself with ever changing places, to have contact with different people, in short to adapt to another version of himself. And so that 'vago paese di Pescara/ dove un medicinal balsamo è l'aria' [beautiful town of Pescara/ where the air is a restorative balsam], whose praises are sung by that lighthearted and goliardic 'Musa balnearia' [seaside Muse], tends to become a locus of anguish, precisely because with every return the new man is forced to confront the child who has stayed behind at the window, looking out over the courtyard and listening to the sounds of the road. It is an arduous, almost unbearable, task, so much so that the returns themselves will become less and less frequent. More than a place to frequent, Pescara is destined to become a place of memory, part of the cocoon in which the author's purest affections are ideally preserved. There, in the old house in Corso Manthoné, his elderly mother waits for him, now in poor health:

> Non pianger più. Torna il diletto figlio
> a la tua casa. È stanco di mentire.
> Vieni; usciamo. Tempo è di rifiorire.
> Troppo sei bianca: il volto è quasi un giglio.

[Cry no longer. Your beloved son is returning/ home. He is tired of lying./ Come; let's go out. It is time to blossom again./ You are too pale: your face resembles a lily.][15]

Yet, at the moment of leaving for Pescara the poet's worry grows great: he is afraid of his melancholic disposition and of his past. A faint sense of pain and tiredness steals over him as he falls prey to 'fantasmi crudeli' [cruel phantasms]. He communicates these feelings to Donatella Cross who was his neighbour before his exile to France. The letter is dated 17 March 1910:

> Che giornata di strazio dissimulato! Partii iersera da Firenze, con un abbattimento indicibile, in una orribile solitudine interiore. Il viaggio è lungo e penoso, perché il treno non ha *sleeping-car*. Sono giunto qui a mezzogiorno, stanchissimo, senz'aver dormito. E il mio primo incontro con mia madre è stato angoscioso. È così debole che qualunque emozione la mette in pericolo. Prima di riacquistare il dominio di sé, ha passato un'ora di vera demenza. Ah, come ti dirò la mia pena?

> Tutto m'intenerisce e tutto mi ferisce qui. Vivo in ogni cosa, e sono ad ogni cosa estraneo. Sento in tutte queste creature il mio medesimo sangue, e sono infinitamente lontano da loro. E la vecchia casa è pur sempre impregnata dalla mia vita puerile come se pur ieri ne fosse uscito fanciullo.
>
> Oggi sono andato a rivedere la foce del fiume, là dove voglio essere sepolto; e poi sono tornato qui, e ho dovuto ricevere i parenti, gli amici, tutto questo popolo che mi adora come un dio sorridente.
>
> Verso sera mi sentivo così stanco che ho chiesto di rimanere nella mia stanza. Mi son seduto su l'inginocchiatoio di cui ti ho parlato una volta, sul vecchio inginocchiatoio delle preghiere infantili. Ho appoggiato il capo alla sponda del letto; e nei rumori della casa, nei rumori della strada ho udito cose che non potrò mai raccontare. Poi mi sono addormentato; e quando ho riaperto gli occhi, mia madre mi guardava — venuta silenziosamente — e piangeva. E non ho mai avuto tanto terrore del mio destino velato.
>
> [What a day of hidden suffering! I left Florence yesterday evening with an inexpressible feeling of despondency, in a terrible state of inner loneliness. The journey is long and arduous as the train doesn't have a sleeping car. I arrived here at midday, shattered, not having slept. And the first meeting with my mother was a painful one. She is so weak that emotion of any kind puts her in danger. Before regaining her composure, she suffered an hour of veritable madness. Oh, how am I to tell you what I suffer?
>
> Everything moves and wounds me here. I live as part of everything, and am a stranger to it all. I feel my own blood flowing in all these creatures and yet I am infinitely distanced from them. And the old house is still saturated with my childhood existence as if only yesterday I had emerged from it as a young boy.
>
> Today I went to see the river estuary again, the spot where I want to be buried. And then I came back here and I had to receive relatives, friends, all these people who worship me as though I were a smiling god.
>
> Towards evening I felt so tired that I asked to stay in my room. I sat down on the kneeling stool that I told you about once, that old kneeling stool I used for my childhood prayers. I rested my head on the edge of the bed, and amongst the sounds of the house, the sounds of the road I heard things that I could never recount. Then I fell asleep; and when I reopened my eyes, my mother was looking at me — come silently to my bedside — and was crying. And I've never felt so afraid of my uncertain destiny.][16]

Moreover, these emotions which he experienced in real life had been prefigured in his work of literary fiction, *Il trionfo della morte* [*The Triumph of Death*], in the episode in which his protagonist Giorgio Aurispa, clearly an alter-ego of the author, goes back to his paternal home in Guardiagrele. The pages of this novel of 1894 appear almost to be a palimpsest of the author's subsequent actual return in 1910, as though he had been mulling over those feelings for a long time in his mind:

> Quando sentì che doveva senza altri indugi accorrere là dove era il vero dolore, fu occupato da una torbida angoscia in cui la primitiva pietà filiale venne a poco a poco sopraffatta da una irritazione crescente che aumentava d'acredine come più chiare e più spesse sorgevano nella coscienza le immagini della lotta prossima e come più alte sonavano dal profondo le voci dell'egoismo intollerante. E quella irritazione si fece così acre che in breve dominò sola, durevole, mantenuta dai fastidii materiali della partenza, dagli strazii del commiato.

[When he felt that without further delay he ought to hasten to that place where there was real pain, a troubled anxiety took hold of him in which his early filial piety was gradually overcome by a growing anger which became more bitter the clearer and more often the images of his future strife sprang into consciousness and the more the voices of an intolerant egoism could be heard rising up from the depths. And that anger became so bitter that, in short, it ruled alone, steadfast, and was kept going by the physical nuisances of leaving and by the pain of saying goodbye.][17]

Giorgio had also experienced that strong conflict between belonging and not belonging to one's native land which distance had merely exacerbated and aggravated:

> Giungendo a Guardiagrele, alla città natale, alla casa paterna, egli era così estenuato che nell'abbraccio la madre pianse come un fanciullo. Eppure né da quell'abbraccio né da quelle lacrime provò conforto. Gli pareva d'essere nella sua casa un estraneo; gli parve d'essere in mezzo a una famiglia non sua. Quel singolar sentimento di distacco, ch'egli era già altre volte aveva provato verso i consanguinei, ora gli risorgeva più vivo e più molesto.
>
> [Arriving at Guardiagrele, his native city, and at his father's house, he was so tired out that his mother wept over him like a child. And yet he found no comfort in that embrace nor in those tears. He felt a stranger in his own home; he felt he was in the midst of a family that wasn't his own. That peculiar feeling of detachment that he had already felt towards his relatives on other occasions, now came back to him yet more alive and more troubling.][18]

Guardiagrele is thus superimposed upon Corso Manthoné, and Giorgio-Gabriele experiences a restless night amidst the objects and noises of his childhood:

> Entrò nelle sue stanze, si chiuse. La luna di maggio splendeva su i vetri dei balconi. Ed egli aprì le imposte, provando un gran bisogno di respirare l'aria della notte; si appoggiò alla ringhiera, bevve, come a lunghi sorsi, la freschezza notturna [...] Stette in ascolto. Gli giunse nel silenzio, da una stalla vicina, lo scalpitio d'un cavallo; poi, un tintinnio fioco di sonagli. Guardò la finestra illuminata; e vide, nel rettangolo di luce, passare alcune ombre, ondeggianti, come di persone che nell'interno si agitassero.
>
> [He went into his rooms, shut himself up there. The May moon shone on the windows of the balconies. He opened the shutters, feeling a strong need to breathe in the night air; he leant against the balustrade, and took deep gulps of the freshness of the night.(...) He stood listening. The sound of a horse pawing the ground reached him from a nearby stable; then, a faint ringing of harness-bells. He looked at the lit-up window and saw a series of shadows passing across the rectangle of light, in waves, like people who were moving restlessly inside.][19]

The *nóstos* towards his 'piccola patria' [little homeland] will resurface in unforgettable fashion also during D'Annunzio's exploration of the world of shadow in *Notturno* [*Nocturne*], where the familiar setting of the city and the author's childhood abode are destined to renew the visionary writer's eternal anxiety:

> Le mura di Pescara, l'arco di mattone, la chiesa screpolata, la piazza coi suoi alberi patiti, l'angolo della mia casa negletta. È la piccola patria. È sensibile qua

e là come la mia pelle. Si ghiaccia in me, si scalda in me. Quel che è vecchio mi tocca, quel che è nuovo mi ripugna. La mia angoscia porta tutta la sua gente e tutte le sue età.

[Pescara's city walls, the brick arch, the crumbling church, the square with its sickly trees, the corner of my rundown house. This is my little homeland. It is sensitive in places like my skin. It freezes in me, grows hot in me. What is old here touches me, new things repulse me. My anxiety carries with it all that city's people and all its ages.][20]

His imagination will inspect the objects most dear to him, 'il letto bianco' [the white bed], the 'vecchio armadio dipinto' [old painted wardrobe] and the much cited 'inginocchiatoio' [kneeling stool] where he used to sit 'in corruccio' [angrily] and 'ammutolito' [in silence]. The wave of memories does not abate and when donna Luisa disappears, everything will assume an indefinable quality of holiness, intimately nourished within the memory of the lonely old man, 'prigioniero atterrito' [the terrified prisoner] in the Vittoriale, who is destined never to return to the city which had witnessed his birth. Even then, with the weight of the years and with the terrible presage of death, the images of his past life and of the errors of his youth spent in Corso Manthoné do not disappear, continuing to shape an identity that is tormented but never denied:

> La mia infanzia la mia puerizia la mia adolescenza son rimaste intatte, come tre piccole sorelle Belle immobili. Quando arrivo, a troppi lunghi intervalli, tutt'e tre si svegliano; e mi sembra che ciascuna mi dica le stesse parole della Principessa al Principe grazioso: 'Ah, come vi siete fatto attendere!'.
>
> [My infancy, my childhood, my adolescence have all remained intact, like three small motionless Sleeping Beauties. When I arrive, with too much time between visits, all three of them wake up; and it is as though each of them says to me those same words the Princess spoke to Prince Charming: 'Oh, how long you have made me wait for you!'][21]

A Convent on the Sea

The convent on the sea, set deep within a calm and natural landscape, is perched on a hill overlooking the blue stretch of the Adriatic on one side, and on the other looking out towards the hills and mountains of Abruzzo. Nestling between the sea and the mountains it becomes symbolic of the two different souls of a single region of Italy imagined for centuries to be on the very borders of reality, in an almost fantastical space — 'piú là che Abruzzi' [further than the Abruzzi], Boccaccio's Calandrino would say, when he wanted to indicate the whereabouts of the philosopher's stone. A wild and inhospitable place according to popular belief and to the English Romantic writers: Ann Radcliffe described it as an exotic land, full of lush vegetation and African palms, craggy rocks and gloomy cliffs. But Abruzzo was, in reality, a cradle of civilization and Boccaccio himself was well aware of this when he left Florence for Naples, following the merchants' route or so-called 'via degli Abruzzi' [Abruzzi road]. Merchants have always brought culture with them, as well as wealth and progress.

Amongst the many cycles of civilization recorded in the Abruzzi over the centuries, the most important period is that between the eighteenth and nineteenth centuries when the Enlightenment culture that had emerged in Naples spread throughout the country nourishing a circulation of ideas on a European scale. Later, after Italian Unification, culture in Abruzzo developed in leaps and bounds thanks to its proximity to the capital city of Rome and to the birth of the railways. Travelling from Rome to Abruzzo and vice versa was therefore much easier than it had been in the past, and city intellectuals often went to the region to take a break from the frenzied pace of the big city, whilst local intellectuals went to Rome to restore their energies and keep themselves up to date with cultural issues of the time. The result was a profitable and vital exchange between the two sides.

There even existed a stage in the history of Italian culture when one did not count for much unless one was 'abruzzese': namely, the period of the 'artists' circle' in Francavilla. The full range of the arts, from literature to painting, sculpture and music were all represented at a high level. The names of Gabriele D'Annunzio, Francesco Paolo Michetti, Costantino Barbella and Francesco Paolo Tosti dominated the cultural milieu in Rome, forming a unified group unto themselves.

★ ★ ★

As is well known, in 1883 Michetti bought the Convent of Santa Maria del Gesù to live there and install a studio for himself. The convent complex dated back to the fifteenth century and stood close to the walls of the old village of Francavilla. It belonged to the Minori Osservanti order of friars, popularly known as the Zoccolanti [Clog-wearers] because of the style of shoes they wore. It was a place of meditation and reflection, and no one could have predicted that one day, amidst those same walls consecrated to the spirit, D'Annunzio would write the sensual and sinful pages of *Il piacere* [*The Child of Pleasure*].

The church adjacent to the Convent is dedicated to Santa Maria del Gesù even if D'Annunzio called it Santa Maria Maggiore, which is actually the name of the Chiesa Madre of Francavilla. Few traces remain of the fifteenth-century structure, but a few years ago a striking fresco from that period was discovered depicting Saint Francis receiving the stigmata. The circumstances of this find are singular to say the least: one night thieves stole a sixteenth-century canvas and underneath it was discovered the fresco which no one had known about beforehand.

The harmonious portico with five arches which opens onto the front of the church also dates back to only a slightly later period than this. Half-way through the eighteenth century the Convent was renovated: the refectory had a new stucco vault fitted and the church was embellished with new baroque altars, other fresco paintings, large church windows and two side chapels. Of the three original bell towers, only one remains today because of the destruction suffered at the hands of the Germans in the winter of 1943–44 (it must be remembered that Abruzzo was a key theatre of a bloody World War).

The Zoccolanti lived in the Convent until 1867 when the laws of the new Kingdom of Italy led to the dissolution of many religious communities. At that point the Convent passed into the hands of the town council. That was when Michetti, a young painter from Tocco Casauria, devised the plan to transform the Convent into a small community of artists all driven by the same desire to celebrate their native region, each using his own expressive medium. The town council proceeded to sell the Convent to Michetti, thus making his dream a reality. The painter made a series of changes to the Convent: he renovated the cloisters, had a fourteenth-century double lancet window installed in one of the outside walls, and fitted two circular church windows, one of which looked out over the sea, the other over the open fields (intending in this way to recreate the circularity of the eyes' movement and the effect of a vision of nature).

★ ★ ★

The Convent was thus transformed little by little into a meeting place, a community and a refuge for a group of young artists and their friends who were passionate about art. Permanent members included Michetti himself, D'Annunzio, Barbella and Tosti, but others also came to stay there, mainly from Rome: the painters Giulio Aristide Sartorio and Basilio Cascella, the writers Edoardo Scarfoglio and Matilde Serao, the translator Georges Hérelle, Paolo De Cecco, and, in turn, the women D'Annunzio loved, Barbara Leoni, Maria Hardouin di Gallese and Maria Gravina. Nunziata, Michetti's wife, cooked for everyone, but the artists often tried their hands too at cooking. D'Annunzio spoke of them as the 'bella compagnia di amici' [wonderful group of friends] and as the Bohemians of Abruzzo.

Towards the end of his life, falling back into his nostalgic habits, D'Annunzio was to write that: 'Nel bel tempo, in terra d'Abruzzi, a Francavilla su l'Adriatico, io vivevo con i miei fratelli accordati in una specie di fràtria monda di ogni altra gente estranea [...] nella casa ospitale di un amico che solo in tutti i miei anni potei chiamare altamente "mei dimidium animi"!' [In the good old days, in the land of Abruzzo, in Francavilla on the Adriatic, I lived with my brothers joined together in a kind of brotherhood from which all outsiders were excluded (...) in the welcoming house of a friend who alone, in all my years, I was able to nobly call 'one half of myself'].[22] In *La chimera* [*The Chimera*], D'Annunzio was to write of Michetti: 'Tu signor de 'l pennello, io de la rima,/ fingeremo beltà meravigliose!' [You lord of the paintbrush, I of verse,/ we shall create things of outstanding beauty!][23]

In fact those 'beltà meravigliose' [things of outstanding beauty] soon became a reality: Michetti did indeed paint his most beautiful canvases in Francavilla and D'Annunzio wrote his three most important novels there, *Il piacere*, *L'innocente* [*The Victim*] and *Il trionfo della morte* [*The Triumph of Death*].

Michetti's studio still retains today that calm and slightly mystical air which the painter wanted to give it, in keeping with the Convent's architecture and with the light of the landscape. It is made up of three huge interlinking rooms, open to no one else except Michetti up until his death. Here he painted his masterpieces: *Il voto* [*The Vow*], *La processione delle serpi* [*The Procession of Serpents*], *Gli storpi* [*The Lame*], pictures both fascinating and appalling at the same time, which explored the religious and idolatrous traditions of his native Abruzzo. In his work, objective and photographic Naturalism gives way to a transfigured vision of events, which I would say is almost pre-Symbolist. Michetti makes use of the camera only to gather useful materials to rework in the confines of his studio and not merely to imitate, but rather in fact to transfigure. In this respect his outlook is very close to D'Annunzio's own poetics, which always aimed at going 'beyond the surface of things' to grasp their essence. To the uninitiated eye Michetti's canvases would make the viewer think of episodes from folklore, whilst in reality it would have been possible to perceive in them already the onset of developing synthetic tendencies. Thus he would rely only on colour to achieve the requisite figures, dimension and perspective of a particular painting. Compared with the masters he followed from the Neapolitan school, such as Morelli and his fellow-Neapolitan Palizzi, Michetti's figurative language already displayed, from his time at the Convent onwards, a study of the real, but infused with feeling, thus opening up his native culture to a European dimension. He ended up privileging pastel over oil so as to obtain the greatest effect of luminosity, giving to the whole a quality of intangibility, very similar to the use of *fading* in D'Annunzio's descriptions. In *Il voto* (1883), for example, through detailed preparatory studies and with the aid of photography, Michetti turns out a sumptuous painting depicting an episode centred on the faithful of Miglianico (as D'Annunzio does in *San Pantaleone*). He highlights the wretchedness, superstition and social evils on a large canvas full of intense drama. But Michetti is far from dwelling on social polemic: the work's content takes second place to the technical ability of the painter. If anything the figures in the painting provoke a sense of repulsion and magnetic attraction which goes well beyond the realms of ideological invective.

Besides, Michetti's work was linked to D'Annunzio's and to the Aestheticist climate associated with the journal *Cronaca bizantina* [*Byzantine Chronicle*], which was the bible of the entire artistic circle of Francavilla even though it had never drawn up a programme of its own activities. *Il canto novo* [*The New Poem*] was born from that milieu, as were *Il piacere*, *L'Isotteo*, and *La chimera* later on. A faint Alexandrian and Parnassian trend hung in the air, and the pursuit of beauty and sensation was of utmost importance.

It is in this perspective that we should read the famous pages of D'Annunzio's *Il trionfo della morte* and the corresponding canvases by Michetti *en plein air* (such as *Gli storpi*) which were the product of his sensational photographic collection. In both there is a desire to shock and to frighten, which puts the degradation of humanity firmly on show.

★ ★ ★

There are many accounts of the long days spent in the Convent in D'Annunzio's work; in fact it is fair to say that there is not a single corner of that place that was not described by the author or did not arouse certain feelings and emotions in him. What attracted him above all were the peace and harmony of nature in a village defined as the 'ospizio di rondini' [shelter for swallows]. He lived there in stillness and silence: 'Sono qui al Convento' [I am here at the Convent] — he wrote to Barbara Leoni —

'Nelle mie stanze nulla è mutato; ma in tutto l'edificio ritrovo cambiamenti strani: vasche, bagni, fontane, scale miracolose, un orto prospero, inscrizioni indecifrabili su i muri; terrazze aeree, tutta un'architettura fantastica. Il mare è magnifico; il colle è opulento' [Nothing has altered in my rooms; but throughout the building I find strange changes: basins, baths, fountains, miraculous steps, a thriving kitchen garden, indecipherable inscriptions on the walls, lofty terraces, a whole fabulous architecture. The sea is magnificent; the hill opulent].[24] Elsewhere he wrote (also in a letter to Barbara): 'Sono stato un poco giù sotto il portico del convento a guardare la luna nuova che, fina come un gioiello, tramontava dietro la collina oscura, in un cielo soave' [I stayed a little while down there, underneath the convent's portico to watch the new moon setting, delicate as a jewel, behind the dark hill, in a soft sky].[25] Moreover, D'Annunzio loved the cloisters and the gardens: they are said to have inspired him (along with Giambattista Marino of course) to write the famous description of the song of the nightingale in *L'innocente*.

From the balcony he perceives the beauty of the sea and enjoys the peaceful climate to be found in the kitchen gardens, especially during October evenings: 'Si viveva così obliosamente. La sera, mentre il plenilunio ottobrale saliva alla marina, i nostri cuori risuonavano nella tranquillità degli oliveti, sotto l'incerto biancicare argentino dei rami. Di tratto in tanto, Messere il Vento veniva a strimpellare questo vecchio colascione che è il Convento' [We lived so forgetfully. In the evenings, whilst the full October moon rose over the shore, our hearts resounded amidst the tranquillity of the olive groves, underneath the uncertain whitish silver of the branches. Now and again, His Honour the Wind would come to strum away on this old lute that is the Convent].

In July 1888, having left Rome, the author has in his possession the bundle of notes and cuttings from his society chronicles published in *La Tribuna* [*The Tribune*] to work on the draft of *Il piacere*. A guest of Michetti's in Francavilla, he began his novel on 26 July and despite considerable difficulties worked at it feverishly up to December. In fact, written at the end of the manuscript, we find the dates 'July-December 1888'. He worked in the left-hand corner of his little room — from then on called 'la stanza del *Piacere*' [The *Piacere* Room]) — and he reports on his progress to Barbara Leoni:

> Lavoro tutto il giorno, infaticabilmente. Ieri dopo aver lavorato cinque ore la mattina, rimasi nel pomeriggio sette ore di seguito al tavolino, senza mai levarmi. Quando smisi, morivo di stanchezza; ma mi pareva d'esser diventato una creatura immateriale, leggera, fluida, quasi direi psichica, alata, spiritualizzata, purissima. […] Io ho risoluto di non muovermi di qui se non avrò finito il mio libro, perché amo il mio libro sul quale ho sudato e spasimato; e non ho il coraggio di abbandonarlo.

> [I work tirelessly the whole day long. Yesterday, having worked five hours in the morning, I stayed at my little table for another seven hours solid in the afternoon, without getting up. When I stopped working, I was dying from exhaustion, but felt as if I had been transformed into an ethereal being, light, fluid, almost psychic you might say, a winged creature, spiritualized and extremely pure. (...) I have resolved not to move myself from here until I have finished my book, because I love this book that I have sweated and racked my brain over; and I don't have the courage to abandon it.][26]

The long and difficult writing of the novel took place in the Convent, which explains why, when it was published in 1889, it was dedicated to the friend who had put him up during that period: 'Questo libro, composto nella tua casa dall'ospite bene accetto, viene a te come un rendimento di grazie, come un ex-voto. Nella stanchezza della lunga e grave fatica, la tua presenza m'era fortificante e consolante come il mare' [This book, composed under your roof where I was a most welcome guest, comes to you as a token of my thanks, as a votive offering. Through the weariness of that long and grievous trial, like the sea, your presence gave me strength and consolation].[27]

But what did Michetti's closeness really signify? D'Annunzio himself provides us with the answer when he emphasizes 'la limpida semplicità del *suo* ragionamento' [the clear minded simplicity of *his* reasoning], the advice he received from him; he recognizes in him 'l'esercizio e lo sviluppo della più nobile tra le facoltà dell'intelletto: [...] l'abitudine dell'osservazione' [The exercise and development of the noblest of the faculties of the intellect: (...) the practice of observation].[28] In these words we find encapsulated D'Annunzio's poetics of *invention* or, to put it another way, his discovery of things and their reworking within the domain of writing. In dedicating the work to Michetti, D'Annunzio smiles at the realization that a work which examined 'tanta depravazione e tante sottilità e falsità e crudeltà vane' [so much depravity, so many subtleties, falsities and vain cruelties] had been written 'in mezzo alla semplice e serena pace' [in the midst of the simple and serene peace] of the Convent.

A few years later, still in Francavilla, D'Annunzio wrote *L'innocente* (1891) and again there are several references to the little, silent room where he worked. While writing, he remarks on the song of the nightingale: 'Soffia il maledetto garbino, un vento micidiale che spezza i muscoli e i nervi e dissecca il cervello orribilmente. Ahimé io scrivo; e nell'orto canta un usignolo, se bene piova. Come canta!' [The cursed *garbino* blows through here, a biting wind which cuts through muscles and nerves and withers the brain in horrendous fashion. Poor me, I am trying to write; and in the kitchen garden a nightingale sings, even though it's raining. How it sings!] (From a letter to Barbara).[29] The work was completed on 2 August 1891 after 'quattro lunghi mesi' [four long months]. The ritual of reading out the pages still wet with ink continued, each time Michetti made his way up to the 'cella remota' [remote cell] during his breaks from work. The same was also true of *Il trionfo della morte* when 'nella grande quiete conventuale, mentre fumigava entro le tazze la bevanda favorita [...] parevami si spandesse nell'aria il calore delle nostre intelligenze' [in the great quiet of the convent, whilst steam rose up from the cups full of our favourite drink (...) it seemed to me as though the heat of our intelligence expanded into the air].[30] D'Annunzio writes in the dedication of *Il trionfo della morte*: 'Era dolce per me quella tregua e molto aspettata, dopo l'acerba lotta diurna in compagnia di colui che comprende tutto' [That moment of peace was sweet for me and much awaited after the bitter daytime struggle in the company of him who understands everything].[31] Michetti — D'Annunzio tells us — was the first to appreciate the poetry of the people of Abruzzo, which *Il trionfo* carries imprinted in its pages, especially those dedicated to Casalbordino, in which the figures previously seen in Michetti's photographs resurface. The preface to this book, once again dedicated to the leader of the Cenacolo, Michetti, includes a place and date as follows: '*Dal Convento di S. Maria Maggiore nel calen d'aprile 1894*' [*From the Convent of S. Maria Maggiore, the Calends of April 1894*].

It is generally held that the sculptor Costantino Barbella also formed part of the 'quadrumvirate' of artists in Francavilla and that his work contributed to Italian intellectuals' interests shifting back onto the Abruzzi. Critics called him 'the great sculptor of tiny statues'. Barbella, like Michetti, took his inspiration from the observation of the real, but gave his terracotta works a 'lyrical' quality, nurturing his extraordinary penchant for the poetic. The artistic representation of the reality of Abruzzo was communicated through features which tended towards transfiguration, features which could be defined as late-Arcadian.

'Accanto a me'– D'Annunzio recollects — 'Costantino Barbella plasmava la divina creta canticchiando. Ai tocchi fini della stecca e del pollice le forme feminee balzavano fuori con una viva freschezza di gioventù, con una movenza balda di vita. Intorno, nella nitidezza del bronzo, arridevano i suoi occhi felici maggiaioli' [Next to me (...) humming to himself, Costantino Barbella moulded the divine clay. Under the touch of his palette knife and thumb those female forms thrown into relief with a youthful and vivid freshness, a bold appetite for life. In the clarity of the bronze shone reflections of the maytime happiness of his eyes].[32]

Amongst the sculptor's best known works one must mention *Il canto d'amore* [*The Love Song*], created roughly at the same time as the *Processione del Corpus Domini* [*The Procession of Corpus Domini*] by Michetti, both exhibited at the National Exhibition of the Belle Arti in Naples, to great critical acclaim. In 1889 terracotta gives way to bronze, and the figures acquire a greater degree of perfection thanks to their metallic surface which gives softness and lightness to the composition. A critic of the period, Giovanni Duprè, describes Barbella's work as follows:

> The sculpture consists of three young ladies who sing and walk and almost seem to be embracing one another. They are wearing a strange, ornate style of clothing native to the mountains of Abruzzo, and those outfits on such young and beautiful bodies, made supple and life-like by the walking movement, and the joy which emanates from their faces thanks to the grace and power of their song, create a whole that is appealingly elegant [...]. The smallness of the figures and the material on which they are based seems to disappear and one seems to feel instead the power of their song, their living breath and their joy.[33]

These are impressions made on the spur of the moment, certainly, but they express the gracefulness that the sculptor wanted to give his figures, in keeping with a tradition which looked back to the Neapolitan *figurinai*, those heirs to the refined art of the eighteenth-century makers of nativity cribs.

D'Annunzio himself seems to make reference to the three girls in his short story 'Fra' Lucerta' in *Terra vergine* [*Virgin Earth*], but the author's often crude and primitive tones generally do not blend well with the gracefulness which emanates from Barbelli's world.

And there were songs by Tosti, born in Ortona, a few kilometres from Francavilla. His Romances, as is well known, were world-famous during a period in which that genre was at the height of fashion. The refined taste he exhibited in fusing together words and music gave his compositions a technical perfection and expressed the languor and sighs of the whole of aristocratic salon society. Amongst the friends of the Convent, Tosti was definitely the most reserved and the most elegant.

His friendship with D'Annunzio went back to 1880, before his transfer to London. Their collaboration, which extended far beyond the Francavilla years, resulted in numerous works, the most famous of which are *Ninna Nanna* (for Giorgio Michetti: D'Annunzio alludes to Michetti's son also in the preface to *Il piacere*) and *A' vucchella*, in Neapolitan dialect: 'Francesco Paolo Tosti che non anche era diventato un puro britanno cantava a bassa voce, con modulazioni d'una inimitabile finezza, le sue romanze più belle, quelle romanze dove spesso rivivono in tutta la loro nativa freschezza le canzoni della patria e dove una così limpida vena di melodia corre e scintilla tra le sottili fioriture dell'armonia accompagnante' [Francesco Paolo Tosti, though he had not become a pure Briton, sang his most beautiful romances in a low voice, with modulations of an inimitable subtlety, those same romances in which the songs of the homeland are brought back to life in all their native vigour and through which runs such a clear chain of melody that it sparkles amidst the subtle embellishments of the accompanying harmony].[34]

There are many anecdotes recounted by biographers regarding D'Annunzio's and Tosti's friendship, some of which are even amusing, but what is important is the fact that the texts written for the musician are little more than a game for the poet, even if D'Annunzio demonstrates that he was well aware of his gifts as a 'lyricist', always ready and able to vary his writings in response to the demands of the music. He senses the difference between the *fixity* of the poetic text and the *mobility* of any text to be set to music. Their pairing became popular thanks to the popularity which that kind of 'light' music (we would call it today) enjoyed. Tosti, like the others, dreamt of a modern culture for Abruzzo which at the same time had its roots in tradition. Other musicians lined up behind him, all driven by the same goal: Paolo De Cecco, Camillo De Nardis, Ettore Montano, Vittorio Pepe, Guido Albanese, the founders, amongst other things, of the much celebrated 'canzone abruzzese d'autore' [canzone *d'auteur* of Abruzzo].

In 1878 Tosti had begun work on the *Canti popolari abruzzesi* [*Popular songs from Abruzzo*]. Four songs are in fact dedicated to Michetti who had helped him with his research. Michetti drew inspiration for his painting *La mattinata* [*Morning*] from them, in which Tosti is also depicted. On the subject of Tosti's *Canti popolari*, D'Annunzio wrote the following to Giselda Zucconi: 'Quelle canzoni lì bisogna sentirle cantare in coro dalle donne in lontananza: sono una meraviglia, sono le più belle canzoni popolari d'Italia. C'è fra le altre una ch'è composta d'una frase breve e semplicissima, poche note; séntile, e proverai un rimescolamento, e ti salirà il pianto agli occhi' [You should hear those songs sung by a chorus of women in the distance: they are a marvel, the most beautiful popular songs in Italy. One of them is composed of a single short phrase, with few notes; listen to them and you will feel a certain stirring in your heart, and find your eyes welling up with tears].[35]

★ ★ ★

This period, however, was destined to come to an end and D'Annunzio emphasizes his regret for the passing of that carefree creativity that the group of friends shared: 'Oh dolcissime notti di Francavilla! Dov'è dispersa ora quella bella compagnia di amici? Paolo Tosti è in Inghilterra, tra il fumo e tra la nebbia, e di tanto in tanto manda una sua romanza malinconica dove non di rado pare a noi di sentire un lontano ricordo delle canzoni del paese [...]' [Oh such sweet nights spent in Francavilla! Where has that wonderful group of friends dispersed to? Paolo Tosti is in England, amongst the smoke and the fog, and from time to time he sends a melancholic romance in which we often find a distant memory of Abruzzo songs (...).][36]

Much has been written about the artists' circle in Francavilla: it has even been suggested by one person that it never existed but was merely the product of the retrospective 'mythicisation' which D'Annunzio indulged in on several occasions. But recent research has unearthed many documents which prove not only the existence of the circle but also the profitable collaboration amongst its members. Certainly, as Luigi Lodi wrote, there were formal differences between them, but 'an intimate and undeniable sense of community' linked them to each other. One cannot deny that there was a connecting thread linking the variety and richness of their individual modes of expression: 'La *Canzone d'amore* del Barbella sembra un'illustrazione al *Canto novo* di D'Annunzio come nelle pagine di *Terra vergine* erano persone che parevano uscire dal *Corpus domini* di Michetti' [Barbella's *Canzone d'amore* seems to be an illustration of D'Annunzio's *Canto novo* just as amongst the pages of *Terra vergine* there were characters who seemed to have walked straight out of Michetti's *Corpus Domini*].[37] In turn, Francesco Paolo Tosti's music provided the unifying force and, as it were, the sound-track for a current of feeling founded on the *joie de vivre* and the successful projection of Abruzzo culture on a national and European scale.

In that almost hermit-like existence which the four friends claimed to practise there was in fact an opening up towards the world and a desire to weave a vast network of human and artistic relations. And in the light of what Walter Pater would go on to write about the principle of the harmony of all the arts, the artists' circle in Francavilla fully articulated the poetics which was to become the basis of the entire Decadent movement.

Aware of the level of importance that the Francavilla group had achieved in that Convent so conducive to the arts, Michetti himself, who was the owner, submitted a proposal to the Italian Government in 1927 when D'Annunzio was already at the Vittoriale: to hand the Convent over to the state as a gift for D'Annunzio and to turn it into a museum dedicated to him. Nothing of the sort happened partly because the poet was involved in a thousand and one projects arising from his fame, but mainly because he was by now afflicted by the depression that came with old age and his days were already taken up reflecting on life and death. Soon after this, in 1929, D'Annunzio was to receive the news of Michetti's death and wrote in a telegram that: 'Egli era fratello vero della mia anima e la lontananza ed il silenzio non mai ci separarono' [He was the true brother of my soul and neither distance nor silence could ever divide us].[38]

From the Hermitage to the Sanctuary

> 'Verresti tu a passare l'estate con me, qui, in Abruzzo, in una casa solitaria sul mare, lontana da Francavilla, sicura?'
>
> [Would you come and spend the summer with me, here in Abruzzo, in a lonely house by the sea, safe, and far from Francavilla?][39]

With these words, written on 11 July 1889, Gabriele invited Barbara Leoni to spend several peaceful days of love and work with him in a refuge close to San Vito, against the backdrop of 'un'estate magnifica, regale, piena di profondi silenzi' [a magnificent and regal summer, full of profound moments of silence], overlooking 'un mare prodigioso' [miraculous sea].[40] There D'Annunzio would work on *L'invincibile* [*The Unconquerable*] (which became *Il trionfo della morte*) in the company of the woman who was at the same time the true protagonist of the story. 'Moriresti tu, con me?' [Would you die along with me?] — he wrote in another passage of the letter, thereby anticipating the tragedy that was to befall Giorgio and Ippolita at the end of the book, though Barbara was unaware of this. And again on 22 July he wrote from Pescara: 'Ti racconterò la *natività* del mio romanzo avvenuta nel mio cervello jeri, sul promontorio dei Sogni. Sono ancora pieno d'una certa ebrezza intellettuale' [I'll tell you all about the *birth* of my novel which took place in my brain yesterday, on the promontory of Dreams. I am still full of a kind of intellectual drunkenness].[41] The remote house had been found for him by Michetti, to whom he communicated his total enthusiasm for the project: 'Potrà venire in Abruzzo e passar con me l'estate. Quella casa di S. Vito, che io non conosco, mi pare già luminosa. Oh se io potessi, questa volta, dedicarti veramente un capolavoro! [...] Barbarella verrà a raggiungermi quando l'alloggio sarà pronto, l'impazienza mi divora' [She can come to Abruzzo and spend the summer with me. That house in S. Vito, that I am not familiar with, already glows bright. Oh, if only I could truly dedicate a masterpiece to you this time! (...) Barbarella will come and join me when the accommodation is fixed up, the impatience is killing me!].[42] To Barbara herself he would subsequently confide his feelings of worry, as they were to remain in his mind forever: 'Così Barbara' — he was to write during his later years in the *Libro segreto* — 'mi fu ridonata dalla tristezza e dalla poesia, a similitudine d'una foglia d'un fiore tra le pagine d'un libro esculto. Ella divenne Ippolita Sanzio. Il libro s'intitolò *Trionfo della morte* come l'allegoria dipinta a fresco dall'Orcagna nel Camposanto pisano' [Thus Barbara (...) was restored to me through sadness and poetry, like a leaf from the flower between the pages of a forgotten book. She became Ippolita Sanzio. The book was entitled *Trionfo della morte* like the allegory painted in fresco by Orcagna in the Camposanto in Pisa].[43]

His letters to Barbara inevitably leave a gap precisely in the two memorable months between 23 July and 22 September when the two young people spent long days working together in that 'solitudine selvaggia' [wild solitude], in a frenzy of creativity, whilst the feeling which bound them together found expression in 'infinite soavi malinconiche carezze' [infinite, soft, melancholic caresses]. The very day of her departure D'Annunzio would be able to write to her from Francavilla: 'Ormai le nostre due vite sono legate. Io ti ho conosciuta buona, dolce, amabile, sempre eguale. Io non potrò mai compensarti di questi due mesi felici. Nessuna, nessuna cosa mi pare e *mi parrà mai* preferibile alla solitudine con te sola, con te!' [Our two lives are already bound together. I have known you as good, sweet, lovable, changeless. I can never repay you enough for these two happy months. I prefer nothing more, I will never prefer anything more, than this solitude spent with you alone, with you!] (22 September 1889).[44]

D'Annunzio was to leave a trace of that solitude in his novel *in fieri* thanks to the clever game of superimposing reality and literary fiction that he found so congenial:

> Trovò L'Eremo a San Vito, nel paese del ginestre, su l'Adriatico. Trovò l'Eremo ideale: una casa construita in un pianoro, a mezzo del colle, tra gli aranci e gli olivi, affacciata su una piccola baia che chiudevano due promontorii.
>
> Era una casa d'una architettura primitiva. [...] La casa non ad altro serviva che ad albergare forestieri nella stagione dei bagni, secondo l'industria comune del contado di San Vito, lungo la costa. Distava circa due miglia dal borgo, all'estremo confine d'una contrada detta delle Portelle, in una solitudine raccolta e benigna come un grembo. Ciascuno dei due promontorii era traforato, e si scorgevano dalla casa le aperture delle due gallerie. La strada ferrata correva dall'una all'altra, in prossimità del lido, per una lunghezza di cinque o sei cento metri, in linea retta. Dall'estrema punta del promontorio destro, sopra un gruppo di scogli, si protendeva un Trabocco, una strana macchina da pesca, tutta composta di tavole e di travi, simile a un ragno colossale.

[He found the Hermitage in S. Vito, in the land of the broomflower, on the Adriatic coast. He found the Hermitage ideal: a house built on a plateau, half way up the hill, amongst orange and olive trees, overlooking a little bay closed by two promontories.

It was a house with a primitive architecture. (...) The house had no other purpose than to provide foreigners with a place to stay during the bathing season, in keeping with the common industry of the area around San Vito, along the coast. It was situated approximately two miles from the village, at the outermost boundary of a district known as Le Portelle, in a solitude as cosy and benign as a womb. Each of the two promontories was cut through and you could see the entrance to the two tunnels from the house. The railway ran from one to the other, close to the shore, for a distance of five or six hundred metres, in a straight line. From the furthest point on the right promontory, above a clump of rocks, a Trebuchet stretched out over the sea, a strange fishing machine, all made of planks and beams, that looked like a huge spider].[45]

Left on his own, Gabriele torments himself with the regret and memory of the happy days spent together with Barbara in that house. Whilst he continues to work, the woman's presence lingers in those rooms where the objects she has left behind add to his suffering, to the point where the poet is stifled by it. Even surrounding nature has already changed its aspect and seems to be decaying in the first autumn rains, and Michetti's visit from Francavilla can do little to lighten the lonely stay. Finally D'Annunzio relocates there, to the Villa del Fuoco, where he recreates a corner of the Hermitage with those left-over objects:

> Stamani, svegliandomi, ho sentito più forte e più inconsolabile il rammarico. Tutto mi pareva definitivamente risoluto, senza più speranza. La visione delle stanze vuote e in disordine, là giù, mi risorgeva nello spirito; e avevo lucidissimo il sentimento dei giorni che non sono più, che non tornano più!
>
> Ho portato qui tutta la mia roba ch'era a San Vito. Nella stanza da letto ho composto coi paraventi un angolo come quello che avevamo; e ci sono i medesimi oggetti. E' forse una tortura. Leverò i paraventi, leverò tutto. Il ricordo delle dolci intimità scambievoli mi farebbe troppo spesso mescolare le lacrime alle acque matutine.
>
> [This morning, when I woke up, the feeling of sorrow hit me more strongly and inconsolably than usual. Everything seemed determined once and for all, with no room left to hope. The sight of the empty, untidy rooms, down there, came back to mind; and I had a crystal clear feeling of days that are no more and which will never come back again!
>
> I brought all of my things here that were at San Vito. In the bedroom, with screens, I made a corner just like the one we had; and using the same objects. It is perhaps a torment. I'll take the screens away, take it all away. The memory of those sweet, mutual intimacies would cause me too often to mix tears with my morning ablutions.] (From a letter to Barbara, dated 24 September 1889)[46]

The letters, as mentioned earlier, say nothing — naturally — about how the poet spent his long stay at the hermitage. But the developing novel carries every possible trace of it, being transformed into a kind of coded diary of that stay. The impressions, feelings and emotions, joys and anxieties experienced in reality become the material of fiction, and even Barbara's responses by letter are redeployed in the context of the story and attributed to Ippolita. In short, as the novel puts it, 'La vita ebbe per lui [Giorgio] in quei primi giorni il sapore dolce e profondo che ha soltanto per il convalescente' [In those first days, life had for him [Giorgio], that sweet deep flavour which is reserved for the convalescent].[47] Meanwhile the surrounding countryside and sea are a delight, and the desire to learn about local customs and to proceed with 'the exploration of the surrounding area' grows more pronounced. And it is in this part of the novel that we find included the long and vibrant pages dedicated to the Sanctuary of the Madonna dei Miracoli in Casalbordino.

Certainly, if the festivities fell, as they still do today, on 10 and 11 June, Gabriele and Barbara could not have attended them together, but within the realms of novelistic fiction anything is possible, even the adapting of an experience which took place two years earlier (1887) and enjoyed by Gabriele alone during some of his excursions around Abruzzo. He would travel to Guardiagrele, Casoli, Lama dei Peligni, Palena, Rapino, Faro Cipollara, the 'gran madre Maiella' [great mother Maiella], always on horseback, with a notebook in hand to jot down ideas, but also furnished with writing paper to send letters to Barbara recounting what he had seen each day, especially the extraordinary experiences he had on Saturday 11 June in the 'hell' of Casalbordino:

> Jeri mattina, prima dell'alba, partimmo per Casalbordino. La chiesa della Madonna dei Miracoli è in mezzo a una pianura limitata dal mare. Una moltitudine di fanatici si agitava intorno alla chiesa gridando. Lo spettacolo

era terribile. Dinanzi all'Immagine centinaia di femmine cenciose, tutte sanguinanti, si trascinavano nella polvere. Gli urli, i pianti, gli strepiti salivano al cielo. Una polvere ardente avvolgeva ogni cosa, e il sole bruciava come una viva fiamma su la pianura aperta. Siamo rimasti lì sette ore. La moltitudine si rinnovava di continuo. Non ti dirò quel che ho veduto! [...] Ai lati della strada, di tratto in tratto, stavano distesi in mezzo alla polvere certi esseri deformi che non avevano apparenza di creature umane: uomini malati d'elefantiasi, che mostravano una gamba nericcia, enorme come un tronco d'albero; uomini storpii che tendevano le mani ritorte come radici; ciechi che avevano li occhi incavati e rossi, d'onde sgorgavano materie purulente; lebbrosi tutti coperti di piaghe; donne idropiche che scoprivano il ventre gonfio, per muovere la pietà; tutte le più miserabili deformità e le infermità più ributtanti erano lì tra la polvere, al pieno sole.

[...] Avevo il cuore così gonfio che non sapevo più trattenere il pianto. Quei miserabili urlavano ancora, mostrandomi le loro piaghe, tendendomi i loro moncherini, guardandomi con i loro occhi bestiali dalle palpebre infiammate. Intorno, la campagna ondeggiava nella sua bella opulenza; e, al fondo, il mare vaniva in un colore virginale, tra il verde del berillo e l'azzurro della turchese.

[Yesterday morning, before sunrise, we left for Casalbordino. The Church of Madonna dei Miracoli is in the middle of a plain next to the sea. A crowd of zealots milled about the church, shouting. It was a terrible spectacle. In front of the sacred Image, hundreds of ragged women, all bleeding, dragged themselves through the dust. The screams, the cries and the shouts rose into the sky. A scorching dust shrouded everything and the sun burned like a living flame on the open plain. We stayed there seven hours. The crowd was constantly renewed. I won't tell you what I witnessed! (...) Every now and then, on the sides of the road, deformed creatures which didn't look like human beings, could be seen sprawled amid the dust: men suffering from elephantiasis with a blackish leg on show, as large as a tree trunk; crippled men who stretched out their hands twisted like roots; blind men who had sunken red eyes, from which purulent substances flowed out; lepers all covered in wounds, dropsied women baring their swollen stomachs to incite pity; all the most wretched deformities and most revolting illnesses were there among the dust, in the full light of day.

(...) My heart was so heavy that I could no longer hold back the tears. Those wretched souls continued to yell, showing me their wounds, holding out their stumps to me, looking at me with their animal-like eyes, with swollen eyelids. Around them, the countryside rolled out in its beautiful richness and, in the distance, the sea fused into a virginal colour, between beryl green and turquoise blue.][48]

This letter to Barbara is a prototype for what D'Annunzio will do in his novel, diluting and expanding his images, whilst not altering his sense of dismay and repulsion at this nightmarish vision of a degraded humanity milling around '[la] Casa della Vergine' [The House of the Virgin].

Moving from the general to the particular, the eye of the observer surveys the frightening and deafening crowd; sometimes the pen is ruthless in recording the blood-curdling details, whilst all this powerful upheaval is set against the apparent tranquillity of open space, dazzling beneath a silent blue sky heralding the start of summer:

> Tutte le cose intorno rendevano più tragica l'ora evocando l'immagine biblica d'un cammino di desolazione che conducesse alle porte d'una città maledetta.⁴⁹
>
> [Everything around made the hour more tragic, conjuring up the biblical image of a road of destruction leading to the gates of a cursed city.]

An 'ansietà angosciosa' [distressing anxiety] takes hold of the two characters who overbearingly demonstrate their desire to distance themselves from that filthy crowd, to find some space to breathe and to enjoy a sort of atavistic and virtual purification rite. The view of the sea fulfils this function perfectly; the waters wash away the stains and regenerate the spirit from the ground up:

> E l'onda si dileguò; e, in una curva della discesa, il Santuario scomparve. E, all'improvviso, quasi un alito fresco passò sopra le larghe mèssi che fluttuarono. E una lunga lista cerulea secò l'orizzonte.
>   'Ecco il mare! Ecco il mare!' proruppe Giorgio, come se in quel punto avesse toccata la sua salvezza.
>   E il cuore gli si dilatava.
>   'Su, anima! Guarda il mare!'
>
> [And the wave petered out; and, in one of the bends of the descent, the Sanctuary disappeared. Then, suddenly, it was almost as though a fresh breeze blew over the expansive crops that swayed about. And a long cerulean line cut across the horizon.
>   'There's the sea! There's the sea!' burst out Giorgio, as though at that moment he had touched salvation.
>   And his heart swelled.
>   'Rise up, my soul. Look at the sea!']⁵⁰

Translated by Francesca Southerden

Notes to Chapter 5

1. Gabriele D'Annunzio, *Libro segreto*, in *Prose scelte*, ed. by Gianni Oliva (Rome: Newton Compton, 1995) p. 572. Quotations from works by D'Annunzio are taken from this and the following editions: Gabriele D'Annunzio, *Tutte le poesie*, ed. by Gianni Oliva, 3 vols (Rome: Newton Compton, 1995); *Tutte le novelle*, ed. by Gianni Oliva (Rome: Newton Compton, 1995); *Tutti i romanzi*, ed. by Gianni Oliva, 3 vols (Rome: Newton Compton, 1995).
2. For the extensive bibliography on D'Annunzio and the Abruzzo, a good bibliographical overview is provided by G. Cipollone, 'Rassegna di studi critici su D'Annunzio e l'Abruzzo', *Critica letteraria*, 5.17 (1977), 787–800. Amongst more specific studies, the following are worth noting: *'Gloria alla terra!' Gabriele D'Annunzio e l'Abruzzo* (Pescara: Editrice dannunziana abruzzese, 1963); M. Vecchioni, *L'Abruzzo di G. D'Annunzio* (Pescara: Editrice Italica, 1983); O. Giannangeli, *D'Annunzio e l'Abruzzo: Storia di un rapporto esistenziale e letterario* (Chieti: Solfanelli, 1988); and especially the proceedings from the 10th Conference on D'Annunzio (Pescara, 5 March 1988), *D'Annunzio e l'Abruzzo* (Pescara: Centro Nazionale di Studi Dannunziani, 1988), with articles by E. Paratore, I. Ciani, R. Colapietra, U. Russo, E. Circeo, O. Giannangeli, F. Desiderio, V. Moretti. See also: *La capanna di bambusa: Codici culturali e livelli interpretativi per 'Terra vergine'*, ed. by Gianni Oliva (Chieti: Solfanelli, 1994); E. Circeo, *L'Abruzzo in D'Annunzio: Studio critico con antologia* (Pescara: Centro Nazionale di studi dannunziani, 1995); F. De Rosa, *Pescara e i luoghi dannunziani*, 2ⁿᵈ edn (Pescara: Edizioni Tracce, 1996). For a general account see Annamaria Andreoli, *D'Annunzio e l'Abruzzo* (Rome: De Luca, 2001), whilst for more specialist contributions see: V. Moretti, *D'Annunzio pubblico e privato* (Venice: Marsilio, 2001); *D'Annunzio*

e la terra d'Abruzzo: Il ritorno del poeta, catalogue of the exhibition in Pescara (Museo delle Genti d'Abruzzo, 12 March-31 May, 2003) (Rome: De Luca, 2003), with articles by G. Oliva, G. Papponetti, W. Tortoreto, A. Lombardinilo, A. Andreoli and F. Minnucci.
3. *Libro segreto*, p. 245.
4. G. D'Annunzio, *Lettere a Enrico Nencioni (1880–1896)*, ed. by R. Forcella, *Nuova Antologia*, 1 May 1939, pp. 3–30.
5. G. D'Annunzio, *Tutte le novelle*, p. 18.
6. From 'La vergine Orsola', *Tutte le novelle*, p. 68.
7. *Libro segreto*, pp. 556–57.
8. From *Primo Vere*, in *Tutte le poesie*, I, 47.
9. From *Canto Novo*, in *Tutte le poesie*, I, 451.
10. *Tutte le poesie*, III, 89.
11. *Tutte le poesie*, I, 49.
12. *Tutte le poesie*, I, 53.
13. *Tutte le poesie*, I, 54.
14. *Tutte le poesie*, II, 29–30.
15. *Tutte le poesie*, I, 359.
16. G. D'Annunzio, *Lettere di Gabriele D'Annunzio a Natalia de Goulubeff (1908–1915)*, ed. by Andrea Lombardinilo (Lanciano: Carabba, 2005), pp. 388–89.
17. *Il trionfo della morte*, in *Tutti i romanzi*, II, 56.
18. *Il trionfo della morte*, p. 69.
19. *Il trionfo della morte*, p. 70.
20. *Notturno*, in *Prose scelte*, p.149.
21. *Prose scelte*, p.37.
22. *Libro segreto*, p.426
23. *La Chimera*, in *Tutte le poesie*, I, 281.
24. *Lettere a Barbara Leoni*, ed. by Bianca Borletti (Florence: Sansoni, 1954), p. 140.
25. *Lettere a Barbara Leoni*, p. 156.
26. *Lettere a Barbara Leoni*, pp. 84–85, 92.
27. *Il Piacere*, in *Tutti i romanzi*, p. 9.
28. *Il Piacere*, in *Tutti i romanzi*, p. 9.
29. G. D'Annunzio, *Lettere a Barbara Leoni*, p. 294.
30. *Il trionfo della morte*, in *Tutti i romanzi*, p. 10.
31. ibid.
32. G. D'Annunzio, 'Frammento autobiografico', *Fanfulla della domenica*, 7 January 1883.
33. M. Vecchioni, *Il cenacolo dannunziano di Francavilla* (Chieti: Solfanelli 1982), p. 39.
34. G. D'Annunzio, 'Il concerto classico', *La Tribuna*, 12 January 1888.
35. G. D'Annunzio, *Lettere a Giselda Zucconi*, ed. by Ivanos Ciani (Pescara: Centro Nazionale di Studi dannunziani, 1985), p.138.
36. G. D'Annunzio, 'Alfonso Muzii', *La Tribuna*, 8 April 1887.
37. Ibid.
38. In F. Di Tizio, *D'Annunzio e Michetti. La verità sui loro rapporti* (Casoli: Ianieri 2002), p. 377.
39. G. D'Annunzio, *Lettere a Barbara Leoni*, p. 142.
40. *Lettere a Barbara Leoni*, p. 142.
41. *Lettere a Barbara Leoni*, p. 147.
42. In F. Di Tizio, *D'Annunzio e Michetti*, p. 95.
43. *Libro segreto*, p. 429.
44. *Lettere a Barbara Leoni*, p. 149.
45. G. D'Annunzio, *Il trionfo della morte*, pp. 141–42.
46. *Lettere a Barbara Leoni*, p. 152.
47. *Il trionfo della morte*, p. 110.
48. *Lettere a Barbara Leoni*, pp. 5–7.
49. *Il trionfo della morte*, p. 178.
50. *Il trionfo della morte*, p. 203.

Llewelyn Lloyd, 'Self-portrait' (private collection)

CHAPTER 6

❖

British Material for the Biography of a Tuscan: Llewelyn Lloyd (1879–1949)

T. Gwynfor Griffith

During the last two decades there has been a resurgence of interest, not by any means confined to Italy, in the works of the *macchiaioli* and *postmacchiaioli*. In this country, we were shown a fine collection of paintings from the former school at Manchester and Edinburgh in 1982.[1] In Italy, a splendid selection of works of artists who could be considered to fit the latter description was on view in Rome in 1993–94.[2] In addition, there have been numerous opportunities to study individuals connected with both groups, either in one-man shows or in other exhibitions of Tuscan art brought together under various headings.[3]

All this has given new prominence to Llewelyn Lloyd (Livorno 1879 – Florence 1949). There have been paintings by Lloyd in the Uffizi and the Pitti in Florence and in the Galleria Nazionale d'Arte Moderna in Rome since the first half of the twentieth century (to mention only the most prestigious of the galleries, from Novara to Lima, which have displayed something by him). If, in the decades following his death, signs of active interest in his work seemed fewer than Lloyd deserved, the last decade has brought compensation. Naturally, attention has been concentrated on his achievement as a painter; the Rome exhibition of *postmacchiaioli*, to give one instance, gave him a generous share of the space available. But there has been evidence that some consideration has also been given to what he wrote. And references to his writing and his presence in bibliographies suggest that scholars have been less interested in his slim volume on *La pittura dell'Ottocento in Italia* (Florence: Nemi, 1929), with its enthusiasm for his master Fattori and Fattori's associates and pupils, than in the posthumous *Tempi andati*, prized for the careful witness Lloyd bore to the development of friends and close colleagues, like Oscar Ghiglia and Amedeo Modigliani, and the assessments he made of other contemporaries on whose works he had meditated for years.[4] *Tempi andati* is also very valuable, of course, because of the accuracy of the chronological list it contains of paintings by Lloyd himself, a list known to be based on the admirable records he kept for decades in his diaries, and which must be the basis for any catalogue.

Llewelyn was the son of William Lloyd (1835–1884), who left Wales for Italy in 1859,[5] and who had a successful career as a merchant in Livorno, where he was joined in 1865 by his youngest brother and future partner Robert (1848–1923).[6] After the death of William, Robert assumed responsibility for his brother's children, as well as for the direction of William Lloyd and Co., the firm William had established. Since Llewelyn was not yet five years old when his father died, his uncle Robert was to have an important part in his life.

Authors of works on Llewelyn Lloyd have not always been accurate in what they have written about Lloyd's family and Welsh background. In this essay, I propose to limit myself to correcting some misconceptions and to commenting on the nature of some of the evidence available, much of it unused. We can begin with what should be a relatively simple matter: the artist's name.

Ugo Ojetti was an influential critic and editor who wrote favourably about Llewelyn Lloyd's work. One of his essays begins:

> Llewelyn Lloyd. Sotto questo inglesissimo nome che nelle orecchie di noi italiani ha un suono quasi femmineo si nasconde un toscano, meglio un livornese, tranquillo e ragionevole, alto e ben quadrato, di là dei quarant'anni, il quale ormai dei suoi antenati inglesi non ha che gli occhi azzurri, la pacata favella e i modi cerimoniosi.[7]

> [Llewelyn Lloyd. Under this very English name, which to the ears of us Italians sounds almost feminine, hides a Tuscan, or rather a Livornese, a quiet and reasonable man, tall and well built, in his forties, who of his English ancestors now has only the blue eyes, calm speech and formal manners.]

Since Ojetti's imprecision in linguistic matters seems here to have been the basis for unjustifiable assumptions concerning Lloyd's ancestry, we may perhaps be pardoned if we begin by stressing the obvious: the surname Lloyd is derived from the Welsh *Llwyd*. Of that name a recent authoritative work offers the following interpretation:

> *Llwyd* is usually understood as the adjective 'grey', but [...] also includes shades of brown: 'dŵr llwyd' refers to the brown waters of a river in flood , 'papur llwyd' refers to old-fashioned wrapping paper or 'brown paper'. It is very likely that when used of younger men 'llwyd' referred to brown or mouse-coloured hair. But 'llwyd' could of course be used also to refer to the grey hair of old age, and was occasionally found in compounds with 'gwyn' (white).[8]

The Lloyds did not determine their own surname; the choice of Llewelyn as a Christian name is more interesting. If we look at boys' names borne by Lloyds of Hendrefigillt, from the time we first encounter them there until the birth of the painter, we find that, before we come to those chosen by the painter's father, the family had been content with names like Edward, John and Robert, none of them specifically Welsh, with the sole exception of Evan, which occurs only once. Indeed, the repetition of a small number of such names, from generation to generation, and for cousins of the same generation, sometimes makes study of individuals in the family quite tricky. It was Llewelyn's father, in exile in Italy, who introduced into the family tree such conspicuously Welsh names as Llewelyn, Idris, and Emrys. That suggests that he may have had a strong sense of national identity, and that impression is confirmed by the two letters from William Lloyd (one in Welsh, one in English) that survive. Such a man would be conscious of the fact that Llewelyn (or Llywelyn)[9] was the name borne by two famous Welsh rulers: Llywelyn ap Iorwerth, called *Llywelyn Fawr* 'Llywelyn the Great', who died in 1240, and Llywelyn ap Gruffudd, known in Welsh as *y llyw olaf* 'the last prince', who was killed in 1282 while at war with the English Crown.

But would not *Llewelyn* have been a rather inconvenient Christian name for a boy brought up in Livorno? Roberto Papini obviously thought it unpronounceable and suggests that other friends shared his view: 'Con Lloyd (nessun amico l'ha mai chiamato col suo nome gallese irto di doppia elle, di doppio vu e d'ipsilonne) [...]'[10] [With Lloyd (none of his friends ever addressed him by his Welsh Christian name, bristling with double l, w, and y) (...)]. This makes one wonder what Llewelyn's own attitude was, or how Welsh he was. His mother, Luisa Bianchini, was an Italian speaker who belonged to a family which had come to Livorno from Canton Ticino. Lewis Allan, who had the benefit of acquaintance with the painter's elder son William, was doubtless right when he wrote that Llewelyn did not speak Welsh, but he recorded that:

> Among his most personal possessions, the sketch books and notebooks of his youth, I came across an English-Welsh dictionary, yellowed and coverless, printed in the last century by William Evans of Carmarthen [...] He had preserved it as a kind of heirloom [...].[11]

It is certainly notable that, although he was baptized Llewelyn Edoardo Guglielmo Lloyd, the painter never used any Christian name other than Llewelyn. The signature on his paintings is usually either Llewelyn Lloyd or Ll. Lloyd. His use of the latter suggests that he at least knew enough Welsh to understand that in that language *ll* stands for a different sound from *l*, and is therefore considered a separate letter in the Welsh alphabet. Illustrations which he made for books he sometimes labelled simply LLOYD in capital letters.[12] I know of only one instance of his choosing to translate his name: a youthful self-portrait bears the words: 'Leolinus Lloyd se ipsum pinxit. Anno Domini MCMI.' As for Llewelyn's own pronunciation of his name, I recall that when I discussed his works with his younger son, the Florentine architect Roberto Lloyd, I was stopped more than once by his desire to hear me repeat his father's name. My pronunciation of *Llewelyn*, he said, was exactly that of his father, to which he added sadly that the name sounds rather different now in Via Llewelyn Lloyd, Livorno, or in the Viale Llewelyn Lloyd named after the painter on the island of Elba.

Among publications on Llewelyn Lloyd, Ferdinando Donzelli's *Llewelyn Lloyd (1879–1949)* is of fundamental importance.[13] The author has attempted a catalogue of the artist's works, given us a brief account of his career, and discussed movements, like Divisionism, with which he was connected. The text is accompanied by a number of good illustrations. The least satisfactory part of the book is the section on Lloyd's origins and family; here the author has clearly lacked access to Welsh sources. The first feature that struck me as odd when I read the book was that the author informs the reader that the family came from Hendrefigillt in Wales, but fails to tell him where that house or farm (which was what the name suggested to me) could be found. As I read on, it seemed obvious that the author believed Hendrefigillt to be a town and presumably large enough not to need further location. This puzzled me until I discovered an article in an Italian periodical based on an interview with Margaret Lloyd Cricchio (1910–2000), the daughter of Robert Lloyd.[14] Margaret, as I discovered when I met her in 1998, had taken a keen interest in what her father had told her, and what she could gather from the papers he left, about the history of the family. And she had told the interviewer quite correctly that the Lloyds to which she belonged were Lloyds of Hendrefigillt. She and her son had also given the editor of the periodical a number of photographs from a family album suitable for use as illustrations. One of these appeared in the article over the caption *Hendrefigillt (Galles)*. It is, in fact, a photograph of the High Street of the town of Mold in Flintshire.

The Hendrefigillt which was home to the Lloyds was a farm in the parish of Halkyn (Welsh *Helygain*) in that county.[15] The Lloyds were tenant farmers there from 1749 until 1874. There has for centuries been mining and quarrying around Halkyn mountain, and Hendrefigillt, after the departure of the Lloyds, became the property of a mining company. The house was pulled down in the nineteen-twenties, and the site is still being worked as Hendre Quarry. The first Lloyd to have been a tenant of Hendrefigillt, Peter, died in 1771, and was succeeded in the tenancy by his widow Elizabeth. She had several sons, and in 1778 she took on, in addition, the tenancy of a neighbouring farm, Llety'r eos, Rhosesmor. At her death in 1782, the tenancy of both farms passed to her son Edward. In 1783 he ceded Llety'r eos to his brother Peter Lloyd, who in that year had married Margaret Bellis, and would presumably have then needed a farm of his own in which to raise their family. By the end of the eighteenth century, therefore, one of the sons of Peter and Elizabeth was settled in Hendrefigillt and another in Llety'r eos.[16] Both these men were to have descendants who were to play a prominent part in the economic life of Livorno.

Llewelyn Lloyd and his elder son William worked on a family tree during and after their visit to Wales in 1938. A copy of their work was given to me by Llewelyn's other son Roberto. I used information from registers of parish churches in Halkyn, Cilcain and Mold, from census returns, and from assessments for contributions to poor relief, much of it previously gathered by Bryn Ellis, in order to compile a more accurate table showing all members of the Lloyd family who lived in Hendrefigillt between 1749 and 1874. This was published in my *O Hendrefigillt i Livorno* (see above note 6).

In the different table that accompanies the present essay, I have included only those of them who are both descended from the original Peter and Elizabeth Lloyd of Hendrefigillt and mentioned in my text as relevant to the history of the Lloyds in Tuscany. But I have also included those descendants of Peter Lloyd and Margaret Bellis who, although also descended from the original Lloyds of Hendrefigillt, lived in Llety'r eos before (as we now know) going to Livorno.

Since my main concern on this occasion has been to cast light on Llewelyn Lloyd's family background, I have not continued his line beyond the time of his children. And I have mentioned only one of the children of his uncle Robert. Both Llewelyn and Robert had (and have) descendants in later generations.

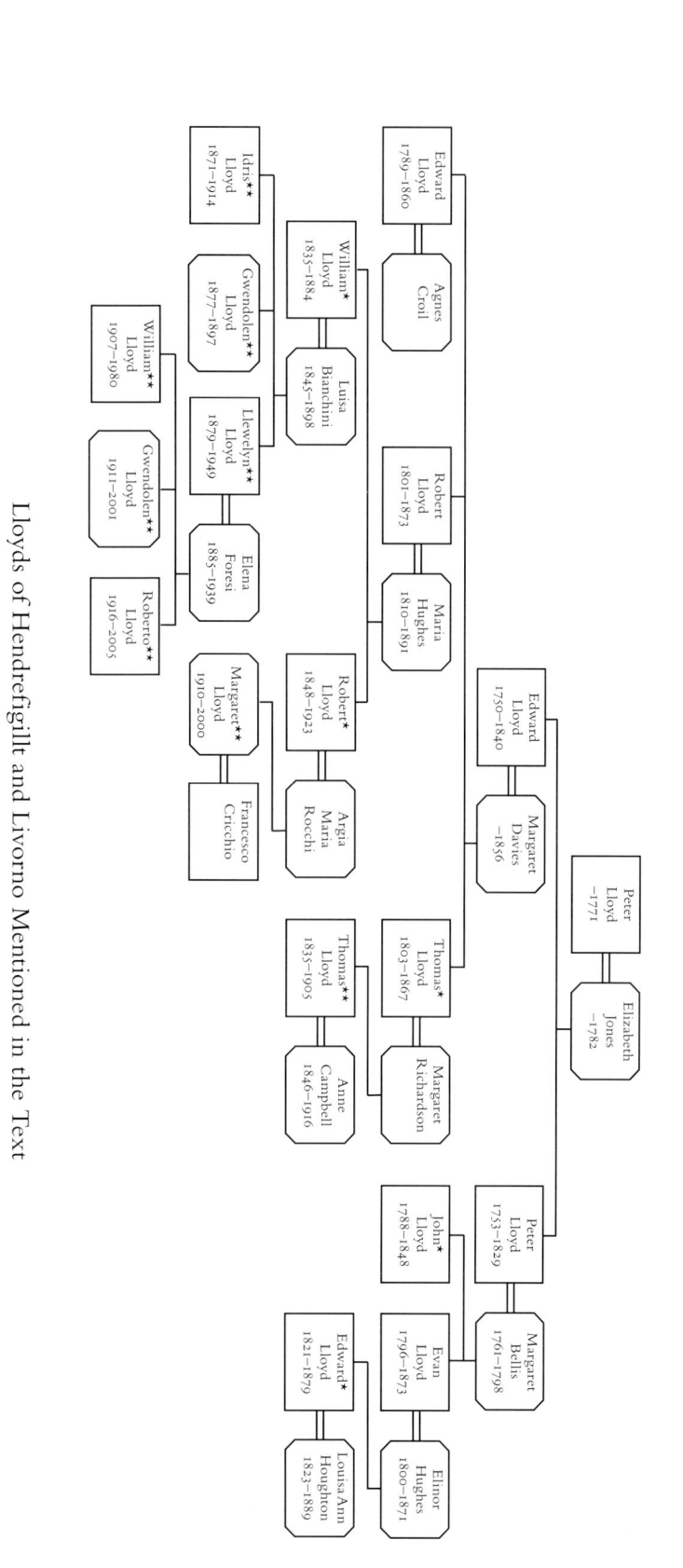

Lloyds of Hendrefigillt and Livorno Mentioned in the Text

★ Left Wales for Italy
★★ Born in Italy

Researchers who venture into this field will find that their work has now been made much easier than it would have been in 1938 by the members of Cymdeithas Hanes Teuluoedd Clwyd/ the Clwyd Family History Society, who have transcribed church records of those births, marriages and deaths which took place before civil registration became the norm. But research can still be made difficult, not only by the large number of the inhabitants of the region sharing a few names (e.g. Thomas Lloyd), but also by other local or family complications, of which I shall cite one by way of illustration. Since Hendrefigillt is in the parish of Halkyn, I expected to find in the church registers there the details of the births of William and Robert Lloyd, the father and the uncle of the painter. They were not there, although other Lloyds of Hendrefigillt were. Luckily, at this stage I consulted Bryn Ellis, local historian (and Chairman at that time of the Clwyd Family History Society). He pointed out to me that, since William Lloyd was born in 1835, his father (another Robert Lloyd) had not at that time become the tenant of Hendrefigillt, as Robert's father Edward (1750–1840) was still there, near the end of a tenancy that had lasted since 1782! Doubtless for that reason, Robert became the tenant, first of a farm called Tarth-y-dŵr, and then of a farm called Tŷn twll, both in the parish of Cilcain. The first three of Robert's children were therefore to be found in the register of Cilcain parish church (and William, the eldest, naturally among them). In 1840 Robert succeeded his father at Hendrefigillt, and, as I had expected, the next two children (born in 1841 and 1842) were recorded in Halkyn parish registers. But there were four more still to come. Of these, two are still unaccounted for, but Mr Ellis remembered that the other two (of whom Robert was conveniently one) were baptized in a Nonconformist chapel: Ebeneser, the chapel of the Welsh Independents, at Rhes-y-cae. Nonconformity spread rapidly in Wales in the nineteenth century. Unfortunately, we do not know the dates or other details of the family's Nonconformist affiliations. It is quite possible that the two missing children's names will eventually be found in another chapel register, although we must remember that not all the Nonconformist churches kept records of baptisms. As it happens, Robert was born late enough (1848) to be included in civil registration of births; but I did not know when I first looked for information about him in church registers that one day in Livorno his daughter, then eighty-eight years old, would give me a copy of a certificate of registration of his birth at Holywell Registry Office!

Hendrefigillt was part of an estate owned by a well known family of Welsh landowners, a branch of the Mostyn family, settled in Cilcain Hall.[17] There is every indication that it was a good farm and that the Lloyds were keen farmers. One of their descendants, Mr John Zehetmayr, still has a handsome silver cup which bears the inscription: 'The gift of Thomas Mostyn Edwards to his tenant Edward Lloyd of Hendrefigillt for the best crop of turnips in the year 1814.' The Lloyds could also afford to employ an adequate number of servants to work the land effectively. The census returns of 1841 show that Robert Lloyd, then aged 35, and his wife Maria, then aged 30, lived there with their children William (6), Edward (4) and Thomas (3 months). They had four male and two female servants. But, of course, the Lloyds were tenants, not landowners. Moreover, the family tree shows that they were producing between 7 and 11 children in each generation while at Hendrefigillt.

It is estimated that the population of Wales was half a million in 1770. By 1851 it had more than doubled to 1,163,000. Dr John Davies has pointed out that Wales was now achieving in two generations the kind of increase which had previously taken twelve. And the pace was maintained: the 1,163,000 of 1851 had become 2,523,000 sixty years later.[18] Some of the excess population of the rural areas found employment in the rapidly developing heavy industries in the south and northeast of the country; in this respect, Wales was more fortunate than Ireland. But emigration was still the way of escape chosen by many. But would their knowledge of English not have made it easier for William and Robert to seek their fortune in some part of the British empire, or in the United States? Their sister Mary, who married John Hughes, did so in Fond-du-Lac, Wisconsin.[19] What did Livorno have to attract them?

Medieval Livorno had been an insignificant village. From 1103 it belonged to Pisa, from 1399 to the Visconti, and then from 1407 to the Genoese. But in 1471 the Genoese sold it to the Florentines, who needed a good outlet to the sea. And it was under the Medici that Livorno grew rapidly in size and importance. From 1547, Cosimo I was offering merchants who settled there ten years' exemption from taxes. New residents were attracted also by remission of all penal sentences, other than those imposed for treason and murder. Construction of a fine harbour, the *porto medicéo*, began in 1571. In 1579, Francesco de' Medici laid the first stone of the great new town which Bernardo Buontalenti had been commissioned to design, and his bold plan, with its wide streets and generous piazzas, became a model for planners from other lands; the Livornesi still recall with pride the debt owed by Inigo Jones, in his plan for Covent Garden, to their Piazza Grande. In 1593 Ferdinand I (Grand Duke of Tuscany 1587–1609), through his *Costituzione livornina*, invited people of any nation and any religion to take advantage of the city's privileges, and Livorno rapidly became famous for its relative tolerance. Since it was a place where merchants of all creeds were allowed to practise their own religions, Jews, Muslims, and Protestants lived there alongside Catholics. By the middle of the eighteenth century there were more foreigners than natives, and Livorno was a great port.[20]

Yet there was a cruel irony in the success that Tuscany's rulers had fostered. As the port grew in importance, Tuscany's relative economic position declined, with the result that it became necessary to make the most of Livorno's international, rather than national, status:

> Ne consegue il fenomeno per cui si crea una città staccata quasi completamente dalla vita toscana, che vive quasi indipendentemente dal suo retroterra troppo povero e fa una politica opportunistica di stretta neutralità in mezzo a guerre d'ogni genere e, in materia di religione, si mostra tollerante rispetto alla cattolicissima Toscana.[21]

> [Consequently, we have the phenomenon of a city almost completely detached from Tuscan life, living independently of its very poor hinterland, following an opportunistic policy of strict neutrality in relation to wars of every kind and, in religion, showing itself tolerant in comparison with very Catholic Tuscany.]

From 1676 it was a free port, and so it remained until 1860, when the inhabitants voted in a referendum to join the new united Italy.

The British had been present in Livorno since the sixteenth century, and in the eighteenth the British Factory was an important body. *Factory* in this context meant a council of *factors,* the heads of British businesses in Leghorn, as the English called it. There were times when over half of the cargoes in the port were the property of members of the British Factory. Their golden age came to an end with the arrival of Napoleon. From 1796 onwards they suffered immense losses. Three times they had to leave their warehouses. The longest period of exile lasted from 1803 until 1814. During this period some of the British merchants carried on their business from Malta. Not all of them came back in 1814. The British were never again to be as powerful in Livorno as they had been in the eighteenth century, but once again during the nineteenth they did become a substantial colony, large and active enough to be important in the economic life of the port.[22]

Margaret Lloyd Cricchio, summarizing family tradition, told me that the first Lloyd to venture into business in Livorno was called John and that 'after a few years' he was joined by 'a young relative' called Thomas.[23] Professor Arthur Whellens, in his valuable research on the early history of the Lloyds in Livorno,[24] found a reference to John, as Giovanni Loid, in 1816, and in 1817 he was a substantial payer of tax. He flourished, and in 1826 was President of the Livorno Chamber of Trade. Professor Whellens also noted that in 1827 a ship from Liverpool brought him a cargo which included 345 ingots of lead (a fact which prompts me to wonder whether its ultimate place of origin might be Halkyn mountain). Thomas was a cousin who came to work with John in 1824, and was made a partner in the firm in 1830. Margaret Lloyd Cricchio was adamant that both John and Thomas were 'Lloyds of Hendrefigillt', as she was herself.[25] After John had returned to Britain, the company became known as Thomas Lloyd & Co.[26]

In 1837 another young Lloyd, this time a fifteen-year-old boy called Edward, went to Livorno to join the family firm. He became an intelligent and ambitious businessman and, in collaboration with an Italian chemist, devised a more economic method of processing the boracic acid which was one of the Lloyds' exports. He was made a partner in Thomas Lloyd's company in 1847, but he felt that the terms offered him did not adequately reflect his contribution to the now very substantial profits. Relations between him and Thomas deteriorated and led to litigation, which Professor Whellens has traced.[27] In 1857 it was agreed that Edward should take charge of the London branch of the company, and that he should receive a fixed percentage of the profits made from the export of boracic acid from Livorno. In exchange, he was not to interfere further in the affairs of the company in Tuscany. This settlement, however, was followed by another dispute over Thomas Lloyd's accounting, and to a final separation. The autonomous company over which Edward thereafter presided in London is still in existence. I was unsure of the identity of this Edward (one of the many in the family) until I received a letter from Mr J.W.Ll. Zehetmayr following the publication of my *O Hendrefigillt i Livorno*. He informed me that Edward was his great-grandfather and offered some clues as to his position among the Lloyds. One of these was a letter written by Edward to his wife Louisa in London in 1861, while Edward was on a visit to his parents in Wales. It was headed *Llety'r eos*, and it was therefore possible, with the aid of parish registers and census returns, to establish that this Edward was the son of Evan Lloyd, the son and successor of that Peter Lloyd of Hendrefigillt (b. 1753) who had become the first Lloyd to settle in Llety'r eos.

On the identity of Thomas Lloyd, Donzelli wrote:

> Anche un altro fratello di William e Robert venne in Italia, a Livorno, intorno alla metà dell'Ottocento e precisamente Thomas Lloyd.
>
> Thomas, che era nato nel 1841, anche lui a Hendrefigillt nel Galles, acquistò dei terreni nei pressi dell'Ardenza (alla periferia di Livorno) e una villa situata di fronte all'odierna costruzione dell'Accademia Navale. Questa villa aveva la caratteristica di essere dipinta di rosso, come i piccoli edifici circostanti, e di qui ne derivò una denominazione popolare di 'case rosse': tali case furono anche indicate con l'appellativo di 'case dei Lloyds'. [...] A Livorno un'altra importante villa, oggi denominata villa Fabbricotti, sede della Biblioteca Labronica e del Museo Civico 'Giovanni Fattori', fu villa Lloyd.[28]

> [Another brother of William and Robert also came to Livorno, about half-way through the nineteenth century, to be precise Thomas Lloyd.
>
> Thomas, born in 1841, also in Hendrefigillt in Wales, acquired land in the Ardenza district (on the outskirts of Livorno) and a villa situated opposite what is now the Naval Academy. This villa was painted red, as were also the smaller dwellings around it, and therefore they became known popularly as the red houses, also called the Lloyd houses. (...) At Livorno another important villa, today called the Villa Fabbricotti, the seat of the Livorno Library and of the Giovanni Fattori Civic Museum, was formerly Villa Lloyd.]

I think that here he may have been misled by seeing the partial family tree in the possession of Roberto Lloyd of Florence, which gives a date of birth, but no date of death, for the Thomas Lloyd mentioned by Donzelli. In fact, the Thomas Lloyd born in Hendrefigillt in 1841 died there in 1854, as can be ascertained from the Halkyn parish register and from a tombstone in the Old Cemetery in Halkyn. In Livorno, there were two Thomas Lloyds. The first, obviously belonging to an earlier generation than the boy mentioned above, arrived, as Whellens noted, in 1824. The second, the son and heir of the first, was born in Livorno in 1835.[29] They became wealthy. Today the house at the centre of Parco di Villa Lloyd in Livorno has become the home of the Livorno Tennis Club. It was once the residence of these Lloyds. They also, from 1860 to 1881, owned the villa which subsequently became known as Villa Fabbricotti, now the *Biblioteca Civica*. That, too, is surrounded by a pleasant park.[30] They were active as shipping agents, and as exporters of various products, varying from marble to boracic acid. Unlike William and Robert Lloyd, the father and uncle of the painter, they did not marry Italians, and Thomas Lloyd the Younger left Italy. Margaret Lloyd Cricchio stated that she had been told that he went to Scotland, but she did not know where.

Professor Whellens, after noting the prestige enjoyed by these Lloyds in Livornese society, wrote:

> Nonostante questa posizione invidiabile, il 20 aprile del 1885, Tommaso scrive alla Camera di Commercio di Livorno una lettera in cui annuncia l'avvenuta liquidazione della ditta di Tommaso Lloyd e Co. Poiché dal catasto appare che nel 1905 non vi siano più proprietà immobiliari intestate a Tommaso Lloyd,

si presume che questo tronco principale della famiglia cessi di avere rapporti con Livorno a quest'epoca. Rimane il mistero sul perché di questa repentina scomparsa di una famiglia cosí potente e cosí affermata.³¹

[In spite of this enviable position, on 20 April 1885, Thomas writes to the Livorno Chamber of Commerce to inform it of the winding up of the firm of Thomas Lloyd and Co. Since from the register it appears that in 1905 there were no longer properties in the name of Thomas Lloyd, it must be presumed that the principal branch of the family ceased at this time to have connections with Livorno. The sudden disappearance of so powerful and well established a family remains a mystery.]

After reading that, I thought it might be useful to search in the Flintshire Record Office for any legal documents bearing their names. I found two, both concerned with their purchase of land in Flintshire.³² In those documents, Thomas Lloyd the Elder is referred to as 'Thomas Lloyd of Leghorn' and as 'Thomas Lloyd of Hafod'. In one of them it is also clearly stated that his son and heir was 'Thomas Lloyd of Minard Castle, Argyllshire'.³³ When I enquired there, Mr Reinold Gayre, the owner of Minard Castle, helpfully suggested that I should seek further information from the Scottish writer and scholar Marion Campbell of Kilberry. From her I learnt that, in order to understand the departure of these Lloyds from Livorno, it was necessary to know something of a story that began in Argyll in the eighteenth century with a Scottish landowner called John Campbell. His ancestral estate was known as Knockbuy (a corruption, presumably, of *Cnoc Buidhe*) and centred on Knockbuy House. In 1798 he inherited from a cousin another estate and with it Kilberry Castle. When he died, he left both estates to his eldest son, but with the command that he should provide for his five brothers and four sisters and the widow. John Campbell II of Kilberry concluded that this could be done honourably only by selling one of the two estates. And since Kilberry was entailed, that could most conveniently be accomplished without recourse to the courts, by selling Knockbuy. He did so, although he then had to face the considerable expense of rebuilding parts of Kilberry Castle, destroyed by fire in 1772.

In the years between 1831 and 1874 there were three owners in Knockbuy. The house was greatly enlarged and renamed Minard Castle. After the death of John Campbell II of Kilberry, his widow and daughters went to Livorno, where they lived in the house of Mrs Campbell's brother, Alexander MacBean, a successful businessman and sometime British consul. Thomas Lloyd the Younger married the second daughter, Anne Campbell, in October 1863. At the time, the bride's brother, John Campbell III of Kilberry, was serving with the British Army in India. On his return, he fell in love with his brother-in-law's sister, Margaret Lloyd, and they were married in 1870. They then went to live in their castle in Kilberry, where John became a Justice of the Peace and Deputy Lieutenant. Thomas Lloyd and his wife Anne felt that they too would like a home in the Highlands, and asked 'Iain and Maggie' to look for a suitable house. By chance the latest owner of Minard Castle was by this time bankrupt, and the estate was for sale. Thomas Lloyd realized that he could now buy back the former home of his wife's family, and did so, gradually selling his property in Livorno. He then, like the man who was doubly his brother-in-law, became a Justice of the Peace and Deputy Lieutenant in Argyll.³⁴ But he never relinquished his family's Welsh connections. He kept a house, Cefn Mawr, a mile or two from the Hafod with which his father had been associated, and was buried in Gwernaffield Parish Church. On the wall there is a marble monument bearing the following inscription:

> THIS MONUMENT WAS ORIGINALLY EXECUTED
> IN MEMORY OF JOHN AND JANE CHILDREN OF
> THOMAS LLOYD OF LEGHORN
> THEY DIED 23rd AND 25th SEPTEMBER 1842
> IT IS NOW PLACED IN THIS CHURCH
> TO THE GLORY OF GOD
> AND SACRED TO THE DEAR MEMORY OF
> THOMAS LLOYD HIS SON
> BORN DECEMBER 3rd 1835 DIED JULY 8th 1905
> BY HIS CHILDREN
> WHERE LOYAL HEARTS AND TRUE
> STAND EVER IN THE LIGHT.
> ALL RAPTURE THROUGH AND THROUGH
> IN GOD'S MOST HOLY SIGHT
> NOVEMBER 1905
> ALSO IN EVER LOVING MEMORY OF
> ANNE, WIFE OF THOMAS LLOYD
> BORN JULY 17th 1845, DIED APRIL 9th 1916

Beside this monument a metal plaque records the death of a son of Thomas and Anne's, Walter Lloyd, a captain in the Royal Welch Fusiliers, killed in Gallipoli in 1915.

This still leaves the problem of the exact identity of Thomas Lloyd the Elder unsolved. When I published *O Hendrefigillt i Livorno*, I included in it a genealogical table of the Lloyds of Hafod prepared by Arthur Lloyd of Pantybuarth and given to me by Miss Marion Campbell. I expressed some doubt about the table, pointing out that I had not myself worked on it, as I had on that of the Hendrefigillt family, and adding that I had been unable to confirm some entries in it. One of the statements I had been unable to confirm was the date of birth of Thomas Lloyd the Elder. I have now come to believe that the table is erroneous in the parts concerning the ancestors of that Thomas Lloyd and his birth, but that it is probably correct in the information it gives about his descendants.

In the Flintshire Record Office at Hawarden there is a somewhat battered volume, some eleven inches long by nine inches wide, with a brown spine and marbled grey covers, whose external appearance may at first suggest it is some nineteenth-century schoolboy's exercise book.[35] But the contents are neither translations from Latin nor essays in English composition. They are copies, seemingly autograph, of letters written by one Edward Lloyd during the years 1837–8, mainly from Port au Prince in Haiti. An attached note from the donor, Mrs Susan Mayer, explains that the book came from Hafod, Gwernymynydd, a village near Mold. The house, now the Plas Hafod Country Hotel, was once the home of Edward Lloyd.[36]

The letters are not easy to read. In places the ink has faded to an illegible light brown; in others, darker in colour, it has seeped through the thin paper, rendering the reading of both sides a trial. Recently the Record Office has acquired a helpful typescript based on a transcription of the letters made by Mrs Mayer over thirty years ago. Gaps in it show that even then some of the most faded lines defied interpretation.

Edward Lloyd does not provide us with the names and addresses of most of those destined to receive his letters. Presumably, the salutation in each ('Dear Lark', 'Dear Freeland', 'My dear Parents') would for his purposes have been sufficient record. Some of the letters are clearly to business associates or employees, and refer to conditions of trade in Haiti. Others are either to other Lloyds, or about other Lloyds, or refer to persons connected to them by marriage ('my cousin John Lloyd', 'my brother John', 'my brothers Hugh and Robert', 'my nephew Robert Foulkes'). They give the impression that Edward was the controlling partner in various family enterprises, involving business in widely scattered locations, from Manchester to Haiti, and from Liverpool to Livorno. Some of them are clear enough without interpretation, as where Edward writes to authorize 'my cousin Mr John Lloyd of Manchester to receive from my account any sum which may become due to me from the first dividend of the Hendrevigillt Mining Company, of which I am a partner'.[37] Others, in the present state of our knowledge, are baffling.

On March 3, 1838 Edward wrote to his parents to inform them that

> [...] it is my intention to embark for England by a packet expected to call at Jacmel in this Island about the end of the month, and you may expect to learn [of] my arrival at Falmouth about the 5th of May next [...] and I hope to find you all well and hearty at Hendrevigillt [...] You will be good enough to say to Robert Foulkes that he is to remain at home until he sees me, but most probably will be directed to return to Port au Prince soon after my arrival in England.

In another letter to his parents, dated November 25 1837, Edward had written: 'I observe what you say about Evan's son and now say to John Lloyd that he may go to Leghorn, provided he is likely to be useful to Tom.' And a letter written the same day beginning 'Dear Cousin' (and presumably to John Lloyd) conveys the same decision concerning the employment of Edward: 'I hear that Tom wants E. Ll. — Evan's son — I have no objection to his going to Leghorn provided he can be of use to your concern — my intention was to have employed him either here or at Liverpool.' After his return to England he wrote, on November 3, 1838, to Tom himself:

> Dear Tom,
> I have been harried from place to place so much that I could not be a regular correspondent, but as Lark has gone out to Port au Prince to relieve Dupuy I must be more stationary for the winter and I will be regular in my correspondence. The mine work is promising and profitable as ever — all well at Hendrevigillt [...] We are doing very much better business with Manchester — our supplies go from Glasgow principally — when Depuy comes here in the Spring I intend to accompany him to Paris, from thence to Lyons, Marseilles and Leghorn where I expect to find you and now your large family quite happy and where I will have many pardons to ask and many apologies to make to Maggy. In the meantime keep her in the best temper you can with me and present my sincerest regards to her. As respects the Consulship I suppose it can be best settled when I am in Tuscany. You will hear again from me.
> Yrs affectionately
> Edward Lloyd

The Edward Lloyd writing from Haiti to his parents in Hendrefigillt must be the Edward Lloyd born in December 1789, the eldest son of the Edward Lloyd (1750–1840) who was the tenant of Hendrefigillt from 1782 until 1840. Census returns show that Edward Lloyd 'merchant', was living in Hafod in 1841 and 1851 (when he was 61 years old), and that his widow Agnes and their sons lived there after his death (which occurred at Hafod on 16 May 1860, with his will being proved on 23 July). I believe that the Tom to whom he wrote in Livorno was his brother Thomas born in Hendrefigillt in 1803, and that he is the Thomas described by Professor Whellens as arriving in Livorno 'ventunenne' in 1824. This would explain why Thomas Lloyd the Elder of Livorno is described as 'Thomas Lloyd of Hafod' in a legal document, although census returns show the family of Edward Lloyd living there. Presumably, Thomas Lloyd spent most of his time at home in Livorno, but lived in Hafod while visiting Britain.

The last piece of the family jigsaw puzzle fell unexpectedly into place for me after the original submission of this essay to the editors, and has occasioned the addition of this paragraph. In January 2004 Bryn Ellis, of the Clwyd Family History Society, asked me to respond to an internet request for information about Edward Lloyd of Hafod. I did so. In return, Marjorie Robbins sent me a copy of a will. At the beginning of this will, which was drawn up in 1841, the testator identifies himself as 'John Lloyd of Manchester, in the County of Lancaster'. But a note at the end, concerning the proving of the will in January 1849 in York and in February 1849 in London, describes him as 'John Lloyd of Manchester, in the County of Lancaster, and of Hafod, nr. Mold, in the County of Flintshire'. In the body of the will, John Lloyd makes Edward Lloyd of Hafod one of his executors, refers twice to 'my partner Thomas Lloyd of Leghorn', and names various relatives to whom he makes bequests. One of these is 'my uncle Thomas Bellis of Berthddu'. It seemed to me that it should be possible to use the list of relatives to further identify John, who was obviously the founder of the Lloyd firm in Livorno, and I mentioned the matter to Bryn Ellis. He immediately realized that John was the son (b. 1788) of Peter Lloyd (1753–1829) and Margaret Bellis (1761–1798) of Llety'r eos, and the nephew of her brother Thomas Bellis of Penyparc, Berthddu (1763–1852). Edward Lloyd of Hafod was therefore strictly correct, in his letters from Haiti, in referring to him as 'my cousin Mr. John Lloyd of Manchester'. This identification is consistent with my belief that Edward Lloyd of Hafod and Thomas Lloyd the Elder of Livorno were brothers, and with the assertion by A. Whellens that John and Thomas were cousins. John was also the uncle of the Edward Lloyd (1821–1879) whose partnership with Thomas Lloyd was dissolved. The Lloyds prominent in the commercial and social life of Livorno in the nineteenth and twentieth centuries were thus all closely related: they were all direct descendants of the Peter and Elizabeth who settled in Hendrefigillt halfway through the eighteenth century.

That, however, is less important for the immediate background of Llewelyn Lloyd than the next event in our story. Thomas Lloyd's failure to retain the services of Edward Lloyd and the acrimonious dissolution of their partnership must have left a gap in the office in Livorno. And it was probably that gap which led to the invitation to William Lloyd of Hendrefigillt, the father of the painter, to join the family firm. He was to work for Thomas Lloyd for only five years (1859–64) before he, too, established a business of his own.[38]

William Lloyd seems from the first to have been delighted with Italy, its culture, and especially its music. A letter he wrote to his sister Margaret in 1861 begins *Carissima mia sorella Margherita*, which is then translated into Welsh before William proceeds for four pages in English. It is signed 'Guglielmo'. In it, William mentions, among several other matters, his ideas on importing some Italian music for which Welsh poets could be invited to supply new words in Welsh. I do not know that anything ever came of this idea; it is perhaps just as well that William entrusted his livelihood to the export of olive oil and anchovies. Nonetheless, the relevant passage is not without interest, as also his advice to Margaret on performance:

> [...] You must not allow yourself to be entirely guided by English taste, that nation is certainly not musical. I pride myself that we of Cambrian race are endowed by nature with a truer ear and better appreciation [...] You must therefore study well what I will send you, guided by your own ear, and by the remarks generally used of piano, pianissimo, con anima, con vivacità [...] I feel persuaded that you will eventually succeed and therefore not offend the refined ear of anyone coming from this land of the Muses. From Hendre the imported production of Italy may possibly extend over the whole of Wales, sung to Welsh words, the creation of some man inspired by the divine *awen*, so common in our country as well as in this. I have often thought that there is in this respect some resemblance between Wales and Italy, the character of the two peoples is also not very dissimilar, both have boisterous passions and unruly tempers, the inhabitants of the latter country are certainly more polished and enlightened, the natural effects of thousands of years of civilization.[39]

In 1865 William was joined by his youngest brother Robert. To him William wrote in Welsh while Robert was in port in Genoa on his way to Livorno, instructing him carefully on how he should behave while there.[40]

Five years later, William married Luisa Bianchini, the daughter of Teodoro Bianchini and his wife Sofia, immigrants in Livorno like himself; they had come from Canton Ticino. Idris, the eldest child of William and Luisa, was born in 1871, to be followed by Emrys and Emery, twins, in 1872, another Robert in 1874, Elyn Margaret in 1876, Gwendolen in 1877 and Llewelyn in 1879, as well as by twins still-born.[41]

In 1873, Robert Lloyd, the father of the William and Robert in Livorno, died. Officially, his eldest son William followed him in the tenancy of Hendrefigillt. But William had been settled in Italy since 1859, and he must have accepted the tenancy only in order to have time to put the family's affairs in order. The Lloyds left Hendrefigillt in the following year, and the farm was sold. The widowed Maria and her daughter Margaret, with a female servant, moved to a substantial cottage called Rhyd Alun in the neighbouring village of Rhydymwyn.[42]

William Lloyd travelled frequently to Wales to find customers. On one of his journeys he caught pneumonia. He died in his mother's house, Rhyd Alun, on May 1, 1884, and was buried in Halkyn a week later.[43] Family tradition has it that his brother Robert was so shocked by William's death that he immediately swore that he would not himself get married until he had raised his brother's children. To that task he was conscientiously to devote two decades of his life. Then he, too, married an Italian and had four children of his own.

William's eldest son, Idris, had been sent back to Wales to be educated, and was there at the time of his father's death. On his return to Livorno, he took his place in the family firm, in which he was in due course to become Robert's partner.[44] Idris was also soon old enough to join his bachelor uncle in some of his leisure pursuits. But Llewelyn was not yet five years old when his father died. Too young to join in the life of Idris and his uncle Robert, he was to spend much more time in the company of his mother and his sister Gwendolen.[45] He was also to enjoy a considerable degree of freedom, which allowed him to pursue, in the country and the port, his interests in the study of nature and in painting, which in turn were to lead him to reject the place he too was expected to fill in the company which had been founded by his father, and to become instead a pupil of Guglielmo Micheli's. But that is something that belongs to a later chapter in the story, one to which Llewelyn himself chose to contribute.[46]

Notes to Chapter 6

1. *The Macchiaioli: Masters of Realism in Tuscany* (Manchester City Gallery, 9 June — 24 July 1982; Edinburgh City Art Centre, 6 August — 25 September 1982). An important contribution to knowledge of the subject in the English-speaking world followed with the publication of N. Broude, *The Macchiaioli* (New Haven: Yale University Press, 1988).
2. *I Postmacchiaioli* (Palazzo Ruspoli, Rome, 3 December 1993–28 February 1994).
3. e.g. *Telemaco Signorini* (Palazzo Pitti, Florence, 8 February–27 April 1997); *Geometria della luce: Il paesaggio toscano nella pittura italiana tra Otto e Novecento* (Palazzo Mediceo, Serravalle, 14 July–23 September 2001); *I Macchiaioli a Castiglioncello: Giuseppe Abbati 1836–68* (Castello Pasquini, Castiglioncello, 14 July–14 October 2001); *Da Modigliani a Lloyd* (Marina di Pietrasanta, 3 July–29 August, 2005, and Livorno, 18 September–21 November 2004). See also A. Parronchi, *Coloristi toscani fra Ottocento e Novecento* (Florence: Turati Arte, 1992), published to coincide with an exhibition in the Galleria Parronchi.
4. The original edition of *Tempi andati* was published by Vallecchi of Florence in 1951. A new edition is due shortly from Olschki as part of the first volume in the series 'Arte toscana nel primo Novecento': the text is to be accompanied by a selection of paintings by Lloyd.
5. Through the kindness of Peter Lloyd, the painter's grandson, I have been able to see the unpublished notes on the history of the family left by his father, William Lloyd. Of the date 1859, he wrote: 'Mio nonno venne per la prima volta a Livorno nel 1859 e lo prova il suo passaporto originale che è ancora in mano nostra' [My grandfather came to Livorno for the first time in 1859, and this is proved by his original passport which is still in my hands]. I have seen this passport.
6. This date can be established by a letter in Welsh written by William Lloyd to his brother Robert when the latter was on his way to Livorno. For the text see my *O Hendrefigillt i Livorno* (Llandysul: Gomer, 2000), pp. 54–55.
7. Originally as an introduction to an early exhibition of Lloyd's work in the Bottega d'Arte of Livorno in 1922–3, quoted in Ferdinando Donzelli, *Llewelyn Lloyd 1879–1949. Con testimonianze e contributi di Giampaolo Daddi, Gwendolen e Roberto Lloyd* (Legnano: Edicart, 1995), p. 182.
8. T. J. Morgan and Prys Morgan, *Welsh Surnames* (Cardiff: University of Wales Press, 1985), p. 151.
9. '★*Lugubelinus* is given as the British form which became Llywelyn [...] It is perfectly obvious that it has no connection with *llew* 'lion', but the attraction of 'llew' could not be resisted so that 'Llewelyn' became normal spelling [...] The idea that the first element meant "lion" no doubt helped to produce the anglicised version *Leoline*'. (ibid., p. 147)

10. Roberto Papini, in the *Premessa* to Lloyd's *Tempi andati* (Florence: Vallecchi, 1951), p. 6.
11. Lewis Allan, 'Chi era Llewelyn Lloyd?', *Anglo-Welsh Review*, 24:53 (Winter 1974), 73 — 86. Lloyd was certainly proud of his origins. In the nineteen-thirties, when it was made clear to him that his election to the Royal Italian Academy depended on his taking Italian citizenship, he declined to do so. This was to have serious consequences for him and his family during the Second World War, when he was interned as an enemy alien, and his son William became a prisoner of war in Japanese hands.
12. See, for example, the covers of the two volumes of *La civiltà del Rinascimento in Italia. Saggio di Jacopo Burckhardt. Traduzione italiana di D. Valbusa. Terza edizione accresciuta per cura di Giuseppe Zippel* (Florence: Sansoni, 1928).
13. Ferdinando Donzelli, *Llewelyn Lloyd 1879 — 1949*. The catalogue unfortunately omits Lloyd's work as book illustrator and therefore does not list the item mentioned in the previous note.
14. [Lucia Borghesan], 'I Lloyd di Livorno', *CN. Rivista del Comune di Livorno*, 6 (April-June 1993), 47–54.
15. *Geiriadur Prifysgol Cymru. A Dictionary of the Welsh Language* (Cardiff: University of Wales Press, 1949 — 2002) gives, as the primary meaning of *hendre*, 'winter dwelling located in the valley to which the family and its stock returned after transhumance during the summer months in the *hafod* on the mountain'. It is a common element in names of farms. I know of no other *Hendrefigillt*, but the second element is clearly a personal name, and is preserved in the same neighbourhood in the name of a stream, *Nant Figillt*. H.W. Owen informs us that variants of this name (*Bugil, Bugail, Bigail, Bigel*) survive in other place-names e.g. *Llanfigail, Maen Bigel* in Anglesey (H.W. Owen, *Place-names of Dee and Alun* (Llanrwst: Carreg Gwalch, 1996), pp. 33–34). Dr Owen also points out that the mutation of the initial consonant of the personal name after *hendre* is not unusual, e.g. the treatment of the name *Morfudd* in *Hendreforfudd*.
16. Bryn Ellis, *The History of Halkyn Mountain* (Halkyn: Helygain, 1998). From our standpoint, the book is particularly useful for the section on mining and quarrying, and that on land ownership and holdings. For Hendrefigillt, see pp. 129 — 30. Ellis notes that enlargement of the farm in 1782 brought its acreage up to 145. It was later further extended. See n. 42 below. The author kindly made available to me, before the publication of his book, his extensive knowledge of farm tenancies and family history in the Halkyn area for use in my *O Hendrefigillt i Livorno*. Mansel Lloyd gave me genealogical assistance in the same period.
17. 'It was Thomas, second son of Sir Thomas Mostyn (died 1641) who was the founder of the Cilcain Hall branch, inheriting that part of the vast Mostyn estate. The estate passed, through his daughter Charlotte to her son Thomas Mostyn Edwards' (B. Ellis, p. 98).
18. John Davies, *Hanes Cymru* (Harmondsworth: Penguin, 1990), pp. 307, 384.
19. Information from notes on family history left by William Lloyd (1907–80), the son of the painter.
20. Piero Innocenti, *Il porto di Livorno* (Milan: Giuffrè, 1968); Paolo Scrosoppi, 'Il porto di Livorno e gli inizi dell'attività inglese nel Mediterraneo', *Bollettino storico livornese*, 1 (1937), 339–80.
21. Paolo Scrosoppi, 'Il porto di Livorno', p. 345.
22. H.A. Hayward, 'The British Factory in Livorno' in *Atti del Convegno di Studi 'Gli Inglesi a Livorno e all'Isola d'Elba (sec. xvii-xix)', Livorno e Portoferraio settembre 1979* (Livorno: Bastogi, 1980), pp. 261–67; Gigliola Pagano de Divitiis, 'Il porto di Livorno fra Inghilterra e Oriente' in *Nuovi Studi Livornesi*, 1 (1993), 43–87.
23. This is based on conversation with Margaret Lloyd Cricchio (1910–2000). But it corresponds closely to what she had already told Lucia Borghesan. See L. Borghesan, 'I Lloyd di Livorno', pp. 50–51. However, we should perhaps consider the possibility that John had previously heard of Livorno from other members of the Lloyd family who had been there. There are four Lloyds buried in the old British cemetery in Livorno (Peter, aged 5, who died in 1716; James, aged 5, d.1717; Elizabeth, aged six months, d. 1736; and Thomas aged 44, d.1745). And, according to H.A. Hayward, there are 16 in the cemetery used after 1840: H.A. Hayward, 'Some considerations on the British cemeteries in Livorno', *Atti del Convegno di Studi 'Gli Inglesi a Livorno e all'Isola d'Elba (sec. xvii-xix)'*, pp. 23–30. We do not know if the earlier Lloyds were connected in any way with the Lloyds of Hendrefigillt.
24. A. Whellens, 'Llewelyn Lloyd, "pittore labronico" e i Lloyds di Livorno', *C.N. Le vie del Comune*, 16 (January-March, 1996), 29–40.

25. Thus Margaret Lloyd Cricchio, in conversation with me. Whellens writes: '[...] Nel frattempo Giovanni Lloyd ha chiamato un cugino, Tommaso, che arriva, ventunenne, a Livorno nel 1824. Nel 1830 questo diventa socio, e il nome della ditta perciò risulta essere Giovanni e Tommaso Lloyd. Nel 1842 Tommaso diventa unico responsabile della "casa" di Livorno, essendo Giovanni ritornato in Inghilterra, a quanto pare per curare gli interessi della ditta nella zona di Manchester e Liverpool' [(...) In the meantime John Lloyd invited a cousin of his, Thomas, who arrived in Livorno, aged 21, in 1824. In 1830 this man became a partner, and the name of the firm consequently was given as "Giovanni e Tommaso Lloyd". In 1842 Thomas became the sole person in charge of the Livorno "house", since John had gone back to England, apparently to look after the interests of the firm in the Manchester and Liverpool area]. See 'Llewelyn Lloyd', p. 31. In a footnote to this paragraph, Whellens adds: 'Alla Camera di Commercio di Livorno sono riuscito a trovare diverse "Lettere Commerciali" che ci consentono di ricostruire, almeno parzialmente, la intricata storia della ditta dei Lloyd e dei rapporti tra i vari membri della famiglia'.
26. 'Scomparso John Lloyd, l'agenzia si trasforma nella "Thomas Lloyd & C." assumendo un ruolo di primaria importanza nel porto di Livorno' [After the departure of John Lloyd, the firm became 'Thomas Lloyd & Co.', and took on a prominent role in the port of Livorno]: see Umberto Ascani, 'Agenti marittimi, ricevitori e raccomandatori inglesi a Livorno nell'800', in *Atti del Convegno di Studi 'Gli Inglesi a Livorno e all'Isola d'Elba (sec. xvii-xix)'*, p. 56).
27. Whellens, 'Llewelyn Lloyd', p. 31. I am indebted to Mr J.W. Ll. Zehetmayr for information concerning the dispute between Edward and Thomas Lloyd.
28. F. Donzelli, *Llewelyn Lloyd (1879 — 1949)*, p. 14.
29. The date is given on the monument in Gwernaffield parish church.
30. Whellens notes that they also owned the Villa delle Pianacce between Montenero and Antignano ('Llewelyn Lloyd', p. 38, n. 12).
31. Ibid., pp. 31–32.
32. Archifdy Sir y Fflint/ Flintshire Record Office, D/BC/2644 and D/GW/259.
33. D/GW/259.
34. For the information on Thomas Lloyd the Younger and his wife Anne Campbell, and for that on John Campbell and his wife Margaret Lloyd, I am indebted to the late Marion Campbell of Kilberry, who was the grand-daughter of John Campbell and Margaret Lloyd.
35. Archifdy Sir y Fflint/ Flintshire Record Office, D/DM/843.
36. In a further letter to me, dated 15 April, 1997, Mrs Mayer wrote of the Lloyd letters: 'My husband acquired them from his maternal grandmother Mrs Howard Settle (nee Humphries). She had inherited them from her parents, the Humphries of Parc Arthur farm on the Hafod estate [...] Apart from being farmers, I believe the Humphries acted as stewards to the Lloyds of Hafod.'
37. Since *f* in Welsh orthography represents a voiced consonant, efforts to anglicize (!) the name led to the form *Hendrevigillt*.
38. The dates are given in the notes on the family's history left by William Lloyd, the painter's son. He also observes that in V. Meozzi, *Guida topografica della città di Livorno* (Livorno: Meozzi, 1866), we find: 'Lloyd, Tommaso e C. neg. piazza S. Marco 1. Lloyd, Guglielmo e C. neg. via Borra 12.'
39. I am indebted to the late Gwendolen Lloyd (1911–2001), the artist's daughter, for a copy of this letter. The meaning of *awen* here is 'poetic gift, genius or inspiration, the muse' (*GPC*).
40. See note 6.
41. Information supplied by the Lloyd family.
42. Information supplied by the Lloyd family and by Lyndon Thomas, the present owner of Rhyd Alun. A poster advertising the sale of Hendrefigillt at the Mart, Tokenhouse Yard, London, on July 8, 1874, described it as being then a 'fertile farm' of 'nearly 200 acres'. But it also emphasized the 'rich and valuable mineral properties': Hendre Lime Works and Quarry, Hendre Lead Mine, and Great Hendre Lead Mine (Flintshire Record Office, D/DM/200/1).
43. *Flint Observer*, 22 May 1884.
44. Information in the notes of William Lloyd. We can add that the 1881 census return for Rhyd Alun alleges that a boy called 'Ferris' lived there. But the fact that 'Ferris' was then ten years old

and a British subject born in Italy makes it obvious that 'Ferris' was a mistake for Idris, who was born in 1871 in Livorno.
45. Information from the Lloyd family.
46. Llewelyn Lloyd, *Tempi andati* (Florence: Vallecchi, 1951), pp. 15–31.

CHAPTER 7

Italo Svevo: Journalism and the Life of a Writer

Antonella Braida

Ever since Roland Barthes's influential statement about the need to avoid at all costs any association between an author's life and his work, literary studies have tended to ignore the question of 'agency' in the creation of literary reputation. However, the study of authors such as Italo Svevo has always been problematic in this respect: the autobiographical nature of all his writings defies any attempt to remove the author from his texts, or to ignore his private and public life. Like Joyce, Svevo left traces of his autobiography in all his works, and he did so paradoxically while trying to follow the demands of impersonality in fiction. While this intertwining of life and fiction has already received considerable attention, Svevo's agency in trying to achieve a literary reputation has often been toned down, if not ignored, in obedience to his own claim of having always been an 'amateur writer'. This essay aims to outline the presence in Svevo of a highly refined consciousness of the making of a literary reputation: from his earliest journalistic writing to his last short stories, Svevo's work pays special attention to the mechanisms of literary academies, of the publishing industry and of the creation of the literary canon.

This attitude was not unique to Svevo. In fact, as pointed out by Pierre Bourdieu in relation to Flaubert and Baudelaire,[1] since the second half of the nineteenth century authors were forced to participate in the creation of their own social role (*habitus*) and to develop a clear awareness of the power relations within their own society. Despite his relatively late recognition by the Italian literary establishment,[2] Svevo developed such an awareness from an early stage in his career. In the short story *Una burla riuscita* [*A Literary Hoax*] Svevo communicates ironically his experience of the workings of literary reputation:

> Tutta la storia della letteratura era zeppa di uomini celebri, e non già dalla nascita. A un dato momento era capitato da loro il critico veramente importante (barba bianca, fronte alta, occhi penetranti), oppure l'uomo d'affari accorto [. . .] ed essi subito assurgevano alla fama. Perché la fama arrivi, non basta che lo scrittore la meriti. Occorre il concorso di uno o più altri voleri, che influiscano sugli inetti, quelli che poi leggono le cose che i primi hanno scelto. Una cosa un po' ridicola, ma che non si può mutare.[3]

[The whole history of literature was full of famous men, and not from birth. At a given moment, a really important critic (white beard, lofty brow, piercing eyes) or a shrewd businessman had turned up (...) and they rose to fame. For fame to arrive, it's not enough for a writer to deserve it. It needs the help of one or more other wills, the sort that influence the helpless, those who read what others choose for them. The system's a bit ridiculous, but there's no changing it.][4]

Written in the years 1926–28, this late short story reveals the irony and consciousness of an author who has finally won the attention of mainstream literary criticism. In fact Svevo's first works already display some knowledge of the mechanisms of the 'literary industry': *Una vita* (1892) and *Senilità* (1898) have a considerable metanarrative component. The protagonists of the two novels, Alfonso and Emilio, aspire to be authors; both possess a healthy self-critical ability. Alfonso rejects as unsatisfactory the plot for a novel co-written with Annetta and laid out by her, while Emilio realises that his autobiographical novel is turning into morbid decadence.[5] Furthermore, the social *milieu* of Trieste becomes in both novels the protagonist of the narrative. Svevo's use of the town is different from Joyce's use of Dublin: Svevo's city lives and exists through the lives and profession of its inhabitants. It always has a dynamic atmosphere. Within this portrait of Trieste one should place Svevo himself, an author torn between social and career aspirations and his literary ambitions. Svevo's autobiographism, critical like his realism in its self-referentiality and introspection,[6] is also a sociological representation of the Trieste of his time.

This article aims to contribute to the study of Svevo's biography by focusing on his early beginnings as a journalist with literary aspirations.[7] It will be argued that Svevo's journalism, often neglected by critics, offers in fact an important starting point for the analysis of his first steps on the road to literature and literary criticism.

Journalism and literature in Trieste: the contribution of *L'Indipendente*

Svevo's decision to start his career as a writer for a newspaper is not surprising when one considers the development of Italian literature and of the literature of Trieste in the 1880s: both are characterised by writers' increasing involvement with journalistic ventures.

Studies on the evolution of periodical publications in Trieste refer to a 'boom in journalism' starting from the creation of the new 'Municipalità' in 1861: in the course of about forty years more than 550 new titles were registered in Trieste.[8] This produced a new class of professional journalists as well as new infrastructures in the publishing industry, a phenomenon that placed Trieste well above other Italian towns with a far older journalistic tradition. According to Silvana Monti Orel, very important for this development was the transformation of typographers into publishers and the involvement of the merchant middle class in the sponsorship of the new publications. Thus, despite a perceived lack of significant literary production, as noted by Scipio Slataper,[9] Trieste was nevertheless a dynamic city rich in cultural clubs — notably the 'Società di Minerva' founded by Domenico Rossetti — and in periodical publications.

In fact the slow development of the literary production of Trieste,[10] corresponded to a crisis and transition for Italian literature, too. The attempt to demonstrate the existence of a national literature had its foundation in De Sanctis's *Storia della letteratura italiana* (1870–71) and its symbols in the figure of the national poet, embodied by Dante thanks to the Florentine Dante celebrations of 1865 and by Carducci's monarchic and patriotic evolution in the 1880s. This unity is, however, a claim rather than a reality: critics agree in identifying in the eighties the birth of a literary industry that forces writers to redefine their role and their product.[11] This change in the dynamics of the literary market is due to the emergence of journalism as a profitable cultural venture promoted by new entrepreneurs who are themselves writers or who aim to involve writers into their cultural projects. Edoardo Scarfoglio and Gabriele D'Annunzio's experiences are significant in order to understand this evolution.[12] Both collaborate on Angelo Sommaruga's literary journal *Cronaca Bizantina* (1881–86), which represented, according to Alessandra Briganti, 'la prima occasione consistente che si offerse ai letterati di inserirsi organicamente nelle moderne strutture economiche' [the first substantial opportunity offered to literary intellectuals to become an organic part of modern economic structures].[13] Equally important was the experience of the periodical publication *Don Chisciotte*, in which a new mechanism was put to the test: 'un nucleo di giornalisti dilettanti con dichiarate aspirazioni letterarie si appoggia ad un gruppo di autori di successo (nel caso specifico: Serao, Scarfoglio, De Amicis, Pascarella, Vamba, Trilussa, D'Annunzio con lo pseudonimo Mario de' Fiori)' [a group of amateur journalists with openly declared literary aspirations drew for support on a number of successful authors (in this particular case: Serao, Scarfoglio, De Amicis, Pascarella, Vamba, Trilussa, and D'Annunzio who used the pseudonym Mario de' Fiori)].[14]

While Italian intellectuals discover the economic potential of journalism, Trieste is characterised by a closer relationship between journalism and literature and by a significant prevalence of the former over the latter. Italo Svevo's beginnings respond, therefore, to a current development in his town and in Italy in the 1880s: being a journalist was the closest possible experience to being a writer able to receive some economic return for his work.

Italo Svevo and *L'Indipendente* (1880–1890)

Not only did Svevo begin his published literary career with journalism, but he did so by choosing a newspaper of strong political inspiration.

In the 1880s, the press in Trieste was divided among the different nationalities present in the town, but the cultural politics of individual papers were not always clear and coherent. Thus while the *Triester Zeitung*, the official newspaper of the Austrian government, aimed at promoting German culture and literature, the equally pro-Austrian newspaper *L'Adria* simply followed readers' taste and published translations of popular fiction, especially French novels. According to Silvana Monti Orel, generally political affiliations caused a widespread lack of cultural engagement and a blind promotion of individual national cultures:

> Sia nel caso che venga radicalizzata la scelta di una cultura in opposizione alle

altre e quindi a svantaggio di un'apertura veramente critica verso il dibattito europeo, sia che per attirare il pubblico meno colto e politicizzato venga favorita la letteratura d'evasione, il risultato è sempre quello di alienare la massa dei lettori.[15]

[The papers either offered a radical choice of one culture over others, thus losing out on a truly critical engagement with European debates, or they favoured escapist literature in order to attract a less cultured and politicized readership, but the result was always one of alienating the mass of readers.]

The newspaper *L'Indipendente* deserves special attention because of its central role in attracting intellectuals and writers who sympathised with 'irredentismo' and who felt therefore closer to the Italian cultural field. *Il Nuovo Tergesteo*, directed by the intellectual Ugo Sogliani, in its only year of life (1877), already stands out for Alberto Boccardi's drama reviews and for the publication of short stories by Italian authors of some reputation as well as serial novels. Its successor, *L'Indipendente*, printed by Giuseppe Caprin, though initially edited by Enrico Matcovich, replaced it in 1877 and maintained the same formula but opened the collaboration to intellectuals not necessarily engaged in 'irredentismo'. The numerous bans by the Austrian Government are well known; the most noticeable challenge concerned the moving article on Guglielmo Oberdan's death in 1883, penned by the editor Enrico Jurettig. Many collaborators were arrested in the course of its publication, among these Jurettig himself who was to die a few years after his release from prison: in thirty seven years of life (1877–1914) the newspaper was withdrawn by the authorities as many as 1,016 times.[16] Eventually, the editors decided to discontinue the newspaper just before the outbreak of the First World War.

Svevo's contribution belongs to the most important phase of the history of the newspaper, from Caprin's editorship (1877–1883) to that of Riccardo Zampieri (1883) and of Marco Bassich (1883–84), through to the most difficult year, 1889, when all the editors were imprisoned on charges of conspiracy and treason.

The *Indipendente* was a publication in-folio, four-pages long in four columns. The first page typically included a long editorial, some brief correspondence from Italian and European cities ('Nostri Telegrammi'), often written in the form of quotations from other newspapers, and a novel or a short story in instalments. The second page continued the political news, but dealt mainly with local news, grouped in brief paragraphs under the title 'Gazzettino di città' ['City Gazette']. The sections 'Di qua e di là' [Here and There] and 'Echi mondani' [Society Echoes], dealt respectively with curiosities and society events or with some items of interest in the second. The third page consisted mostly of brief news items, 'Notizie telegrafiche' and 'Posta', and advertisements. The most significant critical contributions were usually on either the second or third page, after the local news or sometimes included within it and this was the case for most of Svevo's articles. This was for instance the case of Svevo's first published review, 'Shylock', published as a commentary on the performance of the *Merchant of Venice* in Trieste under the direction of Ernesto Rossi.

The most noticeable quality of the newspaper, rarely pointed out by critics, is not literary commitment but a commitment to the promotion of high-quality journalism: this is clear from the choice of collaborators and from the models on which the *Indipendente* is based. Most of the external collaborators on the newspaper are well-known journalists of some reputation in Italy.[17] Both under Giuseppe Caprin's editorship and Zampieri's and Bassich's, the *Indipendente* aimed to secure high-quality contributions from journalists from the Roman and Neapolitan press. Rome and especially Naples are in fact the towns in which the most significant journalistic enterprises of the 1880s and 1890s develop and succeed.[18] Less strong, on the contrary, is the relationship with the new literary periodicals, *Vita Nuova*, *Cronaca Bizantina* and later *Il Convito* (1895) and *Marzocco* (1896).[19] These literary periodicals are at the forefront of the aesthetic turn in Italian literature in the 1890s and they conduct an open polemic against positivism and naturalism.[20] As pointed out by Gatt-Rutter, they rarely publish contributions on Darwin, Comte, Spencer, Lombroso or Nietzsche, and among the writers that are almost ignored one can cite Max Nordau, George Bernard Shaw and Turgenev.[21]

L'Indipendente deals precisely with the authors just quoted and in general with those largely ignored by the Italian press, thus maintaining a notable eclecticism in literary tastes. The significance of Svevo's collaboration on the newspaper is evident already from his similar rejection of D'Annunzio's aestheticism and Fogazzaro's spiritualism. Furthermore, his contributions to the newspaper illustrate his broad interests in European literature that go beyond the general tendency found in Italian contemporary newspapers and periodicals. As Livia Veneziani Svevo recalls:

> Ammiratore entusiastico di Wagner, fu il primo a Trieste a sostenere attraverso il giornale l'estetica Wagneriana. Conservo ancora una copia del giornale del 22 dicembre 1884 recante l'articolo 'l'autobiografia di Riccardo Wagner'. In esso dà sfogo a tutta la sua appassionata ammirazione per il grande maestro, morto da qualche mese. Possiedo altre copie ingiallite da lui conservate, con gli articoli migliori: una recensione del *Libro di Don Chisciotte* di Edoardo Scarfoglio (8 settembre 1884), e 'La verità su un discorso tenuto da Ernesto Renan nella sua città natale' (14 agosto 1884). Essi dimostrano la varietà dei suoi interessi e sono un indice degli orizzonti di cultura verso i quali si orientava. Ma la creazione letteraria continuava ad essere la sua aspirazione più ardente.[22]
>
> [He was an enthusiastic admirer of Wagner, and the first person in Trieste to write about Wagner's aesthetic ideas in the newspaper. I still have a copy of the issue of 22 December 1884, with the article 'The Autobiography of Richard Wagner', expressing Ettore's admiration for the great composer who had died a few months earlier. I have other yellowing copies he kept, with his best articles: a review of *Il Libro di Don Chisciotte* by Edoardo Scarfoglio (8 September 1884) and 'The Truth about a Talk Given by Ernest Renan in his Native City' (14 August 1884). They show the wide range of his interests and the cultural horizons towards which he was looking. However, it was to creative literary work that he most ardently aspired.][23]

Livia Veneziani Svevo was the first biographer who underlined the significance of Svevo's collaboration on *l'Indipendente*. In *Vita di mio marito*, transcribed by Lina Galli, she opens the account of her husband's literary interests with a detailed summary of his collaboration with the newspaper. Svevo's interest in journalism is explained as the obvious consequence of the special cultural situation of Trieste:

> [*L'Indipendente*], vessillo dell'irredentismo giuliano, diretto da Giuseppe Caprin, brillante rievocatore dei tempi andati, poi dal battagliero Riccardo Zampieri, amico di Oberdan, raccoglieva gli articoli dei migliori scrittori triestini. [...] esso era l'unica palestra in cui i giovani delle province irredente, inclini alla vocazione letteraria, misuravano le loro forze.[24]
>
> [(*L'Indipendente*) was the flagship of Irredentism in Venezia Giulia. Its first editor was Giuseppe Caprin, brilliant at evoking past times, its second editor was the militant journalist Riccardo Zampieri, a friend of Oberdan. The paper published the articles of the best Triestine writers. [...] It provided the only outlet for young writers of the irredentist provinces to go through their paces.][25]

Livia Veneziani and Lina Galli's contextualisation underline Svevo's consciousness of the mechanisms of the literary industry in Trieste. A similar analysis is included in the biographical profile by Giulio Cesari, later revised and rewritten by Svevo himself. Cesari identifies in the friendship with the painter Veruda the beginnings of his introduction to the cultural life of Trieste; a further involvement was encouraged by the writers he met through the *Indipendente*:

> Si legò d'amicizia anche colla piccola pleiade di poeti e di romanzieri allora in voga a Trieste, e questi lo indussero a scrivere per i giornali e per il teatro. Italo Svevo fu così portato alla redazione dell'*Indipendente*.[26]
>
> [He became a friend of the small *Pléiade* of poets and novelists that were then in fashion in Trieste; they encouraged him to write for newspapers and for the theatre. This was how Svevo arrived at the editorial offices of *L'Indipendente*.]

Silvio Benco, the young and prolific contributor to the newspaper, added important information on Svevo's presence at the office when the editor was arrested in 1889:

> Ogni mattina egli si levava per tempo, e prima d'andare al suo ufficio, passava alla redazione per riassumere gli articoli di politica estera dei giornali tedeschi e inglesi. Lo fece per quasi un anno: benché, nella sua qualità di corrispondente d'una grande banca, fosse gravato di non poco lavoro.[27]
>
> [Every morning he would get up early and before going to his office, he would stop by the editorial office to write a summary of the articles on foreign affairs published by German and English newspapers. He did this for almost a year, despite the fact that his job as correspondent for an important bank was very demanding.]

Benco is one of the few early biographers who described Svevo's daily work at the newspaper. No trace is left among Svevo's manuscripts of this time spent as editor of the foreign press. Livia Veneziani explains that this was the work of a team that included Giulio Cesari, Salvatore Barzilai, Alberto Gentilli and Camillo de Franceschi.[28]

Svevo published twenty-seven articles in the newspaper with a frequency that ranges from one or two articles per year (1880, 1882, 1885, 1886, 1888, 1889, 1890), to as many as five and seven articles in the years 1884 and 1887. In 1884 Svevo's more significant collaboration was due to his stronger ties with the editorial board which included his friend the poet Cesare Rossi. The intense activity of the year 1887 can be ascribed to the stimulation provided by the 'Circolo artistico', which he had joined in 1886 and where he met the painter Umberto Veruda.[29] In fact one should also consider the most significant result of this fruitful year to be the composition of his first novel *Una vita*, begun according to Svevo in 1887.[30]

Svevo's articles stand out from contemporary reviews, such as Giulio Cesari's or Giuseppe Caprin's, for his European interests. The articles are devoted to French (seven articles)[31], English (one article)[32], Russian (one article)[33] and German literature.[34] However, Svevo does not neglect Italian literature, to which he devotes more than four articles.[35] His choice of topics, as Brian Moloney points out,[36] is the result of his interests in philosophy, in the novel, and in theatre; his approach to these fields and genres is always comparative and most articles move across national literatures using the experience of one to evaluate another. One must note a particular interest in the theatre, to which Svevo devotes six articles.[37] From the brief list just cited, one notices an overriding interest in French literature; after his enthusiasm for German literature during his school years at Segnitz (Germany), which also saw the birth of his enthusiasm for Shakespeare, Svevo dedicated himself to contemporary French literature and in 1882 his brother Elio documents his enthusiastic reading of Zola.[38]

There has been a tendency to identify recurrent themes in Svevo's articles.

Both Brian Moloney and John Gatt-Rutter point out a philosophical devotion to truthfulness that can be identified in the articles *La verità*, *Per un critico*, and *Del sentimento in arte*, and a central autobiographical concern.[39] Moloney finds the first approach to be the dominant one in the article on the popular French novelist Georges Ohnet (1848–1918). Here truthfulness is identified as the essential quality of all good fiction that the popular novelist is seen to lack. For Moloney:

> Svevo finds in a commercially successful writer a superficiality and a falsification of reality which are incompatible with his austere ideal of the high seriousness of art.[40]

According to Gatt-Rutter, Svevo approaches truth in a more philosophical and political sense as he would like writers to be philosophically and politically engaged:

> Through the apparent jumble of his critical articles he was carrying on a provincial literary campaign of his own which was part of the large-scale campaign pursued by Zola and his school to involve literature more seriously and effectively in live human and social issues. Naturalism was Svevo's real starting-point and the fertile matrix of his entire development as a writer.[41]

Gatt-Rutter's account of Svevo's relationship to Zola suggests a sociological reading of his approach to fiction. The analogy between the two authors can be explored further especially as far as their shared preoccupation with contemporary society is concerned. Essential in order to clarify Svevo's approach to Zola is his review of the novel *La joie de vivre*, completed only a few months after the publication of the novel in France.[42] Svevo's interest in Schopenhauer explains his predilection for one of the most pessimistic of Zola's novels, one in which the French novelist was in the process of moving beyond his earlier form of naturalism which had been accused by its detractors of being far too scientific in approach. Svevo understands the ambiguity of Zola's latest novel and points out the importance of Schopenhauer's philosophy as well as the autobiographism criticized by Edoardo Scarfoglio:[43]

> Polemico è lo scopo del romanzo perché il carattere di Paulina ha delle grandi somiglianze con quello di Zola stesso. Così portano ambidue amore alla scienza naturale ed odio a quanto è astratto. Ambidue odiano la musica. Paulina ama e s'interessa a quanto esiste, al bello e al brutto come Zola. Zola vuole evidentemente dimostrare che la sua arte nacque dall'amore alla vita.[44]

> [The novel has a polemical aim, since the character of Paulina resembles Zola himself. Both reveal their love for natural science and their aversion to abstraction. Both hate music. Pauline loves and shows interest in life at large, in what is good or bad, like Zola himself. Zola wants to show clearly that his art was born out of his love for life.]

Zola's truthfulness consists in the autobiographical turn of his fiction, now less concerned with a system in order to leave space for life and its contradictions.

In his articles Svevo has a philosophical, secular approach to the truth that can be compared to the eighteenth-century *philosophes*' desire to wage war on prejudice and misconceptions of all kinds, as shown by his article 'La Verità' which was occasioned by a statement made by the historian Ernest Renan and commented on in Parisian newspapers.[45] Svevo's attack on the author of *La Vie de Jésus* (1863) points out the contradiction of Renan's claim of having loved the truth while maintaining an ambiguous approach to the Catholic religion. Svevo criticises especially his hypocritical enthusiasm for the religion he claims to disprove: 'Le sue più belle pagine sono dedicate alla glorificazione di ciò che egli nega' [His best pages are devoted to the glorification of what he denies].[46] A similar search for coherence and sincerity informs many of Svevo' articles[47] since he always applies this same approach to writers, critics and philosophers, as if his only standard for their evaluation were their sincerity and truthfulness.[48] This preoccupation will become a central one in the literature from Trieste and in particular in the works of Slataper and Stuparich. The similarities between the two younger authors and Svevo are not surprising if one accepts Bruno Maier's claim that Svevo's works left a considerable legacy to the literature of Trieste. This idea of truthfulness in fact is often Svevo's method of ascertaining an author's ability to resist the corrupting influence of 'Academies' or of economic gain. Thus a central focus of his articles, also connected with his interest in autobiography and so far disregarded by critics, stems precisely from his consciousness of the workings of the literary system he will explore so vividly in *Una burla riuscita*. Six articles in particular can be said to form a reflection on the artist's relationship to the literary market and to the public: *Riduzioni drammatiche* (1882), *Il pubblico* (1883), *Una commedia in lingua impossibile* (1884), *Il Dilettantismo* (1884), *Accademia*, (1887), *L'Immortel* (1888).[49] They all share the same interest in the tension for the artist between the dangers of being swept away by the audience's admiration and the isolation of the artist who relies solely on his art. The Italian playwright Paolo Ferrari had fallen into the first mistake by following his public's wishes and thus losing the unique talent displayed in *Goldoni e le sue sedici commedie*.[50] Svevo is consistent in condemning the increasing number of theatre adaptations of novels, a literary fashion from France that the 'veristi' were introducing into Italy.[51] As Moloney points out, Svevo could here take advantage of from the critical reception of the stage adaptations of Zola's *L'Assommoir* (1879) in France, soon to be followed by *Nana* (1881).[52] Svevo reflects on the difficulties faced by the writer of stage adaptations:

> Scilla e Cariddi quindi: o si ridà il romanzo com'è, e non si fa una buona commedia, o lo si modifica e non si soddisfa il pubblico.[53]
>
> [It is between Scylla and Charybdis, then: either you reproduce the novel just as it is, and you do not get a good play, or you modify it and the public is not happy.]

The solution is therefore to avoid adaptations altogether in favour of a direct imitation of reality. Svevo's advice is more than pertinent to the Italian stage at the turn of the century: as the theatre critic Giovanni Cauda pointed out, many companies were forced to make up for the lack of good authors by using adaptations, parodies and in general by re-working well-established texts.[54]

While the reaction of the public is a central concern for the playwright, the writer can face different, but no less dangerous pressures. In a situation like the one in Italy at the turn of the century, writers could and did in fact scorn the public and the progressive democratization of art. Baudelaire in France had set the example for the *poète maudit*, especially after his trial in 1857. A similar, but more accepted attitude of scorn towards the public was encouraged by the new aesthetic turn in literature that characterises the last decades of the nineteenth century in France and Italy.[55] Svevo's journalism is not interested in symbolism and displays a very open rejection of aestheticism and spiritualism. He was certainly aware of it, but his silence testifies to his reservations. In *Una burla riuscita* Svevo has Mario Samigli reading Fogazzaro's spiritualist novels to his sick brother in order to help him to sleep. Also significant is Svevo's knowledge of Max Nordau, whose *Entartung* (1892–1893) will include a severe criticism of French symbolism.[56]

Svevo seems to typify, therefore, the lack of sympathy for symbolism and aestheticism evident in the collaborators on *L'Indipendente*. The writers he focuses on are not priests of a new religion, but professionals struggling to control and understand the changing mechanisms of acceptance and consolidation of one's position within the literary system. Svevo's championing of Zola and Daudet, both of them writers who were openly supporting change in the French literary establishment, suggests a positive attitude towards the democratization of art. His reflections on the difficult temptations facing the writer are expressed in the article *Accademia*, published in two parts in 1887.[57] Svevo accuses literary academies, and especially the Académie Française, of encouraging duplicity and hypocrisy. The appointment of Leconte de Lisle to membership of the Académie Française on Hugo's death gives him the opportunity to approach the theme of the author's relationship with official distinction. The opening of the article clarifies his position:

> Le accademie sono organismi complessi e lo schiamazzo ne è la fisionomia soltanto; il carattere ne è il formalismo e l'amore della menzogna.[58]
>
> [Academies are complex organisms and rumour is only part of their exterior character; their inner character consists in their formalism and love of lies.]

Svevo's accusation stems from the hypocrisy of Leconte de Lisle's speech: Victor Hugo, a poet and writer who certainly attracted much debate and controversy during his life, is freed from any controversy and he becomes an '*irréprochable artiste*'.

The hypocrisy of the literary world engages Svevo again the following year when he decides to review Daudet's novel *L'Immortel*.[59] Svevo found Daudet's work stimulating and original and he first quoted it in a previous review of the same year in order to demonstrate the inadequacy of the popular French novelist Cherbuliez.[60] Svevo's gives a detailed and perceptive reading of Daudet's novel: he compares *L'Immortel*, today among the least appreciated of his novels, to his acknowledged masterpieces, the short stories *Les Contes du lundi* (1873) and the Tartarin cycle (1872, 1885). Svevo is interested in Daudet's satire of the structure of the Académie and of its obsolete electoral system, equally criticised by Zola. However, he is also interested in Daudet's treatment of heredity: the novelist deals extensively with the origins of the protagonist, a farmer who succeeds in becoming a writer. He inherits his father's stubbornness as well as his mother's ruthlessness. Svevo finds Daudet's use of Darwin successful because he is able to create a tragedy:

> È una figura degna dello Shakespeare, tracciata con una chiarezza meravigliosa, senza esitazioni; se il Daudet lo compiange è per spingerlo con maggior facilità in giù.[61]
>
> [He is a character worthy of Shakespeare, drawn with beautiful clarity and no hesitation; Daudet pities him only to cause his downfall more easily.]

Svevo does not consider Daudet a naturalist *tout court*; he certainly had read the contribution of French critics and reviewers who had emphasised the originality of Daudet's work, appreciated by Zola but also by his detractors.[62]

A similar concern for the working of the literary system is present in one of the few articles Svevo devotes to Italian literature: a review of Verga's *Mastro-don Gesualdo*. Svevo's apparent lack of interest in Italian literature is in fact selective. Probably because of his enthusiasm for French literature and for the established association between Verga and naturalism, Svevo ascribes to Flaubert's influence Verga's evolution from the early novels to the acclaimed works *I Malavoglia* and *Mastro-don Gesualdo*.[63] In fact, as Moloney points out,[64] Svevo overestimated the influence of French literature on his work, although his analysis reveals his awareness of the potential marketability of *Mastro-don Gesualdo*:

> Crediamo che questo romanzo potrà avere maggiore diffusione dei *Malavoglia*. Ci troviamo in un contorno di nobili e di popolani molto vicini alla borghesia; è un ambiente che ci è più vicino, più facile di quello del basso popolo di una provincia lontana.[65]
>
> [We believe that this novel will be more popular than *I Malavoglia*. Here the novel is set among noblemen and townsfolk who are very close to the bourgeoisie; the milieu is thus closer to us, easier to understand than the one of the lower classes of a remote province.]

This statement shows Svevo continuing with a personal exploration of the nature of critical success and marketability of literary works. He was thus sharing the preoccupations of the new literary reviewers, working for newspapers of more or less large circulation and targeting a more or less composite readership. Svevo's work for the *Indipendente* was, therefore, more than a preparation for his literary vocation. One can in fact identify in his articles his interest in journalism and in the new genre of journalistic literary criticism, as is shown by his reviews of Salvatore Grita's *Polemiche artistiche* and Edoardo Scarfoglio's *Il libro di don Chisciotte*.[66] Both critics played a central role in the change in Italian journalism that eventually was to attract intellectuals and writers into the field. Scarfoglio's collection leads Svevo to a vindication of the recent French tradition and in particular of Balzac and Zola's fiction. Svevo asserts the need for a deeper understanding of the definitions of naturalism and romanticism as they developed in France:

> Il romanticismo appare agli occhi di tutti, a quelli del Carducci e a quelli di Zola, non solamente quale un rinnovamento e un allargamento. Il romanticismo spostò le colonne di Ercole a segnare le frontiere del territorio allargato, ma disse quelle frontiere i limiti estremi del mondo, mentre non lo erano.[67]

> [For both Carducci and Zola Romanticism did not represent merely a renewal and an expansion. Romanticim shifted the columns of Hercules to mark the boundaries of the new territory, but it claimed that those were the limits of the known world, when they were not.]

In the reviews of Scarfoglio and Grita, Svevo criticizes gratuitous controversy and easy categorisations. In that of Scarfoglio, he claims, 'Il modo della polemica, violento e personale, non si lascia più discutere, dopo l'esempio di maggiori di lui, e dopo l'esperienza fatta dell'efficacia di questa moda' [One is not allowed to call into question any more this style of violent, personal polemic, after seeing the example of those who are more important than him, and after we have experienced how effective this fashion is].[68] In Salvatore Grita Svevo admires the 'carattere originalissimo del Grita' the strength of which consists in his sincerity as well as in his fervour.[69]

Just as he later introduces in his novels the figure of the amateur writer, Svevo did reflect on the role of the reviewer in his articles. In 'Il dilettante', Svevo implicitly identifies the amateur with the literary critic:

> [Il dilettante] dannoso quando fa della letteratura che vuol essere originale, sua, è utilissimo quale individuo che diffonde le idee altrui. Anche il dilettante sente il bisogno di tenersi al corrente del movimento letterario. Legge settimanalmente i giornali domenicali, il nuovo romanzo di Zola, molti elzeviri e, se è della miglior specie, i libri di Carducci.[70]

> [(The amateur) is dangerous when he wants to produce literature with a claim to originality, but he/she is extremely useful as someone who spreads other people's ideas. The amateur also feels the need to keep up to date with literature. He reads the Sunday papers, Zola's latest novel, many reviews, and, if he is a top-class amateur, Carducci's works.]

Despite the humour in the tone of the article, Svevo is clearly applying this definition to himself, a literary critic in an environment that is simultaneously provincial and international, where the most important foreign newspapers and publications can circulate in the original language.

Svevo's writings for *L'Indipendente* are significant ones, and crucial for an understanding of his own attempt to develop an awareness of the mechanism of publishing and of literary recognition in general. This consciousness is present in *Una Vita* e *Senilità*, the two novels he wrote while he was still writing for *L'Indipendente*; Svevo's relative literary isolation at the time prevented the novels from achieving more than a passing notice. However, the friendship with James Joyce enabled Svevo to be put into contact with writers of international reputation and thus break through the encircling restrictions of Italian literary culture. A study of Svevo's early articles shows that his analysis of contemporary Italian and French literature had given him a mature understanding of the role of the writer and his/her relationship with society. His articles, therefore, cannot be accounted for simply as a replacement or preparation for literature, as Svevo himself claims in his fictional auto biography written in collaboration with his friend Giulio Cesari;[71] they represent an important contribution to the study of his (auto)biography and of his future literary production. Svevo was a perceptive journalist, sensitive to new developments in literary fashion and, most importantly, one who saw his role as reviewer in terms that were common in Trieste: a journalist committed to searching for and writing about the truth.

Notes to Chapter 7

1. Pierre Bourdieu, *Les règles de l'art* (Paris: Éditions du Seuil, 1992) : I have used the 1998 edition.
2. The acknowledgment of Svevo's contribution to Italian literature started with Montale's essay in the Milanese journal *L'Esame*: 'Omaggio a Italo Svevo', *L'Esame*, 4 (1925), 804–13.
3. Italo Svevo, *Racconti, saggi, pagine sparse*, ed. by Bruno Maier (Milan: Dall'Oglio, 1968), pp. 813–14. All references to Svevo's articles will be to this edition. All quotations from them have been checked with the original publication in *L'Indipendente*. See also the recent English translation *A Perfect Hoax*, trans. by J. G. Nichols, foreword by Tim Parks (London: Hesperus, 2003).
4. *A Perfect Hoax*, p. 10.
5. See *Una vita* in Italo Svevo, *Romanzi*, ed. by Bruno Maier (Milan: Dall'Oglio, 1969), p. 235; and *Senilità*, in *Romanzi*, p. 524.
6. Svevo's realism typifies and anticipates to some extent twentieth-century psychological realism for its attention to characters 'in the making', and in the process of confronting the new bourgeois reality of Trieste. On this subject, see the study by Aurelio Finzi, 'Il realismo critico di Italo Svevo', *Aut aut*, 3 (1959).
7. For the biography, see John Gatt-Rutter, *Italo Svevo: A Double Life* (Oxford: Clarendon Press, 1988). Svevo's articles were first published in 1954, in Italo Svevo, *Saggi e pagine sparse*, ed. by Umbro Apollonio (Milan : Mondadori, 1954). Leone De Castris and Edoardo Saccone were the first critics to study the articles. Leone De Castris, 'La giovinezza e la formazione letteraria di Italo Svevo', *Studi Urbinati*, 27:1–2 (1953), 179–221; Edoardo Saccone, 'Note Sveviane', *Annali della Facoltà di Lettere e Filosofia dell'Università di Bari*, 2 (1955), 215–65. Ruggiero Rimini's further discovery of unknown articles by Svevo is in his articles 'Una lotta e Critica negativa. Due scritti del giovane Svevo', *Belfagor*, 26 (1971), 599–600, and 'Il teatro negli scritti critici di Italo Svevo', *Belfagor*, 27 (1972), 453–78. This was followed by their publication by F. Carlini in *Paragone* 30:264 (1972), 61–72; and 'Uno scritto sconosciuto di Italo Svevo', *Umana*, 1 (1972), 14–15. Bruno Maier and Brian Moloney published previously unknown articles by Svevo in the 1970s: Brian Moloney, '*Londra dopo la guerra*: Five unknown articles by Italo Svevo', *Italian Studies*, 31 (1976), 59–81; 'Count Norris Changes Trams: an unknown article by Italo Svevo', *Modern Language Review*, 71 (1976), 51–53; 'Italo Svevo e *L'Indipendente*: sei articoli sconosciuti', *Lettere Italiane*, 25 (1973), 536–56. Bruno Maier, 'Due articoli sveviani su *La Nazione*' and 'Italo

Svevo di Giulio Cesari', in *Italo Svevo oggi. Atti del Convegno: Firenze, 3–4 febbraio 1979*, ed. by Marco Marchi (Florence: Vallecchi, 1980), pp. 221–51. Tullio Kezich then published 'Che cosa ne dite', reprinted in *Svevo e Zeno. Vite parallele* (Milan: All'insegna del pesce d'oro, 1970), and F. Carlini *Critica negativa*, in *Umana* (January-April 1972) pp. 12–15, and 'Storia dello sviluppo della civiltà a Trieste nel secolo presente' was published by G. A. Camerino in *Critica Letteraria*, 5 (1977), 763–70, and in *Italo Svevo* (Torino: UTET, 1981), pp. 421–30. The most significant studies on Svevo's journalism are Flavio Catenazzi, *Italo Svevo e 'L'Indipendente'. La lingua e lo stile di un giornalista* (Bologna: Patron, 1984), and most recently a new anthology: Brian Moloney and John Gatt-Rutter (eds.), *'È tanto differente questa Inghilterra...'. Gli scritti londinesi di Italo Svevo* (Trieste: Comune di Trieste, Biblioteca Civica, 2003). Further studies by Brian Moloney are forthcoming.

8. Silvana Monti Orel, *I giornali triestini dal 1863 al 1902* (Trieste: Lint, 1976).
9. In an article published in the journal *La Voce* in 1909, Scipio Slataper claimed that 'Trieste non ha tradizioni di coltura' [Trieste has no traditions of culture]: see Scipio Slataper, *Scritti politici*, ed. by Giani Stuparich, 2nd edn (Rome: Alberto Stock, 1925; Milan: Mondadori, 1954), p. 11. In fact his statement expressed a doubt rather than a certainty: as Cesare Pagnini has pointed out, Slataper wrote his article in Florence and his attempts to acquire further information on contemporary writers from his town did not succeed. To counteract Slataper's statement, one can say that Trieste had its 'umanesimo provinciale' [provincial humanism], as Ara and Magris defined it: Angelo Ara e Claudio Magris, *Trieste: un'identità di frontiera* (Turin: Einaudi, 1982, 1987), p. 8.This 'provincial humanism' was concerned with the study of local history (Domenico Rossetti), or with attempts to follow Italian literary fashions (like the 'carducciani' Riccardo Pitteri and Giuseppe Picciola, or the late romantics Pasquale Berseghi, Michele Fachinetti and Giuseppe Rovere).
10. See especially Maier's discussion in the preface to the anthology *Scrittori triestini del Novecento*, ed. by Bruno Maier and Carlo Bo, 2nd edn (Trieste: Lint, 1991). According to Maier, 'se lo Slataper, anziché riferirsi unicamente a Trieste, avesse preso in considerazione la piú vasta area culturale giuliana, avrebbe probabilmente temperato la sua asserzione' [If Slataper had taken into consideration the wider area of Venezia Giulia, instead of referring solely to Trieste, he would probably have toned down his statement] (*Scrittori triestini del Novecento*, p. 38).
11. For the analysis of the role of the intellectual in the second half of the nineteenth-century, see Antonia Acciani, 'Dalla rendita al lavoro', in *Letteratura italiana*, ed. by Alberto Asor Rosa (Turin: Einaudi, 1982-), II: *Produzione e consumo* (1983), 413–44; Gian Franco Venè, *Il capitale e il poeta* (Milano: Sugarco, 1972) and Alberto Abruzzese et al., *La classe dei colti* (Bari: Laterza, 1970).
12. Both D'Annunzio and Scarfoglio would pursue their relationship with journalism, despite their repeated statements concerning the negative effect of the democratisation of art carried out by periodical publications. Both would reveal an interest in the cultural industry and would reshape their roles accordingly: Scarfoglio would found and be editor of the newspaper *Il Mattino*, which would become an important instrument for Neapolitan intellectuals, D'Annunzio would aspire to become the intellectual aware of the new media, by playing an important part in the staging and direction of his plays and by his experience of cinema.
13. Alessandra Briganti, *Intellettuali e cultura fra Ottocento e Novecento. Nascita e storia della terza pagina* (Padova: Liviana, 1972), pp. 19–20.
14. Alberto Abruzzese and Ilena Panico, 'Giornale e giornalismo', in *Letteratura italiana*, ed. by Alberto Asor Rosa, II, 783.
15. Monti Orel, *I giornali triestini dal 1863 al 1902*, pp. 40–41. The newspapers that stand out for their cultural awareness reflect the interest of the liberal, upper-bourgeois minority, thus alienating the large majority of readers. The most significant nineteenth-century journals of this kind are *La Favilla* (1836) *L'Alba* (1871) and *Il Nuovo Tergesteo* (1876). *La Favilla*, the organ of the liberals who took part in the uprisings of 1848, had a certain following at national level, but did not survive once the intellectuals who supported it left Trieste. *L'Alba* was to some extent the continuation of *La Favilla* with which it shared the same radical programme inspired by Giuseppe Mazzini; however, in the eleven years of its publication (1871–1882) the newspaper progressively changed its political tendency and became increasingly conservative. The town was also characterized by some socialist consciousness. At the end of the century the following

Socialist periodicals were published in Trieste: *Il Lavoratore* (1895), *Il Proletario* (1892), *L'Ordine* (1895), *La Critica del Popolo* (1901) and *L'Internazionale* (ceased publication in 1901): see Monti Orel, *I giornali triestini dal 1863 al 1902*, p. 39.

16. The two main studies of *L'Indipendente* by Leone Veronese and Bruno Coceani focused mainly on the political struggles carried out by the newspaper: Leone Veronese, *L'Indipendente. Storia di un giornale* (Trieste: Silvio Spazzal Editore, 1932) and Bruno Coceani, *Un giornale contro un impero* (Trieste: Semec, 1932). Cesare Pagnini and Silvana Monti Orel have paid greater attention to the literary and journalistic contribution of the newspaper. The present study is based on their analysis as well as on my reading of the *L'Indipendente* for the years 1878, 1882 (second semester), 1885 (second semester), 1886, 1890 (first semester). I am grateful to the Biblioteca Civica 'Attilio Hortis' in Trieste for allowing me to consult the newspaper. Unfortunately not all volumes are yet available for consultation. See also Enrico Ghidetti, *Italo Svevo: la coscienza di un borghese triestino* (Rome: Editori Riuniti, 1992), p. 84.
17. Arturo Colautti (1851–1914) was a collaborator on *Il Dalmata*, *La Difesa*, *L'Avvenire* and eventually was appointed editor of the *Corriere di Napoli* and of the *Corriere del mattino*; Federico Verdinois (1844–1927), after working at the *Fanfulla*, was Colautti's successor as editor of the *Corriere di Napoli* and of the third page in the *Corriere del Mattino*; Luigi Lodi (1857–1933), was editor of many newspapers among which was the *Domenica letteraria*, and he achieved some renown for his collaboration on *Cronaca Bizantina* and for a debate he had with D'Annunzio; Luigi Arnaldo Vassallo (1852–1906), *nom de plume* Gandolin, was well known for his contributions to the satirical newspapers *Capitan Fracassa* and *Don Chisciotte*, and was the editor of the *Messaggero*.
18. It is significant that the local journalist Salvatore Barzilai decided to move to Rome, where he also pursued a successful political career while working as correspondent for the newspaper. Barzilai also established and maintained links with Bologna, where the newspaper *Eco del Popolo* could boast the collaboration of prestigious poets and critics such as Giosuè Carducci, Giovanni Pascoli, Olindo Guerrini and Guido Mazzoni.
19. With these the *L'Indipendente* had in common the occasional contribution of authors such as D'Annunzio, Contessa Lara (Eva Giovanna Antonietta Cattermole Mancini), poet and writer of children's novels and short stories, the novelists Matilde Serao and Girolamo Rovetta.
20. As Patrizia Zambon has pointed out in her study of literary periodicals in Florence and Milan at the turn of the century, 'da un punto di vista di storia letteraria, riescono a divenire immediatamente luogo privilegiato per la partecipazione di scrittori e critici all'attività della stampa periodica' [from the point of view of literary history, they managed to become a privileged space for writers and critics wanting to collaborate on the periodical press]; Patrizia Zambon, 'Riviste Fiorentine e Milanesi dell'Ultimo ottocento nella corrispondenza Neera-Angiolo Orvieto', in *Miscellanea di studi in onore di Vittore Branca*, ed. by Armando Balduino, 5 vols (Florence: Olschki, 1983), V: *Indagini Otto-Novecentesche*, p. 200.
21. John Gatt-Rutter, *Italo Svevo. A Double Life*, p. 159. Some attention is given to Zola, Gide, Tolstoy and Chekhov.
22. Livia Veneziani Svevo, *Vita di mio marito* (Trieste: Edizioni dello Zibaldone, 1950), pp. 20–21.
23. Livia Veneziani, *Memoir of Italo Svevo*, trans. by Isobel Quigley (London: Libris, 1989), pp. 14–15.
24. Livia Veneziani Svevo, *Vita di mio marito*, p. 20.
25. Livia Veneziani, *Memoir of Italo Svevo*, pp. 13–14.
26. Silvio Benco, *Italo Svevo scrittore/ Italo Svevo nella sua nobile vita* (Milan: Edizioni Zara, 1985), p. xiii.
27. Ibid., pp. 18–19.
28. Livia Veneziani Svevo, *Vita di mio marito*, p. 45. Benco considers equally significant the articles Svevo wrote after the war: 'Ma il nome di Italo Svevo ricomparve in pubblico soltanto dopo la guerra, per alcuni acutissimi articoli sulla vita e il carattere inglese che egli pubblicò nella *Nazione* di Trieste. Pochi italiani conoscevano l'Inghilterra a fondo al pari di lui. Furono quegli articoli che ricondussero Ettore Schmitz alle lettere' [But the name of Italo Svevo appeared in public only after the war, through some very perceptive articles on the life and character of the English, articles he published in Trieste's *La Nazione*. Few Italians knew England in depth like him. It was these articles that led Ettore Schmitz back to literature]. See Benco, *Italo Svevo scrittore/ Italo Svevo nella sua nobile vita*, pp. 20–21.

29. Ghidetti, *Italo Svevo*, p. 97.
30. Svevo mentions this date on his twenty-eighth birthday, 19 December 1889. See *Romanzi*, pp. 813–14.
31. 'La joie de vivre di Emilio Zola' (8 March 1884), 'Giorgio Ohnet' (12–13 May 1885), 'Accademia' (11–12 April 1887), 'Le memorie dei fratelli Goncourt' (30 June 1887), 'La vocazione del conte Ghislain' (23 June 1888), '*L'Immortel*' (26 July 1888).
32. 'Shylock' (2 December 1880).
33. 'Poesie in prosa di Ivan Turgenjeff' (29 January 1884).
34. Svevo's articles include explicit and implicit references to German literature. See his reference to Heine in the article 'Shylock' and the articles 'L'autobiografia di Riccardo Wagner' (22 December 1884), 'Giordano Bruno giudicato da Arturo Schopenhauer' (20 February 1885), and 'Il vero paese dei miliardi' (12 June 1883).
35. '*Brandelli* di Olindo Guerrini' (26 September 1883), '*Il libro di don Chisciotte* di Edoardo Scarfoglio' (18 September 1884), 'I libri nuovi' (17 December 1889).
36. *Italo Svevo* (Edinburgh: Edinburgh University Press, 1974), p. 11.
37. 'Shylock' (2 December 1880), 'Riduzioni drammatiche' (22 November 1882), 'Il pubblico' (2 October 1883), 'Una commedia in lingua impossibile' (2 April 1884), 'Il dilettantismo' (11 November 1884), 'Una frase sulla *Mandragola*' (11 February 1887).
38. *Lettere a Svevo. Diario di Elio Schmitz*, ed. by Bruno Maier (Milan: Dall'Oglio, 1978), p. 89.
39. This reading has been explored especially in Noemi Paolini Giachery, *Italo Svevo. Il superuomo dissimulato* (Roma: Edizioni Studium, 1993). Giachery devotes an entire chapter to Svevo's journalism, pointedly entitled 'A partire da Shylock. Ettore Samigli recensore autobiografico' ['Starting from Shylock: Ettore Samigli, autobiographical reviewer']. Psychoanalytical readings abound in her analysis: in the review of *The Merchant of Venice*, 'la componente ebraica è solo un'occasione come un'altra di un'identificazione voluta per più profonde ragioni' [the Jewish component is merely an excuse for a feeling of identification desired for other deeper reasons]; in the review of Zola's novel *La joie de vivre*, 'l'autore sa bene chi rassomiglia a Lazzaro' [the author knows full well who resembles Lazarus]; in the article 'Il Dilettantismo', 'l'autore si presenta subito [. . .] come uno della categoria' [presents himself immediately as one who belongs to that group] (*Italo Svevo. Il superuomo dissimulato*, pp. 43, 49, 52.)
40. Moloney, *Italo Svevo*, p. 13.
41. Gatt-Rutter, *Italo Svevo*, p. 64.
42. '*La Joie de vivre* di Emilio Zola', *L'Indipendente* (8 March 1884). Also in *Racconti, saggi e pagine sparse*, pp. 575–77.
43. See '*Il libro di don Chisciotte* di Edoardo Scarfoglio', in *Racconti, saggi e pagine sparse*, p. 590.
44. "*La Joie de vivre* di Emilio Zola', p. 577.
45. *L'Indipendente* (14 August 1884).
46. *Racconti, saggi e pagine sparse*, p. 587.
47. See for instance 'Il vero paese dei miliardi', *L'Indipendente* (12 June 1883), 'Polemiche artistiche di Salvatore Grita', *L'Indipendente* (23–24 May 1884), 'Per un critico', *L'Indipendente* (20 March 1887), 'Una frase sulla *Mandragola*', *L'Indipendente* (11 February 1887).
48. See for example his statement on Machiavelli: 'Si potrebbe ammettere in Machiavelli un errore, non una malafede.' Discovered and reprinted by Brian Moloney, in 'Italo Svevo e *L'Indipendente*: sei articoli sconosciuti', p. 543.
49. The articles were published as follows: 'Riduzioni drammatiche' (22 November 1882), 'Il pubblico' (2 October 1883), 'Una commedia in lingua impossibile' (8 March 1884), 'Il Dilettantismo' (11 November1884).
50. *Racconti, saggi e pagine sparse*, pp. 568–69.
51. 'Riduzioni drammatiche', in *Racconti, saggi e pagine sparse*, pp. 559–60.
52. Moloney, *Italo Svevo*, p. 13.
53. *Racconti, saggi e pagine sparse*, p. 35.
54. Giuseppe Cauda, *Sulla scena e dietro le quinte. Figure, tipi, aneddoti, impressioni, confronti* (Chieri: Premiata Officina Grafica Gaspare Astesano, 1914), p. 55.
55. On Italian literature at the turn of the century see Neuro Bonifazi, *L'alibi del realismo* (Florence: La Nuova Italia, 1972); Giuseppe Antonio Camerino, *Italo Svevo e la crisi della Mitteleuropa*, nuova edizione ampliata e completamente riveduta (Naples: Liguori, 2002); Marco Forti, *L'idea del*

romanzo italiano fra Ottocento e Novecento (Milan: Garzanti, 1981); Giorgio Luti, *Narrativa italiana dell'otto e novecento* (Florence : Sansoni, 1964); Gian Franco Vené, *Il capitale e il poeta. Storia dei rapporti tra il capitalismo e la letteratura italiana dall'illuminismo a Pirandello* (Milan: Sugarco, 1972); and the essential volumes in Asor Rosa's *La letteratura italiana* (Turin: Einaudi, 1982-), vol. I: *Il letterato e le istituzioni* (1982) and vol. II: *Produzione e consumo* (1983).

56. Svevo reviews Max Nordau's *Studi e schizzi parigini*, in 'Il vero paese dei Miliardi', *L'Indipendente* (12 June 1883). See also Gianni Nicoletti, 'Max Nordau e i primi critici del *Simbolismo* in Italia', *Studi francesi*, 3 (1959), 433–38.
57. *L'Indipendente* (11–12 April 1887). Discovered and reprinted by Brian Moloney in 'Italo Svevo e *L'Indipendente*: sei articoli sconosciuti'.
58. *Ibid.*, p. 544.
59. *L'Indipendente* (26 July, 1888).
60. 'La vocazione del conte Ghislain', *L'Indipendente* (23 June 1888).
61. *Racconti, saggi e pagine sparse*, p. 616.
62. Roger Ripoll, in his introduction to Daudet's novels, writes: 'The Académie welcomed Daudet, certainly he received better treatment than some of his colleagues equally committed to the renovation of the novel: *Fromont jeune* and *Risler aîné* won an Académie prize in 1875. When one considers critics' attitude to Daudet's novels one undertands why he was given this welcome: Daudet's novels could be approved by the supporters of naturalism as well as by its adversaries' (my translation): see Alphonse Daudet, *Oeuvres*, ed. by Roger Ripoll, 3 vols (Paris: Gallimard, 1994), III, 1273–74.
63. *L'Indipendente* (17 December 1889), reprinted in Moloney, 'Italo Svevo e *L'Indipendente*: sei articoli sconosciuti', pp. 554–56.
64. Moloney, 'Italo Svevo e *L'Indipendente*: sei articoli sconosciuti', p. 556. Verga expressed his reservations about *Madame Bovary* to Capuana.
65. Moloney, 'Italo Svevo e *L'Indipendente*: sei articoli sconosciuti', p. 556.
66. *L'Indipendente* (23–24 May 1884), (18 September, 1884).
67. *Racconti, saggi e pagine sparse*, p. 591.
68. *Ibid.*, p. 588.
69. *Ibid.*, p. 581.
70. *Ibid.*, p. 595.
71. See *Racconti, saggi e pagine sparse*. See also Italo Svevo, *Racconti e scritti autobiografici*, ed. by Clotilde Bertoni (Milan: Mondadori, 2004).

PART III

❖

Self-Images in Fascist Culture

CHAPTER 8

❖

Intellectual (Auto-)Biography in Bontempelli

Jon Usher

In *La cognizione del dolore*, first published in instalments between 1938 and 1941, Carlo Emilio Gadda acerbically imagines the national obsequies of the great poet of the imaginary South American country of Maradagàl, Carlos Caçoncellos, who, it was said, had written over two hundred thousand alexandrines and twenty-three thousand iambic tetrameters, and of whose manuscripts but a minor part had been printed in 'fifty or so volumes'. Behind the phallogenic cedilla and the immediately emasculating diminutive suffix of the poet's name (which with exquisite typographical economy turns him from a shit into a little prick), and behind the insistent capitalisation of his various appellations ('Vate'; 'Vegliardo'; 'Poeta', and even 'Estinto') and behind the reference to the 'Villa Giuseppina' as the 'sacrario' and much discussed locus for a monumental sepulchral complex, it is easy enough to discern the outline of a recently deceased Gabriele D'Annunzio and the indulgent self-commemoration of the Vittoriale.[1] Gadda's portrait of the great man is surprisingly ferocious, given his past record of admiration and even of imitation,[2] but he had recently become irritated by sanctimonious over-reaction to the gossipy biography of the poet written by Tom Antongini,[3] and this irritation found its release in an eruption of brilliantly sardonic savagery.

Part of the national obsequies for the real D'Annunzio, who died in 1938, involved a funeral oration delivered on 27th November in the poet's birthplace, Pescara, by an *Accademico d'Italia* who had already specialised in valedictories, having pronounced the funeral speech for Pirandello (1937) and an anniversary commemoration for Leopardi (1937). Subsequently the same *Accademico* (but now an ex-*Accademico*) would also honour Verga and a number of Italian composers, but with rather less enthusiastic official support. The public orator's name was Massimo Bontempelli: he was one of the most prominent literary figures of the inter-war years, having been, in addition to a successful novelist, playwright, theatre composer and journalist, an architectural critic, translator, school anthology compiler, founder of the first Italian cine-club (Rome, 1929) and even duellist (with Ungaretti, 1930).[4]

More pertinently, he had been the founding secretary of the writers' union, the 'Sindacato fascista autori e scrittori' (1928), a timely cultural contribution which may well have been partially instrumental in his swift elevation to the Reale Accademia only two years later (the Academy was founded in 1929). As an *Accademico*, he was in demand as a visiting lecturer, acting as a flag-waver for Italian culture in Europe, the Middle East and South America. By the time of D'Annunzio's death, however, rumours were already beginning to circulate that Bontempelli was perhaps not as politically dependable as the regime might have wished. A discreet sign of this was his principled refusal, in the same year 1938, to occupy the chair of Italian literature vacated by Arnaldo Momigliano as a result of the infamous racial laws.

The Pescaran valedictory for the Vate of the Vittoriale was to prove a very public parting of the ways, but, though the most visible, it was only one of a number of breaks in Bontempelli's literary career, and one which had been long sign-posted, for those with the ability to engage with the clues in his earlier writings, both critical and fictional.

Whilst the official funeral took place in the presence of the Duce,[5] the Pescara speech commemorating D'Annunzio was given before lesser, but still prominent members of the regime, including Giuseppe Bottai,[6] a *gerarca* who by this time, distancing himself from the rhetoric of Action, and indeed from his own thuggish past as an *ardito* and *squadrista*, was trying, as minister of education (supposedly a safe place to park somebody awkward), to present a more sophisticated, liberal face to Fascism. Bottai's antisemitism would have made him wary, perhaps, of Bontempelli's independent stance on Momigliano, and he might have therefore been on his guard even when an *Accademico* was delivering an apparently innocent obituary.

Bontempelli's valedictory starts innocently enough,[7] stressing D'Annunzio's mighty gifts, calling him a 'prodigio', a 'meteora', and emphasising that behind the intuitive genius there was also a meticulous, patient craftsman with a strong sense of duty towards art.[8] At this point in the discourse, and seemingly out of the blue, Bontempelli launches into the theme which will enrage Bottai and others in the front row, and lead not only to his formal expulsion from the Partito Nazionale Fascista,[9] but also to a temporary prohibition to publish, to a very mild *confino*, agreeably passed in Venice, and to *radiazione* from the Reale Accademia itself. When he was quietly allowed back into public life, just over a year later, the regime made sure that the only commemorations Bontempelli would be able to give from now on were for the safely long-deceased: Verga (1940), Scarlatti (1940), Pergolesi (1941).

D'Annunzio's sense of duty towards art, Bontempelli now argues in his valedictory, was fatally compromised by his even stronger sense of duty towards action. His return from France to agitate for and participate in the Great War, a return described in Garibaldian terms as the voyage from Paris to Quarto and from Quarto to Fiume,[10] arguably marked the beginning of the end for D'Annunzio's genius. Genius itself was a word to be taken with caution, if coming from the lips of Bontempelli.[11] Instead, D'Annunzio's art was replaced by a 'feticismo della violenza' [fetish of violence] and a 'coltivata barbarie' [cultivated barbarism], elencated in a slightly tongue-in-cheek rush, an ultimately dismissive catalogue of D'Annunzio's military exploits:

> Enumeriamo insieme, discorso di Quarto, partenza per il fronte, azione sul cacciatorpediniere 'Impavido', missioni dagli idrovolanti e perdita dell'occhio, volo su Trieste, volo su Trento, combattimento all'isola Morosina,

> bombardamento delle aerorimesse di Parenzo, azioni con i fanti al Veliki e al Faiti, voli sul Timavo, incursione aerea sulle bocche di Cattaro, Beffa di Buccari, volo su Vienna, Marcia da Ronchi, Fiume ... (p. 878)

> [Let us go over them together: the Quarto speech, going to the front, seeing action on the destroyer 'Impavido', seaplane missions and losing an eye, the flight over Trieste, the flight over Trento, fighting on Morosina island, bombing the aircraft hangars at Parenzo, infantry engagements on Veliki and Faiti, flights over the Timavo, the air-raid on the mouth of the Cattaro, the Buccari exploit, the flight over Vienna, the March from Ronchi, Fiume... .]

The poet, Bontempelli declares, had been prey to an overwhelming, untreatable addiction to history, which had left him ill-prepared for the subsequent peace. Only anti-history, the orator announced, can be the well-spring of true literature. D'Annunzio's misguided quest — through derring do — for 'una splendida biografia' (in Maurice Barrès's tellingly ambivalent phrase) had diminished the poet's claim to artistic greatness. To rub things in even further, Bontempelli had already made an unflattering comparison. Dante had had the good fortune to be rebuffed when he had tried to take part in history, and thus had ended up a true poet. D'Annunzio, on the other hand, was now denied his place in art because history had welcomed him too readily.

This line, delineating the matter of history from the matter of poetry, would become a consistent part of Bontempelli's ideology, receiving a clear enunciation, for instance, in his introduction to *Lirica italiana* (1943):

> Mentre procede il viaggio sanguinoso della storia, che è mantenimento di barbarie, vi sorge parallelo il mondo della poesia; [...]. Lungo cammini isolati, improvvisi elevarsi di sommità s'accampano fuori del tempo, irraggiungibili dalla matta bestialitade.[12]

> [As history, which keeps barbarism going, proceeds on its bloody way, there arises parallel to it the world of poetry; (...). Along lonely tracks, sudden high spots rise up which are lodged outside time, inaccessible to 'mad brutishness'.]

The Dantean quote (*Inferno* XI, 82–83) at the end of this declaration is an explicit denunciation of the cult of violence, and simultaneously a defence of that art which in its universal value is able to rise above the melee. The criticism Bontempelli offers his audience in the town hall of Pescara is stinging because it not only affects the poet: it also concerns his readership. If D'Annunzio the earlier writer had been able to surround himself with disciples, as was fitting, the later celebrity would be the focus and rallying point for mere nobodies:

> Perciò intorno al veggente sono pochi discepoli amati e con lui collaboranti; invece intorno al potente sta, gli è necessaria, una folla anonima di gente celebrante da lui disprezzata. (p. 882)

> [So around the seer there are few beloved disciples working with him, but around the man of power there is something he must have, a nameless crowd of people talking him up, though despised by him.]

D'Annunzio had sold out to facile acclaim, to the here and 'NUNC' (an abbreviation of D'Annunzio's own device, witheringly reprised here by Bontempelli),[13] and had abandoned his art. By extension, those who affected to admire him as an embodiment of virile nationalism (and were, by implication, all too present in the front row at the town hall in Pescara) were deluding themselves that they were culturally informed. Had the authorities been properly attentive readers of Bontempelli's welter of pronouncements on literature, they would have seen that this dismissal of contemporary favour as a criterion for art was far from a new position, even with regard to Fascism. In an essay of 1929, *Canzone all'Italia* (written in prose!), later included in *L'avventura novecentista*, Bontempelli had exclaimed:

> Il contemporaneo crede [...] che un romanzo dove si parli di Italia fascista sia ipso facto più fascista [...] che un romanzo ove non si parli, per esempio che d'amore o di viaggi per mare; mentre tra cento anni un romanzo di pura fantasia potrà apparire aderente allo spirito fascista assai più di uno che metta in scena la Marcia su Roma. (p. 776)

> [People today think (...) that a novel which talks about Fascist Italy is ipso facto more Fascist (...) than a novel which talks only about, say, love or sea travel; whereas a hundred years from now a novel of pure imagination may appear a lot more in keeping with the spirit of Fascism than one which portrays the March on Rome.]

The rhetoric in Bontempelli's speech at Pescara now becomes even more insistent: under the influence of lurid patriotism, D'Annunzio's one-time lyricism has become crude and vulgar:

> Fu pervaso da una decisione di conquista; sentì con delizia l'odore di sangue, uscì dalla torre di cristallo e cercò la ressa degli uomini che sudano; [...] il delirio del piacere lo vedemmo nelle sue mani trasmutarsi a volontà di potere, l'ermetismo monodico sboccare nel desiderio popolare del coro e il liuto diventare fanfara. (pp. 884–85)

> [He was filled by a sudden urge for conquest, he smelt with delight the smell of blood, he left the crystal tower and sought the crush of men who sweat; (...) we saw the delirium of pleasure change in his hands into a will for power, the solo voice of hermeticism come out as popular desire for chorus, and the lute turn into a military band.]

This fracture between history and art, specifically forged to confront D'Annunzio, is also used in Bontempelli's account of Verga, just over a year later, where he makes a controversial distinction between the artistic failure of *Mastro-don Gesualdo*, fatally forced to 'rientrare nel tempo', and the timeless 'poema' constituted by *I Malavoglia*. Bontempelli's reading here is forced, taking no notice of Verga's explicit views on history in his ideologically charged, consciously programmatic cycle of 'I vinti'. Few Verga critics (let alone the ghost of Verga) would agree with him, but it is nevertheless indicative of Bontempelli's own idiosyncratic take on the enduring values of literature.

Bontempelli's valedictory reveals that, despite superficial niceties, he had come to bury D'Annunzio, not to praise him or his followers and sponsors. Perhaps Bottai should not have been so surprised, for already Bontempelli, during the notorious 'polemica Carducciana' of 1910, had written equally ferociously about D'Annunzio, but from a diametrically contrary point of view:

> L'arte del D'Annunzio conquistò anzitutto le signore. Fu la prima arte vera che penetrasse largamente nei salotti. In secondo luogo essa penetrò un altro campo, rimasto fino allora negato a ogni soffio di poesia: la provincia; e nelle farmacie, tra la politica e il pettegolezzo, l'affare e lo sport, si cominciò a parlare con ardore di Gabriele D'Annunzio; sioccamente, se vogliamo; prima dei suoi vestiti che delle tragedie e delle laudi.[14]

> [D'Annunzio's art won over ladies especially. It was the first real art to get into drawing rooms on a wide scale. Secondly it got into another environment, hitherto absolutely impervious to any whiff of poetry: the provinces; and in chemist's shops, between talk of politics and gossip, business and sport, people began to speak enthusiastically about D'Annunzio; stupidly, perhaps, and first about his dress sense rather than about his tragedies and his *laudi*.]

Despite the lively tone, this passage is quite artfully contrived. Bontempelli proceeds by meta-literary insinuation. As with the Dantean reference to 'matta bestialitade' earlier, a prominent sub-text alerts the reader to the real message. The sly combination of provincialism, feminine readership and pharmacies here indicates Bontempelli's implicit dismissal of *dannunzianesimo* as a mere pandering to a past-its-sell-by-date Bovaryism. The hint then becomes explicit when Bontempelli lashes out against the cult of empty form and complaisant referentiality verging on plagiarism, and against the idea of the poet as somebody with a social status. A similarly anti-D'Annunzian slant can already be seen in Bontempelli's 'preface' to *L'avventura novecentista*, composed in 1914, and pointedly inserted as a prophetic 'statement' into a collection primarily made up of articles from the 1920s and '30s. Even this early, Bontempelli was in good (if controversial) company in thinking D'Annunzio was a has-been. Bontempelli's adherence to Futurism, especially in its war-mongering phase, would undoubtedly have caused him to come into contact with Marinetti's pithy demolition of D'Annunzio in *Guerra sola igiene del mondo* (1915):

> Bisogna ad ogni costo combattere Gabriele D'Annunzio, perché egli ha raffinato, con tutto il suo ingegno, i quattro veleni intellettuali che noi vogliamo assolutamente abolire: 1° la poesia morbosa e nostalgica della distanza e del ricordo; 2° il sentimentalismo romantico grondante di chiaro di luna, che si eleva verso la Donna-Bellezza ideale e fatale; 3° l'ossessione della lussuria, col triangolo dell'adulterio, il pepe dell'incesto e il condimento del peccato cristiano; 4° la passione professorale del passato e la mania delle antichità e delle collezioni.[15]

> [We need to fight Gabriele D'Annunzio come what may, because he has distilled, with all his cunning, the four intellectual poisons which we want absolutely to abolish: 1st the unhealthy, nostalgic poetry of distance and memory; 2nd romantic sentimentalism dripping with moonlight, which wafts towards that ideal and fatal Lady Beauty; 3rd the obsession with lust, with the triangle of adultery, the pepper of incest and the spice of Christian sin; 4th the professorial passion for the past and the mania for antiques and collecting.]

The Bontempelli of the D'Annunzio valedictory, in other words, was consistent in his dismissal, and had a long track-record of doubts about the Vate, even though these changed considerably in focus. Though the authorities should have seen it coming, the consequences of this all-too-public Pescaran denunciation, not only of D'Annunzio the man, but also of the cult of the hero and Italy's strident place in history, were predictable. Though Bottai probably felt the same about some of the excesses of revolutionary nationalism, and in cultural terms had undergone a similar ideological iter to Bontempelli,[16] moving steadily away from the shared heady days of *Roma futurista*, the fact that the funerary orator had had the temerity to criticise a national icon, for the very features and quest for a place in the pantheon which had endeared him (somewhat guardedly) to the Fascist leadership, was bound to cause embarrassment. Bottai, whose own position was becoming increasingly difficult within the Party, would have to show his own loyalty by an act of zeal, publicly calling Bontempelli to order.

Bontempelli's break with received (if not expert) opinion about D'Annunzio, and indeed his break with his own previous criticism of the Vate, shows him in a characteristic light: that of polemicist always ready to change tack. The judgment on D'Annunzio as unaware that he has been left behind by the very history he was pursuing also implicitly corresponds to a marked interest in periodization in Bontempelli's critical writing, and would lead inevitably to his unlikely pairing of D'Annunzio and Marinetti as the last vestiges of Ottocento romantic agony. This periodization was expressed by Bontempelli as an eccentrically millenarian sequence of three ages: classical, romantic and now ... virile. The first epoch stops with the Advent of Christ, the second lasts from the Sermon on the Mount to the Great War (or the Ballets Russes, as he says on one occasion), whilst the third, still to be fully realised (with the timely help of *Novecentismo*), is just beginning in the Dopoguerra. One of the themes most strongly developed in the funeral oration was the sense in which D'Annunzio had belonged (despite occasional moments of cultural prophecy) to the old, romantic order. His oeuvre:

> È la gran catasta di profumate legna sulla quale in gloria e in una specie di nervosa gioia si consumava l'ultima vita d'un costume spirituale di diciannove secoli, la Seconda Epoca della umanità civile d'Occidente; soprattutto vi bruciavano con allegrezza gli estremi atteggiamenti del decimonono, il secolo duro a morire. (p. 884)
>
> [Is the great stack of perfumed fire-wood on which, in glory and in a kind of nervous joy, the ebbing life of nineteen centuries of a way of thinking, the Second Age of Western civilization, was consumed; what burnt merrily were above all the final attitudes of the nineteenth, the century that just wouldn't die.]

The new age, in particular, had to break totally with the old. In its programmatic iconoclasm (and even in much of its phrasing), Bontempelli's periodization is a highly qualified derivative of Marinetti's Futurist rhetoric. These ideas on epochs can be found more fully developed in Bontempelli's collection of essays, ranging from 1926 to 1936, entitled *L'avventura novecentista*.[17] Though professing a respect for the notion of centuries as real, meaningful divisions, Bontempelli argues that the last of the three ages of Man does not correspond with the opening of the twentieth century. The third, modern age is only starting to begin in the aftermath to the Great War, whose long drawn out closure arguably did not correspond with the

Armistice, or the Treaty of Versailles. This skewed periodization, with its shadowland between 1900 and 1920, corresponds precisely to the years of Bontempelli's own maturation as a writer, and leads him to a febrile adoption, and equally repeated rejection, of previous models and influences,[18] including the Vate, D'Annunzio, and that supreme iconoclast of nineteenth-century constructs, Filippo Tommaso Marinetti.

In *L'avventura novecentista*, though there are occasional references to previous writers, such as Pascoli, Bontempelli reserves most space for Futurism, as it was the movement whose salutary destructiveness and glorious failure provided the specific raison d'être for his own brand of poetics, *Novecentismo*:

> Noi professiamo una grande ammirazione per il futurismo, che nettamente e senza riguardi ha tagliato il ponte tra Ottocento e Novecento. [...] nessuno di noi novecentisti, se non fosse passato attraverso le persuasioni e le passioni del futurismo, potrebbe oggi dire le parole che aprono il nuovo secolo.
>
> [We are open about our great admiration for Futurism, which cleanly and brutally cut the bridge between the nineteenth and twentieth centuries. (...) none of us *novecentisti* could say today the words which open the new century, without having passed through the convictions and passions of Futurism.]

By and large, though, the essays of *L'avventura novecentista* are notably coy about Bontempelli's own sequential transfer of cultural allegiances, and less illuminating in that respect than the comments of his one time collaborator (and then arch-rival) Curzio Malaparte in *Strapaese e stracittà* (1927),[19] and certainly a good deal less frank than Elio Vittorini's juvenile effusions in *Scarico di coscienza* (1929).[20] It is nevertheless possible to trace Bontempelli's intellectual autobiography quite closely through another channel, namely a number of autobiographical statements masquerading as biographical fictions which display some interesting technical features. Bontempelli's most significant critical statements are frequently articulated as short stories.

Even early in his creative writing career, Bontempelli faithfully projected his own literary and intellectual vicissitudes into his characters. In 'Sotto i torchi',[21] one of the early novellas of his 1908 collection of short stories about the life of provincial school-teachers, *Socrate moderno*, Bontempelli relives his own doomed attempts to pass the *concorso a cattedra* to teach in the *liceo*, despite a double degree in philosophy and in letters. The character, Enzo Battei, desperately tries to augment his scarce 'titoli' by engaging a local printer to publish a single rushed copy of his forgotten, festering, handwritten graduating thesis in Hellenistic philosophy. The deadline for the *concorso* is close, and proof-reading the modest printer's doomed attempts to render the convoluted arguments and dense Greek quotations requires a heroic effort. The attempt to revisit his student past and his now unfamiliar, utterly irrelevant classical erudition forces Enzo painfully to re-evaluate his own limitations and former ambitions. Life can be regression as well as progress. In another story of the same collection, 'Il divino ozio',[22] the protagonist, blissfully unaware of his own aesthetic limitations, maps out for himself a future literary career of breathtaking conventionality, very close to the real Bontempelli's early efforts. The reverie occurs at the opening page of the novella, after hesitations about espousing classical or modern theatre:

> Andava virtuosamente ordinando in pensiero la sua opera futura, e [...] si leggeva e si rileggeva all'infinito, in sulla prima pagina immaginaria d'uno qualunque dei suoi libri futuri, il dolce elenco delle sue opere: — Le Opere di Giovanni Albieri: POESIA 'Poema de la Donna'; ROMANZI 'I Volgari'; TEATRO... Frattanto non aveva ancor messo mano a nessuna, sebbene grande fosse l'ardor del lavoro.
>
> [In his mind he virtuously ordered his future output, and (...) he read to himself again and again, on the imaginary front page of one or other of his future books, the sweet catalogue of his works: The Works of Giovanni Albieri: POETRY 'Lady Poem'; NOVELS 'The Vernaculars'; THEATRE ... actually he hadn't got round to starting any of them, even though he was dying to get to work.]

The literary models are easy to pick out: the hesitation between an unrealisable Aeschylus and the now inevitable Ibsen in theatre,[23] the strong suggestion of Carducci, Pascoli and D'Annunzio in poetry, and the looming examples of Capuana and Verga (but arguably seen through D'Annunzio-tinted lenses) in prose. Bontempelli, though only thirty, is providing an ironic commentary on his own earlier influences, now safely discarded. It is a model of self-separation we shall shortly see taken to extremes in another meta-literary 'novel'. *Socrate moderno* itself would later be repudiated, along with much of Bontempelli's early poetry and drama including a verse drama, *Costanza*, 'di tipica industria dannunziana' according to Luigi Baldacci, once the writer was elected an academician in 1930.

One of Bontempelli's preferred narrative devices, showing a clear debt to Pirandello, is his use of doubles,[24] a feature perhaps most prominent in *Il figlio di due madri* (1929), but also very evident in his short story about the cinema, 'La mia morte civile', where the actor begins to confuse his feelings with that of the character he is playing in the film.[25] Gradually it is the character who comes to dominate. One of the most interesting, but least commented examples of doubling occurs in 'Il romanzo dei romanzi', the last of the mini-sequences in *La vita intensa*, which was published as a volume by Vallecchi in 1920. *La vita intensa* is a set of micro-novels which came out as instalments, from March through to December 1919, in *Ardita*, the monthly supplement to Mussolini's daily *Il popolo d'Italia*. The collection as a whole, whose subtitle is also 'Romanzo dei romanzi', is characterised by an extraordinary degree of meta-literary references and reflexiveness, neatly summed up by the final conceit of the first of many prefaces:

> E allora per chi e perché scrivo questo romanzo?
> Lo scrivo per i posteri. Lo scrivo per rinnovare il romanzo europeo.
> Questa duplice dichiarazione non deve maravigliare. Uno che scrive un romanzo, e ci mette la prefazione, non può assolutamente dichiarare meno di tanto. (p. 8)
>
> [So who do I write this novel for, and why?
> I am writing it for generations to come. I am writing it to renew the European novel.
> This double declaration shouldn't surprise anyone. Nobody writing a novel, who puts in a foreword, can possibly declare anything less.]

The last novella, 'Il romanzo dei romanzi', is a piece of writing very close to Pirandello's 'La tragedia di un personaggio' and 'Colloqui coi personaggi', in that characters from various parts of *La vita intensa* come together to remonstrate with the author, complaining about their fixity, which has been imposed merely for the convenience of writer and reader, crassly desirous of beginnings, middles and ends. But Bontempelli goes one step further than Pirandello, indeed perhaps in deliberately conscious rivalry. Even Bontempelli's author is now doubled into a character whom the real author can observe interacting with the other characters,[26] and with whom he can converse:

> – Scusa: a chi di noi due ha detto 'Voglio rivederti'?
> L'altro mi rispose:
> – Tu sei tu, tu uomo vivo, scrittore di romanzi eccetera. Io sono tu come personaggio dei romanzi stessi. Ci sono gli altri, non potevo mancare io. (p. 140)

['Excuse me: to which one of us two did you say: "I want to see you again"'?
The other answered me:
'You are you, you the living man, writer of novels etc. I am the you as a character in the novels themselves. The others are here, so I couldn't stay away.']

The author is introduced by his double into his own study, where one of the characters from an earlier section of the *Vita intensa* is holding forth unstoppably:

> – Questo è il futurismo — gridò Marinetti dominando dall'angolo estremo della stanza — è una grande vittoria del neodinamismo antiplastico sul fetido spazio passatista.
> – *El ga resòn el Marinett!* — urlò il mio portinaio, lettore assiduo, oltre che della *Vraie Italie* come s'è visto a suo luogo, anche di tutti i giornali e giornaletti futuristi postfuturisti e avanguardisti che mi piovono a casa settimanalmente traverso sua portineria.
> Marinetti abbracciò il portinaio e cominciò a improvvisare una conferenza sulla necessità imperiosa di abolire il punto e la virgola. (p. 140–41)

['This is Futurism,' Marinetti cried, dominating from the furthest corner of the room, 'it is antiplastic neo-dynamism's great victory over stinking passéist space.'
'He's right, that Marinetti!', shouted my concierge, a keen long-time reader not just of *Vraie Italie*, as we saw at the appropriate point, but also of all the Futurist, post-Futurist and avant-garde newspapers and bulletins which pour into my home every week through his lodge.
Marinetti hugged the concierge and started to improvise a lecture on the absolute necessity of abolishing the full stop and the comma.]

Apart from a fleeting reference to Alberto Savinio, tumultuously playing the piano to drown out the assembled characters of 'Il romanzo dei romanzi',[27] this mention of Marinetti is the only reference to a character who is a real, historical contemporary. Despite the surreal comedy, deliciously reinforced by the Milanese dialect of the concierge,[28] the details are not entirely invented. Marinetti's Futurist manifestos did indeed advocate the suppression of punctuation;[29] 'dinamismo', 'plastico', 'fetido' and 'passatista' really are characteristic vocabulary from the rallying cries of the Futurists (though '*neo*dinamismo' and '*anti*plastico' are naughty distortions of Boccioni's pronouncements on Futurism and the visual arts).[30] Even Bontempelli's complaint about the avalanche of unwanted Futurist junk mail rings true. *La Vraie Italie* was a short-lived French language publication, edited after the Great War by Papini and Soffici.

Though embedded in a fiction, what we have before us, projected through a series of lenses (pseudo-biographical, yet autobiographical), is a genuine part of Bontempelli's contact with the world of literary schools and movements.

Marinetti's particular walk-on part in 'Il romanzo dei romanzi' derives from his appearance in another micro-novel sequence in the *Vita intensa*, namely 'Mio zio non era futurista'. The preface to this particular sequence advertises Bontempelli's characteristically explicit metaliterary stance: 'Sotto specie di romanzo d'avventure, questo è anche, e soprattutto, un esempio di "romanzo storico d'ambiente letterario"' (p. 92) [Beneath the appearance of an adventure novel, this is also and above all an example of a 'historical novel in a literary setting'].

'Avventura' looks like the generic term for standard fictional fare, but it is also Bontempelli's cypher for intellectual development, as witnessed by the title of his collection of essays, *L'avventura novecentista*. The basic structure of this 'romanzo d'avventure' is the account of the unstinting efforts by an unnamed but youngish protagonist to develop the latent literary genius of his unnamed uncle, a mature if inertly elitist product of late nineteenth century aestheticism. The paradoxical relationship between guided uncle and guiding nephew begins whilst the nephew is still at *liceo*:

> Qualche volta passavo settimane intere da lui, nella grande biblioteca bruna, ne' suoi salotti pieni di collezioni varie e di cose belle. Mentre egli mi leggeva i suoi versi, io guardavo le cose belle e ascoltavo in estasi. (p. 94)
>
> [Sometimes I spent weeks on end at his house, in the great, dark library, in his drawing rooms full of various collections and beautiful objects. Whilst he read out to me his poetry, I was looking at the beautiful objects, and listening ecstatically.]

On the surface, the remark is a perfunctory element of plot-building, establishing the relationship between the uncle and the nephew, and indicating the solid (perhaps stolid) cultural roots of the uncle. Though dictated by the needs of narrative economy, the reference corresponds closely to a draft idea for a larger autobiographical narration recorded in consciously Leopardian outline[31] in *Il bianco e il nero*:

> GIOVINEZZA NUOVA. L'esaltazione del fanciullo in casa del nonno, sognando gloria letteraria, leggendo Ariosto e Cervantes e pensando a Molière mi ricorda quella di quando ero fanciullo. [...] Indifferenza del padre, morboso amore per la madre che [*lacuna*] quando ho 7 anni: — amicizia col nonno che mi ha scoperto in biblioteca. (pp. 212–13)
>
> [NEW YOUTH. The exaltation of the small boy in his grandfather's house, dreaming of literary glory, reading Ariosto and Cervantes and thinking about Molière, reminds me of the feelings I had as a boy. (...) My father's indifference, my unhealthy love for my mother who [text missing] when I was seven: friendship with my grandfather who discovered me in his library.]

In 'Mio zio non era futurista' there follows a typology of the uncle's writings, all characterised (like the imaginary bibliography of Giovanni Albieri in *Il divino ozio*) by a conspicuous conservatism and formal preference for externals: rare sonnet forms not used since the Renaissance, eclogues, verse tragedies. As Enrico Falqui[32] and later Luigi Baldacci[33] have pointed out, this is an exaggerated but none the less faithful self-portrait of the precious, classicizing young Bontempelli. We thus have an elegant, paradoxical conceit at the heart of what should be a *Bildungsroman*. If the nephew represents the author after his literary conversion to Futurism and post-Futurism, the older uncle is Bontempelli as a young, neoclassicising fogey. This back-to-front (but chronologically coherent) fictional device finds an almost perfect match in a statement made by Bontempelli in 1930 (the year of his election to the Academy) about the surprising effect participation in the Great War had had on him:

> Molti [...] s'erano tanto maravigliati quando tornando nel '19 con l'anima fresca, ho rinnegato, buttato via, calpestato tutto quanto (sette od otto volumi) avevo scritto prima, per ricominciare in pieno...[34]
>
> [Many (...) were very surprised when, coming back in 1919 with a fresh spirit, I disowned, chucked out, trampled on everything (seven or eight volumes) I had written previously, in order to restart again in full flow...]

A glimpse at some of the items repudiated when the real Bontempelli gained his seat at the Academy underlines the pointedly autobiographical nature of this description of the uncle-young Bontempelli figure:

> *Egloghe* (1904)
> *Verseggiando: Intermezzo in rime* (1905)
> *Costanza* (verse drama) (1905)
> *Odi siciliane* (1906)
> *Giosuè Carducci* (published lecture) (1907)
> *Amori* (novellas) (1910)
> *Settenari e sonetti* (1910)
> *Odi* (1910)
> *Santa Teresa* (comedy) (1916)

As an eloquent contrast, Bontempelli follows up the description of the uncle's output with an indication of the nephew's volatile literary tendencies: 'Ora è necessario sapere che quand'io facevo la licenza ginnasiale ero dannunziano, ma appena presa la licenza ginnasiale diventai antidannunziano, come accade' (p. 94) [You need to know that when I was preparing my middle school exams I was a D'Annunzian, but as soon as I had taken the exams I became an anti-D'Annunzian, the way these things happen].[35] The placing of such a momentous literary conversion at a banal rite of passage in secondary education, combined with Bontempelli's throw-away qualification 'come accade', indicates that D'Annunzio's place in the Novecentista canon is far from secure. This is confirmed a few sentences later. The uncle is a genius precisely because he doesn't ape the current vogue for D'Annunzio:

> Aveva il coraggio di scrivere e pubblicare a quel modo, nel tempo in cui tutti navigavano e pescavano nella scia di licenza poetica lasciata dal passaggio della *Laus vitae*.

> Io lo convinsi ch'egli era un neoclassico, e che la sua scuola sarebbe stata il vero e solo rimedio alla decadenza della lirica segnata dall'imperante dannunzianesimo. (p. 94)

> [He had the courage to write and publish that way, at a time when everybody was sailing and fishing in the wake of poetic licence left by the passage of the *Laus Vitae*.
> I convinced him that he was a neoclassicist, and that his school would be the one and only remedy for the decadence of lyric poetry, marked as it was by the D'Annunzianism that was in fashion at the time.]

But Bontempelli is still not finished with the Vate. After a belated reading of Croce's *Estetica*, the nephew gives a luxuriously bound copy to his unnamed uncle on his name-day. This casual detail maps Bontempelli's own impatience with Croce, which found its most amusing outlet in a spoof Crocean reading of the then anonymous[36] children's ditty, *La farfalletta*, in which a little girl catches a butterfly and then decides to let it go. Bontempelli's faux-Crocean criticism carries the title *La vispa Teresa: Saggio di critica filosofica*, and is one of the funniest contributions to the 'polemica carducciana'.[37] It is possible that Bontempelli's sardonic highlighting of the children's poem led to Trilussa's controversially goliardic additions to it (1917), inspired by the actress Dina Galli,[38] and to the eventual newspaper competition to find out who had actually written the poem.

The uncle's neo-classicism imperceptibly begins to crumble under the perfectly fused weight of intuition and expression. He now pens programme sonnets 'a Giosuè Carducci' and 'a Gabriele D'Annunzio'. The pastiche tercets of the latter cruelly highlight both the artistic limitations of the uncle (the earlier Bontempelli) at a literal level, and, at a figurative level, are a confession of the younger Bontempelli's anxiety of influence with regard to the 'Poeta di Pescara':

> Quei che vati son detti, or dai pantani,
> tizzi male arsi, all'aria pigra in gara
> fumigano i modesti animi vani.
> Tu su lor raggi una tua luce amara.
> Qualche restio, remoto dai profani,
> in lei riguarda, e l'avvenir prepara. (p. 95)

> [Those who are called bards, now as half-burnt embers from the swamps compete to fumigate, in the stale air, modest empty minds. You shine upon them your bitter light. Some restless spirit, far from the vulgar throng, looks into that light and prepares the future.]

Whether Bontempelli is referring to himself as the 'restio', absorbing the D'Annunzian lesson but already thinking of something different, is all the more effective an insinuation for not being made clear. The literary construction of such verse proves that the uncle, despite the comically timid abandonment of capital letters for each line of verse, is still a Carduccian at heart. So, perhaps inevitably, Carducci is the next apparent focus of 'Mio zio non era futurista'.

Bontempelli now introduces into the story his own role as an agitator in the 'polemica carducciana' (supposedly about free verse but actually an argument about the merits of Crocean philosophical criticism versus Carduccian literary criticism), for the nephew slips into the uncle's pile of unread, conservative *Cronache letterarie* copies of the much more adventurous *La Voce*. Bontempelli knew what he was talking about here for, once he had abandoned school teaching, he had taken the job of editor, at Sansoni, of *Cronache letterarie*, and was instrumental in cranking up intellectual and literary rivalries and polemics in order to boost circulation. The episode of intercalation in 'Mio zio non era futurista' is a precise clue about a real-life prank when, in 1911, a group of collaborators from *La Voce* put together a counterfeit issue of *Cronache letterarie* with the almost identical title *Croniche letterate*. The real Bontempelli appears in this fake as Minimo Maltempelli, a conventional commentator on a rigidly defined canon of Italian classics including Boccaccio. Bontempelli is describing his own experience, thinly disguised as comic fiction. The writing is funny enough on its own, but Bontempelli's friends, in the know, must have been vastly amused by these details.

The self-reference in 'Mio zio non era futurista' is extended even to the mention of the subsequent anthology of the Carduccian polemic, a volume 'con la copertina gialla', edited by Ettore Romagnoli,[39] which, as we have already seen with the spoof Crocean criticism, actually contains a number of Bontempelli's own contributions to the debate. Amongst these, D'Annunzio again figures as a target:

> Un vero spirito d'annunziano non vi fu, o non fu durevole. L'influsso dell'arte d'annunziana fu soprattutto in diffusione, e il suo valore più grande fu la diffusione per l'appunto, la volgarizzazione di certo modo di considerare l'arte, l'educazione di taluni ceti, per l'innanzi affatto retrivi, a interessarsi all'arte, a un'arte pura e degna.[40]

> [There never was a true spirit of D'Annunzianism, or rather it didn't last. The influence of D'Annunzian art was in its spread, and its greatest merit lay indeed in this dissemination, the popularisation of a certain way of considering art, the training of certain social classes, previously impervious to culture, to become interested in art, in pure, worthwhile art.]

It is the same critique Bontempelli will make in the Pescaran speech, only uttered a quarter of a century earlier. D'Annunzio just did not know how to create a school. All he managed to gather around him were groupies: women first, followed by social snobs and then by *gerarchi*, but none of them was capable of applying the lessons to be learnt.

Again, the contrast between the uncle's insensitivity to these new currents, and the nephew's enthusiastic espousal of them, only serves to provide an autobiographical gloss on Bontempelli's own 'late' conversion to modernity. Having failed by positive means, the nephew has to resort to negative ones: he removes from the uncle's study the intellectual underpinning of Carduccian-style literary criticism: the volumes of literary history by D'Ancona, Renier, Flamini, Casini, Rossi, etc., plus the weighty tomes of German positivist linguistic scholarship, the various *Grundriss* and *Wörterbuch* [sic].

It is only at this point that Bontempelli addresses the reader on the issue of his characters' lack of delineation, suggesting that some readers may find the uncle is as featureless as the portrait of the *Dio ermafrodito* by Carrà. There is indeed a real painting by Carrà which certainly fits the bill, but with a slightly different title (*Idolo ermafrodito*). It hangs in the Collezione Mattioli in Milan, and looks like an unclothed tailor's or artist's dummy, sitting on a box in the corner of a bare room with its right arm and hand aloft, with visible stitching down the centre-line of the asexual, straw-stuffed body.[41] By this reference, Bontempelli is intimating that the absence of distinguishing features in the uncle is deliberate, and the reader is to make of the writer's dummy what he will. Bontempelli nevertheless offers a broad hint: he himself has been given imaginary features by his readers: a great blond beard and glasses.[42]

The remainder of 'Mio zio non era futurista' deals with the creation of an environment conducive to the conversion of the uncle to Futurism (and genius). Already Marinetti's manifesto has begun to echo throughout Italy:

> Squillò nel cielo di Firenze, dopo aver animato già tanta parte d'Italia e del mondo, l'Annunzio Futurista. (p. 99)
>
> [After having already galvanised so much of Italy and the world, there pealed out in the Florentine sky the Futurist Annunciation.]

The capitalised 'annunzio', apart from its wickedly 'D'Annunzian' spelling, introduces a mock-messianic element which will be picked up a few sentences later in an equally capitalised 'Evangelista'. Futurism is the Gospel according to San Marinetti. The nephew immediately recognises the target of Marinetti's pronouncements. It is people who think like his uncle:

> 'Sviate il corso dei canali, per inondare i Musei', gridava il nuovo Evangelista. E mio zio viveva, si può dire, in un museo! [...] Quei salotti pieni di cose putride: quadri d'autore, stampe, avori, metalli lavorati, tessuti morbidi; ecco la tomba imminente del genio di mio zio, se io non sapevo liberarlo. (p. 99)
>
> ['Deviate the flow of canals, to flood museums', shouted the new Evangelist. And my uncle was living, one could say, in a museum! (...) Those drawing rooms full of rotting things: signed paintings, prints, ivories, fine metalwork, soft furnishings, here was the imminent tomb of my uncle's genius, unless I could find a way to free him.]

This incorporates a quote from the Italian version of the founding manifesto of the Futurists,[43] immediately following the declaration: 'Suvvia! Date fuoco agli scaffali delle biblioteche!' [Come on! Set fire to the bookshelves in libraries!] (which Bontempelli slyly omits, for the deliberate destruction of the classics of Italian literature by fire is about to be carried out by the nephew). This overstuffed, bourgeois environment — hostile to the creation of new art — bears a striking resemblance to the interiors of D'Annunzio's fictions, and anticipates the Vate's last and most monumental autobiographical fiction, the sequence of rooms in the Vittoriale.

The nephew arranges to donate this Ottocentista paraphernalia to a museum, despoiling the 'Villa Artemide' to make it into a 'Villa Dinamo'. The occasion for this rebaptising of the uncle's residence was a chance visit to the Florentine café, the famous *Giubbe Rosse*. There the nephew witnesses the 'magnetica fluidità del corpo di Giovanni Papini, che svolgeva allora la sua rapida "esperienza futurista"' [magnetic bodily fluidity of Giovanni Papini, who at that time was carrying out his brief 'Futurist experiment'] (p. 100). The anti-D'Annunzian *par excellence*, Papini was the founder of *Lacerba*, and was defined by his one-time admirer Croce as amongst 'amongst the most louche and untrustworthy adventurers of the mind'.[44] *Esperienza futurista* was, as it happens, the title of one of Papini's works (1919), relating to his short-lived flirtation with Futurism. Bontempelli is again showing, in fictional garb, his own real circle of acquaintances and influences.

The nephew goes to meet Marinetti. The encounter emphasises the two contradictory sides to Marinetti. The apostle of Futurism lives in a grand bourgeois manner, in a house full of creature comforts and oriental luxury, serviced by a house-keeper. In its stuffy indulgence and ottocentista bric-a-brac, it could pass for the residence of D'Annunzio. Then all changes once they enter the 'fucina del lavoro collettivo del Movimento Futurista' [the furnace of the Futurist Movement's Collective Output]. There the nephew is assailed by simultaneous stimuli to all his senses:

> La violenza caotica dei capolavori d'ogni arte che scrollando e sibilando vi si aggrovigliavano. Ero ebbro. Mi pareva che i colori ballassero rumorosamente nella stanza, le linee cantassero, i quadri scivolassero dalle pareti per venire a portarmi via la sedia su cui F. T. mi accennava di accommodarmi. (p. 102)

> [The chaotic violence of masterpieces of every art form which writhed there jostling and hissing. I was drunk. It seemed to me that the colours were dancing noisily in the room, the lines were singing, and the paintings were slipping from the walls to take away from me the seat which F.T. was motioning me to sit in.]

It is a Futurist poetic in miniature, with its ideal breakdown of the generic barriers between the arts, and offering strong suggestions of Soffici-style simultaneities and synaesthesia. The picture is beautifully complemented when the nephew hears through the opening windows, facing onto the Corso Venezia, the symphony of mechanical noise, evidence of an industrial city-soul so dear to the Futurists:

> L'anima della vita grande di Milano: stridori voluttuosamente intricati di tranvai, camion, automobili, motociclette, strilloni. (p. 103)

> [The soul of the great life of Milan, voluptuously intricate screeches of tramcars, lorries, cars, motorbikes, newsboys.]

Marinetti gives the nephew the replacement decor for the Villa Dinamo, wall poems, big coloured posters. Luigi Russolo, the author of the *Arte dei rumori* [The Art of Noises], lends him an 'intonarumori' [noise-intoner]. All is set for a Futurist masterpiece, but time is passing, and we are now in July 1914. After many hesitations, the uncle's blank paper and sharpened pencils produce an appropriately absurdist title: 'Chincaglia dello scimpanzè' [chimpanzee's ironmongery]. The nephew prepares to combine the visual stimulus of the mural poetry and posters with the aural stimulus of the 'ululatore medio' [medium screamer]. The uncle is about to put pencil to paper, when:

> Proprio in quel momento scoppiò la guerra europea. (p. 106)

> [At that very instant, the European war broke out.]

This is where the text terminates. Bontempelli at one level is showing his mastery in producing a shaggy dog story. We have been deprived, apparently, of an ending. But at another level, he is showing the very real outcome of Futurist rhetoric, with its celebration of destruction and its cult of violent cleansing. The real masterpiece of the uncle (and the society he represents) is only now to be genuinely realised. It is to have 'written' or 'performed' the outbreak of modern warfare. Bontempelli's own initial period of adhesion to the edges of Futurism coincided with the interventionist campaigns of 1914–1915 (in which Papini had a major role),[45] and became cemented with the production of a trench-newspaper, *Il Montello*, produced with fellow Futurists in uniform. His association with the movement (along with Bottai) would continue into the early post-war years as the Arditi found a political voice and Futurism itself became absorbed in the Fascist project. Rapidly, however, Bontempelli came to the conclusion that Futurism was not the formation of the new but the last, self-destructive spasm of the old, as he declares in *L'avventura novecentista*:

> Tale opera di sgomberamento il futurismo la compié con una temperatura così alta, che l'assieme di tutti i suoi tentativi di realizzazione costituì di per se stesso una notevole opera d'arte: l'ultima e la più folgorante delle espressioni del romanticismo, che in esso si brucia e gloriosamente chiude la sua lunghissima vita. (p. 767)

> [Such clearance-work was carried out by Futurism at such a high temperature that the whole package of measures to carry it out constituted by itself a noteworthy work of art: it was the last and most striking expression of romanticism, which burns itself out in it and gloriously ends its lengthy life.]

In this section of *L'avventura novecentista*, written in the late twenties, Bontempelli objected to the Futurists' paradoxical concern with ultra-subjectivity. They had merely replaced one time-limited lyricism with another. This verdict might have surprised Marinetti, who believed that he had heralded an age liberated from the limitations of the human ego. But already the cruel depiction of Marinetti's cloying, self-satisfied bourgeois décor of the apartment in corso Venezia in 'Mio zio non era futurista' shows that doubts about the newness of Futurism were surfacing as early as 1919. Bontempelli also objected to the Futurists' concern with form and fashion, to the detriment of the universal and timeless, the mythical. Behind the specific distancing from Futurism, Bontempelli can be seen to be employing exactly the same kind of critique he has advanced against D'Annunzianesimo. But the objections Bontempelli raised were those of a son towards his father:

> Se dovessimo contrapporci con violenza a qualche attuazione o atteggiamento futurista, lo faremmo per quella necessaria ed eroica ingratitudine e ribellione che i figli debbono avere verso i padri per non morire in loro. (p. 767)

> [If we had to violently oppose any Futurist achievement or attitude, we would do it for that necessary and heroic ingratitude and rebellion which children owe their parents, so as not to die with them.]

The pattern of uncle and nephew, employed as a metaphor for cultural succession and *Bildung* in 'Mio zio non era futurista' thus anticipates uncannily the Freudian, proto-Harold Bloomian relationship outlined in *L'avventura novecentista*. Yet again, we can see that Bontempelli's fictional and critical writings were part of a seamless project of autobiographical commentary on cultural succession. D'Annunzio and Marinetti (and Pirandello and Verga, too) were not just figures in their own right. They were stations of the cross in Bontempelli's own eventful literary iter, a complex and paradoxical one which he felt could stand, in its doubts and denunciations, for a whole generation.

Marinetti died in 1944, at a time unsuited to official commemorations, but it is fairly clear that if Bontempelli had indeed been minded (and permitted) to provide a valedictory, he would have consigned the Futurist to the same parking lot of literary development as D'Annunzio. Both writers had tried to hitch a ride on the wagon of history, and both found themselves left behind by it. Neither had been able to transcend the referentiality of their own making: they had tied themselves to their times. Ironically, the same fate was to befall Bontempelli himself, and the catalyst for all three eclipses was the Great War which had sucked them all into its maws as all too willing poet-volunteers.

Notes to Chapter 8

1. The passage can be found in Carlo Emilio Gadda, *Romanzi e racconti*, ed. by R. Rodondi, G. Lucchini and E. Manzotti, 2 vols (Milan: Garzanti, 1988), I, 589–91.
2. For a brief account of Gadda's *dannunzianesimo*, see the excellent entry by Antonio Zollini in the online *Pocket Gadda Encyclopedia*, ed. by F. G. Pedriali, in *The Edinburgh Journal of Gadda Studies* (www.arts.ed.ac.uk/gadda), 2 (2002), supplement 1.
3. T. Antongini, *Vita segreta di Gabriele D'Annunzio* (Milan: Mondadori, 1938).
4. A photograph of the epic encounter can be found reproduced in E. Cecchi and N. Sapegno, *Storia della letteratura italiana*, 9 vols (Milan: Garzanti, 1987), IX.2: *Il novecento*, 357.
5. A photograph of Mussolini attending the funeral is reproduced in *Gabriele D'Annunzio: Volti e maschere di un personaggio*, ed. by S. Costa (Florence: Sansoni, 1988), p. 200.
6. In the *Illustrazione italiana* for the 4th December 1938, there is a photograph bearing the caption: 'S.E. Massimo Bontempelli, Accademico d'Italia, commemora Gabriele D'Annunzio alla presenza delle L.L. E.E. Bottai, Solmi, ed Host-Venturi al Palazzo Civico di Pescara' [His Excellency Massimo Bontempelli, Member of the Italian Academy, commemorates Gabriele D'Annunzio in the presence of Fascist leaders Bottai, Solmi, and Host-Venturi at the Palazzo Civico in Pescara].
7. The speech can be found in M. Bontempelli, *Opere scelte*, ed. by L. Baldacci (Milan: Mondadori, 1978), pp. 861–93. All subsequent page numbers from Bontempelli's writings, unless otherwise indicated, refer to this volume.
8. This corresponded closely to Bontempelli's own position: 'Uscito in pieno dal costume romantico, vogliamo che il nostro poeta (di qualunque arte, e vi comprendo pure il filosofo) anche nel modo e nel contegno materiale del suo lavoro abbandoni l'attitudine di tempestosa semidivinità che ci aveva insegnata certa poetica romantica del genio. Se uno è genio, non lo possono sapere che i posteri. Da vivo nessuno ha il diritto di pensare d'essere un genio. Sia dunque egli, come tutti gli uomini devono essere, un lavoratore; e il suo non un fuoreggiare invasato, ma un lavorare quotidiano, intenso e modesto. L'arte è un mestiere col quale si raggiunge talvolta (ma sempre senza esserne certi) la poesia. Un racconto una sinfonia una statua un quadro una piazza, non meno che gli oggetti del gusto e dell'utile quotidiano che escono dalla bottega dell'artigiano. Le Opere' [We want today's artist (in whatever art, including philosophy) to cast aside Romanticism totally and to abandon, also in his style and material approach, the attitude of stormy semi-divinity that a certain kind of Romantic poetics of genius had taught us. If someone is a genius, only posterity can know. While alive, nobody has the right

to think he is a genius. Let our artist then be, as all men must be, a worker; and his behaviour not the actions of someone possessed, but a daily shift of work that is intense and modest. Being an artist is a job through which one sometimes reaches (but always without being certain) the heights of poetry: a story, a symphony, a statue, a painting, a piazza, but equally the objects of everyday taste and usage that emerge from the artisan's workshop. Works]. See M. Bontempelli, *Il bianco e il nero*, ed. by S. Cigliana (Naples: Guida, 1987), p. 118. The entries in this 'inventario' (probably conceived as a companion to Savinio's 'encyclopaedia') are difficult to date, but some of them may go back to the early 1940s.

9. Bontempelli claims, rather disingenuously, that his membership of the Fascist Party was not a sign of political conviction but a mere 'anagrafe' [official act of registry] (see the entry 'Confessione' in *Il bianco e il nero*, pp. 58–59, which also provides an attempted slant on the supposedly Fascist sympathies of the members of the R. Accademia d'Italia).

10. On 5 May 1915, D'Annunzio used the occasion of the inauguration of a monument to the embarkation of Garibaldi's One Thousand at Quarto to launch an impassioned plea for Italy's entry into the hostilities. Cardarelli would later describe the inflammatory appeal to patriotism at Quarto as 'quello scherzo letterario con cui l'Italia entrò in guerra' [that literary joke whereby Italy entered the war]: Vincenzo Cardarelli, *Opere complete* (Milan: Mondadori, 1962), pp. 605–06.

11. In *Il bianco e il nero*, p. 83, Bontempelli records gnomically: 'GENIO. Non si nega che il genio possa farsi eslege: ma deve assumersene la responsabilità' [GENIUS. It cannot be denied that the genius can become an outlaw: but he has to take responsibility for it]. In this semi-Nietzschian statement, he is almost certainly thinking about D'Annunzio.

12. The introduction can be found reprinted in M. Bontempelli, *Introduzioni e discorsi* (Milan: Bompiani, 1945), p. 277

13. D'Annunzio played on the Latinisation of his name, NUNCIUS, as can be seen in his printed *ex libris*.

14. *Polemica carducciana*, ed. by E. Romagnoli (Florence: Quattrini, 1911), p. 124.

15. See F. T. Marinetti, *Teoria e invenzione fascista*, ed. by L. De Maria (Milan: Mondadori, 1983), p. 304.

16. F. T. Marinetti, in *Futurismo e fascismo* (1924), places both Bottai and Bontempelli amongst the Futurists absorbed into Fascism as a result of *Roma futurista*: see F. T. Marinetti, *Teoria e invenzione futurista*, p. 495.

17. A representative selection from the collection, first published as a volume in 1938 by Vallecchi, can be found in M. Bontempelli, *Opere scelte*, pp. 749–803.

18. For Bontempelli's problems in establishing a chronological canon of Italian literature, see the entry 'superstiti' in *Il bianco e il nero*, pp. 167–69. D'Annunzio has to share an anthological mention with Carducci and Pascoli, whereas Pirandello has to give up his position to... Alfredo Panzini.

19. Malaparte's article appeared in *La fiera letteraria*, 30 October, 1927. On the cultural context of Bontempelli's attitude to 'strapaese' and 'stracittà' positions, see L. Mangoni, *L'interventismo della cultura: Intellettuali e riviste del fascismo* (Bari: Laterza, 1974).

20. Vittorini's article appeared in *L'Italia letteraria*, 41 (1929). A section of it is reproduced as 'Maestri cercando' in his *Diario in pubblico* (Milan: Bompiani, 1957), pp. 9–11.

21. In M. Bontempelli, *Primi racconti* (Milan: Mondadori, 1934), pp. 29–36.

22. Ibid., pp. 74–83.

23. A cross between Greek theatre and Ibsen was exactly what Eleonora Duse had asked D'Annunzio to write for her.

24. This theme is analysed *passim* in F. Airoldi Namer, *Massimo Bontempelli* (Milan: Mursia, 1979).

25. In *Miracoli: La donna dei miei sogni e altre storie d'oggi*. See Bontempelli, *Racconti e romanzi*, ed. by Paolo Masino, 2 vols (Milan: Mondadori, 1961), I, 714–21.

26. Given that Pirandello's *Sei personaggi in cerca di autore*, in which there is a projection of the author figure, was first performed in 1921, it is legitimate to speculate whether Bontempelli's extension of the earlier Pirandello's granting of autonomy to characters to the doubling of the author wasn't a contributing element in the construction of that play.

27. '[Il] tumultuare ariostesco del pianoforte su cui Savinio aveva attaccato il primo atto di *Perseo*'

[the Ariostesque thundering on the piano with which Savinio had started the first act of *Perseo*] (*Opere scelte*, p. 142). Unless Savinio is one of the many unnamed characters (who play important catalytic roles in Bontempelli's fiction), his appearance in the 'Romanzo dei romanzi' is otherwise unexplained. He may indeed be one of the anonymous figures from the musically-themed sixth novel of *La vita intensa*. However, the reference to the first act of the *Perseo* is genuinely topical. The score, composed in Paris just before the war, had recently been revived in an impressive piano reduction by Savinio which had been performed at the Milan conservatoire in 1919 to great critical acclaim. Bontempelli, who was a composer and accomplished pianist himself, was an ardent admirer.

28. He appears in the second novel of *La vita intensa*, in the ninth chapter 'Il portinaio della vera Italia'.
29. See paragraph six of the *Manifesto tecnico* (1912): 'Abolire anche la punteggiatura. Essendo soppressi gli aggettivi, gli avverbi e le congiunzioni, la punteggiatura è naturalmente annullata, nella continuità varia di uno stile *vivo* che si crea da sé, senza le soste assurde delle virgole e dei punti' [Abolish punctuation as well. Having suppressed all adjectives, adverbs and conjunctions, punctuation is naturally eliminated in the variegated continuity of a *living* style which creates itself, without the absurd pauses of commas and full stops]. The text can be found in F. T. Marinetti, *Teoria e invenzione futurista*, p. 47. Needless to say, the declaration by Marinetti above suffers from absurd pauses, containing as it does both adjectives and adverbs and the offending commas and full-stops.
30. The later, ex-Futurist Bontempelli had some dismissive things to say about dynamism: on 'dinamico' and 'dinamismo', see *Il bianco e il nero*, p. 69. *Valori plastici* was the title of an avant-garde art review published by Mario Broglio from 1918 to 1922.
31. The library is modelled on that of Leopardi's father, Monaldo, at Recanati.
32. E. Falqui, *Novecento letterario* (Florence: Vallecchi, 1960), p. 374.
33. L. Baldacci, *Massimo Bontempelli* (Turin: Borla, 1967), p. 19, n. 4
34. The passage is quoted in F. Airoldi Namer, *Massimo Bontempelli*, p. 26, n. 4.
35. Bontempelli is probably taking a dig at Gian Pietro Lucini's bold para-Futurist critique *Antidannunziana* (1914).
36. The real identity of the author was eventually established by Alfredo Panzini, who named him as the Milanese schoolteacher Luigi Sailer.
37. *Polemica carducciana*, pp. 202–05. A long extract of Bontempelli's Crocean spoof can be found in F. Tempesti, *Bontempelli* (Florence: La Nuova Italia, 1974), pp. 8–10.
38. The work is not in Trilussa's *Opere*, ed. by P. Pancrazi, (Milan: Mondadori, 1951), but can be found on the net at http://www.associazioneimmagine.it/curiosita/cur-001.htm. It is not impossible that Bontempelli's subsequently reprised the now Trilussian Teresa-figure as the malodorous 'tabaccaia' in the fourth story of *La vita intensa*, 'Il dramma del 31 aprile: Ovvero delitto e castigo'.
39. *Polemica carducciana*.
40. *Polemica carducciana*, p. 124.
41. The painting is reproduced in *Storia della letteratura italiana*, ed. by E. Malato (Rome: Salerno, 1999), vol. 8, p. 388, plate 16.
42. Features which make him curiously like the commonest photographs of Carducci, whose luxuriant locks and beard, white with age, look blond in the black and white plates.
43. The passage can be found in F. T. Marinetti, *Teoria e invenzione futurista*, pp. 12–13.
44. In the epilogue to his *Storia d'Europa* (Bari: Laterza, 1932).
45. Papini's bloodthirsty article 'Amiamo la guerra' in the October number of *Lacerba* is typical of this current. It is reproduced in G. Getto and G. Solari, *Il novecento* (Bergamo: Minerva italica, 1982), pp. 181–86.

CHAPTER 9

❖

Italian War-Correspondents and The Spanish Civil War: Propaganda and Autobiography

Charles Burdett

Between 1937 and 1939 the Spanish Civil War became, for months at a time, the dominant subject of Italian national daily newspapers — even relegating the chronicling of the colonization of Mussolini's newly acquired African Empire to a secondary position. Leading Italian newspapers sent their most seasoned reporters to cover the development of hostilities and the stages of Italian military participation. The *Corriere della sera* initially sent Achille Benedetti, Renzo Segala and Cesco Tomaselli. From 1937 Guido Piovene reported from Spain accompanied by Mario Massai. Piovene's stay in Spain was to last until December 1938 and to prove a formative experience in a prolific literary and journalistic career. Massai remained in Spain until the fall of Madrid, piloting his own plane and covering the aerial operations of the war. As the Republic began to slide towards defeat in early 1939, the *Corriere* dispatched Virgilio Lilli and Ciro Poggiali to follow the concluding chapter.[1] *La Stampa* sent Riccardo Forte, Giovanni Artieri and Sandro Sandri to Spain, while Curio Mortari wrote from France on the trail of supplies sent by the democratic powers to the beleaguered Republic. Lamberto Sorrentino, a veteran of the First World War, Fiume and the Ethiopian campaign, wrote on the war for *La Gazzetta del Popolo*. Luigi Barzini, with a highly distinguished career as a foreign correspondent stretching back to the beginning of the century and involving such famous episodes as his car journey from Peking to Paris (1906), wrote on the war for *Il Popolo d'Italia*.[2] Gian Gaspare Napolitano acted as the war correspondent for Leo Longanesi's *Omnibus* while from the offices of *El Norte de Castilla* in Valladolid, Stanis Ruinas worked as the editor of *Il Legionario* — the paper for the Italian combatants in Spain or rather the vehicle through which the Italian expeditionary force was subjected to the propaganda of the regime.[3] Other journalists entrusted with giving Fascist Italy's view of the war and who all published books on either the war's origins or its progress included Concetto Pettinato, Nello Quilici and Alessandro Volta.[4] Though the reporters sent by all Italian dailies were men, in February 1939 the *Corriere* printed one of the few accounts of the war written by Italian women. In three extended articles, Luigi Barzini's daughter, Emma, published a detailed description of the time that she and her husband had been compelled to spend in Republican Spain.[5]

Franco was certainly conscious of the importance of securing sympathetic coverage in the foreign press and, as Glauco Licata has documented in his history of the *Corriere della sera*, each foreign journalist was provided, where necessary, with a car, an interpreter and a Falangist escort. In the early stages of the war, Italian journalists would send as a rule one telegram a day to their respective newspapers while photographs could be sent by air from Seville. The situation was made easier from the end of January 1938 when Italian newspapers could use as their base St Jean de Luz in France.[6] From the details contained in many of the dispatches sent from Spain and particularly in the collections of articles that several journalists subsequently published, it is possible to gain a sense of the daily life of the war correspondent and especially the close contact with Italian troops.[7] The groups of reporters tended to be based in the same towns (Salamanca when reporting from the Aragon front, Talavera when following offensives against Madrid) and to stay in the same hotels. Virgilio Lilli describes in some detail the life of a reporter in the Grand Hotel at Zaragoza requisitioned by Italian and Nationalist forces close to the Aragon front.[8] At times of relative calm in the fighting the various correspondents would travel daily to the front although they all referred to the difficulty of finding transport either during a successful Nationalist offensive or when needing to travel rapidly to Saint Jean de Luz.[9] Correspondents from different newspapers tended to associate together and to travel in the company of other foreign observers such as *The Daily Telegraph*'s Pernbrook Stephens or W. P. Carney of the *New York Times*.[10] In many of the photographs reproduced in Renzo Segala's collection of articles groups of Italian correspondents are seen posing for the camera against the backdrop of a deserted or newly 'liberated' Spanish town.[11]

The itinerary that Italian journalists followed through Spain was dictated by the nature of the regime's interest in the conflict and by the deployment of the Italian expeditionary army. Shortly after the outbreak of the Civil War the Italian press was ordered to restrict coverage to simple news stories.[12] Unsurprisingly, no mention was made of Italian planes being dispatched to ferry Franco's troops from Spanish Morocco to the mainland. The decision to send combat troops to the aid of Franco was reached gradually and it was not until December 1936 that massive numbers of Italian soldiers began to arrive in Cadiz.[13] Italian intervention in Spain was motivated not only by the fear that a victory of liberalism or Communism in Spain might encourage dissent at home or by the perception of the need to secure the western side of the Mediterranean.[14] One of the most important factors in deciding large-scale military commitment was a desire for the prestige of Fascism to be enhanced both at home and abroad through a series of spectacular victories in Spain. Italian troops were organized as a separate corps to be used in decisive military operations and the friction between Franco and Mussolini derived largely from the latter's desire for offensive action when the Nationalist command was in favour of the consolidation of territory.

Any study of the articles written by Italian journalists from within Nationalist Spain together with the often terse bulletins from the front or the collected writings of Italy's war correspondents is unlikely to reveal the complexity of human experience which writers such as Hemingway or Orwell, or photographers like Robert Capa or David Seymour, were able to capture from the opposing side. Yet, this type of writing does expose the nature of the exploitation of the Civil War within the official culture of the late 1930s — with its facile reduction of the ideological complexities of the time to the certainty of a struggle between good and evil, its exaltation of military prowess and its insistence on maintaining a triumphalist tone.[15] At the same time, it provides some indication of how elements of introspection and autobiography are threaded into a genre of writing whose primary function was propagandistic. As Sciascia wrote in his commentary on the articles of Virgilio Lilli, all reporters had in some sense to confront, amidst the extremities of the situation, aspects of their own beliefs — the meaning of their Catholic faith, the depth of their allegiance to Fascism, or their feelings towards people, fragments of whose lives they witnessed.[16] In what follows I want to examine how in representing the Republican enemy, the morale of the Italian troops and the march towards victory, the journalists from Italy's official newspapers betrayed both deep-seated attitudes as well as allegiances that were to prove transitory. I wish to conclude with some speculation on how the correspondence from the front might have been read and how a few of its authors looked back on the pressures that acted upon its composition.

In the preface to his book, Lamberto Sorrentino referred to the Spanish Civil War as the 'most complex war of religion that humanity has ever seen'.[17] The allegorical interpretation of the war as a struggle between competing religions was necessarily substantiated by the idea that Italian troops in Spain were aiding the Nationalists in a struggle against Communism. The main thesis of Francesco Belforte's text on the Civil War was that Italian intervention was in response to the massive interventionist programmes of France and Russia and to save Spain from the hell of Bolshevik revolution.[18] The notion that everything in Spain pointed to an imminent Communist take-over was one that the corps of journalists rarely tired of repeating and one of the most frequently deployed strategies for denigrating Republican Spain was to present it as merely a puppet in the hands of Bolshevik masters.[19] Those Spaniards who remained loyal to the government were either the servants of a non-European ideology or the agents of a foreign power. The repetition of the idea that the Republic was merely a 'colony of Moscow' or the magnet for social agitators from around the globe may not have reflected the nature of the government in Madrid at the time of the revolt or indeed the conflict between legitimacy and revolution that lay at the heart of Republican resistance.[20] It did, however, facilitate the presentation of the enemy along the lines of a sinister, orientalizing fantasy. In accounts of the war the Communist enemy was evoked not only as a threat but also as an object of disgust. The metaphor of a disease spreading across Spain was one that was often used: Communism was seen as an Asiatic virus or the 'red plague', its adherents were portrayed as refuse.[21]

The supporters of the Republic were defined as guilty of pretty criminality, extreme cruelty and senseless violence while remaining essentially inscrutable. Nello Quilici maintained that the insurrections, killings and burnings that, in his view, characterized Republican Spain, reflected the 'obsession with violence' of Russian Bolshevism.[22] Most Italian journalists provided lurid details of the violent suppression of resistance on the other side of the front.[23] In the three articles she published as a captive in the 'inferno of Communist Spain', Emma Barzini gave an account of the Republic seen through the eyes of an unequivocal supporter of the Nationalist uprising. In Madrid she witnessed the population of the capital being terrorized by squads of militiamen, the killing of suspected sympathizers of Franco and the spectacle of women and children going to see the victims of such purges.[24] In Barcelona she insisted on the contrast between the wealth of government officials and the dire poverty of the city's ordinary inhabitants.[25] When Barcelona fell on 26 January 1939, the iniquities (both real and imagined) perpetuated in the 'Marxist capital' were documented by all Italian correspondents.

The description of food shortages, strife between opposing political factions (the riots in Barcelona in May 1937 received wide coverage in Italy), daily sequestrations and killings were intended to play on basic fears and, like all propaganda, to influence contemporary opinion. But the correspondents for Italy's major newspapers concentrated also on painting a picture of the destruction to the country's urban landscape, social fabric and religious institutions that they believed was the legacy of the Republic. The apocalyptic vision of the end of civilization or the triumph of evil was achieved through a variety of strategies. As the war correspondents followed the Nationalist advance first in Andalusia and the Basque region and subsequently into Catalonia, they gave an account of the destruction left in the wake of the Republican retreat that was not lacking in literary or historical parallels. On the fall of Malaga, Benedetti evoked the condition of the city's population by calling to mind Manzoni's descriptions of Milan during the plague.[26] When attributing the devastation in Guernica to the 'reds', Segala asserted that they had in razing the town to the ground shown the same savagery as marauding medieval armies.[27] Images of violence perpetrated against the institutions of the Catholic Church were fully exploited by the Italian press. The desecration of religious icons was, in the view of Piovene, not only proof of the godless materialism of the Republicans; it provided a further indication of their essential sadism. Reporting from Vitoria on the damage done to the artistic heritage of northern Spain, he suggested that the 'cemeteries of mutilated statues' reflected a desire not so much to destroy venerated artefacts as to inflict physical torture.[28] The same emphasis on the brutality displayed towards objects of worship is to be found in one of the most resolutely Christian interpretations of the war, Lilli's *Racconti di una guerra* (1941).

It was not only the ruins of buildings and churches but the cost in human life that many of the correspondents found staggering. Every reporter sent to Spain was confronted both with the unexpected extent of the carnage and the problem of representing either through words or images the after-effects of the ferocious battles of the Civil War or the reprisals of both sides. In a kind of postscript to *Racconti di una guerra*, Lilli reflected on the inability of his photographs of the war's dead to convey an adequate sense of the experience of following the front (p. 167). On returning to Rome after having covered the war in the north for ten months, Sorrentino maintained that he and his fellow journalists had grown used to seeing piles of men who had been 'shot down like human ribbons' (*Questa Spagna* (1939), p. 235) but that the stench of death had proved overpowering and something against which no one could become inured (p. 176). In his view, Spain had become an inferno or a 'terra di morte' [land of death] and for the average Spaniard life was simply 'un modo polemico di essere di fronte alla morte' [a polemical way of existing faced with death].[29] Similarly for Piovene the scale of the killing was such that it was possible to give an idea of the reality of Spain only through metaphor: to come to Spain was, to paraphrase his words, to enter a tragedy where individual protagonists disappeared against a 'magnificently bloody backcloth'.[30] Perhaps the most revealing moments in the contemporary accounts of the war are those instances where the writer observes the aftermath of violence: it was then that individual journalists betrayed the degree to which they had succeeded in dehumanizing the enemies of Fascism.

Of all the correspondents working in Spain, Alessandro Volta was the most confident in his belief that the opposing side conformed entirely to the negative stereotype created by Nationalist propaganda. His text on the Civil War, *Spagna a ferro e fuoco* (1937), obeyed a simple narrative structure. On the one hand, it represented, through writing supported by a series of closely related photographs evidence of atrocities committed by both Anarchists and Communists in central and southern Spain. On the other hand, it documented the violent revenge that was, in the author's opinion, justly wreaked on the 'bestial Marxist rabble'.[31] Volta was certainly not alone in documenting the details of punishment meted out against supposed subversives. While Koestler's *Spanish Testament* (1937) had been written in the shadow of the shootings in Seville's model prison, many Italian journalists referred to the invitation to witness the execution of prisoners.[32] Ruinas described seeing the shooting of two Anarchists from Asturias in the courtyard in the prison of Seville and reflected on the stoicism and defiance they showed at the moment of their deaths.[33] Unlike Ruinas, Volta displayed little interest in the individuality of captured prisoners and his representation of summary killings excluded any sense of compassion. The text presented the action of rebel firing squads as necessary and sanctioned by the highest order: to witness the killing of prisoners was to see justice at work and order being restored. In the small town of Montoro, close to Malaga on the Andalusian front, Volta described the following scene:

> Otto miliziani cecoslovacchi [...] furono immediatamente portati sulla piazza e allineati davanti al plotone di esecuzione: 'Un giorno l'Europa sarà grata alla Spagna di averla liberata dai rifiuti sociali affluiti qui dai bassofondi di tutti i paesi', mi disse il cappellano militare quando giustizia fu fatta. Su quella stessa piazza, segnata ancora da una vastissima pozza di sangue, fu celebrata a mezzogiorno la messa di Natale. (Volta, *Spagna a ferro e fuoco*, p. 213)

> [Eight Czech militiamen (...) were immediately brought to the square and lined up in front of the firing squad. When justice had been done, the military chaplain told me: 'One day Europe will be grateful to Spain for having liberated it from the social refuse that have come here from the slums of every country.' In the same square, still marked by an enormous lake of blood, at midday, the Christmas Mass was celebrated.]

Other correspondents, while never questioning the objectives of the war on Communism, rarely represented the dead of the opposing side with the same absolute lack of humanity. Writing for the *Corriere* both Lilli and Piovene showed some interest in the life stories of the troops opposing the Nationalist advance into Aragon and Catalonia. Both described in detail the boy soldiers sent to the front and both sought to gain a sense of the lives of the Republican dead by reading letters found in the squalor of deserted trenches.[34] In one of the most carefully constructed of his 'stories', Lilli described travelling towards the front and discovering a wallet belonging to a British member of the International Brigades. From its contents (a photograph of its owner, his wife and children, a driving licence, the receipt for a piano) he attempted to recreate the life story of Frank J. Th. from Liverpool (*Racconti*, pp. 117–18). He speculated on his identity as husband and father, suggesting that: 'Non era un soldato caduto, non era un miliziano abbattuto, non era un nemico' [He was not a fallen soldier or a dead militiaman, he was not an enemy]. The 'story' ends as Lilli comes face to face with the corpse of the militiaman and returns the wallet, in an act of *pietas*, to its owner.

In the course of following the progress of the war on its different fronts all Italian journalists made lengthy journeys through the regions of Nationalist Spain. As they did so they wrote on the components of Franco's army and gave some perception of life immediately behind the front line. Segala, for example, gave a long description of the fighting qualities of the army of Africa while Volta and Sandri wrote in detail on the mentality of the staunchly Catholic *Requetés*.[35] Covering the assault on Catalonia, Piovene evoked the atmosphere among soldiers' relatives in Zaragoza while many of Lilli's reports from Spain, written quite self-consciously as stories, focused on the war's casualties.[36] 'Vengono dal fronte' [They're Coming from the Front] (*Racconti*, pp. 27–31), one of the most effective examples of the 'corrispondenza-racconto' [article in the form of a short story] describes a car journey from Pamplona to Zaragoza that is interrupted when Lilli's Spanish driver stops to help repair another car that has broken down in the pouring rain.[37] While the driver works on the engine, the narrator observes the occupants of the other car; especially the two women huddled in the back as they struggle against the freezing cold. He also observes the large trunk strapped to the roof of the car, covered with a grey tarpaulin and soaking wet. He watches as the older of the two women insists that one of the two men checks that the tarpaulin is properly strapped to the roof and is not becoming excessively soiled by the journey. Only when his driver returns to the car does the narrator realize that what he has taken for a trunk is the body of a dead soldier that his relatives are taking home, strapped to the roof of the car, for burial in Pamplona.

Descriptions of journeys through areas of the country occupied by rebel forces were not intended only to produce a picture of sacrifice and mourning; their primary function was to give an account of what was being defended by Italian intervention. By suggesting that the Nationalists were fighting in order to maintain the traditions of the past, the narrated journeys through Franco's Spain gave a sense of the reactionary nature of Mussolini's priorities. Italian journalists were ready to see the inspiration of Italian Fascism in the Falange's corporativist principles and in its regimentation of social life, but the identification with the Falange only partially concealed the contradiction of a supposedly revolutionary regime supporting a coalition of unashamedly conservative authoritarians.[38] The lack of a serious inquiry into the differences between Fascist ideology and Franco's view of Spain's future was further obscured by the emphasis in most reporting on the importance of Italian involvement. Participation in the Spanish conflict was presented both as a decisive action on the stage of world events and as the opportunity for the Fascist nation to display its essential characteristics.

As in reporting on the conquest of Ethiopia, it was the foot-soldier, defined as the legionary or volunteer, in whom journalists of the national dailies saw the clearest reflection of the qualities that the regime identified as those of the nation. In his journeys from one region of Spain to another, Ruinas was, as he did not tire of reminding his reader, engaged in a parallel search for the soul of the Italian nation. His search achieved its object when he wrote on the Italian expeditionary force. In Valladolid he visited the cemetery where the Italian legionaries were buried and was drawn to the military hospital where the casualties of Guadalajara had been taken.[39] In this 'austere building', listening to the stories of the wounded and watching the effects of radio transmissions as they were broadcast in the wards, he professed to feeling more than in any other place the nearness of the spirit of 'la Patria' (*Vecchia e nuova Spagna*, p. 145). Without being able to match the same degree of pomposity, Piovene wrote a series of articles in the spring of 1938 on the heroism of ordinary Italian soldiers, listing the values that, in his view, were represented by the *Corpo Volontari*.[40] Such values included the simplicity of the troops' devotion to the cause for which they were fighting, their indifference to hardship or personal injury and their concern for the well-being of their fellow soldiers. The values that Piovene identified were more or less the same as those Luigi Barzini extolled in his 1940 work on Italian legionaries in Spain.[41] Writing in 1938 on the conquest of Santander, Segala (*Trincee di Spagna*, p. 220) wrote of the Nation's pride in its 'magnificent soldiers' while Ruinas, describing the same event, drew a familiar parallel between the contemporary Italian presence in Spain and the example of ancient Rome.[42]

There is no reason to doubt that the majority of journalists who wrote on Spain were genuinely moved or impressed by the courage and stoicism they witnessed among Italian troops. Writing more than fifty years after the conflict, Artieri recalled the lives of soldiers he had known personally and who had been killed in action and other correspondents recorded similar feelings of grief.[43] Yet the language used by the newspapers of the time to characterize the attitude of front-line troops tended to view the individual soldier simply as the vehicle through which abstract qualities supposedly belonging to the collective found expression. Though principally the symbols of the Fascist values of aggression and obedience, the soldiers of the CTV (*Corpo Truppe Volontarie*) were, in the writing of one correspondent after another, presented as the armed defenders of the faith. In the context of photographs of *Requetés* receiving the sacrament before battle or of Spanish priests making the Fascist salute, correspondents were keen to stress that Italian intervention was part of the same crusade against Communism and that the religious devotion they witnessed among Franco's troops was shared by Italian soldiers. In the eyes of most reporters aspects of the behaviour of ordinary soldiers indicated the dual existence of Christian and Fascist beliefs. In the military hospital of Valladolid, Ruinas was struck by examples of the most hardened soldiers grasping sacred images with intense and emotional devoutness (*Vecchia e nuova Spagna*, p. 146). A more subtle and less typical elision of the cult of the military with the representation of more established system of worship is to be found in Lilli's *racconto-articolo*, 'Freccia nera' [Black Arrow] (*Racconti*, pp. 37–42). The piece describes the sight of a dead soldier (initially it is uncertain whether he is Spanish or Italian) lying by the side of the road as the front advanced towards Lleida. The soldier's corpse, left unburied from one day to another and in changing states of decomposition, serves as the subject of different representations. In death the body assumes the attributes of a marble statue (p. 39) as the writing suggests a transition from human being to symbol of military sacrifice and by so doing implies a concept of the after life of the military hero. But more explicit is the Christian notion of death and rebirth as Lilli speculates on the passage of the soldier from this world to the next and imagines a silent communication that takes place between the soldier and his God during the days that he lies unburied.[44]

If it is true that Italian correspondents in Spain represented the Civil War as a clash of religions or as the defence of civilization against barbarism, then underlying this representation was a narrative of the march of Fascism towards ultimate victory. Defeat at Guadalajara was, at least in part, the result of the haste with which the regime had set its sights on securing a dramatic end to the war that would announce to the world the irresistibility of its power. With the exception of the disaster to the north-east of Madrid, the repetition of the idea of a glorious march through Spain was a staple of reporting both in the printed media and in the newsreels of the time.[45] Reporters for the Italian dailies were employed to witness the spectacle of victory — a spectacle that obeyed its own narrative logic. The pack of correspondents would often be among the first to enter a town evacuated by the Republican retreat, they would wait for the arrival of Nationalist or Italian troops, then describe the scenes of joy as the advance guard approached. Lastly, they would report on the victory parade that inevitably followed. Describing the atmosphere in Malaga shortly before the entry of the main body of the CTV, Benedetti wrote of being mobbed by overjoyed men and women, 'come se avessi io liberato Malaga' [as if I myself had liberated Malaga].[46] When reporting on the parade of Italian soldiers through Santander, Segala wrote of the 'apotheosis' of the legionaries.[47] Celebrations and official acts of thanksgiving in Italy echoed the rhythm of one triumph after another that was more or less maintained in the Italian press. On 20 October 1938 ten thousand Italian troops returning from Cadiz disembarked at Naples where, under the eyes of the King, they paraded through the city's streets.[48] In Spain Italian reporters recorded the aftermath of victory through descriptions of towns and cities awakening from what they characterized as the nightmare of Communist rule.

The correspondence of those journalists who covered the Spanish Civil War for the Italian press was of course written under certain forms of surveillance: reports from the front were submitted to the official censor for approval and were then further scrutinized by the editorial authority of each newspaper.[49] The extent to which reporters believed in the accuracy of their interpretation of the conflict is therefore difficult to assess and can only be known partially by piecing together reflections made by the journalists themselves in the years following the collapse of Fascism and the end of the Second World War. A related question concerns that of the nature of individual writers' allegiance to the regime. Already within the apparently uniform representation of the conflict, shifting levels of personal investment, are woven into what was almost always presented simply as observation. Through occasional and for the most part inadvertent admissions, Lilli gives a sense of himself in his writing as an established member of Rome's bourgeoisie, as a Catholic and as a conservative. A sense of defending an existing order against the possibility of radical subversion pervades his writing and defines his support for Italian intervention in Spain. The relative complexity of his position contrasts with that adopted by Stanis Ruinas who, proud of his Sardinian origins and describing himself as a 'man of the people' (*Vecchia e nuova Spagna*, p. 249), rarely missed an opportunity to affirm his identity as a committed follower of Mussolini and, apparently untroubled by the support for the forces of conservativism in Spain, his view of Fascism as a working-class revolt against the standards of the middle classes.

In collections of autobiographical reflections that have appeared at different stages in the decades since the end of the Civil War a similarly wide spectrum of beliefs concerning the legitimacy of Italian action in Spain is to be found: a spectrum that reflects the fact that many journalists enjoyed lengthy and successful careers beyond 1945.[50] As late as 1995, in one of his many books of popular history, Giovanni Artieri, addressing the question to what extent the correspondents of the time had identified with the regime, suggested that for the majority little difference existed between a feeling of loyalty to the Italian state and loyalty to Fascism.[51] He also repeated, almost word for word, the interpretation of Italian intervention in Spain that had served as the mantra of the 1930s. In his view, reiterated over fifty years after the conflict, 'l'autorità dell'Ordine' [the authority of Order] had triumphed over the forces of chaos, Franco had won because he had represented the 'l'anima immortale della Spagna' [the immortal soul of Spain] and Mussolini's generous supply of arms and troops had served no other purpose than to guarantee 'la libertà del continente dal comunismo' [the freedom of Europe from communism].[52] The unshakeability of his confidence in the role that Italy had performed, and by implication his and his colleagues' reporting of the event, should be contrasted with other recorded memories where the relationship between the writing self of the past and present is far more problematic. Guido Piovene, looking back on his career at the *Corriere della sera*, referred to the necessity of writing copy the falsity of which was approved both by the editor and by the other journalists on the staff.[53] His evocation of the five months he spent as a war correspondent reporting from the Aragon front from the autumn of 1938 (*Le Furie*, pp. 213–22) focused on impressions of violence and destruction while supplying details lacking in his original reports.[54] Though the later account fell short of addressing the contradictions inherent in Italian support for Franco, it did refer unequivocally to the evident but unacknowledged purges that took place in the wake of the Nationalist advance in to the north east of Spain (*Le Furie*, p. 219) and the climate of silence that surrounded them. A feeling of having been professionally compromised by the actions of the past did erupt occasionally in the text with statements such as: 'I pochi capaci di scrivere che stavano dalla nostra parte, dopo le falsificazioni servili, si sono vergognati o hanno taciuto per far dimenticare la loro sciocchezza' [The few who were able to write on our side, after their servile falsifications, became ashamed or kept their silence so as to let their stupidity be forgotten] (*Le Furie*, pp. 213–14).

If the question of the degree to which the Italian correspondents who followed the war believed in the veracity of their own reporting is complex, then the reception of their writing among the Italian public is even more difficult to assess. Though an analysis of the Italian public's responses to war in Spain as it was reported in the national press lies well beyond the scope of this essay, Sciascia's reflections on reading the war correspondence of the time give some indication of the ways in which the writing could have been read. For Sciascia, writing in the 1980s, the recollection of the events of the Civil War was a memory of the way in which those events were relayed to a public with no knowledge that a sizeable group of Italians of differing political persuasions were ranged against the divisions of the CTV or that the Republic offered an example of popular resistance to Fascism. He wrote of reading about the battles of the Civil War himself as a boy in his late teens in Sicily, of being convinced of the objectivity of the reporting in the press and of the rightness of Franco and of Italian intervention.[55] Suggesting that most people were entirely convinced of the legitimacy of Italian support for Franco (*Ore di Spagna*, p. 53) he also described the correspondence of Virgilio Lilli, with its strongly Catholic undertones, its sense of the necessary defence of order yet its horror at the cost in human lives as nothing less than: 'testimonianza del sentire della maggior parte degli italiani di fronte alla guerra spagnola' [testimony of the feelings of the majority of Italians with regard to the war in Spain].[56] Yet, though Sciascia implied in *Ore di Spagna* that the majority of Italians were prepared to accept the simplified and, to a large extent, allegorical vision of the war as an epic struggle between the forces of civilization and those of barbarism that was transmitted through the news media of the time, he also pointed to ways in which the intended reception of the vision of a righteous crusade against the excesses of Communism could be subverted and how his own naïve experiences of reading changed over the years of war's duration. Despite the efforts of the regime to silence or minimize the defeat of its troops in March 1937, he remembered the proliferation of cautious rumours and whispers of Guadalajara (*Ore di Spagna*, p. 54). Yet, his most revealing observation did not concern the circulation of rumours in his native Sicily so much as the way in which hearsay, snippets of information gleaned from returning soldiers, observable realities like the 'conscription' of volunteers or the *podestà* informing a local family of the death of a serving soldier (p. 52) encouraged an awareness of a different kind of conflict, an awareness that could be brought to the biased reporting from the front. He wrote of the possibility of reading the reports of those correspondents who followed the war from one theatre of action to another not as they were intended to be read but *against* themselves — or to use his words 'in un certo modo' [in a certain way] (p. 52) — and of developing an interpretation of events which, though it derived from the officially sanctioned version of the war, was at odds with it.[57] The way in which autobiographical reflection was threaded into the correspondence of the journalists who followed the Nationalist advance was certainly among those sources that enabled some readers at least to discover a counter-narrative to the official representation of the Spanish Civil War.

Notes to Chapter 9

1. In her preface to the collected articles of her father, Virgilio Lilli, *Racconti di una guerra* (Palermo: Sellerio, 1988), originally published 1941, pp. 12–13, Laura Lilli makes the point that although he considered himself a foreign correspondent, he was for much of the 1930s and 1940s a war reporter, covering first Ethiopia, then Spain, then Greece and finally Russia.
2. Barzini's career as a war correspondent had involved the Russo-Japanese war 1904–1905, the conquest of Libya in 1911, and various theatres of action in the First World War. He was an early convert to Fascism. John F. Coverdale points out that Mussolini himself was keen to read the dispatches he sent from the front during the war in Spain, *Italian Intervention in the Spanish Civil War* (Princeton: Princeton University Press, 1975), p. 157.
3. *Il legionario* was founded in March 1937 by Guglielmo Danzi. Journalists working for the paper included, Buonaventura Caloro, Lamberto Sorrentino, Raffaello Patuelli, Giuseppe Valentini, Gian Gaspare Napolitano, Sandro Sandri and Mario Massai. For a history of the paper together with that of *Il Garibaldino*, the journal of Italian volunteers fighting in the International Brigades see P. Corti and A. Pizarróso, *Giornali contro: Il Legionario e Il Garibaldino, la propaganda degli Italiani nella guerra di Spagna* (Alessandria: Dell'Orso, 1993).
4. C. Pettinato, *La Spagna di Franco* (Varese-Milan: Istituto per gli Studi di Politica Internazionale, 1939); N. Quilici, *Spagna* (Rome: Istituto nazionale di cultura fascista, 1938); A. Volta, *Spagna a ferro e fuoco* (Florence: Vallecchi, 1937).
5. Emma Barzini was married to the Spanish airforce officer, Alessandro Gomez Spencer. The outbreak of the Civil War caught the two in Madrid by surprise and they were forced to spend the duration of the conflict on the Republican side of the front.
6. G. Licata, *Storia del Corriere della sera* (Milan: Rizzoli, 1976), p. 287.
7. See Lilli, *Racconti*; R. Segala, *Trincee di Spagna. Con i legionari alla difesa della civiltà* (Milan: Treves, 1938); L. Sorrentino, *Questa Spagna: Avventure di una coscienza* (Rome: Edizioni Roma, 1939).
8. Lilli, *Racconti*, p. 83.
9. Guido Piovene, *Le Furie* (Milan: Mondadori, 1975), originally published 1963, p. 218.
10. Segala, *Trincee*, p. 208.
11. Ibid., p. 112.
12. Coverdale, *Italian Intervention*, p. 264.
13. Figures for the composition of these forces are given by Coverdale, *Italian Intervention*, p. 175. By February 1937 the total number of Italian ground troops shipped to Spain had reached almost 49,000. Of these, 40% formed part of the army; the other 60% were from the Fascist militia. The soldiers fighting in Spain were organized into four purely Italian divisions that formed the Corpo Truppe Volontarie (CTV). On the actual meaning of the term 'voluntary' see Coverale, p. 183.
14. Ugo D'Andrea, 'Fascismo e communismo nel Mediterraneo', *Il Mediterraneo*, 8 (August 1938), p. 2, provides a good example of contemporary justifications for Italian intervention in Spain.
15. Discussing the reclamation projects to the south of Rome and the conquest of Ethiopia, Simonetta Falasca Zamponi has examined the ways in which the propaganda of the regime cast the progress of its domestic and foreign policy in terms of a melodramatic struggle between good and evil: see 'War and Melodrama' in her *Fascist Spectacle: the Aesthetics of Power in Mussolini's Italy* (Berkeley: University of California Press, 1997) pp. 148–82.
16. In Lilli, *Racconti*, p. 180.

17. Sorrentino, *Questa Spagna*, p. 10.
18. F. Belforte, *La guerra civile in Spagna: Gli interventi stranieri nella Spagna rossa* (Rome: Istituto per gli studi di politica internazionale, 1938). Belforte was the pseudonym of General Biondi-Mora of the Italian army historical office: see Coverdale, *Italian Intervention*, p. 246.
19. See Sorrentino, *Questa Spagna*, p. 13, p. 41; Volta, *Spagna*, p. 21, p. 52; Lilli, *Racconti*, p. 16.
20. Volta, *Spagna*, p. 24; Quilici, *Spagna*, p. 107.
21. Sorrentino, *Questa Spagna*, p. 328; F. Cremascoli, *Inferno a Barcellona* (Milan: Mondadori, 1939) pp. 35–44; S. Ruinas, *Vecchia e nuova Spagna* (Milan: Garzanti, 1940), p. 235. In the work of a number of correspondents and at the time when the race laws were being introduced in Italy, the denuniciation of 'i rossi' carried undertones of anti-Semitism. For example, Segala, *Trincee*, p. 70; Ruinas, *Vecchia e nuova Spagna*, p. 90, p. 259.
22. Quilici, *Spagna*, p. 96.
23. See, for example, Volta, *Spagna*, p. 153.
24. Emma Barzini, 'Da Madrid alla fosca prigione di Murcia', *Corriere della sera*, 16 February 1939, p. 3.
25. Emma Barzini, 'Un'italiana, sfuggita miracolosamente alla morte, racconta la sua tragica vita e le peripezie che l'hanno ricondotta a un valico dai Pirenei', *Corriere della sera*, 14 February 1939, p. 3; 'Incubo quotidiano di Barcellona', *Corriere della sera*, 17 February 1939, p. 3.
26. A. Benedetti, 'In Malaga liberata con le colonne vittoriose', *Corriere della sera*, 9 February 1937, pp. 1–2.
27. R. Segala, 'Guernica distrutta dai rossi e liberata dalle truppe di Franco', *Corriere della sera*, 30 April 1937, p. 5.
28. Guido Piovene, 'Mutilazioni d'arte e di vita', *Corriere della sera*, 27 October 1938, p. 3.
29. Sorrentino gave the following figures for the death toll in Spain: 1,200,000 in a population of 24 million (*Questa Spagna*, p. 178). In the light of such horrific figures, he and other Italian observers were often ready to speculate on Spanish attitudes towards death. Piovene wrote: 'E non è vero che i soldati spagnoli siano soldati che odiano fino alla ferocia il nemico. Soltanto guardandosi dentro sembra che stimino cosa da poca importanza il morire per se stessi e per gli altri' [It is not true that Spanish soldiers have a ferocious hatred of the enemy. It is only when they look into themselves they consider their own death and that of other people to be of little importance] ('Eroica semplicità del volontario italiano', *Corriere della sera*, 21 March 1938, p. 4).
30. Piovene, 'Gli irresistibili volontari italiani', *Corriere della sera* (2 April 1938), p. 1.
31. Volta, A., *Spagna*, p. 199. The photographs referred to are printed on the following pages of the text: p. 37, p. 53, p. 180.
32. Arthur Koestler, *Spanish Testament* (London: Gollancz, 1937).
33. Ruinas, *Vecchia e nuova Spagna*, p. 118.
34. See Lilli, *Racconti*, pp. 60–73, pp. 43–47; Piovene, 'Eroica semplicità del volontario italiano', *Corriere della sera*, 21 March 1938, p. 4.
35. Segala, *Trincee*; Volta, *Spagna*, pp. 43–65; Sandri, 'Requetès', *La Stampa*, 15 June 1937, p. 5.
36. Piovene, 'La bambola di Pilarin', *Corriere della sera*, 9 December 1938, p. 3.
37. The *racconto* was first published in the *Corriere della sera* on 6 January 1939 with the title 'Automobile con baule lungo', p. 3.
38. Pettinato, *La Spagna di Franco*, p. 75; Sorrentino, *Questa Spagna*, p. 14; Volta, *Spagna*, p. 61.
39. *Vecchia e nuova Spagna*, pp. 143–51.
40. Piovene, 'Eroica semplicità del volontario italiano'; 'Gli irresistibili volontari italiani'; 'La guerra delle caverne', *Corriere della sera*, 2 July 1938, p. 3.
41. Luigi Barzini, *Legionari di Roma in terra iberica (1936–1939)* (Milan, 1940).
42. *Vecchia e nuova Spagna*, p. 166. Repeated in many of the books on the Civil War was the notion that Italian intervention in Spain was legitimated by the earlier presence of imperial Rome. Thus the description of Spanish culture was a way of indirectly characterizing the 'spirit' of ancient Rome and following the advance of Mussolini's troops was a means of reliving an episode from the history of Rome. In the words of Ruinas: 'Tutta la civiltà spagnola è prevalentemente innestata sul tronco sempre rigoglioso della civiltà romana' [The whole of Spanish civilization is largely grafted onto the ever-green trunk of Roman civilization] (*Vecchia e nuova Spagna*, p. 197).

43. See G. Artieri, *Le guerre dimenticate di Mussolini* (Milan: Mondadori, 1995), p. 185 and also Lilli, *Racconti*, pp. 77–84.
44. The article first appeared in the *Corriere della sera* on 24 February 1939. In the preface to *Racconti*, Lilli imagines God looking down at the carnage in Spain and affirms unproblematically that He is on the side of the victors (p. 24).
45. See *Le guerre del Duce*, ed. by G. Giraudo, videocassette, vol. 5, 'La guerra di Spagna' (Bresso: Hobby and Work, 1997).
46. Benedetti, 'In Malaga liberata con le colonne vittoriose'.
47. Segala, 'Apoteosi dei legionari a Santander', *Corriere della sera*, 29 August 1937, p. 1.
48. See Coverdale, *Italian Intervention*, p. 371.
49. Licata recounts how Indro Montanelli was required to return to Italy and was struck off from the professional register of journalists for having reported that the surrender of Santander was not so much the result of the Italian offensive action as the inevitable outcome of the defenders lacking the munitions to continue to resist (*Storia del Corriere della sera*, pp. 286–87).
50. Segala, for example, was the editor of the daily *Tempo* from 1945–46 and from 1947 to 1955 the editor of the weekly *Epoca*. After the war, Lilli worked for the *Corriere* until 1973 with short spells working also for *Il Tempo*, *Il Giornale della sera* and *La stampa*: see Licata, *Storia del Corriere della sera*, p. 603, pp. 631–32.
51. Artieri, *Le guerre dimenticate*, p. 220.
52. Artieri, *Le guerre dimenticate*, pp. 220–22.
53. Piovene, *Le Furie*, pp. 39–42.
54. The later work, pp. 215–16, gives details, for example, of the atmosphere in Zaragoza behind the Nationalist front line with thousands of women, widowed by the war, living in poverty and working as prostitutes. Such information is lacking from Piovene's earlier description of Zaragoza, 'La bambola di Pilarin'.
55. Leonardo Sciascia, *Ore di Spagna* (Marina di Patti: Pungitopo editrice: 1988), p. 46.
56. See Lilli, *Racconti*, p. 181.
57. Sciascia's well known short story, 'L'Antimonio' (1958), like the later *Ore di Spagna* (with its journeys to the sites of the most ferocious battles forty years after the conflict), represents a specifically Italian memory of the Spanish Civil War in the way that it represents narratively the difficulty of understanding the dynamics of the struggle and its human tragedy, hidden as they were by the rhetorical certainties of Fascist propaganda.

PART IV

❖

Autobiographical Strains in Contemporary Italian Writing

CHAPTER 10

❖

Concessions to Autobiography in Calvino

Martin McLaughlin

The first two critical monographs on Italo Calvino were published within a year of each other, between 1967 and 1968.[1] Both Germana Pescio Bottino and John Woodhouse in preparing their volumes had written to the author requesting biographical information. Calvino replied to both scholars, but in widely differing tones and at differing lengths. His letter to Pescio Bottino, written on 9 June 1964 was curt and ironic: in four brief paragraphs amounting to less than a page, he first expresses his alarm, as until then he thought he was safe from such monographs, then his relief, since usually such publishing enterprises founder. Her request for biographical information is given short shrift:

> Dati biografici: io sono ancora di quelli che credono, con Croce, che di un autore contano solo le opere. (Quando contano, naturalmente). Perciò dati biografici non ne do, o li do falsi, o comunque cerco sempre di cambiarli da una volta all'altra. Mi chieda pure quello che vuol sapere, e Glielo dirò. *Ma non Le dirò mai la verità*, di questo può star sicura.
>
> [Biographical data: I am still one of those people who, like Croce, believe that it's an author's works that count. (If they count at all, of course.) So I don't give biographical details, or I give false ones, or always try to vary them on each occasion. By all means ask whatever you want to know, and I will tell you. *But I shall never tell you the truth*, of that you can be sure.][2]

The final paragraph rejects her request for an interview, though he is happy to meet her for the sole purpose of discouraging her from the enterprise.

The statement that an author's works are more important than any biography is repeated on several occasions by Calvino, yet when John Woodhouse wrote just under three years later with a list of 21 factual-biographical questions, Calvino painstakingly replied to all of them in a lengthy, five-page letter of 5 April 1967.[3] He gave precise answers to questions about his place of birth, his current residence, his university studies, the date of resignation from the Communist Party, etc. For further biographical information he refers the English scholar to *La strada di San Giovanni* [*The Road to San Giovanni*] (1962), and to his important autobiographical chapter in *La generazione degli anni difficili* [*The Difficult Generation*] (1962); he also sends him the longer, original version of that chapter which had initially appeared in the journal *Il Paradosso* (1960), as well as the 1964 edition of *Il sentiero dei nidi di ragno* [*The Path to the Spiders' Nests*], with the new preface, which he explains does contain autobiographical references, unlike the novel itself.[4] In short he furnishes Woodhouse with a complete bibliography of his own autobiographical writings up to that point. It is striking that he does not refer Pescio Bottino to those accounts, though all were in print when she wrote her letter.

When Woodhouse's study of the trilogy appears, Calvino responds with an enthusiastic letter written on 16 September 1968, expressing 'grande emozione' at what he considers the first genuine book on his work, since he discounts Pescio Bottino's work as a 'pasticcio senza metodo e senza idee' [mess, devoid of method and ideas] (*L*, p. 1011). As a literary Anglophile, Calvino is thrilled that this first serious study is published in England, since his own literary formation owed so much to English literature. The rest of this second letter is also worth examining. After praising particular chapters of Woodhouse's study, and giving him advice on contacting Einaudi for the annotated edition of *Il barone rampante* [*Baron in the Trees*] for Manchester University Press,[5] he is sceptical about the English scholar's other project, a comprehensive volume on Calvino's life and works, for Oxford University Press: 'Ma una *vita* su cui si possa scrivere qualcosa non mi pare proprio d'averla' [But as for a *life* about which to write, I don't really think I have one] (Calvino's italics, *L*, p. 1012); and he reiterates the view already expounded to Pescio Bottino and others that an author's life consists mainly of his works. When pushed, then, Calvino was prepared to divulge autobiographical information for the sake of accurate scholarship, but even towards scholars of whom he approved he was adamant that a biography was not a valid project.

Nevertheless, despite this and many other cautious statements warning of the irrelevance of an author's biography to an understanding of his works,[6] Calvino repeatedly wrote autobiographical pieces at curiously regular nine-year intervals, as Mario Barenghi has pointed out:[7] from the autobiographical trilogy *L'entrata in guerra* [*The Entry into War*] (1953), to the shorter pieces *La strada di San Giovanni* (1962) and *Dall'opaco* [*From the Opaque*] (1971) to the self-portrait of a committed intellectual in his first selection of essays, *Una pietra sopra* (1980).

The publication in 2000 of over 1,000 of Calvino's letters, along with the 300 or so published in 1991,[8] now allows us a more accurate assessment of the status of these and other more fictionalised autobiographical writings. For instance, it is now clear that the impulse to write about himself was connected with moments of crisis and rites of passage (indeed Calvino intended to publish a number of autobiographical pieces under the title *Passaggi obbligati*):[9] his father's death (1951), his fortieth birthday and his marriage (1963–64), and major periods of depression (1971 and 1980). Nor is it an accident that the most sustained output of autobiographical works in the mid-1970s — 'Ricordo di una battaglia', 'Autobiografia di uno spettatore', 'Eremita a Parigi' (all 1974); 'Il mio 25 aprile' (1975); 'La poubelle agréée' (1974–76) — takes place in the middle of the unparalleled period of creative crisis (1973–78) that preceded the writing of *Se una notte d'inverno un viaggiatore* [*If on a Winter's Night a Traveller*] (1979). Calvino returns to similar topics in the last year of his life: in April 1985 he writes another piece for the anniversary of the Liberation ('Tante storie che abbiamo dimenticato'); and the letters also show that in this same period he was planning to write a major autobiographical story based on his experiences of 1948–50, involving the poet Alfonso Gatto and his wife Graziana Pentich (*L*, p. 1531). Interestingly the letter which attests to this late autobiographical project is dated 18 March 1985, and we shall see that that date had a particular significance in Calvino's life.

This chapter will examine Calvino's oscillating attitude towards autobiography in both these explicit and other implicit autobiographical writings in the light of the letters, firstly considering a series of verbal portraits of his parents in some semi-fictional works, and secondly examining his accounts of the most decisive years of his life, the years of the partisan war. It will also consider Calvino's important reflections on the complex relationship between lived experience, the process of remembering, and writing, and suggest a roughly decennial recurrence of works concerned with his time in the Resistance.

Calvino's most explicitly autobiographical work was the brief trilogy, *L'entrata in guerra*, published in 1954, but the precise dates of composition of the three tales help to determine some of the motivation behind them: the first story to be written, 'Gli avanguardisti a Mentone' [A Trip to Mentone], was composed between 25 November 1952 and 18 January 1953. Calvino's father had died on 25 October 1951, so what ultimately became an autobiographical trilogy about a young man's entry into war began as a homage to his recently dead father, exactly one month after the first anniversary of his death.

However, before dealing with this realist trilogy, it is worth recalling that Calvino had already portrayed his father, while he was still alive, in a strikingly large number of fictional tales. His first three post-war stories, all written in 1945, were initially published in *Ultimo viene il corvo* [*The Crow Comes Last*] (1949), but he later felt uneasy about them because of their 'emotive' qualities: so much so that he cut them from his collected *Racconti* (1958), and from the 1969 edition of *Ultimo viene il corvo*.[10] In the first of these tales, 'La stessa cosa del sangue' ['In the Blood'], there are a number of autobiographical elements including an allusion to the fact that because their two sons had refused to enrol in the army of Mussolini's Fascist republic of Salò, Calvino's parents had been taken hostage by the Germans who had pretended to shoot the father three times in front of the mother. This detail surfaces at the start of the story when the younger brother is told: 'L'esse esse ha arrestato tua madre. Tuo padre è sceso per vedere se la liberano' [The SS have arrested your mother. Your father has gone to see if they'll release her] (*RR*, I, 222). There is also one of the author's first self-portraits in fiction, when the older brother is described as always having a book in his hand, being rather absent-minded, like someone from another planet, and maybe not even able to load a pistol (*RR*, I, 224). And there is a mention of the parents' bravery when arrested, since the father is described as feigning illness to try to have the mother released, and she, although being held as a hostage, was still sending messages warning her sons to be careful and not to worry about her (*RR*, I, 226). It was presumably because the story offered a portrait of the whole Calvino family and the traumatic experiences they had undergone in the war that the author felt uneasy about it. Nevertheless, many other portraits of his father are to be found in his early tales.

In the second of these 1945 stories, 'Attesa della morte in un albergo' ['Waiting for Death in a Hotel'], we find the first brief description of his father, as Claudio Milanini has convincingly shown.[11] The protagonist of this tale, like Calvino himself, had been caught by the Germans, put into the Santa Tecla prison at San Remo harbour, then transferred to a hotel which was being used as a bigger prison, before managing to escape when the prisoners were in transit to the Marassi prison in Genoa. He remembers that while he was in the cramped harbour prison, amongst the inmates was 'Un vecchio con la barba bianca, vestito da cacciatore, padre d'uno di loro' [An old man with a white beard, dressed in hunting clothes, father of one of the prisoners] (RR, I, 229–30). Calvino's father had always seemed old to him, having been born in 1875 (hence nearly sixty when Italo was born), and he had been a passionate hunter: these two elements, the white goatee beard and the hunting jacket, become leitmotifs in a strikingly regular series of paternal descriptions. In the third story, 'Angoscia in caserma' ['Anguish in the Barracks'], we find similar allusions to a father held prisoner (RR, I, 243), though there is no physical description of him here. What we do find is another autobiographical motif that will surface several times in later evocations of the partisan war: the fact that Calvino's role in an attack on the hilltop town of Baiardo was to carry the heavy munitions box that chafed at his shoulder (RR, I, 240).[12] As Milanini has pointed out, often in Calvino this kind of third-person autobiography is more detailed and revealing than first–person accounts.[13]

Paternal portraits also surface in five other early tales which Calvino clearly felt happier about, since these did appear in the 1958 *Racconti*. Here they were grouped together as the first part of a separate section entitled 'Le memorie difficili' ['Difficult Memories']; the second part of the section was occupied by the more explicitly autobiographical trilogy *L'entrata in guerra*, thus suggesting that the link between these 'difficult memories' is that of autobiography. In the earliest of the five tales, 'Uomo nei gerbidi' ['Man in Wasteland'], first published in June 1946, the first-person narrator describes his father going out hunting as having his chest and back swathed in boots, capes, hunting jacket, satchels, water-cans, and cartridge-holders, 'in the midst of which sprouted a white goatee beard' (RR, I, 186). Here the bare descriptions of the earlier stories (white goatee and hunting jacket) are enriched with a list of the many other hunting items his father would put on for these expeditions.[14] In 'I fratelli Bagnasco' ['The Bagnasco Brothers'], first published September 1946, no father figure is present but one of the two brothers dons a similar array of hunting gear.[15] In 'L'occhio del padrone' ['The Master's Eye'], first published March 1947, the anger of the hard-working father at his lazy son is channelled into his dragging out sacks of fertilizer for the fields, while the son is consumed with remorse when he returns from the cities he prefers to be in (RR, I, 192–93). Both motifs will surface elsewhere, notably in the most substantial autobiographical tale he ever wrote, *La strada di San Giovanni* (1962). The following year we find another paternal description in 'I figli poltroni' ['The Lazy Sons'], first published in January 1948. Here again he is described as fussing around with fertilizers, pesticides and seeds (*RR*, I, 200), but the picture is enriched by two further leitmotifs: the sound of his metal-tipped boots, as he stamps through the house roaring at his lazy sons to get up, and his morning expectorations of catarrh as he makes his way along the lane to their land up the valley (*RR*, I, 198–200). Interestingly there is also in this story the first, contrasting, portrait of Calvino's taciturn mother: 'Mia madre non fa rumore ma è già in piedi anche lei in quella grande cucina' [My mother makes no noise but she too is already up and about in that big kitchen], and this motif of her silence is emphasized on two other occasions in this first brief maternal portrait (*RR*, I, 198). There will be fewer portraits of Calvino's mother, but they will be significant.

The last fictional story in 'Le memorie difficili' is 'Pranzo con un pastore' ['A Goatherd at Luncheon'], published in September 1948. In this tale of the awkward lunch in the bourgeois house to which the father has invited a shepherd, we find a first physical description of the mother: 'Entrò mia madre, alta e vestita di nero, coi bordi di pizzo e la scriminatura impassibile tra i capelli bianchi e lisci' [Now my mother came in, tall, dressed in black with lace trimmings, her smooth white hair rigidly parted].[16] The austere woman is just as she appears in photographs,[17] and she also resurfaces in caricature form as Cosimo's mother, the Generalessa, in *Il barone rampante* [*Baron in the Trees*] (1957). What strikes one about these family portraits in Calvino's early post-war short stories is firstly the annual regularity with which the father figure recurs, and the consistency of his elderly, irascible character; less frequent but equally striking are mentions of the taciturn severity of the mother, and the self-portrait of the lazy, intellectual son filled with remorse at preferring the city to his father's agronomist passions.

The final fictional portraits of Calvino's father before his death occur in *Il visconte dimezzato* [*The Cloven Viscount*]. Both parents are visible in the Huguenots episode: old Ezechiele, 'che urlava senza posa coi pugni levati al cielo, tremando nella bianca barba caprina' [forever shouting with fists raised to the sky, his white goatee beard atremble],[18] is clearly Calvino senior, while his wife's austere, silent authority, firmly convinced of her own 'secret religion', shows she is a version of the author's botanist mother (*RR*, I, 396–97).[19] Medardo's father, Aiolfo, is also a portrait of Calvino's father: both men had an enthusiasm for hunting that was accompanied by a passion for ornithology and a capacity to imitate all manner of birdsong, and to confirm this link Aiolfo's name even contains the three vowels of Mario Calvino's first name.[20] In chapter 3 he is described as world-weary but as retaining his passion for birds (*RR*, I, 376), so much so that he ends up living with them inside a huge aviary, feeding them and imitating their chirps (*RR*, I, 379). This motif of Mario Calvino's brilliance at imitating bird-sounds will recur frequently in other evocations of the father, but here the chapter ends with Aiolfo dying of grief at Medardo's mutilation of one of his pet birds (*RR*, I, 380). At the time Calvino wrote these words, between July and September 1951, his father was still alive, but it is clear from the recently published letters that he had been seriously ill at least since March of that year (*L*, p. 318), and that at the time the author wrote *Il visconte* he knew his father had not long to live (*L*, p. 320).

Mario Calvino died on 25 October 1951, while Italo was in the USSR, as part of a Communist Youth Delegation, and thus only learnt of his father's death on his return to Italy. The distance Calvino felt from his father both during his life and at his death is worked out in a later death-scene, in Chapter 16 of *Il barone rampante*, where Cosimo's father dies. The list of the latter's disappointments includes the fact that his eldest son is still living in the trees, and his wife is too authoritarian (*RR*, I, 673–74). Cosimo's preference for the trees represents the younger Calvino's decision to opt for the world of ideas, books and cities. The sense of distance emerges most memorably in the description of the old Baron's funeral: Cosimo from his tree places a branch on his father's coffin, and his brother Biagio concludes: 'Io pensavo che da mio padre eravamo sempre stati tutti distanti come Cosimo sugli alberi' [We had all, I thought, been as far removed from my father as Cosimo was on the trees.][21]

The first portrait of Calvino senior after his death occurs not in a fictional work but in two brief mentions in the earliest story of *L'entrata in guerra*, namely 'Gli avanguardisti a Mentone' ['A Trip to Mentone']: he is described as being dismayed by the damage done to the countryside by the war and as volunteering to go once a week with his wife to look after gardens near Mentone, which had been the property of 'enemy subjects' (*RR*, I, 502);[22] when they return with rare plants they were trying to save, the narrator remarks: 'Perseveravano in quei gesti di pietà vegetale, in un tempo in cui già i popoli morivano falciati come l'erba' [They persevered in those actions of botanical *pietas* at a time when people were already dying mown down like hay] (*RR*, I, 504). This sentence, with its ironic contrast between the parents' excessive botanical *pietas* and the horrors of the war, also makes it clear that in *Il visconte dimezzato* behind Dottor Trelawney's pointless researches and the Good Half's uselessly pious actions resides Calvino's father once more.

In the second autobiographical tale, 'L'entrata in guerra' ['The Entry into War'], written in the summer of 1953, we find an emphasis on two aspects of his father's character: his being out of sorts with the times and his hunting prowess (*RR*, I, 488). This lack of harmony with the times resurfaces in caricature form in Cosimo's father in *Il barone rampante* (*RR*, I, 550–51).

The fact that his father's recent death is still a prime motivator for the whole autobiographical trilogy is confirmed when we read the final page of the last story, 'Le notti dell'UNPA' ['UNPA Nights'], written in September 1953, a finale which is a lengthy homage to the man from whom Calvino had always felt distant, but which offers us in its closing words an attempt at closeness on the part of the son. It begins with the by now familiar emphasis on the father's hunting gear: 'A quell'ora mio padre s'era già alzato, s'era affibbiato ansando i gambali, e infilato la cacciatora gonfia d'arnesi' [At that hour my father was already up, and panting all the time had fastened on his leggings and donned his hunting-jacket bristling with hunting equipment] (*RR*, I, 545). After a silent breakfast with his dog, he sets out, and here the other physical leitmotifs are emphasized: his white goatee wrapped in his scarf, and his constant coughs and expectorations. This morning walk to San Giovanni is seen as one of his rare moments of serenity, and the passage ends with a final mention of his delight in the dawn chorus: 'E forse i soli momenti suoi felici erano questi dell'alba, quando passava col suo cane per le note strade, liberandosi i bronchi del catarro che l'opprimeva la notte, [...] e riconoscendo il fischio degli uccelli mattinieri uno per uno' [And perhaps these dawn moments were his only moments of happiness, as he took his dog along the familiar paths, freeing his chest of the catarrh that afflicted him at night, (...) and recognizing the sounds of the morning birds one by one] (ibid.). This lengthy paragraph describing his morning excursion to San Giovanni is followed by a very brief concluding paragraph to the story, in which the son-narrator reveals for the first time his affection for his father: 'Così, seguendo col pensiero i passi di mio padre per la campagna, m'addormentai; e lui non seppe mai d'avermi avuto tanto vicino' [So, with my thoughts following my father's footsteps through the countryside, I fell asleep; and he never knew that he had had me so close to him] (*RR*, I, 545).

Here, then, even within the confines of these brief autobiographical tales, we can observe the gradual growth of Calvino's homage to his father, culminating in this full-page moment of closure and rapprochement at the end of the third story of the autobiographical trilogy. Where all previous mentions of the father had been brief and had stressed his age and distance from his sons, this unusually lengthy passage ends on the very word 'vicino'.

However, partly because of this eulogistic finale, Calvino felt dissatisfied with *L'entrata*, since immediately after completing it he tells Elio Vittorini that he has no desire to write other such tales (*L*, p. 381); and just after the book is published he tells a reviewer that he is satisfied but also bewildered, since such autobiographical work prompts the crucial question: 'Se ci si mette sulla strada dell'autobiografismo, dove ci si ferma?' [Once you start on the road to autobiography, where do you stop?] (*L*, p. 408). This uneasiness about autobiography would continue: in a 1968 letter to Guido Fink he would explain that he turned to the memorialistic mode of *L'entrata* under the influence of Giorgio Bassani's works and in order to escape the impasse into which his first post-war style had led him, but he considers this turn an involution and is genuinely disappointed that Fink remembers the stories so well and quotes them twice (*L*, pp. 1004–05).

Before leaving them, it is worth considering the changes made in the three stories between first publication and the later version in the collected *Racconti*. In the first tale written, 'Gli avanguardisti a Mentone', there are no fewer than ten major cuts over the first twenty-two pages of a twenty-five page story, perhaps because this was Calvino's first full-scale autobiographical tale, and in this first venture into 'la letteratura della memoria' he was initially too expansive about close friends.[23] In the second tale written, the title story 'L'entrata in guerra', there are nine altered passages, but these occur only over the first four pages of a fourteen-page story, most of them concerning an aristocratic friend. Since in the final tale, 'Le notti dell'UNPA', he feels the need to excise just one passage about a peripheral character, it seems as if Calvino was gradually adapting to the autobiographical mode, and the fact that, in the midst of this pruning of excessively personal memoirs, he retains the long closing page describing his father, reinforces its significance as an act of literary *pietas* in the context of what Barenghi has called Calvino's 'contrastato memorialismo' [difficult attitude to memoirs] (*RR*, I, 1319).

La speculazione edilizia [*A Plunge into Real Estate*], written in 1956–57, was intended partly as a kind of ten-year survey of Italy since the Liberation, charting the country's involution in the protagonist's abandonment of his Resistance ideals and his corruption by the economic boom.[24] This novella contains both a negative self-portrait in the failed intellectual protagonist Quinto (the name Calvino had also given himself in 'Pranzo con un pastore'), and — paradoxically in a plot largely concerned with socio-political issues — a positive homage to his mother in three lengthy portraits of Quinto's mother in the story, strategically placed at the beginning, middle and end of the novella.[25] At the start, in chapter 2, she is portrayed in the fertile plot of garden that her sons have decided to sell off to a property speculator. This detailed evocation of the 'terreno della vaseria' [flowerpot-area] is a wonderful example of Calvino's powers of description of nature, but it ends on an image of his mother standing in this favourite spot: 'Là piú che in ogni altro luogo aiolato e inghiaiato del giardino alla madre piaceva di sostare' [It was there rather than among the gravel paths and flower beds of the garden that Signora Anfossi liked to pass her time].[26] Unlike early portraits of the silent mother working indoors, and the caricature of Ezechiele's wife in *Il visconte*, here she is always outdoors with her beloved plants and flowers. Halfway through the novella, the end of chapter 13 describes the mother staring from what is left of the garden at the sold-off plot that is now being dug up, and in the final words of the chapter retreating once more into the greenery: '... poi si ritirava nel suo verde' [... then she would turn back to her green].[27] Finally at the close of the whole book, the end of chapter 24, we find the mother busy with her flowers, trying not to raise her eyes too high in order to blot out the new buildings: 'La madre era in giardino. I caprifogli odoravano. I nasturzi erano una macchia di colore fin troppo vivo. Se non alzava gli occhi in su, dove da tutte le parti s'affacciavano le finestre dei casamenti, il giardino era sempre il giardino' [The Signora was in the garden. The scent of honeysuckle was in the air, the nasturtiums were an almost too vivid splash of color. If she didn't raise her eyes to the ranked windows of the apartment buildings all around, the garden was still the garden].[28] Once more, the maternal figure is portrayed amidst the greenery, in the gathering gloom, as the new building is finally finished and excludes the light. None of these portraits is as lengthy as the description of Calvino's father at the end of 'Le notti dell'UNPA', but there are three of them evenly distributed in this short novella, and they go some way to filling out the mother's portrait and balancing this family album.

The fact that in a 1958 letter Calvino couples *La speculazione edilizia* with *L'entrata in guerra* confirms that he saw this as very much an autobiographical novella (indeed the whole story of the sale of parental land to a builder, and of the concomitant tax problems, are autobiographical and are echoed in his correspondence). A long letter of 21 May 1958 to Alberto Asor Rosa makes this clear. Talking of *La speculazione edilizia*, which Asor Rosa had praised in his review, Calvino worries that it is

>terribilmente decadente: l'autobiografismo, l'introspezione, l'egocentrismo, tutte cose che io ho sempre odiato e combattuto. [...] *L'entrata in guerra* e *La speculaz. edilizia* sono stati due *cedimenti* all'autobiografia (il primo in chiave di autoesaltazione, con un 'io' modello di tutte le virtú come quello di Carlo Levi;

> il secondo in chiave di autodenigrazione [...] è autobiografia al 95%, tanto che non so se potrò mai pubblicarla in volume, perché i personaggi sono tali e quali e riconoscibilissimi e i fatti quasi tutti veri.)
>
> [terribly decadent: autobiographical writing, introspection, egocentricity, all things I have always hated and fought against. (...) *L'entrata in guerra* and *La speculaz. edilizia* were two *concessions* to autobiography (the first in self-promotion mode, with an 'I' who is the model of all virtues as in Carlo Levi; the second in self-denigration mode (...) is 95% autobiography, so much so that I am afraid I will never be able to publish it as a book, because the characters are exactly the same in reality and very easily recognizable, and the events are all true.] (*L*, pp. 548–49)

One of the problems with *L'entrata in guerra* was that the first-person narrator was portrayed in a superior moral light to those around him, rather like the narrator in Levi's *Cristo si è fermato a Eboli*, whereas with *La speculazione* Calvino now went to the opposite extreme, in portraying a feckless intellectual in the grip of *mauvaise foi*. But neither approach solved the problem of 'autobiografismo': in fact the complicated editorial vicissitudes of this novella, from its publication in the journal *Botteghe Oscure* (1957) to the abridged version in the *Racconti* (1958) to the final redaction published as a separate volume (1963), reflect the considerable difficulties Calvino experienced when handling autobiographical and biographical material of this kind.[29]

A different portrait of the austere or garden-loving mother appears in that 1960 interview for *Il Paradosso* that Calvino sent to John Woodhouse. In response to the question why he made the political choices that he did, Calvino replied that it was primarily due to his partisan experiences, but he adds a paragraph about the exemplary courage she displayed in two areas, in encouraging her two sons to become partisans, and in behaving with dignity and courage before the SS and the Fascist militia, who held her hostage for a long time, and pretended to shoot her husband in front of her. He concludes: 'I fatti storici a cui partecipano le madri acquistano la grandezza e l'invincibilità dei fenomeni naturali' [The historical events which mothers take part in acquire the greatness and invincibility of natural phenomena].[30] Significantly this passage of almost exaggerated homage to his mother's courage was omitted by the author when he rewrote the chapter for the book based on the journal's responses, *La generazione degli anni difficili* (1962):[31] Calvino always regarded a published book as having a much louder voice than a journal, hence his modest pruning of this passage. This pattern of stating and then retracting autobiographical material, already evident elsewhere, is a further indication of Calvino's difficult relationship with personal memories. But Calvino will return to his mother's heroism at a later date.

Calvino's gradually expanding verbal homages to his father seemed to have culminated in the final page of 'Le notti dell'UNPA', but were counterbalanced by the less serious, caricature figure of Cosimo's father in *Il barone rampante*. They would then resurface some years later in a more serious vein, in a 20-page autobiographical story dedicated to his memory, *La strada di San Giovanni* (1962). Claudio Milanini points out that this story, written in January 1962, was meant as a 'moving testimony to the memory of Calvino's father' (*RR*, III, 1204), since its date of composition follows closely on the tenth anniversary of his death (25 October 1961); and the same critic cites a letter written just a week after that anniversary which makes clear that Calvino was aware of this tenth anniversary: the author did not feel any shock at the time, but as the years went by the pain of this paternal absence continued to grow (*RR*, III, 1204).[32] This most expansive tribute to his father is prompted not just by the tenth anniversary of his death, but also by Calvino's own growing appreciation of his father in the years since then, and by his own need to justify his decision not to follow him into the world of agronomy. *La strada di San Giovanni* recounts the morning journey from San Remo to the family's land up the valley at San Giovanni, but the return journey does nothing to bring the two men closer together: the son still cannot wait to get back to the town, to the cinemas, the beach, and the girls.

La strada contains many of the father's leitmotifs already noted in the fictional tales, such as his hunting gear, leggings and hobnailed boots (*RR*, III, 7). Another attribute also taken up from the end of 'Le notti dell'UNPA' is his capacity to imitate all varieties of birdsong (*RR*, III, 12).[33] Apart from these mentions of the hunter's clothes and his love of birdsong, *La strada di San Giovanni* also reworks the final page of 'Le notti dell'UNPA' with echoes of 'I figli poltroni', recalling how his father would try to wake his sons, then prepare the baskets full of insecticides and compost, before setting off on his own, coughing and spitting catarrh (*RR*, III, 13–14).

However, in this story too, as in 'I figli poltroni' and *La speculazione edilizia*, Calvino inserts mini-portraits of his mother, both deliberately hidden within parentheses to reflect her less strident character. In the first one, the narrator initially seems to hear her shouting at the two boys to get up and join their father at San Giovanni, but then he says it is not her voice he hears, and she retreats from the story, much as she had done in *La speculazione*:

> (No, non è la voce di mia madre che ritorna, in queste pagine risuonanti della rumorosa e lontana presenza paterna, ma un suo dominio silenzioso: la sua figura si affaccia tra queste righe, poi subito si ritrae, resta nel margine. Ecco che è passata nella nostra stanza, non l'abbiamo sentita uscire, ed il sonno è finito per sempre). (*RR*, III, 14)

> [(No, it's not so much Mother's voice that comes back to me, in these pages echoing with my father's noisy and distant presence, but a silent authority she had: she looks out between these lines, then immediately withdraws, is left in the margin; there, she came into our room and is gone, we didn't hear her leave and our sleep is over forever.)][34]

Later, when the father returns with too much produce, we learn of her horror of waste, and another parenthesis explains that this fear of waste was also a fear of passion, whereas she preferred the dispassionate study of the carefully labelled plants in her garden and underneath her microscope (*RR*, III, 15; *The Road to San Giovanni*, p. 16).[35] But this cold sublimation of passion into duty was also a strength, particularly as it also explains both her conviction that her sons should join the partisans and her courage when threatened by the Nazis.

One particular feature of Calvino's later autobiographical writing is his rejection of hindsight, a constraint that starts in *La strada di San Giovanni*. The first-person narrator refuses to check the exact names of the plants his father would name to him in their morning walk to San Giovanni. He prefers to use the invented names that have stayed in his memory, since checking them in a botanical dictionary would have been to 'cheat', to refuse to accept the loss of memory that he had inflicted on himself (*RR*, III, 12). Interestingly, in another parenthesis, he adds that to have checked the names would have been an act of humility and *pietas*, an act of reconciliation with his father, even one of maturity (*RR*, III, 12). *La strada di San Giovanni* is, then, also about a failure to achieve humility, reconciliation and maturity.

This elimination of hindsight is similar to the constraint deployed in other autobiographical essays, particularly the other three in the projected *Passaggi obbligati* volume: in 'Autobiografia di uno spettatore' ['A Cinema-Goer's Autobiography'] (1974), he declines to consult filmographies to say which precise films he saw in his adolescent years (*RR*, III, 38); in 'Ricordo di una battaglia' ['Memories of a Battle'] (1974), his memoir of the battle of Baiardo, he refuses to add more details to explain the broader military picture into which this microcosm of a battle fitted, since that would overlay his memories with hindsight rather than reawaken them (*RR*, III, 53); and in 'La poubelle agréée' (1974–76), he leaves a note in parenthesis reminding himself to insert a description of the positive aspects of the kitchen when he rewrites this piece, but the note remains in the form of a parenthetical pro-memoria.[36]

Very soon after *La strada di San Giovanni* Calvino returns to autobiographical matters in his substantial preface written for the definitive 1964 edition of his first novel. The preface has since become a major document for a definition of neorealism in Italian literature, but it is an equally important reference-point for Calvino's autobiography. The main emotion caused by his decision to caricature his closest partisan companions in the novel, is one of remorse, a word that crops up as the key motif of the central section of the preface, repeated five times in as many pages (*RR*, I, 1190–94). Indeed at one point he declares that remorse ought to have been the starting point of the whole preface (*RR*, I, 1190).

The close of the preface has the most important things to say about the fragility of memory. Reversing the usual claim that literature immortalizes events and people, Calvino notes that a writer's first book is actually destructive, cutting the threads that link him to the facts and destroying the treasure of memory (*RR*, I, 1203); it leaves him with a changed memory instead of a complete set of recollections with their fuzzy outlines. Continuing his polemic against literature, he sees literary rewriting of memory as something not living but solid and inert, whereas it is memories that have a living existence: 'La proiezione letteraria [...] ha fatto sbiadire, ha schiacciato la vegetazione dei ricordi in cui la vita dell'albero e quella del filo d'erba si condizionano a vicenda' [The habit of projecting things onto a literary plane (...) has faded and crushed the crop of memories in which the life of the tree and of the blade of grass mutually nourish each other].[37] Experience, which he says consists of the memory, plus the wound, plus the change it has wrought in you, may give shape to a work of literature but it immediately 'withers and dies' ('insecchisce, si distrugge', ibid.): once again a natural, organic metaphor is used. In the last paragraph of the preface the image shifts to make the contrast between the distant, misty past and the false solidity of the written pages, and the author ends up praising the fuzziness of memory over the false 'esattezza' of literary reconstruction. Although Calvino praises precision as a key literary value in the late Harvard lectures, it is perceived as a dangerous quality here in the realm of autobiographical writing.[38] The elegant concluding paradox suggests that memories and experiences could allow the writer to compose all his books, but his first work has already started the process of destroying memory, and in the end only provides enough material for that first slim novel (*RR*, I, 1204; *The Path*, pp. 29–30). Yet we shall see that in the end Calvino never freed himself of the burden of these memories and he turned again and again to that 'esperienza' to write some of his last works.

The importance of the preface in autobiographical terms is confirmed by the recently published letters. After its publication, he calls it an ever-expanding preface ('questa prefazione-fisarmonica'), he is haunted by other things he should have included in it, and feels he could publish an even more expanded version except he is afraid he would look obsessive (letter of 12 November 1964 to Gian Carlo Ferretti, *L*, p. 836). He says something similar in the following month to Gianfranco Contini, noting that the minute he wrote the Preface it stirred avalanches of other topics in him, so much so that he feels he has still not finished it, and that the real things he wanted to say are not in it (*L*, p. 840). What the letters do is to underline the personal as well as the literary significance of the preface to his first novel. Calvino's feelings that he still had more to say on these subjects would be borne out ten and twenty years later in a series of anniversary revisitations of this material in the mid-1970s and 1980s.

Remorse is a key word in Calvino's autobiographical writings, but remorse stemmed not just from his neorealist distortion of his fellow-partisans but also, as we have seen, from his sense of having abandoned his father's rural ideals. This also emerges in the later autobiographical piece, 'La poubelle agréée' (1974–76). Here he claims that he feels, in common with the North African immigrant in Paris, a remorse that was to last for years for having contravened his father's will and abandoned an agricultural world in crisis.[39] The feelings of remorse for not having followed his father's vocation remained with Calvino throughout his life: in a letter of March 1963 perhaps in the wake of the memories stirred up by *La strada di San Giovanni* he expresses remorse at opting to live in the city after his utopian country upbringing (*L*, pp. 739–40); in April 1967 he appreciates Benvenuto Terracini's review of *Le cosmicomiche* [*Cosmicomics*] which first brought out the links between 'Un segno nello spazio' ['A Sign in Space'] and the recurrent theme of remorse in Calvino's prefaces, and he adds: 'è un tema che darebbe da pensare a un critico-psicologo' [this is a theme that would provide a psychological critic with food for thought] (*L*, p. 954);[40] and one of the last mentions of the term in his letters also concerns his father: a few months after his mother's death in March 1978, Calvino admits to feelings of remorse for not collecting his father's memoirs (letter of 20 August 1978, *L*, p. 1381).

The final section of this chapter is devoted to the partisan essays written in the last decade of Calvino's life, which concentrate more on his own experiences and less on his relations with his parents. 'Ricordo di una battaglia' (25 April 1974) is the most extended example of his concentration on the processes rather than on the contents of memory.[41] He begins with a natural or even mineral metaphor, saying that all his memories are still intact in the damp bed of sand deposited at the bottom of the stream of his thoughts (*RR*, III, 50). Mario Barenghi has indicated in the titles of Calvino's two essay collections (*Una pietra sopra* [literally *A Stone Over It*] and *Collezione di sabbia* [*Collection of Sand*]) the importance of such mineral metaphors (*S*, I, p. XXXII), and in this memoir the sand-bed image reminds us of the organic metaphors used in the Preface to *Il sentiero* written exactly ten years previously; in fact the two works have much in common. Later he varies the fluvial metaphor by comparing these undisturbed recollections to eels lurking in the wells of his memory: so all it needs is for him to lift one of the big boulders marking the confines between present and past in order to discover the little caverns behind his forehead where forgotten things lurk. The piscatorial metaphor is developed when he claims that nearly thirty years after the event he has decided to draw in the nets of his memories to see what they have caught, and this sentence encapsulates the technique of the whole essay, as he shifts from the present groping for memories in the dark to the narrative of the morning of nearly thirty years ago:

> Eccomi qui ad annaspare nel buio, come se il mattino non volesse piú cominciare, come se non riuscissi a spiccicare gli occhi dal sonno, e proprio questa imprecisione magari è il segno che il ricordo è preciso, quel che ora mi sembra mezzo cancellato lo era anche allora, quella mattina la sveglia era stata alle quattro, e subito il distaccamento di Olmo era in marcia giú per il bosco nel buio [...].
>
> [I find myself groping in the dark, as if that morning didn't want to begin again, as if I were unable to unglue the sleep from my eyes, and perhaps it is precisely this imprecision that guarantees that the memory is precise, what now seems half erased was so then too, that morning they woke us at four and immediately Olmo's detachment was on the march down through the woods in the dark (...).][42]

The blurred nature of the present act of remembering is an analogue of the grogginess of that morning march, and from now on Calvino proceeds to establish a whole series of analogues between the act and the content of remembering: the processes of memory are compared to the approach march the partisans themselves are involved in (*RR*, III, 51); he hopes to come upon a solid memory, like the solid road his feet hit, after emerging from the wood onto the road to Baiardo; the rips ('gli strappi', *RR*, III, 52) in the uniforms the partisans wore are paralleled by the many rips ('strappi') in his memories (*RR*, III, 54), and so on. The most striking analogue comes when he says that for years he had believed that in order to remember everything about that morning all he would have to do is remember the relief he felt when removing the stiff boots from his feet to make less sound, the feeling of the earth underneath his socks, and the stings from the chestnuts and thistles through his socks. This textile metaphor fits perfectly with or indeed is evoked by the content of the memories, in a passage that contains a highly wrought alliterative evocation of the prickles coming through the layers of holed socks:

> Pensavo che mi sarebbe bastato ricordarmi questo momento e tutto il resto sarebbe venuto dietro come lo sgomitolarsi d'un filo, come il disfarsi di quei calzettoni sfondati sugli alluci e sui calcagni, sopra altri strati di calzettoni pure sfondati e dentro tutte le spine le spighe gli stecchi, lo spolverio vegetale del sottobosco impigliato alla lana. (*RR*, III, 54)
>
> [I thought all I'd have to do was remember this moment and all the rest would follow on naturally like a ball of wool unravelling, like the unravelling of those socks with their holes at the big toe and the heel, over other layers of socks likewise with holes and inside all the prickles the grass spikes the twigs, the vegetable dusting of undergrowth caught in wool.] ('Memories of a Battle', pp. 83–84)

In 'Ricordo di una battaglia' the partisan plan to take Baiardo goes wrong, since as they approach the town, they realize the Fascists have resisted and are chanting *Giovinezza*, so the next thing the narrator remembers is fleeing through olive groves. At this point his personal memories end, but he is now in the paradoxical position of being able to narrate more clearly thanks to hindsight the battle in Baiardo which he never saw, which leads him to formulate another paradox: his memory of a battle he did not witness can find an order and a meaning more precise than what he really lived through. As in the 1964 preface to his first novel, so here he praises not the 'esattezza' of falsely precise memories but the fuzziness of the confused sensations that clutter his recollections of that day. The memoir ends with Calvino recognizing that in reality he has remembered almost nothing about that morning. The memories of his partisan experiences are clearly among the most precious elements of his autobiography, and as with the preface to his first novel, he still felt he had other things to add to this memoir of a battle.

'Ricordo di una battaglia' was one of Calvino's most substantial autobiographical pieces, and interestingly its plan had been outlined the previous year in a 1973 interview with Ferdinando Camon. To the question how would he write about the partisan war now, Calvino replies: 'sarebbe a livello non macroscopico, ma quasi microscopico, una situazione, un episodio minimo, un momento tra la vita e la morte, momento assolutamente quotidiano in quella vita lí' [it would be not on a macroscopic but on a microscopic level, a tiny episode, a moment between life and death, the kind of moment that was actually a daily occurrence in that life] (*S*, II, 2778). In fact the 1974 evocation of the battle of Baiardo is precisely such a minimal event, one that hovers between life and death, but which was a regular occurrence at that time. In the interview he also says that now he would start with the physical conditions of the partisans, especially their symbiosis with nature, which was crucial for two reasons: first because throughout the winter they had nothing to eat but chestnuts and this lack of vitamins caused partisans to be recognized by the boils on their legs ('ciavèli' in dialect), and secondly because only once the bushes ('custi' in dialect) started to put out new leaves in the delayed spring of 1945, could the partisans move about the hills with some cover (*S*, II, 2778). The two dialect terms he remembers confer a linguistic seal of authenticity on this evocation. He summarises the contents of this hypothetical story as: weapons, chestnuts, munitions, boot laces, the broader military context, but constantly moving back and forward from the macroscopic to the microscopic with concomitant variations in style, highlighting the relationship between natural, cultural and historical events, and focusing on one single, minimal episode, in which some humble, anonymous combatants risk their own and others's lives (*RR*, III, 2780). This is a perfect summing up of 'Ricordo di una battaglia' which Calvino would write the following year.

'Ricordo' also has links with another anniversary evocation of the Liberation, 'Il mio 25 aprile 1945' (*S*, II, 2810–13), written the following year, 1975. In 'Ricordo' Calvino's own memory fails when he hears *Giovinezza* and flees through the olives realizing that the partisans have been defeated, and at this point before moving on to describe the battle of Baiardo that he never actually saw, he says 'Il mio ricordo della battaglia è finito. Ora non mi resta che ripescare il ricordo della fuga nel fondo del torrente coperto da fitti nocciuoli, che stiamo cercando di risalire per evitare le strade' [My memories of the battle end here. Now all I can do is cast about for my memories of the flight over a carpet of hazelnuts along the dry streambed we try to climb up to avoid the roads] (*RR*, III, 56; 'Memories of a Battle', pp. 86–87). A central passage in the 1975 article, 'Il mio 25 aprile 1945', talks of the return of spring in 1945 and the cover afforded by the new leaves, but he specifically mentions again a clump of hazel bushes:

> Le vallate tornavano a coprirsi di foglie e di cespugli, questo voleva dire maggiore possibilità di tenersi al coperto sotto al fuoco nemico, come in quella macchia di noccioli che ci aveva salvato la vita, a me e a mio fratello, una ventina di giorni prima, dopo un'azione sulla strada di Ceriana. (*S*, II, 2811)
>
> [The valleys were starting to become covered again with leaves and bushes, which meant a better chance of finding cover from enemy fire, like that clump of hazel-trees that saved our lives, my brother's and mine, twenty days previously, after action on the road to Ceriana.]

Though twenty days before 25 April would only be the beginning of April, and the battle of Baiardo took place on 17 March 1945, it is possible that Calvino is using 'twenty days' in an imprecise way and that here he is referring to the battle of Baiardo. The battle is, then, important for him since it was a day he nearly lost his life, though of course this is never specified in 'Ricordo'. In fact 'Ricordo', like the preface to the first novel ten years earlier, is in a sense an unfinished text: the month after it was published Calvino acknowledges that the piece was shorter than intended because of the requirements of newspaper space, and he says he still wants to write up the whole story with the help of others (letter of 29 May 1974, *L*, pp. 1239–40). He adds that his first novel and short stories were inspired by those times and places, though he changed the events and the characters involved; but now he feels the need for change, the need not to caricature but to write 'con fedeltà assoluta' [with absolute fidelity] (*L*, p. 1240). The next month he writes a letter where he states that it is only now that he is fifty that he wants to narrate the events of those years faithfully, and not disguised as in his early fiction: those deformed versions are no use to his current need for precision (letter of 21 June 1974, *L*, pp. 1244–45). Calvino thus remained sensitive to anniversaries and birthdays. The following year, in March 1975, he tells fellow ex-partisan Marcello Venturi that he appreciated the 'fedeltà' of Venturi's novel about that period, *Terra di nessuno*, and that he himself has tried to write about the war, but seeing that his memory was fading, and that he was in danger of falling into generalities, he gave up, though he might try again (letter of 12 March 1975, *L*, p. 1270). In fact Calvino did try again.

In his final evocation of the partisan war, written for the last anniversary of the Liberation he would see (April 1985), 'Tante storie che abbiamo dimenticato' ['So Many Stories We Have Forgotten'] (*S*, II, 2912–19), he starts by emphasizing the things that are most forgotten, in particular the importance of the family in that war. In 1943–45 the traumas experienced by Italian families magnified those that existed for every individual. He then adds a detail in parenthesis, as he often did, that in fact was quite personal: '(Lo sapevano le autorità tedesche e repubblichine che prendevano in ostaggio i genitori dei giovani che non si presentavano alla chiamata alle armi [...]. Chi ha vissuto questo ricatto ne porta la ferita per sempre, [anche] quelli che sono andati alla macchia pur sapendo di giocarsi la vita dei propri genitori)' [(This was something known by the German and Fascist authorities who took as hostages the parents of young men who had not enlisted (...). Those who lived through this blackmail carry the wounds of it with them for ever, including those who went into hiding even though they knew that they were risking the lives of their own parents)] (*S*, II, 2913). Once more the wounds first mentioned in the 1964 preface resurface here, though the parenthesis and the vague pronouns — 'chi', 'quelli' — hide the fact that Calvino is talking about himself and his brother. He acknowledges that the family plays a key role in all wars, but it was particularly true in this war since the separation between combatants and the civilian population was more blurred, and the decisive factor was the behaviour of ordinary men and women in extraordinary circumstances. Here he introduces a second parenthesis, but this one contains an explicit eulogy of the heroism of his mother, who had died in 1978: '(Qui voglio ricordare mia madre, la cui forza d'animo sta al centro di quella storia privata senza la quale il 25 aprile sarebbe per me una rispettabile solennità nazionale e nient'altro)' [(Here I wish to remember my mother, whose strength of mind lies at the heart of that private history of mine without which the 25 April would simply be a respectable national anniversary for me and nothing else)] (*S*, II, 2913).

Although his mother appeared here again only in a parenthesis, Calvino instantly regrets this personal turn the recollection has taken, worried that this return to his war memories might falsify them and prevent him from recognizing how he and others really were at that time. Once more we witness this tentative approach to revealing personal memories and experiences. What he does admit is that he himself was an inadequate partisan, not up to the mark: 'Non mi sentivo mai all'altezza della situazione. Ma parlare di se stessi è sempre difficile' [I never really felt up to the situation. But it is always difficult to talk about oneself] (*S*, II, 2917). The Italian phrase used for his inadequacy has Conradian echoes, especially as applied to Lord Jim,[43] and echoes another phrase used twenty years earlier in the preface to his first novel, where he admits that during the war he had not been able to live up to his own dreams when the moment of test came (*RR*, I, 1200). Calvino's enthusiasm for

Conrad is not just a literary cult: it is intimately bound up with his own partisan experiences. The conclusion returns to one of the natural metaphors often used by Calvino in these memoirs, but here applied to the collective not to the individual memory: there is a deep level of a society's consciousness where the memories of wounds are deposited, along with the capacity to tolerate these wounds, and that is the layer that will remain, whereas all the rest will complete its cycle and disappear into dust (*S*, II, 2919).

Two different sets of anniversaries stimulate Calvino into personal memoirs. The first is the period 1943–45, when aged barely twenty, he made the decision to join the partisans and to risk his life for his ideals: the beginning of his twenties coincided with the beginning of his Resistance. The battle of Baiardo on 17 March 1945 seems to have been one of the most significant pieces of action he was involved in, and as a minor battle in which the partisans were defeated, it was ideally suited to Calvino the memorialist, since it offered no scope for a heroic portrayal of the self. It is no accident that ten years after the Liberation is the point at which Calvino decides to take stock of Italian society and its involution in *La speculazione edilizia* (begun on 25 April 1956, but set in 1954): several passages in the novel talk about the degeneration of Italy in this decade. In 1964, shortly after turning forty and getting married, he returns to partisan material, in the lengthy, ever-expanding preface to *Il sentiero dei nidi di ragno*. In 1973, he becomes fifty and admits that since then he has begun to think more about the war: the Camon interview of that year is followed in the next two years by two anniversary pieces, 'Ricordo di una battaglia' (1974) and 'Il mio 25 aprile 1945' (1975), the latter for the thirtieth anniversary of the Liberation. Finally in 1985, for the fortieth anniversary, he returns to the topic with 'Tante storie che abbiamo dimenticato' ['So Many Stories We Have Forgotten']. Significantly, the last mention of an autobiographical project is in a letter to Graziana Pentich written on 18 March 1985, the day after the fortieth anniversary of the battle of Baiardo.

The other set of anniversaries centred round his father. It is Mario Calvino's death that prompts the first extended autobiographical work, begun a year after his demise, *L'entrata in guerra* (written 1952–53). The tenth anniversary of his death also occasions more reflections about his father on Calvino's part and culminates in the homage of *La strada di San Giovanni* (written January 1962). After this date, Calvino wrote little about his father, presumably as his memory of him fades, and as he abandons realism in his narrative works. Instead we find a growing attention to his mother in autobiographical writings (she died aged 92 on 31 March 1978): from the triptych of portraits in *La speculazione edilizia*, to praise of her strength of character during the war, in the 1960 interview for *Il Paradosso*, to her cameo appearances in parentheses in *La strada di San Giovanni*, to the explicit praise of her bravery in his final anniversary celebration of the Liberation in 1985.

In that first letter to John Woodhouse, with which we began, Calvino gave him substantial biographical information, and as we saw, supplied him with the most complete list then available of his autobiographical writings. Not surprisingly, at the end of this lengthy letter Calvino realizes that Woodhouse has made him work for over three hours, but the tone is one of friendly irony and the letter ends with good wishes for the scholar's future work: 'M'accorgo che è da piú di tre ore che Lei mi sta facendo lavorare. Non mi resta che salutarLa, augurandoLe buon lavoro e sperando di leggere presto il Suo studio' [I realize that you have been making me work for more than three hours now. It only remains for me to say goodbye, wishing you every success with your work, and hoping to be able to read your book soon] (*L*, p. 952). Woodhouse never did write a biography of Calvino, but *A Reappraisal and an Appreciation of the Trilogy* would appear in 1968, and along with Pescio Bottino's study would open the floodgates for a torrent of books on Calvino in many languages that even today shows no sign of drying up.

Notes to Chapter 10

1. Germana Pescio Bottino, *Italo Calvino* (Florence: La Nuova Italia, 1967); and J. R. Woodhouse, *Italo Calvino: A Reappraisal and an Appreciation of the Trilogy* (Hull: Hull University Press, 1968).
2. Calvino's italics: see Italo Calvino, *I libri degli altri. Lettere 1947–1981*, ed. by Giovanni Tesio (Turin: Einaudi, 1991), p. 479. The sentence is also quoted at the beginning of the *Cronologia* that appears in the Mondadori editions of Calvino's collected fiction, essays, and letters (cited below), as though to warn the reader to be wary of Calvino's biographical pronouncements.
3. Italo Calvino, *Lettere 1940–1985*, ed. by Luca Baranelli (Milan: Mondadori, 2000), pp. 947–53. Henceforth references to the letters will be given as *L* with page number.
4. Both versions of the chapter in *Il Paradosso* and in *La generazione degli anni difficili* are now in Italo Calvino, *Saggi*, ed. by Mario Barenghi, 2 vols (Milan: Mondadori, 1995), II, 2733–59 (henceforth *S* with page reference); an English translation is to be found in Calvino, *Hermit in Paris. Autobiographical Writings*, trans. by Martin McLaughlin (London: Cape, 2003), pp. 130–56.
5. Italo Calvino, *Il barone rampante*, ed. by J. R. Woodhouse (Manchester: Manchester University Press, 1970).
6. For instance: 'non credo che la biografia dell'autore sia molto importante: gli scrittori contemporanei hanno delle vite molto povere d'avvenimenti' [I don't believe that an author's biography is very important: contemporary writers have lives that are very thin in terms of events] (letter of 8 February 1965 to Edoardo Fea, *L*, p. 851); see also letters from the same period in *L*, pp. 884, 965.
7. Mario Barenghi, 'Per non contrabbandare elegie: aspetti dell'autobiografismo calviniano', *Italo Calvino: Le Défi au labyrinthe*, ed. by Paolo Grossi and Silvia Fabrizio-Costa (Caen: Presses Universitaires de Caen, 1998), pp. 15–43.
8. For publishing details see notes 2 and 3 above.
9. The projected title is mentioned in a 1978 letter to Guido Neri (*L*, p. 1359). For information on the projected works to be included in *Passaggi obbligati*, see Claudio Milanini's notes in Calvino, *Romanzi e racconti*, ed. by Mario Barenghi, Bruno Falcetto, Claudio Milanini, 3 vols (Milan: Mondadori, 1991–94), III, 1201–04, especially his definition of works like *La strada di San Giovanni* and *Ricordo di una battaglia* as ones that hinge on 'un'esperienza vissuta a mo' di svolta' [an experience that has been lived through as a kind of turning-point] (III, 1203). Henceforth all references to Calvino's fiction will be to this edition in the form *RR* plus volume and page number.
10. He defines the three tales as the first things he wrote after the war, attempts at giving narrative shape to recent experiences, but where the evocation of those events was still too tied to 'un appello emotivo' [an emotional appeal] (*RR*, I, 1262–63).
11. Claudio Milanini has unearthed crucial new evidence on Calvino's partisan life: see 'Calvino e la resistenza: l'identità in gioco', in *Letteratura e Resistenza*, ed. by Andrea Bianchini, Francesca Lolli (Bologna: CLUEB, 1997), pp. 173–91; 'Appunti sulla vita di Italo Calvino 1943–45, con novità poetiche', *Belfagor*, 61 (2006), 43–61.

12. Allusions to a partisan carrying machine-gun ammunition is found several times: in an early story, 'E il settimo si riposò' (*RR*, III, 834), in one of the versions of *La speculazione edilizia* (*RR*, I, 1346), and in the autobiographical 'Ricordo di una battaglia' (*RR*, III, 51).
13. Milanini, 'Appunti sulla vita di Italo Calvino 1943–1945', pp. 51–52.
14. For photographs of Mario Calvino, see those contained in *Album Calvino*, ed. by Luca Baranelli and Ernesto Ferrero (Milan: Mondadori, 1995), pp. 12, 13, 45 etc; and now the important photographic documentation in Paola Forneris and Loretta Marchi, *Il giardino segreto dei Calvino. Immagini dall'album di famiglia tra Cuba e Sanremo. The Secret Garden of the Calvinos. Pictures from the family album from Cuba and Sanremo* (Genoa: De Ferrari and Devega, 2004).
15. *RR*, I, 213. There is a similar desription of the father in *La strada di San Giovanni* (*RR*, III, 16).
16. I, 205; 'Goatherd at Luncheon', in Calvino, *Adam, One Afternoon*, trans. by Archibald Colquhoun and Peggy Wright (London: Picador, 1984), p. 30.
17. eg. *Album Calvino*, pp. 8, 22, 45 etc.
18. I, 396; *The Cloven Viscount* in Calvino, *Our Ancestors*, trans. by Archibald Colquhoun (London: Minerva, 1995), p.28.
19. As Calvino admitted in the 1960 preface to *I nostri antenati*, the Huguenots were in a sense an autobiographical allegory of his family (*RR*, I, 1308).
20. Calvino was fond of using names in this allusive way: the most famous was the anagram of his own name, Tonio Cavilla, who writes the 'cavilling' notes to the school edition of *Il barone rampante* (Turin: Einaudi, 1965), but there are other instances: his school-friend Percivalle Roero appears as Jerry Ostero in 'L'entrata in guerra'; in the 'Mitosi' section of the 'Priscilla' tales from *Ti con zero*, the woman Qfwfq is in love with is called Priscilla Langwood and lives in Paris: again the vowels of the first name and the central consonants of the second name are identical to those of Calvino's wife, Chichita Singer.
21. *RR*, I, 673–74; *Baron in the Trees* in *Our Ancestors*, cit., p. 191.
22. Probably the Hanbury Gardens, full of exotic species of plants, near Ventimiglia and Mentone, originally under English ownership, and probably the setting for 'Il giardino incantato' (*RR*, I, 168–72).
23. Two major cuts are descriptions of his best friend Biancone (Duilio Cossu), two concern an enemy schoolboy here called Ceretti, and he also excises other passages describing individual characters: the 'centurion' Bizantini, a Tuscan Fascist, an anecdote about the Fascist leaders Starace and Bottai, and the protagonist's own pessimism and antipathy towards Bizantini and Ceretti: see *RR*, I, 1322–27.
24. See the letter of 15 July 1955 to Angelo Ponsi, praising him for his 'bilancio d'un uomo a dieci anni dalla Liberazione' [assessment of where we stand now ten years after the Liberation] (*I libri degli altri*, p. 161).
25. For the violent negativity of the self-portrait see the fine article by Domenica Scarpa, 'Dall'alto degli anni. Sguardi sul paesaggio calviniano', *Nuova Prosa*, 42 (2005), pp. 245–62; for fuller discussion of the maternal portraits, see Martin L. McLaughlin, '*La speculazione edilizia*: natura e storia in un racconto "difficile"', in *Italo Calvino. A Writer for the Next Millennium*, ed. by Giorgio Bertone (Alessandria: Dell'Orso, 1998), pp. 205–20 (209–11).
26. I, 787; *A Plunge into Real Estate*, trans. by D. S Carne-Ross, in Calvino, *Difficult Loves* (London: Picador, 1985), p. 169.
27. I, 841; *A Plunge into Real Estate*, p. 213.
28. I, 889–90; *A Plunge into Real Estate*, p. 249.
29. See Milanini's notes in *RR*, I, 1338–51, and Martin L. McLaughlin, 'The genesis of Calvino's *La speculazione edilizia*', *Italian Studies*, 48 (1993), 71–85. Later, in an interview with Ferdinando Camon, Calvino pointed out how autobiographical the work was: 'L'ho riletto da poco, e l'ho trovato sempre piú autobiografico, piú vero...' [I reread it recently, and I found it more and more autobiographical, more and more true...] (*S*, II, 2764–65).
30. S II, 2746; Calvino, *Hermit in Paris*, p. 142
31. For full details see Calvino's note in S, II, 2733.
32. This feeling of delayed loss is articulated even more clearly in a brief letter written around the same time to Franco Fortini, whose father had just died. On 29 January 1962, thus in the month he was writing *La strada di San Giovanni*, he writes to Fortini: 'Io ho capito cos'è perdere il

padre solo qualche tempo dopo averlo perduto, e continuo a soffrirne ancora, dopo dieci anni' [I realized what it means to lose one's father only some time after he had died, and I am still suffering from it ten years later] (*L*, p. 699)

33. Calvino's difficulty with this personal memory of his father is in evidence even as late as *Palomar* (1983): in the first newspaper edition of 'Il fischio del merlo' Calvino explicitly evokes his father's knowledge of birdsong, but in the definitive edition of *Palomar* (Turin: Einaudi, 1983) he says simply that it was 'someone' who was an expert in birdsong: see Martin McLaughlin, *Italo Calvino* (Edinburgh: Edinburgh University Press, 1998), pp. 155–56.
34. III, 14; *The Road to San Giovanni*, trans. by Tim Parks (London: Cape, 1993), p. 15.
35. This dislike of waste was genetic, and Calvino was also notoriously parsimonious: see the recent portrait in Ernesto Ferrero, *I migliori anni della nostra vita* (Milan: Feltrinelli, 2005), pp. 49–59.
36. III, 73; 'La poubelle agréée', in *The Road to San Giovanni*, p. 116. Calvino adopted this strategy in other evocations of the partisan war: in 'Il mio 25 aprile 1945' (1975), he refuses to depart from his limited memories in order to describe the broader strategic events of that day (*S*, II, 2810); similarly at the close of his 1983 essay on 'I ritratti del Duce' [The Duce's Portraits], he refuses to check the name of the most famous English caricaturist of the time, even though he could easily find it since the artist had recently died, because he wanted to respect what he calls 'l'impegno d'usare solo la memoria' [my commitment to rely only on my memory] (*S*, II, 2891; 'The Duce's Portraits', in *Hermit in Paris*, p. 219).
37. I, 1203; *The Path to the Spiders' Nests*, trans. by Archibald Colquhoun, revd. by Martin McLaughlin (London: Vintage, 1998), p. 29.
38. In fact, in his Harvard lecture in praise of 'Esattezza', he also maintains that the opposite quality, haziness, can have powerful poetic appeal as well, as Leopardi shows (*S*, I, 679–83).
39. *RR*, III, 71. He had used the same phrase about a remorse lasting for years, when discussing the deformation of his comrades in his first novel (*RR*, I, 1190, 1194). For other examples of remorse as a theme, see McLaughlin, *Italo Calvino*, pp. 153–54.
40. Terracini's insight was later developed in a fine article by Carla Benedetti on the specific links between this story and the 1964 Preface to *Il sentiero*: see Carla Benedetti, 'Calvino e i segni dell'autore', in *Piccole finzioni con importanza. Valori della narrativa italiana contemporanea*, ed. by Nathalie Roelens and Inge Lanslots (Ravenna: Longo, 1993), pp. 79–101.
41. For an acute extended analysis of this story see Massimo Schilirò, *Le memorie difficili. Saggio su Italo Calvino* (Catania: CUECM, 2002).
42. *RR*, III, 50–51; 'Memories of a Battle', in *The Road to San Giovanni*, p. 78.
43. The phrase occurs in the central passage of his main essay on Conrad, 'I capitani di Conrad' (1954), which states that the real message of Conrad's works is: 'Il senso di una integrazione nel mondo conquistata nella vita pratica, il senso dell'uomo che si realizza nelle cose che fa, nella morale implicita nel suo lavoro, l'ideale di saper essere all'altezza della situazione, sulla coperta dei velieri come sulla pagina' [the sense of integration with the world that comes from a practical existence, the sense of how man fulfils himself in the things he does, in the moral implicit in his work, that ideal of always being able to cope, whether on the deck of a sailing ship or on the page of a book] (*S*, I, 815; 'Conrad's Captains', in Calvino, *Why Read the Classics?*, trans. by Martin McLaughlin (London: Cape, 1999), p. 174; an idea repeated verbatim in 'Natura e storia nel romanzo' (1958) (*S*, I, 39). For a survey of the significance of Conrad in Calvino's oeuvre, see Martin McLaughlin, Arianna Scicutella, 'Calvino e Conrad: dalla tesi di laurea alle *Lezioni americane*', *Italian Studies*, 57 (2002), 113–32.

CHAPTER 11

❖

Umberto Eco: Autobiography into Romance

Jane E. Everson

In spring 1991 Umberto Eco gave three public lectures in the Sheldonian Theatre, Oxford. The subject of these lectures, which were introduced and chaired by John Woodhouse, was the history of man's search for the perfect language. This was the theme of Eco's forthcoming publication for the international multilingual publishing venture, *The Making of Europe*.[1] Eco's volume, *The Search for the Perfect Language*,[2] was one of the earliest to be published. The lectures thus aimed to draw attention to the publishing venture generally, and to give Eco a forum for expounding to an English audience some of his intellectual concerns. From the point of view of the publishing consortium, Eco's lectures were a marketing initiative. Although Eco was no doubt aware of this aim, the lectures also provided an opportunity for him to explore serious ideas with a suitable academic and educated public. Eco's first lecture drew a gratifyingly large audience; the Sheldonian was crowded. He spoke eloquently and in detail on the topic, discussing, in particular in this first lecture, early attempts to construct a perfect language; he devoted some attention too, as in his volume, to Dante's considerations on language in the *De Vulgari Eloquentia*.[3] The key issues of the lecture series, as of the volume, related to long-standing concerns of Eco about the nature of signs, about questions of comprehension and expression, knowledge and the interpretation of knowledge and experience through language.[4]

At the end of the first lecture, questions were invited. Eco then seemed surprised, and certainly was irritated, that most if not all of the questions concerned not the topic of the lecture or the general subject of perfect languages and sign systems, but his first novel, *Il nome della rosa*,[5] which had not been mentioned in the lecture. Eco's irritated response to such questions conveyed the impression that there were no links between the subject of the novel and that of his present area of enquiry, and even that no links should be made between a novel (essentially frivolous, he seemed to suggest) and the heavyweight material he had just been discussing.[6] He seemed in short disappointed by the audience's lack of interest in the serious, intellectual matter under discussion. Eco's surprise was disingenuous; for an English-speaking audience, even more than ten years later, Eco and *Il nome della rosa* remain synonymous, as the general public continues largely to ignore his later novels;[7] while his academic interests and scholarly publications, his continuing concerns with comprehension, expression, knowledge and interpretation are mostly confined to practitioners in the same fields of enquiry — literary theorists, Italianists, students of linguistics, comparative literature, and European thought.[8]

His response was disingenuous in another way too (unless it was deliberately calculated to throw his readers off the scent): for Eco, as for virtually any writer, life and literature interact at some level of consciousness. The historical period through which a writer lives, the experiences he encounters, the people he knows or knows of, form the bedrock of his fiction. People, places, events, but also importantly in Eco's case, ideas, intellectual pursuits, cultural interests, mental games and a sense of the Zeitgeist inevitably, if at times not entirely consciously, influence the way in which he writes, the emphases present in his fiction. No writer exists in a vacuum, unaffected by the environment. Eco himself in another forum would readily admit such a truism, the more so since his activities as a columnist for *L'Espresso* required, obliged and encouraged him to reflect on 'real life', whether momentous events or passing trends, enduring traditions or changing fashions. In one sense, however, Eco was right to be irritated by the facile desire of the Sheldonian audience to concentrate on *Il nome della rosa* and to associate it with the enquiry into the search for perfect languages. To do so was not only to make false connections; it was also to ignore that Eco's fiction had moved on. There are some very close links between *The Search for the Perfect Language* and an Eco novel, but these are to the second novel, *Il Pendolo di Foucault*, published only three years previously in 1988, and not to *Il nome della rosa*. It is the purpose of this discussion to demonstrate these links, through an examination of aspects of Eco's lived experiences (his biography), his research and scholarly productions (his intellectual biography), and his writings — the three elements contributing to the genesis of his second novel.[9]

Il Pendolo di Foucault[10]

Eco's second novel is in many respects very different from *Il nome della rosa* and certainly provoked a perplexed reaction in many of the readers who had devoured that first novel. In place of the 'medieval whodunnit' (to use a tag frequently applied to *Il nome della rosa*) readers found themselves confronted by a novel which demanded intellectual engagement of all its readers even at the literal level of the story line. *Il pendolo di Foucault* could not be read, as many had read his first novel, just for the enjoyment of a good story and without regard to the deeper concerns and play of ideas it contained. The second novel seemed almost wilfully erudite, structurally fragmented, peopled by characters less easy to engage with, elusive and finally apparently inconclusive. Though generally well regarded by reviewers, received critical opinion agreed that the readership for this novel would be more restricted.[11] The differences between the two novels inevitably provoke the question: why did Eco, who, following the international success of *Il nome della rosa*, had already become an international best-selling author, turn away from the vein which he had so profitably mined in that first novel?[12] That question has subsequently acquired a renewed relevance with the publication of his third and fourth novels, *L'isola del giorno prima* (1994) and *Baudolino* (2000), and in particular this last, in which

Eco returns to treating a medieval subject and creates a highly sympathetic (if not entirely honest) protagonist, set in a narrative of adventure which can certainly be read on a literal level and with pleasure by the same general public that enjoyed *Il nome della rosa*. If on publication *Il Pendolo* seemed strikingly different from its predecessor, it seems even more strikingly different when compared with all three of the other novels, with its successors as well as its predecessor.[13]

Though certain concerns, preoccupations and hobby horses of Eco's can be traced through all four of the novels, not least the theme of the perception and interpretation of reality, *Il Pendolo* is distinct from the other three in that it is set in our contemporary world, the world of Italy in the late twentieth century. It deals with events and concerns which belong not only to Eco's intellectual life, to his study, but also to the cities, streets, piazzas, universities and railway stations of Italy during the 1970s and early 1980s.[14] The world of *Il Pendolo* is at one and the same time the world about which Eco is writing and the world in which he is (or until recently had been) living. It follows, therefore, that his engagement with his material in the second novel, his use and transformation of sources and incidents, is not just an academic game or an intellectual exercise. It is also a reflection on lived experience, and springs from life and daily experience in the way the other novels do not.[15] Eco, after all, has never been a monk in a fourteenth-century monastery, an explorer marooned on board a deserted ship in mid-Pacific ocean, nor gone adventuring as a soldier of fortune on the crusades of the twelfth century. But he did, as an adolescent boy, live through the partisan campaigns in Piedmont at the end of the war (like Belbo),[16] has been a university student writing a thesis (like Casaubon),[17] did live in Milan during the 1970s, has been closely involved with the world of books, as both author and collector as well as scholar (like his three protagonists), did spend some time in Brazil (like Casaubon) and has delved into arcane universal languages and systems such as the Kabbalah, devoted to codifying the world and human experience (again like the three protagonists). Above all Eco, like all of his contemporaries in Italy, lived through the domestic terrorism of Italy in the 1970s, the 'anni di piombo'. In the face of public anxiety at the terrifying if politically confused propaganda emanating from the different groups, and the unpredictable and random terrorist incidents which seemed to aim at completely destabilizing the state and civic society, Eco, like his contemporaries, tried to understand the aims and motivations of the terrorist groups, to place them in some kind of coherent political framework and to relate them to established political ideologies.[18] As a journalist it was his responsibility to try to make sense of what was happening politically and explain it to the public, and to explain not only the terrorists but also the repeated failures of the police and secret services to arrest and bring to justice those genuinely responsible, to explain also the failure of the judicial system to convict and punish the guilty.[19] Inevitably Eco, whose intellectual engagement had always been with matters of logic, understanding, interpretation and expression, was driven to reflect on the contradictions of those years, both at the time, in his journalism, and subsequently in his second novel. *Il Pendolo di Foucault*, both in its principal narrative and in its apparent inconclusiveness, reflects the confusions and obfuscations of the 'anni di piombo'. The proliferation of conspiracies, plots and secret societies, now working together and now independently, for often conflicting ends, which *Il Pendolo* presents as fiction, was all too much a part of reality in the years between 1969 and the mid 1980s, as at least one later study among others makes clear.[20] But alongside *Il Pendolo*, with its mocking attempt to fit everything into a single explanation or plan, should be set Eco's contemporaneous, serious study of all such attempts in *The Search for the Perfect Language*. For this last work also invites reflection on the dangers of totalitarianism of thought and expression, of attempting to codify and control through language, and above all of the danger so frequently alluded to in *Il Pendolo* of false connections, the danger of 'only connect'.[21]

The publishers' blurb describes *Il Pendolo* as follows: '...tre redattori editoriali, a Milano, dopo aver frequentato troppo a lungo autori "a proprie spese" che si dilettano di scienze occulte, società segrete e complotti cosmici, decidono di inventare, senza alcun senso di responsabilità, un Piano. Ma qualcuno li prende sul serio' [Three editors in a Milan publishing firm, who have been involved for too long with self-financing amateur authors obsessed with the occult, secret societies and cosmic conspiracies, decide to invent, without any sense of responsibility, a Plan. But there are some people who take them seriously].[22] In the publishers' mind the key phrases here are surely '*scienze occulte*' and '*complotti cosmici*', inviting the reader to see Eco's new novel as part of a genre of occult and/or science fiction. More important for the interaction of life and art which concerns us here, however, are other phrases: '*frequentato troppo a lungo*', '*società segrete*', '*alcun senso di responsabilità*' and '*prende sul serio*', as well as the more obvious '*piano*' and '*complotto*'. The key years, also identified here, are 1969–1984; the narrative ends on Midsummer's Day 1984. The dates are highly significant: 1969 was the date of the first terrorist bombing, of Piazza Fontana in Milan; Christmas 1984 the date of the last, that of the train between Florence and Bologna. Though Eco's narrative concludes before that outrage, the composition of the novel obviously postdates it.[23] The concerns highlighted above and the years which provide the framework of the narrative, thus create a triangle of associations, formed respectively of Eco's own biography, the political events of these years and Eco's reflections on them, and his interest in and developing research on theories of the occult, universal systems and philosophies, in particular in the late Renaissance, which bore fruit in *The Search for the Perfect Language*. All three are brought together in *Il Pendolo di Foucault*.

Surface links

Even at a superficial level the connections between the two works are easily discernible. Uniquely among Eco's novels, *Il Pendolo* is divided into sections, named from the ten divisions of the Sefirot.[24] Though allusions to the meaning of these are made in the course of the novel, the reader's understanding of why the novel's sections should be related to these elements is advanced much more quickly by reference to *The Search*, whose second chapter provides a straightforward explanation of the Sefirot and their place in Kabbalistic tradition. For the reader the chapter of *The Search* acts like a commentary to the novel; but for Eco the author it is surely the analysis of the Kabbalah and its intellectual and linguistic traditions, while pursuing research for *The Search* which provides the idea of structuring *Il Pendolo* in ten sections and naming them in this way — a structure of subdivisions not used in *Il nome* and to which he does not return in the subsequent novels.

Il Pendolo is also unique (thus far) in prefixing to each chapter an epigraph, relating to the ideas of that chapter. These are culled from a wide range of reading, from the *Corpus Hermeticum* to Woody Allen, but the dominant impression they leave on the reader is that they are derived from original writings, and studies on esoteric language systems and secret codes and societies. What stand out are the epigraphs of writers on the Kabbalah (Abulafia, Reuchlin),[25] the Rosicrucians (Johann Valentin Andreae, Hoeme-Wronski, Neuhaus),[26] the Freemasons,[27] and the names of Bacon, Trithemius, Kircher and Postel.[28] Most readers of the novel have no way of knowing how many of these are real writers and texts, and probably are satisfied with making the connections within the novel between epigraph and chapter. But again here *The Search* provides both a commentary for the reader and an explanation of many of Eco's choices of epigraph.[29] Moreover a glance down the chapters and subdivisions of *The Search* stresses that Eco's concern there is not just with language understood as grammar and semantics, but rather with attempts to explain and codify experience either for philosophical or for cultic reasons. The second chapter of *The Search* is entitled 'The Kabbalistic Pansemioticism'; the fourth and sixth are concerned with the 'Ars Combinatoria' which lies at the root of all encoding and encrypting systems; Kircher's *Polygraphy* is the subject of chapter nine, and his title again, like Pansemioticism, underlines the attempt to 'write' the whole of experience, to fit everything into a single system. Both *Il Pendolo* and *The Search* bring into play ideas and individuals from the whole of recorded history and from almost every culture and continent; but where in *Il Pendolo* these seem (and indeed are) deliberately mixed up and apparently random in the connections made, not least because of a deliberate blurring of chronology and the game element, in *The Search* the connections are made acceptable largely by the chronological approach which Eco, unlike his fictional alter egos, adopts for his study.

Further surface links between the two works are provided by the diagrams contained in each, and especially by the appearance in both of certain key items. In *Il Pendolo* (ch. 5) these begin with the list of combinations or permutations in which the tetragrammaton (of the name of God) can be cast. The 'source' of this intellectual game is given as the Temurah, and Diotallevi proceeds at this point to a dissertation on the Torah, Abulafia and the world of the Kabbalah (*Il Pendolo*, pp. 34–36).[30] The same set of explanations — on the real or original Torah, acrostic games and the association of numbers and letters, the Temurah and Abulafia — recurs in *The Search* (ch. 2), and is followed there by a discussion of permutations. The relevant diagram appears in the subsequent chapter on Lull and the *ars combinatoria*. Here Eco is discussing Lull's Tabulae or wheels for coding language and experience (*The Search*, p. 57). At this point in his study Eco alludes also to the significant figure of Athanasius Kircher, and to the revival of Lull's *ars* by Trithemius in the sixteenth century. Lull's wheels, and their subsequent developments are, as we shall see, the key to the various interpretations of Ingolf's message, and are consequently illustrated in *Il Pendolo* by diagrams and explanations, both when Ardenti first mentions them (*Il Pendolo*, pp. 110–11) and when Lia offers her decoding of the message (ibid., p. 423).[31]

Eco's biography

The centrality of Eco's biography in terms of lived experience within the seemingly fragmented narrative of *Il Pendolo*, is most evident in what is apparently the most exotic section of the novel, the part of the narrative set in Brazil.[32] At the end of the third section of the novel, Casaubon graduates and, in 1975, leaves Italy for Brazil, where he takes up a post as 'lettore' in a university in Rio de Janeiro. He spends three years in Brazil, returning to Italy in 1978. Eco too spent time at a university in Brazil, in his case the university of Sao Paulo, between 1966 and 1970, but his involvement with Brazilian culture was renewed in the late 1970s — the period of Casaubon's fictional residence there — and synthesized in his essay of 1979: 'Con chi stanno gli Orixà?' ['Whose Side Are the Orixà On?'], published in *L'Espresso* in December of that year.[33]

The narrative of Casaubon's experiences in Brazil (chapters 23–33) can be grouped principally under two headings: Marxism and politics on the one hand; exotic cults and rituals on the other. In Brazil Casaubon studies and comments on both of these and both topics find their way into the Plan he and his friends subsequently construct, and in particular into its dénouement. But the interest, observations and comments of Casaubon are also those of Eco, both in his lived experience, in Brazil, and in his intellectual biography, in *The Search*. Both topics, politics and the exotic, provide evidence of the perils of making connections and the oddities thrown up when diverse elements come together. The Marxist ideology which Casaubon believes he knows by heart reveals itself in Brazil to be profoundly, even completely different from its European counterpart. It is shot through with local traditions, coloured by local folklore and myth and impressed with the particular political confusions and accommodations of South America in that period. Casaubon makes the point again through his reflections both on Amparo and on Marxism.[34]

Casaubon finds such syncretism fascinating, but fails to perceive its inherent dangers, especially when taken to extremes. A political ideology so fused and mixed with other quite disparate elements, no longer has a clear and logical set of values, aims and objectives, can no longer really be called an ideology. Anything can be added to it, any interpretation or emphasis brought to bear, ideas and actions even quite foreign to the original ideology can be promoted in its name. Though Casaubon is aware of these confusions, he fails to address them, and on his return to Italy finds himself, like his contemporaries, bereft of the old political certainties. He and his friends substitute an ironic detachment for political engagement, and intellectual games for active and practical commitment. In due course Casaubon will be made to confront the dangers of ideologies which admit anything and everything, and which have been hijacked by personalities with private agendas, but which still attract those in search of a fervent commitment and a need to give blind loyalty to a cause, however illogical or poorly understood.

The most memorable chapters of the Brazilian section, however, are those which recount Casaubon's participation in the cultic rituals of *candomblé* (chs 26–28) and *umbanda* (ch. 33). Here biography and literature are virtually coterminous, in spite of the exotic, fantastic nature of the subject matter. For the composition of these chapters Eco returns especially to his essay, 'Con chi stanno gli Orixà', and indulges in a rewriting of himself.[35] Indeed he almost plagiarizes himself, since at many points the only difference between the two accounts lies in the shift from the journalistic discourse to the direct speech and dialogue of the principal characters of this part of the novel: Casaubon, Aglié and Amparo.[36]

The objective, descriptive tones of Eco's journalism are broadly retained in the first of Casaubon's two cultic experiences, that of the *candomblé*, in which Casaubon appears as the curious traveller, intrigued by the exotic cult but separate from it and unaffected by it. That tone, however, is progressively lost in the second account, in the *umbanda* tent, in which Casaubon and Amparo become increasingly infected and absorbed by the experience — Amparo in the end completely so. Casaubon on this occasion is forced to recognize that participation in these rites has a price, that beyond a certain point a sceptical rationality offers no protection or defence against the powers of the irrational.

The power of music, incense, dance, ceremony and ritual, and their effects even on a rational Marxist like Amparo, as observed here by Casaubon, also struck Eco in his Brazilian encounters.[37] Casaubon on his return to Italy believes he has left behind such experiences, which he continues to see as somehow foreign, primitive and remote. Aglié, however, in his explanations, has alluded to the negative elements of rituals involving possession and trances (*Il Pendolo*, pp. 143, 171–72). Eco, returning mentally to his experiences in Brazil, retains also that sense. Once a cult, like a political ideology, is uprooted from its origins in time and place, adopted, practised and manipulated by the inexperienced or the power-hungry, it becomes dangerous. Reason is never sufficient against the irrational forces of the emotions, the physical senses, the group psyche, and the need to believe, as Casaubon discovers in the final chapters of the novel, and as Eco's contemporaries discovered as they struggled to understand the obscure and violent politics of the 'anni di piombo'.

Belbo and Casaubon

In fictionalizing his Brazilian experiences, Eco shifts the dates by almost ten years. For the sections of the novel set in Milan, both before and after, the shifts operated are of a different kind. In place of the one alter ego of the Brazilian chapters Eco reflects life (his own and that of his contemporaries) through the two characters of Casaubon — younger than Eco, and Belbo, his exact contemporary in age.[38] Casaubon reflects the ideas and attitudes of students in the 1970s, a group with whom Eco was of course very familiar and with whom he was in daily contact.[39] Belbo on the other hand reflects the attitudes of Eco's own age group, a generation too young to have participated in the partisan struggles at the end of the war though old enough to have sensed the excitement and appeal of that struggle, but equally too old to be genuinely part of the student unrest of '68 and its aftermath. This sense of having missed an opportunity to prove oneself, to show one's commitment by rising to a great challenge or occasion runs like a thread through Belbo's computerized autobiography, as Casaubon readily perceives, and even if such attitudes are not necessarily characteristic of Eco's autobiography, they are certainly an element in the psychology of his generation.[40] In the person of Belbo the unresolved tensions and political allegiances of the end of the war in Italy are inserted into the (fictional) representation of Italy in the 1970s.[41] Thus Belbo is an habitué of Pilade's bar and of its crowd of 'contestatori'; he participates in their political discussions and protest marches, seems to be part of their left-wing rhetoric, but his autobiographical files, which are inserted into these chapters or interspersed with them, are concerned with the uncertain allegiances and the difficulty of distinguishing friends from enemies during the final stages of the war.[42] A comparison with the study of Italian politics by Peter Willan is interesting for the similarities of emphasis:

> In order to understand the origins of the strategy of tension and the directions that terrorism would take in later years, it is necessary to go back to what happened during the Second World War and in its immediate aftermath.[43]

Willan goes on to underline the disparate nature of the Resistance movement and the way in which it attracted to it ex-fascists and bandits, as well as communists and other genuine anti-fascists, commenting also on 'the guilty consciences of those who had failed to make a stand against fascism at the time'.[44]

As Belbo's files reveal, commitment to a great occasion is something that he has spent his whole life searching for; Casaubon too is in search of commitment, as his comments perhaps unwittingly reveal both before and after his trip to Brazil (*Il Pendolo*, pp. 129, 176). Both believe they can be ironic and detached observers, mocking others' commitment in the construction of the Plan. Both find that that becomes for themselves, and in the eyes of others, precisely the commitment they are simultaneously seeking and mocking. A Plan, in Italy in the 1970s, is not value-free. Again Casaubon's comment (ibid., 52) serves for both fiction and contemporary events: 'chi si impegna a fare un mondo si è già compromesso con l'errore e il male' [he who embarks on the creation of worlds is already tainted with corruption and evil (*Foucault's Pendulum*, p. 57)].[45]

Both Belbo and Casaubon function also as alter egos for Eco in his intellectual life. Casaubon's research interests, starting with his 'tesi di laurea' on the Templars, relate him to Eco's interests in the Middle Ages, but without making the two identical. His later researches into the history of metals, alchemy and the like, has links to Eco's interests in the late Renaissance and Baroque, in particular the figure of John Dee, present in both *Il Pendolo* and *The Search*. The Templars form a key component of the Plan, but it is language — its possibilities, decipherment, and application — which constitutes the fundamental basis of this game as evolved by Belbo, Casaubon and Diotallevi.[46] In the initial stages Belbo and Casaubon are playing an innocent game which reflects Eco's own love of abstruse vocabulary and the flexibility of language. The encounter with the mysterious Colonel Ardenti and his secret message changes the tone and nature of the game. In Ardenti's view the message expresses an arcane and esoteric system of communication, behind which lies the Templars' aim to order and control the world. Intrigued and challenged, both by Ardenti's bizarre theories and the incomplete message and its linguistic and semiotic possibilities, Belbo, Casaubon and Diotallevi are precipitated into the world of perfect languages, and especially of coded languages, which is the current research topic of Eco their creator. In the course of the rest of the novel, as the Plan gradually develops, the three are led to consider the Kabbalah, the Rosicrucians, Athanasius Kircher and various other groups whose ideas in the novel seem utterly fantastic. As *The Search* will subsequently show quite soberly, these theories have serious, historical foundations, and Eco here is simply mining his 'schede di ricerca' in a similar way to that practised by Casaubon in the construction and continual additions to the Plan.[47] As Casaubon comments on his research (though the statement also holds good for his creator):

> Mi riusciva sempre più difficile districare il mondo della magia da quello che oggi chiamiamo l'universo della precisione. Ritrovavo personaggi che avevo studiato a scuola come portatori della luce matematica e fisica in mezzo alle tenebre della superstizione, e scoprivo che avevano lavorato con un piede nella Cabbala e l'altro in laboratorio. [...] Ma poi trovo testi insospettabili che mi raccontavano come i fisici positivisti appena usciti dall'università andassero a pasticciare per sedute medianiche e cenacoli astrologici, e come Newton fosse arrivato alle leggi della gravitazione universale perché credeva che esistessero forze occulte (mi ricordavo delle sue esplorazioni nella cosmologia rosacrociana). (*Il Pendolo*, p. 286)

> [It was becoming harder for me to keep apart the world of magic and what today we call the world of facts. Men I had studied in school as bearers of mathematical and physical enlightenment now turned up amid the murk of superstition, for I discovered they had worked with one foot in cabala and the other in the laboratory. (...) But then I would find texts above all suspicion that told me how in the time of positivism physicists barely out of the university dabbled in séances and astrological cénacles, and how Newton had arrived at the law of gravity because he believed in the existence of occult forces, which recalled his investigations into Rosicrucian cosmology. (*Foucault's Pendulum*, p. 360)][48]

The Search for the Perfect Language

In his introduction to *The Search for the Perfect Language*, Eco sets out the scope of the work. Much of the emphasis falls on language systems and on actual, real languages, but even here an equal emphasis is given to artificial languages, those created for a specific purpose. It is also worth noting the category under which Eco himself states that this work falls: history of ideas,[49] and the acknowledgements and the thanks he expresses to Paolo Rossi for his interest in the subject of 'pansophia and world theatres' (ibid., p. 5). In chapter one it becomes clear that the term 'perfect language' must be understood philosophically as much as linguistically, as a means of explaining and expressing the world, experience and reality, and not just as a sign system or syntactic construct. In the same first chapter of *The Search*, Eco slips from discussing specific languages to considering systems of thought, and this is in fact the core element underpinning the choice of material in *The Search*. Even the titles of some of the different chapters and sections are illuminating for comparison with *Il Pendolo*: consider for example 'Cosmic Permutability and the Kabbala of Names' (in ch. 2); the '*Arbor Scientiarum*' (in ch. 4); the 'Etymological Furor', and 'A Dream that Refused to Die' (both in ch. 5), and ch. 8 entitled 'Magic Language' and containing the section 'Perfection and Secrecy'.

In the introduction and chapter one Eco raises a number of ideas which can immediately be related to *Il Pendolo* and have already been fictionalized there. Chapter one begins with Genesis, and the account of the naming of things by God, and then by Adam. Thus, as Eco uncontroversially states here in *The Search*, all things in this account acquire existence through language. By being named they come into being and acquire reality, corporeality. As a comment in a study of how language works to mediate experience, this is an unexceptional, even obvious point.[50] But Eco's comment is striking, and in particular the choice of certain words:

> It is this story [of Babel] that served as the point of departure for any number of dreams to 'restore' the language of Adam. Genesis 10, however, has continued to lurk in the background with all its explosive potential still intact. If the languages were already differentiated after Noah [and before Babel], why not before? [...] If languages were differentiated not as a punishment but simply as a result of a natural process, why must the confusion of tongues constitute a curse at all?
>
> Every so often in the course of our story, someone will oppose Genesis 10 to Genesis 11. Depending on the period and the theologico-philosophical context, the results will be more or less devastating. (*The Search*, pp. 9–10)

If, however, we try to imagine what would happen if the actions of God or Adam actually occurred in real life, then the word 'devastating' seems a mild comment and the relevance of this discussion to *Il Pendolo* is apparent. Belbo, Casaubon and Diotallevi do not so much conjure up things from nothing by giving them names, as take names already in existence and twist them to give them a new meaning and hence a new reality. Either way through naming they create and bring into corporeal existence — a fact only realized by Casaubon towards the very end of the novel:

> Noi abbiamo inventato un Piano inesistente ed Essi non solo lo hanno preso per buono, ma si sono convinti di esserci dentro da tempo, ovvero hanno identificato i frammenti dei loro progetti disordinati e confusi come momenti del Piano nostro, scandito secondo un'inconfutabile logica dell'analogia, della parvenza, del sospetto.
>
> Ma se inventando un piano gli altri lo realizzano, il Piano è come se ci fosse, anzi, ormai c'è. (*Il Pendolo*, p. 490)

> [We invented a nonexistent Plan, and They not only believed it was real but convinced themselves that They had been part of it for ages, or, rather, They identified the fragments of their muddled mythology as moments of our Plan, moments joined in a logical, irrefutable web of analogy, semblance, suspicion.
>
> But if you invent a plan and others carry it out, it's as if the Plan exists. At that point it does exist. (*Foucault's Pendulum*, p. 619)]

It is, too, in *The Search* that the links between word games and the play of language on the one hand, and mystic cults and secret societies on the other, which are the twin poles of the Plan in *Il Pendolo*, are explained. Eco in his introduction to

The Search traces the gradual decline in the universal acceptance of the Greek and Latin languages as systems sufficient to explain human experience, sufficient to give linguistic expression to all human knowledge and experience. A civilization 'showing signs of age' linguistically, philosophically and in its religious observances gradually absorbs and comes to accept and even promote 'revelations beyond reason', mystical cults and systems of 'secret wisdom' which come to be believed as capable of providing explanations which reason and rational language cannot. Eco's summary of some of these sources of 'wisdom' reads like some of Casaubon's musings, and the incorporation of details into the Plan.[51]

As Eco points out, these hermeneutic ideas were to be very influential in the later sixteenth century, a period on which both *The Search* and *Il Pendolo* focus.[52] As he concludes this part of the discussion, Eco makes an important statement, which provides the key to the dynamic the Plan eventually acquires in *Il Pendolo*:

> Since the reason of the philosophers proved unable to supply truths about important matters such as these, men and women sought revelations beyond reason, through visions, and through communications with the godhead itself. [...] there is nothing more fascinating than secret wisdom: one is sure that it exists, but one does not know what it is. In the imagination, therefore, it shines as something unutterably profound. (*The Search*, p. 13)[53]

Many of the phrases which Eco uses in discussing cultural changes in the later Roman Empire could be equally applied to Italy in the period between the mid-1960s and the early 1980s. The questioning of the traditional ways of viewing society, of the traditional classifications of countries, cultures, ideologies, systems of thought, together with a decline in traditional forms of religion, changing social mores and attitudes to the family, the cornerstones of society, are ways of summing up this period of Italian history. Into this questioning of established orthodoxies crept supposedly new creeds and forms of wisdom, sometimes inchoate (like 'flower power') and sometimes revivals, as Eco's comment in *The Search* (p. 15) underlines. The loss of guidelines provided by established tradition and orthodox religion does not lead to agnosticism or sceptical atheism, but rather to an irrational and emotional adherence to everything and anything of a mystical nature. It is significant that Eco quotes Chesterton's famous aphorism, not here as a relevant illustration of his serious academic discussion in *The Search*, but in *Il Pendolo*:

> Ma c'era un altro (forse Chesterton?) che aveva detto: da quando gli uomini non credono più in dio, non è che non credano più a nulla, credono a tutto. (*Il Pendolo*, p. 492)
>
> [And someone else — was it Chesterton? — said that when men stop believing in God, it isn't that they then believe in nothing: they believe in everything. (*Foucault's Pendulum*, p. 620)]

Thus as Eco in *The Search*, writing against the background of the decline, fragmentation and increasing loss of direction, the growing irrationality of Italian politics and culture in the 1970s, is led to such appropriate reflections, so in *Il Pendolo* his alter egos draw into the Plan secret and esoteric societies and individuals from the past together with organizations enjoying a revival in the 1960s and 1970s, not always for harmless reasons, of which the Freemasons are the most notable.[54]

The thirst for alternative religions thought to hold superior forms of wisdom more satisfying to their adherents and explanations of the universe fuller than those of traditional religion is still evident in contemporary society more than a decade after the publication of *Il Pendolo* and *The Search*. The lack of easy answers, which the open-ended nature of the novel suggests, underlines the continuing relevance of these reflections in *Il Pendolo*.

This association in *The Search* between the gradual loss of the universal languages of the ancient world and the absorption into the culture of late antiquity of esoteric cults and arcane wisdom, of mysticism and initiatory rites which Eco studies scientifically in this work has been foreshadowed and explored in *Il Pendolo*. But in the novel the association of these two themes is linked by a third, that of contemporary politics, so that once again the intellectual life and lived experience coincide. Both *The Search* and *Il Pendolo* acknowledge the particular relevance of the power of language for the political sphere. If knowledge is power and knowledge is expressed in language, it follows that political language, its formulation and use, is a powerful weapon. Writing *The Search* in the early 1990s, Eco's political focus is on the increasing unity of Europe following the Single European Act of 1992, and on the lessons to be drawn from the devastation of post-Tito Yugoslavia. His words in *The Search* (p. 19) are broadly optimistic. Writing in the mid 1980s, but reflecting back on the 1970s, as he composed *Il Pendolo*, Eco had transmitted a bleaker picture, a stronger warning against the destruction caused by the wanton abuse or manipulation of language. The focus seems to fall on the playful misuse by Belbo, Casaubon and Diotallevi of the language of esoteric popular cults taken so seriously by their adherents. But the true focus is surely the corruption of political discourse which characterized Italy certainly in the 1970s, both in the language of extra-parliamentary groups such as the Brigate Rosse, and perhaps even more in that of the established political parties, in particular the Christian Democrats and the arch-manipulator of language, Aldo Moro. *Il Pendolo* mentions Moro only in passing,[55] but it is worth recalling in this context Sciascia's description (drawing on Pasolini) of Moro's use of language in *L'Affaire Moro* (1978), and where such use of language led Moro.[56]

Ardenti's message

The triangle of links which has been outlined above, between the contemporary politics of Italy in the 1970s, Eco's academic and research interests in esoteric language systems, and the 1988 novel are particularly evident in the chapters concerned with Colonel Ardenti's message and the various interpretations given to it.

Introduced at the very end of ch. 16, Ardenti is immediately associated with the 1940s and the privations of the war. He reminds Casaubon of the guerrilla fighters on both sides of the partisan divide. As he details his military, colonial past (Ethiopia, Spain, Algeria), it becomes clear that he is an ex-Fascist. In spite of admitting to choosing always 'la parte perdente' [the losing side], he continues to display a dangerous enthusiasm for conspiracies in the cause of world domination and a fascination for semi-secret organizations such as the Templars and the Masons.

Ardenti in short is an ironic (at least at this stage) construct of the not-so-ex Fascist of the 1960s.[57]

Ardenti's fixation on the Templars may strike the protagonists (and the reader) as ludicrous, a response underlined by the author in the following chapter where Ardenti makes a series of false connections in order to prove his argument, and is accordingly consistently debunked by the sceptical Casaubon on behalf of Eco.[58] Ardenti also reveals, inadvertently, that he is not just fascinated by secret societies, but is also actively involved with the secret services and has used questionable techniques to extract sensitive information.[59] Ardenti thus fits even better the stereotype of the right-wing conspirator of the 1960s and later 1970s. The point is further underlined by the concentration in Ardenti's story on military orders and the reference to 1944 as the year in which the grand plan of world domination was to conclude, but did not, leaving unfinished business for the type of right-wing groups with which Ardenti is in sympathy.

The political dimension of the plan and its links to the strategy of tension and obscure conspiracies and associations of individuals in Italy in the 60s and 70s should be clear. The message itself, presented in ch. 19, takes us, however, straight to the concerns of *The Search*. The series of meaningless words is presented by Ardenti as a cypher based on the systems of encryption devised by Trithemius. Though Ardenti stresses the chance element in his application of Trithemius' system, much of his explanation concerning Trithemius is virtually a preview, a summary of the same points discussed more fully by Eco in *The Search*, ch. 6, another case of auto-rewriting by Eco. The secret service and political potential of encrypted messages *à la* Trithemius is already present in Ardenti's words in *Il Pendolo*, but *The Search* carries this aspect of the discussion further, incorporating consideration of magic rituals which Ardenti mentions, but which are not developed until later in the novel, when their ludicrous dimension, noted also in *The Search*, is overlaid by the fanaticism of the adherents of the various groups absorbed into and convinced of the Plan. When the final drama in the Conservatoire des Arts et Métiers begins (ch. 113) the words which Bramanti incites the crowd to chant are precisely those recommended by Trithemius, and explained in *The Search* (p. 126). In this same section of *The Search* Eco stresses the way in which cryptography runs the danger (by definition) of becoming an end in itself, as does the Plan in the novel, an unending and not always sane and sensible game.[60]

Crucial too for the links between the two texts is Eco's penultimate paragraph in this section of *The Search*, in effect a dispassionate, objective summary of the three protagonists' game in constructing the Plan in the novel, and of its intellectual hubris and corruption.

> The steganographers had little interest in the content (or the truths) expressed by their combinations. Steganography was not a technique designed to discover truth: it was a device by which elements of a given expression-substance [...] might be correlated randomly (in increasingly different ways so as to render their decipherment more arduous) [...] all that mattered was engendering new expressions through an increasingly mind-boggling number of purely syntactic operations. The letters were dealt with as unbound variables. (*The Search*, p. 128)

The same approach is evident in the three protagonists' use of random computer-generated links and deliberately anachronistic associations in the generation of the Plan.

Trithemius's encrypting circles return later in *Il Pendolo* when Lia provides her decryption of the message of Ingolf. Her interpretation starts from one of Eco's favourite medieval philosophers, Ockham, and unravels the message by eschewing complex number associations in favour of historical and topographical data. Her revelation subsequently of how Ingolf has used Trithemius' wheels both seriously and playfully is intended in the novel to debunk the interpretations both of Ardenti, and of Belbo, Casaubon and Diotallevi. Her tones as she does so are, however, predominantly didactic, and her explanation reminiscent of her creator, though longer than that offered in *The Search*. Through Lia Eco has already demonstrated the extremes of ambiguity and uncertainty attendant upon the decipherment of messages thought to be encrypted, and the dangers deciphering them presents. There is no need for Eco to dwell again at length on this in *The Search*; here it is *Il Pendolo* that provides the commentary to *The Search* instead of vice versa.[61]

Among the items explored in ch. 7 of *The Search*, are the problems of trying to decipher a language (or a code) when one has no key or certain starting point, and the fanciful theories current in the sixteenth and seventeenth centuries on the multiple meanings of symbols and the even more fanciful explanations for the relationship between symbol and meaning (*The Search*, pp. 146, 147). The survey of the attempts to decipher Egyptian hieroglyphs confronts the reader directly with the fusion of linguistic science and the attraction of secret cults, mystic lore and lost civilizations (ibid., p. 148) which has earlier formed such a prominent and potent mixture in the Plan of *Il Pendolo*. Indeed the summary Eco gives (ibid., pp. 148–49), though not a rewriting of his earlier words, is nonetheless an accurate synthesis of the dangerous games of Belbo, Casaubon and Diotallevi. As the chapter of *The Search* continues, it acts as a commentary to the novel, addressing the distortions imposed on understanding and interpretation by assumptions about authorship and the direction of one's reading (ibid., pp. 152–54, especially p. 153). The key quotation here (p. 154) is from Kircher. His evident support for linguistic symbols as intrinsic elements of secret wisdom underlines not only Kircher's centrality to the search for perfect languages as discussed here, but also his centrality for *Il Pendolo*. In his systematic collection of data, his precise transcriptions, his involvement with a wide range of languages and cultures in the name of science, Kircher is a model for Casaubon, in particular as he elaborates the history of metals, and Casaubon, like Kircher, will reveal himself to be, for all his scientific scepticism, hopelessly trapped in his own prejudicial assumptions about the decipherment of linguistic texts, while the debunking of Kircher by Champollion is worthy of Lia's debunking of the mystical messages of Ingolf.[62]

The association of Kircher with *Il Pendolo* and with the distortions of language by political and terrorist groups, and secret societies which lurk behind the fiction of the Plan in the novel, and in the contemporary milieu in which it was composed, are encapsulated when Eco talks of Kircher's 'ideology' (section title) — a strange word to use in the context of linguistics but, as Eco stresses, entirely appropriate given the context of seventeenth-century politics. Most telling of all, though, for the links between Kircher and the protagonists of the novel, is the phrase used by Eco of Kircher in *The Search*: 'The hieroglyphic configurations had become a sort of machine for the inducing of hallucinations ...' (p. 162). Kircher's dreams of world harmony and the imposition of a single, 'divine' order may indeed seem hallucinatory, but the word recalls rather the hallucinations of the Diabolici and of their would-be manipulators and mockers, Belbo, Casaubon and Diotallevi, and the final catastrophic hallucinations in the Conservatoire. Having raised the spectre of the hallucinatory and destructive force of language, Eco concludes the section by pointing back to a series of figures whose ideas are linked to those of Kircher, but who also underpin the Plan: Postel, Lull, the Rosicrucians, the German Empire and its latter-day manifestation — the Reich that would last for a thousand years (ibid., pp. 164–65). Dreams of perfect harmony, of order in every sphere of existence may seem harmless and even beneficial in the confines of the intellectual's study (Kircher) or mildly diverting amidst the tedium of the publishing house (Belbo, Casaubon), but they are serious and dangerous in a society disturbed by social and economic upheavals, and characterized by political paralysis and judicial inertia. In such a context extremists of both left and right can too easily adopt and manipulate such perfect systems and the language in which they are articulated to justify their actions. Postel repeatedly proclaimed the ideals of universal peace and non-violence; but his wild imaginings, summarized by Eco in *The Search* (pp. 77–78), are almost exactly those satirically imported into the Plan by Belbo and Casaubon and which in the end destroy them. It is no accident that Postel's wanderings constitute almost a blueprint for the locations of the Plan, nor that he is especially associated with Paris where the Plan reaches its dénouement, nor, above all, that the Abbey of St. Martin-des-Champs, where the Conservatoire des Arts et Métiers is housed, is the place where Postel, the utopian but also the potential totalitarian, died. Eco in *The Search* does not draw parallels with Italy in the 1970s and 1980s. Rather he concludes his discussion on the topic of what was the original language and whether all languages had a common root, with an allusion that is nowadays milder because historically more distant, and yet, as the figure of Ardenti and those he represents remind us, one that still constitutes a threat: Eco concludes with reference to the Aryan myth, but the words are still thought-provoking:

> Unfortunately, this is not just a story of the gullibility of scientists. We know only too well that the Aryan myth had political consequences that were profoundly tragic. (*The Search*, pp. 105–06)

The conspiracy interpretation of the message, cynically but energetically promoted by Belbo, Casaubon and Diotallevi, becomes in the novel a reality for the shadowy groups both on the Left and on the Right which characterized Italian politics in the 1970s and early 1980s. Casaubon, in particular, has spent several years engaged in research on the writers who underpin *The Search*, but, unlike Eco, he has not made the valid and obvious connections between politics and language. All three protagonists have also failed to understand either human nature or politics. Yet from the perspective of the new millennium Eco's optimism about the new order in Europe after 1989 now seems misplaced. Political violence in Italy did not die with the 1980s, unsolved mysteries remain, and shady figures like Gelli are still at large. Eco's return in *L'isola del giorno prima* to a novel set in historic times, and continued in *Baudolino*, is perhaps a confession of pessimism in the face of continuing political and judicial shenanigans.[63] It is certainly an abandonment of the triple genesis of his second novel, of the combination of biography, research interests and fiction, in favour of the simpler, perhaps less threatening dual combination of just research and fiction.[64]

Notes to Chapter 11

1. The series was promoted by a group of European publishers, including for the UK Basil Blackwell, which sponsored the Sheldonian lecture series. For the publication details of these lectures see Peter Bondanella, *Umberto Eco and the Open Text: Semiotics, Fiction and Popular Culture* (Cambridge: Cambridge University Press, 1997), p. 205.
2. This appeared first in the original Italian from Laterza, the Italian collaborator, in 1993, and then in English in 1995. All quotations here are taken from the English version, Umberto Eco, *The Search for the Perfect Language* (Oxford: Blackwell, 1995). A number of the topics first treated in *The Search* are further explored, in some cases more fully, in the essays collected in *Serendipities, Language and Lunacy*, trans. by William Weaver (London: Weidenfeld and Nicolson, 1999; Italian edition, 1998).
3. See Eco, *The Search*, pp. 34–52.
4. For a full and detailed list of Eco's research and publications in this area, see for example Bondanella, *Umberto Eco and the Open Text*.
5. This had appeared in English in 1983, but had been filmed after that: the film appeared in 1986.
6. Subsequently he has overcome this and has engaged with interest in discussions of links between his fiction and his scholarly studies: see Bondanella, *Umberto Eco and the Open Text*; Michael Caesar, *Umberto Eco. Philosophy, Semiotics and the Work of Fiction* (Cambridge: Polity Press, 1999); and most recently Eco's own contribution to *Illuminating Eco. On the Boundaries of Interpretation*, ed. by Charlotte Ross and Rochelle Sibley (Aldershot: Ashgate, 2004), pp. 171–99. JoAnn Cannon, 'The imaginary universe of Umberto Eco. A reading of *Foucault's Pendulum*', *Modern Fiction Studies*, 38.4 (1992), 895–909, suggests that *Il nome della rosa* indirectly confronts the modern political scene in Italy, with the indication that the 'author' found the 'manuscript' in Prague in 1968. Though an interesting point, it seems somewhat tenuous.
7. With the possible exception of *Baudolino*, energetically marketed in William Weaver's translation (London: Secker and Warburg, 2002) for Christmas 2002. On Eco's fifth novel see note 13 below.
8. The development of two often mutually exclusive readerships in the Anglo-American reception of Eco's work, one for the theoretical writings and one for the fiction, is considered by Michael Caesar, 'Eco on the Move', in Ross and Sibley, *Illuminating Eco*, pp. 155–67 (esp. pp. 157–61).
9. Eco himself reflects on some of these links in his essay 'Come scrivo' in *Sulla letteratura* (Milan: Bompiani, 2002), pp. 324–59, now translated into English: 'How I write' in Ross and Sibley, *Illuminating Eco*, pp. 171–92; subsequent references to this essay are to this version, though there is now a complete translation of *Sulla letteratura*, trans. by Martin McLaughlin as *On Literature* (London: Secker and Warburg, 2005).
10. Umberto Eco, *Il Pendolo di Foucault* (Milan: Bompiani, 3rd ed., January 1989). All references will be to this hardback edition. All translated passages are from *Foucault's Pendulum*, trans. by William Weaver (London: Secker and Warburg, 1990).
11. For a range of critical discussions on *Il Pendolo di Foucault*, emphasizing various different approaches see JoAnn Cannon, 'The imaginary universe'; Cristina Degli Espositi, 'The poetics of Hermeticism in Umberto Eco's *Il Pendolo di Foucault*', *Forum italicum*, 25.2 (1991), 185–204; M. Viano, 'Ancora su *Il Pendolo di Foucault*', ibid., 152–61; N. Bouchard, 'Critifictional epistemes

in contemporary literature: The case of *Il Pendolo di Foucault'*, *Comparative Literature Studies*, 32.4 (1995), 495–513; V. Vernon, 'The demonics of true belief: treacherous texts, blasphemous interpretations and murderous readers', *Modern Language Notes*, 107 (1992), 840–54; R. Artigiani, 'Image — Music — Pinball', ibid. 855–76, does talk about language, logic and science, but appeared too early to take account of *The Search*. For a bibliographical overview see J. P. Consoli, 'Navigating the labyrinth: a bibliographical essay of selected criticism of the works of Umberto Eco', *Style*, 27 (1993), 478–514 (esp. pp. 505–07).

12. Caesar, *Umberto Eco* (pp. 134–44, esp. p. 135), takes a slightly different view on this. Eco himself also sheds light on this in his reflections in 'How I write'. Though all of Eco's novels have been commercially successful, as evidenced by their rapid translations into other languages, especially English, none of the subsequent novels has been as widely successful as *Il nome della rosa*, the only one so far also translated into a film version.
13. Since then Eco has published a fifth novel, *La misteriosa fiamma della regina Loana* (Milan, Bompiani, 2004). This appeared after this chapter was completed and so is not treated here. There are some interesting parallels to be drawn between the second and fifth novels. Both, for example, follow a novel set in the medieval world, and turn away from a historical epoch to the period of Eco's own lifetime. Nevertheless the interplay of lived biography, intellectual interests, and fiction present in this fifth novel, though in some respects complementary to that in *Il Pendolo*, is nonetheless based on rather different source texts and time frames, and has rather different emphases and objectives. *La misteriosa fiamma* has been translated into English as *The Mysterious Flame of Queen Loana*. An illustrated novel, trans. by Geoffrey Brock (London: Secker and Warburg, 2005), but in view of its dependence on children's literature and popular culture specific to Italy in the 1930s-40s, its appeal to a global reading public outside Italy is, in my view, likely to be more limited than for any of the previous four novels.
14. See for example the protest march and its aftermath (how to run away), *Il Pendolo*, chapter 15, and Belbo's journey with the case containing a bomb, which is timed to explode in Florence, chapter 108.
15. In 'How I write', 173, 176, Eco draws attention to two incidents from his autobiography which appear in *Il Pendolo*, namely the pendulum, and his playing the trumpet at the funeral.
16. These experiences form possibly an even more important element in the narrative of *La misteriosa fiamma*.
17. And is indeed the author of *Come si fa una tesi di laurea* (Milan: Bompiani, 1977).
18. There is a relatively brief discussion of the links between contemporary politics and *Il Pendolo* in Caesar, *Umberto Eco*, pp. 145–46. See also JoAnn Cannon, 'The imaginary universe', 896.
19. On these issues see, for example, Paul Ginsborg, *A History of Contemporary Italy. Society and Politics 1943–88* (Harmondsworth: Penguin, 1990); Robert Lumley, *States of Emergency: Cultures of Revolt in Italy from 1968 to 1978* (London: Verso, 1990); D. Moss, *Italian Political Violence 1969–1988* (Geneva: United Nations Research Institute for Social Development, 1993).
20. Peter Willan, *Puppet Masters. The Political Uses of Terrorism in Italy* (London: Constable, 1991).
21. See *The Search*, pp. 80–85.
22. My translation. The blurb for the English translation omits some of these elements and conveys a slightly different emphasis.
23. See again ch. 108, and the comments there on the nervousness of passengers on the train.
24. Degli Espositi, 'The poetics', pp. 190–91, and Viano, 'Ancora su *Il Pendolo*', pp. 154–55, refer to the use of the Sefirot in *Il Pendolo*, but do not connect its presence in the novel with *The Search*.
25. *Il Pendolo*, chs 3, 68.
26. Ibid. chs 9, 29, 53, 56, 57, 87, 104, 119. Eco returns to a consideration of the Rosicrucians in his essay 'La forza del falso' in *Sulla letteratura*, pp. 292–323; pp. 305–14 of that essay provide information on many of the figures referred to in *Il Pendolo* and *The Search*. The essay dates from 1994–95.
27. Ibid. chs 19, 38, 76, 94, 95.
28. Ibid. chs 2, 58, 74, 78.
29. Abulafia's work is discussed in some detail in chapter two of *The Search*; the Rosicrucians in chapter eight; Kircher in chapters seven and nine; Postel in chapter five, Bacon in chapter ten, Trithemius in discussions of both the Kabbalah and magic language.

30. Abulafia and Lull are very briefly mentioned by Degli Espositi, 'The Poetics', pp. 192, 194, but only with reference to the novel.
31. The third diagram common to the two works is John Dee's *Monas Hieroglyphica* (*The Search*, p. 186; *Il Pendolo*, p. 332) but little is made of this in *Il Pendolo* except for the joke of the 'false connection' with the pendulum. *Il Pendolo* also contains an illustration from Kircher's *Ars Magna Sciendi* (p. 372) which is discussed but not illustrated in *The Search*.
32. Though some critics consider this section 'trascurabile' and at first sight its relevance to the main narrative of the construction of the Plan is not obvious, Eco confirms its centrality to the novel in 'How I write' (p. 186).
33. Now in Umberto Eco, *Sette anni di desiderio. Cronache 1977–1983* (Milan: Bompiani, 1983), pp. 22–29. Eco's first essays on Brazil appeared in *L'Espresso* in late 1966; for a discussion of some aspects of the links between Eco's experiences in Brazil and those of Casaubon in *Il Pendolo*, see R. Cotroneo, *La diffidenza come sistema. Saggio sulla narrativa di Umberto Eco* (Milan: Anabasi, 1995), pp. 43–48, and my unpublished essay 'Esotismo o controesotismo: l'episodio brasiliano del *Pendolo di Foucault*', given at the XXIII Convegno interuniversitario 'L'Europa e l'esotico', University of Padua, Bressanone, 7–9 July 1995.
34. *Il Pendolo*, pp. 133–34.
35. Interestingly Eco makes no mention of the reuse of journalism when reflecting in 'How I write' on how he composes his novels. Moreover, his comments there on writing with a computer as a continual process of self-correcting and rewriting are contradicted by the virtual copying unchanged of passages about Brazil from the essay to the novel.
36. Cf. the passages both beginning: 'Le case degli Orixà[s] …', in *Il Pendolo*, p. 151, and 'Con chi stanno gli Orixà', p. 25, with interesting variants in accents on the proper names between the two texts. For another very close pair see the description of the polychrome statues, *Il Pendolo*, p. 147 and 'Con chi stanno', p. 23; and see also the description of the Ogà, *Il Pendolo*, p. 146 and 'Con chi stanno', p. 22, and several other shorter passages in the two texts. Cotroneo, *La diffidenza*, pp. 43–48, notes the close parallels in the passages concerning the 'figlio di Oxalà', and also that about the 'psicologa tedesca' who fails to enter a trance, but does not notice that this latter incident in *Il Pendolo* occurs during the *umbanda* ritual, where in 'Con chi stanno', it occurs during the *candomblé* celebrations; similarly he fails to note that the fifteen-year old girl who is possessed in 'Con chi stanno', and on whom Amparo's reactions in *Il Pendolo* are partly based, is possessed by Ogùn, a more benevolent deity than the Pomba-Gira who possesses Amparo, again in the *umbanda* not *candomblé* ritual. The 1979 essay refers to a number of visits to *candomblé* ceremonies, but only en passant to a previous attendance at *umbanda* rituals. In the novel there is only one visit to each type, clearly differentiated and narrated in distinct chapters.
37. See the final paragraph of 'Con chi stanno', pp. 28–29.
38. Eco's use of alter egos in the novel is treated by Viano, 'Ancora su *Il Pendolo*', p. 155, but a theory of ten alter egos, advanced there, seems somewhat exaggerated and unnecessary. All characters to some extent bear the imprint of their creator, but do not necessarily function as alter egos.
39. Eco reflects in another essay in *Sulla letteratura*, 'Il mito americano di tre generazioni antiamericane' (pp. 274–91), on responses to America by the generations of Belbo and Casaubon. His conclusions (pp. 290–91), on young left-wing Italians in the 1970s and their need to escape from Italy are particularly relevant to *Il Pendolo*. The essay was originally published in 1980, and thus constitutes another piece of prior writing absorbed into the novel.
40. See for example Casaubon's comment: 'Nei files di Abulafia ho trovato molte pagine di uno pseudodiario che Belbo aveva affidato al segreto dei dischetti, sicuro di non tradire la sua vocazione, tante volte ribadita, *di semplice spettatore del mondo*' [In Abulafia's files I found many pages of a pseudo diary that Belbo had entrusted to the password, confident that he was not betraying his often-repeated vow to remain *a mere spectator of the world*] (my italics; *Il Pendolo*, p. 52; *Foucault's Pendulum*, p. 56); and the file (pp. 94–97) which opens thus: 'Sono scappato davanti a una carica di polizia o di nuovo davanti alla storia? E fa differenza? Sono andato al corteo per una scelta morale o per mettermi ancora una volta alla prova davanti all'Occasione? Va bene, *ho perduto le grandi occasioni perché arrivavo troppo presto, o troppo tardi, ma la colpa era dell'anagrafe*' [Was it from a police charge or, once again, from history that I ran away? Does it

make any difference? Did I go to the march because of a moral choice or to subject myself to yet another test of Opportunity? Granted, *I was either too early or too late for all the great Opportunities, but that was the fault of my birth date*] (my italics; *Il Pendolo*, p. 94; *Foucault's Pendulum*, p. 112).

41. Similar unresolved tensions also characterise much of *La misteriosa fiamma*, which ends on precisely such a note, but with the emphasis on the personal rather than the political.
42. See esp. ch. 49, Belbo's account of his uncle Carlo's capture and release by the partisans, but also chs 15, 37. I would take issue here with Cannon's view, 'The imaginary universe', p. 897, where she seems to suggest that the period of the Resistance was one when political allegiances were clear cut. Eco/Belbo does not seem to me to express 'nostalgia for the *clarity* of the Resistance' (my italics).
43. Willan, *Puppet Masters*, p. 30.
44. Ibid., p. 31. In this same section, Willan also points to the other significant political phenomenon which emerged at the end of the war and which was to have disastrous consequences from the 1970s onwards, the Mafia, promoted and used first by the Allies and subsequently by unscrupulous politicians.
45. 'Impegno' translating the French 'engagement' is a particularly significant word in the context. 'Impegno', 'essere impegnato' were vital concepts in the period and especially among the young. For a study of 'impegno' and writers, see Jennifer Burns, *Fragments of 'Impegno': Interpretations of Commitment in Contemporary Italian Narrative* (Leeds: Northern Universities Press, 2001), in particular pp. 13–58, for the situation prior to 1980.
46. See especially *Il Pendolo*, ch. 12.
47. Cf. *Il Pendolo*, pp. 313–15 and *The Search*, pp. 178–81, on Rosencreutz; on John Dee cf. *Il Pendolo*, pp. 317–18 and *The Search*, pp. 185–90.
48. See note 10.
49. '[...] were it up to me to decide under which heading this book should be filed in a library catalogue [...] I would pick neither "linguistics" nor "semiotics" [...] I would pick rather "history of ideas"' (*The Search*, p. 5).
50. It is explored at some length in Eco's later study *Kant and the Platypus. Essays on Language and Cognition* (London: Secker and Warburg, 1999; the Italian original, *Kant e l'ornitorinco* appeared in 1997).
51. Cf. *The Search*, pp. 10–18, with the discussion of the Persian magi, the Egyptian Thoth-Hermes, the Chaldeans, Pythagorean and Orphic traditions, and especially the quotation from Diogenes Laertius, p. 13, and *Il Pendolo*, pp. 332–37, and 353–55. See also Aglié's comments on religion and mystic cults in the late Roman Empire, *Il Pendolo*, pp. 147–50.
52. See *The Search* chs 5–10; and the emphasis in *Il Pendolo* on John Dee, Postel, Bacon and the Rosicrucians.
53. Cf. also the conversation between Aglié and Casaubon on Amparo's reactions to *umbanda* (*Il Pendolo*, pp. 171–72), on the power of the irrational and the dangerous attractions of initiatory rites.
54. Eco's incorporation of the P2 affair in *Il Pendolo* is touched on by Cannon, but there is much more to be said on this.
55. *Il Pendolo*, p. 176.
56. Leonardo Sciascia, *L'Affaire Moro*, trans. by S. Rabinovitch (London: Granta Books, 2002; 1st ed. Carcanet, 1987; Italian ed. 1978) — see introduction (by N. Belton) p. 3; and Sciascia himself, pp. 18–19, 33–38, 114–16.
57. Eco may have in mind here figures like Generals De Lorenzo and Miceli.
58. See for example Casaubon's comment on Nostradamus and the haycart legend (*Il Pendolo*, p. 102).
59. See his enthusiasm for, and ability to appreciate the underground passages of Provins: 'quelle gallerie sembrano fatte per i commandos' (*Il Pendolo*, p. 104)['those tunnels are tailor-made for commandos' (*Foucault's Pendulum*, p. 125)] ; and his underhand treatment of Ingolf's daughter and her property, with Casaubon's comment: '"[...] l'imbottitura dei divani non va solo tastata, occorre anche infilarvi degli aghi per sentire se non si incontrano corpi estranei ..." Capii che il colonnello non aveva frequentato solo campi di battaglia' (*Il Pendolo*, pp. 107–08) [" It's not enough, for instance, to feel the stuffing of a sofa; you have to stick needles in to make sure

you don't miss any foreign object ...." The colonel's experience, I realized, was not limited to battlefields (*Foucault's Pendulum,* p. 130)].
60. The quotation Eco gives from Vignère and his comment on this, *The Search,* p. 128, are especially important here.
61. Ardenti's graphic representation of the links between the key places in the Plan, a symbol halfway between a rune and a hieroglyph (*Il Pendolo,* p. 120), is also linked with Eco's researches for *The Search* and in particular the section concerned with the perfect systems of hieroglyphs and ideograms (ch. 7). Central to these discussions is the figure of the Jesuit Athanasius Kircher.
62. Cf. *The Search*, pp. 155–57 and *Il Pendolo*, pp. 419–21.
63. For Eco's own views on the genesis of *Baudolino,* see 'How I write', pp. 182–84.
64. Eco has returned to the period of his own lifetime in *La misteriosa fiamma,* but as far as political issues are concerned, there is a stronger emphasis on the historical dimension — the end of the Fascist era — rather than, as in *Il Pendolo*, on the contemporary world, the years in which the novel has been written.

CHAPTER 12

❖

The Dummy Interlocutor and Oriana Fallaci's Self-Projection in *La rabbia e l'orgoglio*

John Gatt-Rutter

> Mi chiedi di parlare, stavolta. Mi chiedi di rompere almeno stavolta il silenzio che ho scelto, che da anni mi impongo per non mischiarmi alle cicale.
>
> [You ask me to speak, this once. You ask me just this once to break the silence which I have chosen, which for years I have imposed on myself so as not to mix with the chatterers.]

These were the opening words of the mammoth article — over four broadsheet pages of the *Corriere della sera* on 29 September of 2001 — in which Oriana Fallaci (1929–2006) voiced her reactions to the devastation and carnage wrought nearly three weeks earlier upon the Twin Towers of the World Trade Centre and upon the Pentagon. They immediately foreground the speech act itself: particularly, an addressee, and a vocal outburst after a long silence. The life and the voice are made to coincide. Through the voice I shall scan Fallaci's composite self-realization, a *dramatis persona* which is both an end in itself and a prime instrument of her armoury of persuasion or vituperation. As, in varying degrees, in Fallaci's novels and reportage or quasi-reportage narratives, so too in the invective of her response to the atrocities of September 11th, 2001, autobiographical self-projection, while not being the purported aim of the discourse, is one of its strategic components.

But the opening words of a newspaper article never come first. Something else always precedes them, if only a headline — in this case, the title, 'La rabbia e l'orgoglio' [The Rage and the Pride]. And in this case there was also a preamble. This was the work of Ferruccio de Bortoli, the *Corriere*'s editor-in-chief, and it explained how he had personally prevailed on Fallaci, visiting her in her Manhattan apartment, to write the piece. De Bortoli in fact provides the life-writing context, the autobiographical instance of discourse, which Fallaci seizes on in the article. The reader of the newspaper article thus gathers that it takes the form of an open letter addressed to de Bortoli, who is the presumably familiar *tu* [thou] in those opening phrases.

The second person pronoun, the pronoun of direct address, of inter-subjectivity, has recently acquired the reputation of possessing a remarkably protean nature and a potent or presumptuous grip. Jonathan Culler and Barbara Johnson memorably and diversely explored its use in apostrophe embarrassingly to conjure up a vatic status for the *I* or anguishingly to interrogate the animate status as persons of mothers *manquées* and their unborn (whether miscarried or aborted).[1] In either case, the addressed *you* implicates the grounding *I* to which and by which it is inevitably related, and Fallaci's *I* in previous works of hers *is* heavily implicated in effects of this sort, where she foregrounds a *you*. Critics and commentators on Fallaci have in fact regularly complained that the *you* so often foregrounded as the structuring feature of her works is in fact swamped by the discourse of the *I*, even in the interviews of which she is an acknowledged master. In Fallaci's works previous to *La rabbia e l'orgoglio*, her *you* is, with almost invariable injustice, taken to be a dummy interlocutor by reason of the sheer overwhelming emphaticness of the first-person Fallacian persona, invariably reinforced by her autobiographical credentials as a child Resistance fighter and a journalist on various political and military front lines.[2]

In the recently burgeoning analysis of second-person narrative, as well as the *I-you* nexus, much play has been made of the ontological slipperiness or versatility of that *you*, which may double up or do duty as a virtual first-person or virtual third person and which also reaches outside the text to invest the reader who is, after all, the actual *you* of address within the literary act.[3] It is this last that most applies in Fallaci's case. Her books, always referentially anchored, are usually closer to reportage than to novel, and accordingly the identity of the *you* explicitly addressed within her texts is well-defined and stable. Yet, once again, Fallaci's critics have regularly complained that her intratextual *you*, whether as protagonist in the person of Alekos Panagoulis in *Un uomo* (1979), or as discursive and existential interlocutor in the person of her father in *Se il sole muore* [*If the Sun Dies*] (1965) and the child in *Lettera a un bambino mai nato* [*Letter to a Child Never Born*] (1975), insidiously inveigles the reader and browbeats him or her into subjection to the terms of a closed discourse which is nearer to binary opposition than to genuine dialogue in, say, a Bakhtinian sense.[4]

This, when well-founded, is probably the most serious and profound criticism of Fallaci as a writer, and the most relevant to her most recent and, potentially, in political and social terms, her most important (or dangerous) work, *La rabbia e l'orgoglio*.[5] I propose, therefore, to look at the *you* and *you*s in this pamphlet, how they work in terms of discursive theatricality and rhetorical amplification, and, as far as I am able, how they impact on a world that is today perhaps even more frighteningly dangerous than in the days of Mutually Assured Destruction and possible nuclear annihilation. In all this, the role of the *I*, inextricably intertwining autobiographical referentiality and literary *écriture*, remains always pivotal.

This is very much the case in *La rabbia e l'orgoglio* (both in its abbreviated article form and in the ensuing volume). Fallaci's previous works took the form of a narrative debate or discovery process conducted within a narrative 'confessional' *I* (or projected into a third person in the novels *Penelope alla guerra* [*Penelope Goes to War*] (1976) and *InsciAllah* (1990)). In *La rabbia e l'orgoglio*, on the other hand, the debate (or invective) is directed outwards at an array of interlocutors by a 'Fallaci' ('*I*') who firmly identifies her textual with her extratextual persona and pointedly inserts narrative or confessional tesserae of autobiography: from her girlhood participation in the Resistance against Nazism and Fascism to her estrangement from contemporary Italy (pp. 137–38); from her own experience, in her Manhattan apartment, of the destruction of the Twin Towers (pp. 52–55) to her attachment, despite her atheism, to Italy's religious heritage (pp. 132–34); from her meetings with those whom she considers adversaries, like Arafat (pp. 58, 87) and friends like Ali Bhutto (p. 95) or the Dalai Lama (p. 111), to her direct or indirect witnessing of atrocities sanctioned by governments professing Islam (pp. 93–94, 99); from her personal experiences in Teheran (p. 103) to her feud with Italian feminists over her *Lettera a un bambino mai nato* (p. 105).

All this, and much more, some of which will be remarked on in various connections through the remainder of this essay, makes it clear that, while not being autobiographical in intent, *La rabbia e l'orgoglio*, in a different way from Fallaci's previous works, is very largely autobiographical in texture and structure. Autobiography and invective indeed coincide in the present-tense speech act which sums up or subsumes the whole of *La rabbia e l'orgoglio*, as flagged in its very title: Fallaci's *urlo* [scream], her declaration of war against Islamic terrorism and fundamentalism (p. 35). Everything in the book is subordinated to this act, in the name of both the self and the citizen, of both existential and civic responsibility, drawing its values of justice and liberty from Fallaci's interpretation of the ideals of the Resistance and the whole of western civilization, to which she proclaims her fidelity. While she writes no explicit or straightforward autobiography, Fallaci's entire published *oeuvre* (other than her periodical journalism) forms one enormous autobiographical macrotext in which the life-writing is itself a form of action: testimony, commitment, exhortation, challenge. Courageous, or foolhardy, or intemperate, it brings its risks — foremost among them, the disqualification of the other.

If the second-person pronoun has an established role in lyric poetry as a trope in apostrophe, and if it has recently found an often perplexing role also in narrative (though it made its appearance not so recently as a key element in St Augustine's *Confessions*, where it borders on sacramental liturgy and prayer), its natural literary home is on the stage as a mimetic fiction or in letters, where it functions pragmatically and with fully referential deixis. However, in all cases where a putatively private and intimate *I/you* polarity (St Augustine's discourse with the Almighty, Shelley's with the wild west wind) is made public, it immediately becomes theatrical, addressed as it is to a new *you*, the readership, which becomes in effect a theatre audience voyeuristically peeping in on the interaction between a framed-off *I* and *you* which in turn (when deliberately made public by the agent of either or both those textual persons) becomes indistinguishable from an acting performance. Here we have therefore a double deixis. The intratextual deixis, which may originally have been intended as referring to the empirically verifiable real world (however problematically in the case of the Almighty or of the west wind or in other cases also) is now displaced or re-placed in the literary space. This is always in some sense a fictive space. At the same time, the pragmatic deixis of a mutual *I/you* polarity now applies to the relation between text and reader in the world of the reader.

Fallaci in *La rabbia e l'orgoglio* (as, in extremely diverse ways, in several of her previous works) makes full and conscious use of this theatricalization of the intratextual *I/you* polarity in the new, extratextual polarity set up between her text and her readership. My next step, therefore, is to sketch out briefly the primary *I/you* structure of Fallaci's original article and how this is made more explicit in the volume publication that goes under the same title. This will be followed by an exploration of Fallaci's theatricalization and the use to which she puts it: the proliferation of intratextual *you*s and their de-voicing, the exclusion of others (or Others) as intratextual interlocutors, the attempted selection of extratextual *you*s (the readership), and the impossibility of any such selection. I will attempt to comment on at least some of the implications of these inclusions and attempted exclusions, not simply in terms of the structures of the production and reception of discourse (particularly, of civilizational discourse), but in terms of the political and, above all, the ethical implications they bear on the present crisis of human existence on our crowded planet. In all this, Fallaci's autobiographical self-construct is crucial, not in the simple negative terms of the *protagonismo* of which she is regularly accused, but as an ethical and existential investment that combines huge assets with huge liabilities, huge risks and dangers. Her discourse, which is herself, goes right to the centre of the world's present crisis, and is part of that crisis.

The quotation with which this essay opens, and which opens Fallaci's 'letter' to de Bortoli in the *Corriere della sera*,[6] announces, then, the theatricalization of the one-sided dialogue between the two. Fallaci takes care to keep this mimetic fiction going right up to her closing words, which announce her resumption of the silence which had been interrupted by the appalling events of September 11: 'Stop. Quello che avevo da dire l'ho detto. La rabbia e l'orgoglio me l'hanno ordinato. La coscienza pulita e l'età me l'hanno consentito. Ora basta. Punto e basta' [Period. I've said what I had to say. Rage and pride commanded me to do so. A clear conscience and my age have made it possible. And that's enough. Period] (p. 163). Along the way, the *I/you* set-up is constantly emphasized: 'A rompere il silenzio accendo un detonatore che da troppo tempo ha voglia di scoppiare. Vedrai' [To break the silence, I set off a detonator which has for too long felt the urge to go off. You'll see] (p. 52); 'E non chiedermi che cosa ho provato...' [And don't ask me what I felt...] (p. 53); 'Eh! Chissà come friggerebbe il signor Arafat ad ascoltarmi. Sai, il signor Arafat non mi ha mai perdonato...' [Ha! Who knows how Mr Arafat would sizzle as he hears this. You see, Mr Arafat has never forgiven me...] (p. 58); 'Invulnerabilità? Ma come invulnerabilità?!?' [Invulnerability? What invulnerability?!?] (p. 59); 'Perché credi che...?' [For do you think that...?] (p. 60: used four times to introduce theatrically rhetorical questions); 'Quando ci siamo incontrati t'ho visto quasi stupefatto...' [When we met I saw you were almost flabbergasted...] (p. 64); 'Te lo dice una che non è mai contenta...' [It's someone who is never satisfied that is telling you this...] (p. 64); '... lasciami spiegare... Io non so se in Italia avete visto... L'avete visti o no?' [... let me explain ... I don't know whether you've seen, in Italy... Have you seen them, or not?] (p. 69); '...caro mio ... E sai perché?' [... my dear man... And do you know why?] (p. 71); 'Sai perché? Perché...' [Do you know why? It's because...]

(p. 75). And so Fallaci goes on. Here are the closing instances: 'E la cosa più tremenda sai qual è?' [And do you know what is most appalling?] (p. 140); '...lascia che rivolga un discorsino...' [... let me make a little speech...] (p. 145); 'E risparmiati la battuta...' [And save yourself the quip...] (p. 155); 'È con questa gente che vorresti vedermi cicalare quando mi rimproveri il silenzio...?' [Are these the people you'd like to see me chattering with when you deplore my silence...?] (p. 159); 'Qual è la mia Italia, allora? Semplice, caro mio, semplice' [Which, then, is my Italy? Simple, my dear man, simple] (p. 162).

The examples just presented show clearly enough that no real dialogue, or even dialectic,[7] is entertained: this is not a philosophical dialogue of a Platonic kind in which a Socrates at least has to grapple with and demolish an intellectual challenge, a serious argument which is allowed to present itself seriously. The nearest we come to this in *La rabbia e l'orgoglio* is when Fallaci addresses the thesis of Samuel P. Huntington's *The Clash of Civilizations*[8] which de Bortoli had mentioned: 'Vogliamo farlo questo discorso su ciò che tu chiami Contrasto-fra-le-Due-Culture?' [Shall we hold this discussion on what you call The-Clash-Between-The-Two-Civilizations?] (p. 85). This Fallaci demolishes by denying to Islam the status of a civilization. The clash is therefore not, for her, between two civilizations, but between a civilization and a non-civilization, between a civilization and something quite different — a religion. 'Ecco dunque la mia risposta alla tua domanda sul Contrasto-tra-le-Due-Culture' [And that's my answer to your question about The-Clash-Between-The-Two-Civilizations] (p. 89).

But on the whole, Fallaci the *eiron*, the ironic undercutter of complacent pretentiousness, of the *alazon*, makes sure she has things all her own way; the *alazon* stands little chance. Her use of *tu* is cursory and perfunctory, merely sufficient to construct a dummy interlocutor and justify the theatricalization of her own voice. For the real *you* being addressed in Fallaci's open letter to the *Corriere* is her readership. This becomes explicit on one occasion, a key occasion, the third person transforming into the second: 'E a loro dico: sveglia, gente, sveglia! Intimiditi come siete ... non capite o non volete capire che qui è in atto una Crociata alla Rovescia. Abituati come siete al doppio gioco, accecati come siete dalla miopia, non capite o non volete capire che qui è in atto una guerra di religione...' [And to them I say: Wake up, you people, wake up! Intimidated as you are ..., you fail, or refuse, to understand that what we have here is a Crusade in Reverse. Accustomed as you are to duplicity, blinded as you are by myopia, you fail, or refuse, to understand that what we have here is a war of religion] (p. 78). The *I/you* set-up between Fallaci and de Bortoli is a theatrical performance in which the actual relationship is between Fallaci's text and her readership.

That performance was of course itself captive to the medium, the *Corriere*, which sold out on that Saturday morning thanks to Fallaci's contribution. De Bortoli was after all himself the orchestrator of that theatricalization, verbalizing his ownership in his courteous preamble to Fallaci's 'letter'. Fallaci's volume publication of *La rabbia e l'orgoglio*, which appeared two and a half months later, on 12 December, makes structurally explicit the double deixis of the second person, internally addressed to de Bortoli but externally to the public at large. The text proper of

La rabbia e l'orgoglio, running to 114 pages (of which the *Corriere* article was an abridged version), is prefaced by forty-two pages written subsequently and addressed '*Ai Lettori*' [To My Readers].

In this long preface, its difference marked out by being printed in italics as if to show that this is not a performance, there is no explicit sustained address to a *you*. The readers, the actual interlocutors to whom it is dedicated, remain invisible in the background, in keeping with the normal convention of publication. Only in one passage does Fallaci break this convention, in order to overturn what she conceives to be the common notion that the religious leaders of Islam, the Imams, are harmless and inconsequential figures (p. 31): 'Nossignori. L'Imam è un notabile che dirige e amministra con pieni poteri la sua comunità ... Dietro ciascun terrorista islamico c'è un Imam e io vi ricordo che Khomeini era un Imam, che i leader dell'Iran erano Imam. Ve lo ricordo e affermo che nove Imam su dieci sono Guide Spirituali del terrorismo' [No sirs. The Imam is a dignitary who directs and administers his community with full power.... Behind each Islamic terrorist there is an Imam, and I remind you that Khomeini was an Imam, that Iran's leaders were Imams. I remind you of the fact and I declare that nine Imams out of ten are Spiritual Guides of terrorism] (p. 32).

That de Bortoli, the interlocutor within the 'letter' published in the *Corriere*, is not its real addressee, appears clearly in this preface, which, though written after the 'letter', of course precedes it. The opening of the preface links up with the opening of the 'letter': 'Io avevo scelto il silenzio. Avevo scelto l'esilio' [I had chosen silence. I had chosen exile] (p. 7). (The echo of Joyce's — or Stephen Dedalus's — 'silence, exile and cunning' may be fortuitous; its autobiographical valence, however, is over-determined, as, I trust, will become clear in the course of this essay.) As is in the nature of prefaces, this one is largely metatextual, informing us about what is presumptively the main text that is to follow. And one of its key operations is to disqualify and de-voice de Bortoli, to reduce him visibly to a dummy interlocutor, anonymous (neither he nor his newspaper are named at any point), a virtual nonentity. This is how he appears in the preface:

> ... Il direttore del giornale venne a New York. Ci venne per convincermi a rompere il silenzio che avevo già rotto, e glielo dissi. Gli mostrai addirittura gli appunti convulsi, disordinati, e lui s'infiammò come se avesse visto Greta Garbo che tolti gli occhiali neri si esibisce alla Scala in licenziosi striptease. O come se avesse visto il pubblico già in fila per comprare il giornale, pardon, per accedere alla platea e ai palchi e al loggione. Infiammato mi chiese di continuare, cucire tutto con gli asterischi, farne una specie di lettera rivolta a lui, mandargliela appena pronta. (pp. 17–18)

> [... The newspaper editor came to New York. He came to persuade me to break the silence which I'd already broken, and I told him so. I even showed him my jumble of jottings, and he went flaming red as if he'd seen Greta Garbo doing a sexy striptease at La Scala without her dark glasses. Or as if he'd seen the public already queuing up to buy the newspaper — sorry! to get into the theatre stalls, the gallery, the boxes. Flaming red, he asked me to carry on, to stitch it all together with asterisks, to turn it into something like a letter addressed to him, to send it to him as soon as it was ready.]

From this point on he is referred to invariably as 'il direttore infiammato' [the flaming red editor] and exclusively in connection with his mercenary concern to exploit Fallaci and the seriousness of the subject for his newspaper's circulation while disclaiming responsibility, or even respect, for her views.

Even in the preface, however, Fallaci's irrepressible instinct for theatricalization does not desert her. There are minor instances when she appeals to her predecessors in American exile: 'Mi-dia-una-mano, Salvemini. Mi dia una mano, Cianca. Mi-dia-una-mano, Garosci' [Give-me-a-hand, Salvemini. Give-me-a-hand, Cianca. Give-me-a-hand, Garosci] (p. 12), implicitly identifying her anti-Islamist stance with their anti-Fascism; or when she rhetorically invokes the Italian government — 'Signor Ministro degli Interni anzi signor Ministro degli Esterni' [Mr Minister of the Interior, or rather, Mr Foreign Minister] (p. 30) — or rebuts some of her actual interlocutors/readers reacting to her *Corriere* article — 'Eh, no, caro mio, no' [Oh, no, my dear man, no] (p. 39); 'Eh, no, caro Signore o Signora o Mezzo e Mezzo' [Oh, no, my dear Sir or Madam or Half-and-Half] (p. 42). And there is one major instance, which brings us to the heart of the matter, and involves a switch from the third person to the second: after cursing 'the sons of Allah', she adds:

> E se [...] mi distruggessero uno solo di questi tesori, uno solo, assassina diventerei io. Dunque ascoltatemi bene, seguaci d'un dio che raccomanda l'occhio-per-occhio-e-il-dente-per-dente. Io non ho vent'anni ma nella guerra ci sono nata, nella guerra ci sono cresciuta, di guerra me ne intendo. E di coglioni ne ho più di voi che per trovare il coraggio di morire dovete ammazzare migliaia di creature incluse le bambine di quattro anni. Guerra avete voluto, guerra volete? Per quel che mi riguarda, che guerra sia. Fino all'ultimo fiato. (p. 35)

> [And if (they) were to destroy a single one of these treasures, just one, I myself would become a murderer. So just you listen to me, you followers of a god who calls for an eye for an eye and a tooth for a tooth. I'm no twenty-year-old, but I was born and bred in war and I know a thing or two about it. And I have more balls than you, who haven't got the guts to die unless you can slaughter thousands of people including four-year-old girls. Is it war you wanted, is it war you want? As far as I'm concerned, let it be war. To the last gasp.]

This is the *urlo* that Fallaci more than once (pp. 18, 21) characterizes as the essence of *La rabbia e l'orgoglio*. As such, it is theatricalized as authentic, visceral subjectivity and, at the same time, as a call to arms and a declaration of war. Voice and speech-act are one with the autobiographical agent.

Let us take the declaration of war first. This involves a slippage, which becomes explicit. From asserting that for decades an Islamic Jihad or Holy War has been conducted against the West and that 'i seguaci del fondamentalismo islamico si moltiplicano come i protozoi d'una cellula che si scinde per diventare due cellule poi quattro poi otto poi sedici poi trentadue. All'infinito' [the adherents of Islamic fundamentalism multiply like a single-cell protozoan that divides to become two cells, then four, then eight, then sixteen, then thirty-two. To infinity] (pp. 22–24, 78–80), Fallaci's preface goes on to argue that there is more to it than that, that Bin Laden and his like are not the real protagonists of this war: they are just the visible tip of that immovable Mountain called Islam that has not budged for 1400 years and that is irreconcilably hostile to the West. The fundamentalists and the terrorists cannot be distinguished from the body of Islam as a whole: 'nove Imam su dieci sono Guide Spirituali del terrorismo' [nine Imams out of ten are Spiritual Guides of terrorism] (p. 32); 'gli Usama Bin Laden sono decine di migliaia ... e i più agguerriti stanno proprio in Occidente' [there are tens of thousands of Usama Bin Ladens ... and the most committed are in the West itself] (p. 90). As an alarm call, Fallaci's book is addressed implicitly to her readers in Italy and in the West. But as a declaration of war, the addressee is the world of Islam. This consideration will lead to the end point of this essay, but before we get there, let us first listen more closely to Fallaci's voice and then consider her intermediate interlocutors who stand somewhere between the 'direttore infiammato' and Islam.

Fallaci uses her inter-subjective mode, as always, to produce two interlinked effects: that of projecting her speaking voice, and that of personalizing the discourse to the utmost. A passionate existential drama is thus generated, improbably, through the print medium, Fallaci's persona identifying itself with imperilled western civilization. The speaking voice is deployed in terms of timbre and reiterative rhetoric, and somehow amplified so as to turn the printed text into a megaphone. The colloquial register is impeccably theatricalized through the written medium. Fallaci's preface asserts that whereas usually she is meticulously careful in fashioning her writing prosodically — metre, rhythm, cadence, tone — this time, exceptionally, 'la metrica cioè il ritmo fioriva da sé, e come non mai ricordando che le cose scritte possono guarire od uccidere' [the metrics, that is, the rhythm, burgeoned of its own accord, mindful as never before that the written word may heal or kill] (p. 19). Lexical, syntactic and prosodic resources are unleashed to explosive effect. Urgency and reiterative emphasis are at a maximum, and the visceral dimension of the speaking voice is made to connect to the visceral sensors of her audience. Her voice strives in this to outdo that of the muezzin, which she twice reviles as 'la vociaccia sguaiata del muezzin' [the braying of the muezzin] (pp. 121, 131). She uses the most literal physical language to refer to the excretory functions of protesting Muslim immigrants in Italy and the sexual liberty of the West, constructing and appealing to a demotic readership with her straight talk and confirming her less demotic critics' opinions about her crudeness. Let one key example suffice for all. On the very opening page of her main text (as of the 'open letter' published in the *Corriere*) she talks of herself as being impelled against the jeering Italian and European enemies of the United States by 'una rabbia fredda, lucida, razionale [...] che mi ordina di sputargli addosso. Io gli sputo addosso' [a cold, lucid, rational rage (...) which commands me to spit on them. I spit on them] (p. 51). This somatic, desublimated and demotic quality of her voice and rhetoric through the printed form is one of the factors — beyond her outspokenness in articulating many people's repressed fears or misgivings — that may explain the extremely wide readership which the book has reached and which constitutes its actual interlocutor. As Parekh has demonstrated regarding the uproar over Salman Rushdie's *The Satanic Verses*, the intellectual quality of an argument may count less than the mass support or public attention it can command and the emotional forces it can tap and unleash.[9]

One index of the impact of Fallaci's book in Italy is that it sold an unprecedented 700,000 copies in the first two weeks and that during April to June of 2002 it was back at or near the top of the Italian best-seller lists, nudging aside *Harry Potter*, *The Lord of the Rings* and Ken Follett's *Thieving Magpies*.[10] Sales quickly topped one million, and the book went on selling strongly, saturating the Italian readership market. It was also made available as an audio CD, with Fallaci reading her own text, and used as a discussion text in Italian schools. Fallaci's discourse is thus a formidable societal force in Italy, but also beyond Italy as translations appear in other languages. Fallaci was invoked in the Netherlands by Pim Fortuyn, the popular leader of a new party committed to stopping Muslim immigration into the Netherlands, before his assassination in April 2002. Whatever the intellectual failings of Fallaci's message, the importance of its popular impact can not be ignored.

The mass readership, the actual interlocutor of *La rabbia e l'orgoglio*, is the audience to the spectacle of the theatricalization which the book (and before it the open letter) represents. We have seen already how the purported interlocutor, the *direttore infiammato*, is invalidated and demoted to the status of pretext, of occasion or instance of discourse, justifying the pseudo-dialogic rhetoric of speech. But while maintaining this primary theatricalization with perfect consistency and characteristic energy, Fallaci, in the main text to a greater extent than we have seen in the preface, introduces other interlocutors who are equally disqualified by her textual strategy. These are also dummy interlocutors, vocal enough in their own space outside Fallaci's text, but denied the hospitality of Fallaci's text except as dumb targets of her apostrophizing. Yasser Arafat and Usama Bin Laden are invoked in hypothetical sentences early on in the text:

> Chissà come friggerebbe il signor Arafat ad ascoltarmi ... Gli direi: illustre Signor Arafat, lo sa chi sono i martiri? ... E lo sa chi sono gli eroi? ... Il guaio è che ora Lei fa il Capo di Stato ad perpetuum, fa il monarca. Rende visita al Papa, frequenta la Casa Bianca, rinnega il terrorismo, razza di bugiardo, in più manda le condoglianze a Bush. E nella sua camaleontica abilità di smentirsi sarebbe capace di rispondere che ho ragione. Ma cambiamo discorso. (p. 59)
>
> [Who knows how Mr Arafat would sizzle as he hears this... I would tell him: illustrious Mr Arafat, do you know who are the martyrs? ... And do you know who are the heroes? ... The trouble is that now you play Head of State in perpetuity, you play monarch. You visit the Pope, you go to the White House, you renounce terrorism, you thoroughbred liar, you even send Bush your condolences. And with your chameleon-like skill at disclaimers, you might reply that I'm right. But let's change the subject.]

And:

> Gli chiederei: 'Sor Bin Laden, quanti soldi Le vengono non da Suo padre e dal Suo patrimonio personale bensì dai suoi compaesani?' (p. 63)
>
> [I'd ask him: 'Mr Bin Laden, sir, how much money do you get, not from your father and from your personal birthright, but from your fellow countrymen?']

'Caro il mio Arafat' [My dear Arafat] returns on pp. 87–88 to have his claims put down (rather arbitrarily) regarding the historical Muslim contribution to the development of mathematics.

But Fallaci's theatrical dialogue is essentially with the Western world: '(Mi consenta una domanda, Santità: è vero che tempo fa Lei chiese ai figli di Allah di perdonare le Crociate ...?)' [Allow me one question, your Holiness: is it true that a while back you begged forgiveness of the sons of Allah for the Crusades...?] — an aside addressed to the Pope that goes on for over a page (pp. 76–77), immediately followed, after a break in the text, by an address to the real interlocutors:

> Non sto parlando, ovvio, agli avvoltoi che se la godono a veder le immagini delle macerie e ridacchiano bene-agli-americani-gli-sta-bene. Sto parlando alle persone che pur non essendo stupide o cattive, si cullano ancora nella prudenza e nel dubbio. E a loro dico: sveglia, gente, sveglia! Intimiditi come siete dalla paura d'andar contro corrente oppure d'apparire razzisti [...] non capite o non volete capire che qui è in atto una Crociata alla Rovescia. (pp. 77–78)

> [Sure, I'm not addressing those vultures who get a kick out of seeing pictures of ground zero and snigger serves-the-Americans-right. I'm addressing those who are neither stupid nor wicked but who are still swaddled in prudence and doubt. And to them I say: Wake up, you people, wake up! Intimidated as you are by the fear of swimming against the tide or appearing racist, you fail, or refuse, to understand that what we have here is a Crusade in Reverse.]

And for a few pages Fallaci addresses this collective interlocutor while occasionally slipping back to her *direttore infiammato* and then, for a short passage, to her prime minister, addressed as *signor cavaliere*: 'Mi spieghi, signor cavaliere...' [Explain to me, sir knight...] (p. 84), to whom she will return at greater length near the finale for the demolition job of her *discorsino*: 'Discorsino. Egregio signor cavaliere...' [Little speech. Esteemed sir knight...] — which goes on for ten pages and ends 'la Sua Italia non è la mia Italia. Non sarà mai la mia Italia' [Your Italy isn't my Italy. It will never be my Italy] (pp. 145–54). Into this is intercalated a further aside, nearly a page long, in English, to the British prime minister: 'Do you hear me, Mister Blair?' (pp. 150–51). To the Pope and these two named prime ministers, we must add, among Fallaci's prominent interlocutors, a further ex-prime minister of Italy, unnamed, who is made to bear the brunt of part of her long tirade against the shortcomings of contemporary Italy (pp. 127–33).

The complexities of this high-level, one-sided haranguing function not merely as critique or invective but as a validation of Fallaci's voice as being on a par with the voices of elected or consecrated leaders, in keeping with the standing she had established for herself from 1968 onwards as an international figure participating in world events (especially wars) and interviewing, sometimes discomfiting, the world's leaders, as implied by the title of her volume of political interviews, *Intervista con la storia*.[11] In addressing Berlusconi or Blair or Pope Wojtyla, Fallaci is putting herself on their level, at least to the extent that the political interviewer is on the same level as the leaders interviewed. Truth-seeking is the leveller notionally at the service of the eavesdropping community, the interviewer being sanctioned by commitment to the truth on behalf of the community, in parallel with the sanction by election of politicians or of Popes to govern on behalf of their respective communities.

Pamphleteering, of course, is not the same as interviewing, and it is pamphleteering, not interviewing, that is Fallaci's business in *La rabbia e l'orgoglio*, though she herself prefers to class the volume as a *sermon*, a *predica*, an appropriately *oral* genre (p. 36), but Fallaci draws on her international prestige as a political interviewer and on the mass readership which her works spanning the distinction between reportage and fiction[12] have won her in many countries to set herself up on equal terms as an interlocutor. This, however, is still part of the theatricalization, one of the devices for projecting and amplifying her voice before the readership or audience. This *mise-en-scène* disguises the real confrontation between Fallaci and the *cicale* [cicadas (but, more colloquially and contemptuously, the 'yakkers', the chatterboxes, prattlers)], media gurus and public intellectuals, against whom, as a class, she has found herself progressively in deeper and deeper opposition for close on half a century, ever since she came to be known as 'la strega di Piazza Carlo Erba' [the witch of Carlo Erba Square], from her Milan address at the time.[13]

To chart the hows and whys of this confrontation would take us well out of our way, but, on Fallaci's behalf it must be said that it has largely been due to her fierce independence, courage, and forthrightness on behalf of her own strongly held moral and political principles, in fearless disregard of any party or interest group or constituency of political correctness. What is of concern to the present argument is that the real adversarial interlocutors of *La rabbia e l'orgoglio* are indeed the oft-mentioned, and scornfully mentioned, *cicale*, and particularly in their affluent latter-day guise of jet-setters, *le Super Cicale di Lusso* [Super De Luxe Chatterers]. It is over the heads of the *cicale* that Fallaci theatrically addresses the great in the West and more seriously appeals to her mass readership. It is these public intellectuals that she refers to as she nears the climactic conclusion of her diatribe:

> Quelle cicale che dopo aver letto questi appunti mi odieranno più di quanto mi odiassero prima, che tra una spaghettata e l'altra mi malediranno ... Quelle cicale presuntuose, velenose, noiose, che nei dibattiti televisivi rompono le scatole più delle cicale vere. Fri-frì, fri-frì, fri-frì... [...] Quelle malinconiche creature che vestite da ideologi, giornalisti, scrittori, commentatori, cantanti, puttane à la page, dicono solo ciò che va di moda o ciò che gli hanno detto di dire. Ciò che gli serve per entrare o restare nel jet-set politico-intellettuale e godersi i privilegi che esso conferisce. [...] Quanto alle Super Cicale di Lusso cioè ai padroni del jet-set politico-intellettuale, a me sembrano la banda di Barras e Tallien e Fouché. Gli ex Commissari del Terrore ... (pp. 158–59)

> [Those chatterers who, having read these jottings, will hate me more than they hated me before, who, between one dish of spaghetti and the next, will curse me... Those smug, poisonous, tedious chatterers, cicadas whose television forums get up people's noses more than real cicadas do. Trrr-trrr, trrr-trrr, trrr-trrr (...) Those sad creatures tricked out as ideologues, journalists, writers, commentators, singers, up-to-the-minute whores, who say only what's fashionable or what they've been told to say. What gets them into the politico-intellectual jet set or keeps them in it to enjoy the privileges which it confers... As for the Super De Luxe Chatterers, that is, the bosses of the politico-intellectual jet set, they remind me of the Barras-Tallien-Fouché gang. Ex-Commissars of the Terror...]

Fallaci has of course herself been a member of the intellectual jet-set, and though she has distinguished herself, often heroically, her exclusive claim to integrity must be worrying or laughable. Nevertheless, she does raise serious questions of freedom and truth about the discursive economy of Western democracy, and she presents herself, in effect, in this book as an unheeded Cassandra warning that Troy is in danger of destruction. It is precisely in regard to such a crucial issue that Fallaci attempts to deny her fellow intellectuals the role of interlocutors, denying them the dignity and courtesy of second-person address: 'È con questa gente che vorresti vedermi cicalare quando mi rimproveri il silenzio che ho scelto, quando disapprovi la mia porta chiusa?' [Are these the people you'd like to see me chattering with when you deplore my silence, my closed door?] (p. 159).

Silence, the refusal to address a *thou* or a *you*, is in fact the key rhetorical strategy and structure of this vociferous *La rabbia e l'orgoglio*. Both the main text and the preface open by thematizing silence. The main text: 'Mi chiedi di parlare, stavolta. Mi chiedi di rompere almeno stavolta il silenzio che ho scelto, che da anni mi impongo per non mischiarmi alle cicale' [You ask me to speak, this once. You ask me just this once to break the silence which I have chosen, which for years I have imposed on myself so as not to mix with the chatterers] (p. 51). The preface: 'Io avevo scelto il silenzio. Avevo scelto l'esilio' [I had chosen silence. I had chosen exile]. Which is justified by the assertion 'vivere gomito a gomito con un'Italia i cui ideali giacevano nella spazzatura era diventato troppo difficile, troppo doloroso...' [to live elbow to elbow with an Italy whose ideals had been trashed had become too hard, too painful...] (p. 7). So the book's real drama, above and beyond any mere theatricalization, lies in interrupting this silence: 'ma vi sono momenti, nella Vita, in cui tacere diventa una colpa e parlare diventa un obbligo' [but there are moments, in Life, when it becomes wrong to stay silent and speaking out becomes a duty] (p. 13). And its conclusion is a return to silence.

Fallaci's silence, then, is determined by the *cicale*, and her utterance in *La rabbia e l'orgoglio* is aimed at circumventing and avoiding them. But Fallaci cannot quite avoid treating them, ever bitterly and scornfully, as real interlocutors at whom the text is directed as seriously as at the ideal Italian readership which she regards as being morally attuned to her voice and her message. From time to time, they are addressed directly. She wrangles with a *tuttologo* or media guru and various other intellectuals from Italy's communist or ex-communist left on the question of the ethical and political integrity of the various individuals concerned (pp. 140–44). But the great outburst comes with regard to the treatment of Afghan women under the Taliban:

> Ci riguarda tutti, signori e signore Cicale, e [...] Alle cicale di sesso maschile [...] non ho nulla da dire. [...] Alle cicale omosessuali, idem. [...] Alle cicale di sesso femminile ossia alle femministe di cattiva memoria, invece, qualcosa da dire ce l'ho. Giù la maschera, false Amazzoni. Ricordate gli anni in cui [...] ? [...] Vi siete tutte innamorate del fascinoso Usama Bin Laden, dei suoi occhioni da Torquemada, delle sue labbra cicciute, e di quel che sta sotto la sua sottanaccia? Lo trovate romantico, sognate tutte d'essere stuprate da lui? Oppure delle sorelle musulmane non ve ne importa un cazzo perché le considerate inferiori? In tal caso, chi è razzista qui: io o voi? La verità è che non siete nemmeno cicale. Siete e siete sempre state galline [...] (pp. 105–06)

[It concerns us all, gentleman Chatterers and lady Chatterers, and (...) To the male chatterers I have nothing to say (...) To the homosexual chatterers, ditto (...) To the female chatterers, that is, to the feminists with a bad memory, however, I do have something to say. Off with your masks, you phoney Amazons. Do you remember the times when (...)? (...) Are you all in love with the alluring Usama Bin Laden, with his great Torquemada eyes, with his fleshy lips, and with what's under his kirtle? Do you find him romantic, do you fantasize about him ravishing you? Or is it that you don't give a fuck for your Muslim sisters because you consider them inferior? In which case, who's the racist: I or you? The truth is that you're not even cicadas. You are and have always been hens...]

We can see here why the silence has not been only on Fallaci's side and why, in the past, the usual response by Italian intellectuals to Fallaci's provocations has been to bury them as much as possible in silence. Each side has ostracized the other. But the ostracism is not complete. Having here excoriated her female counterparts or adversaries addressing them in the second person, and having, as we have seen above, done the same using the third person with *le Super Cicale di Lusso* (pp. 158–59), she makes sure that there can be no mistaking her target in the concluding apostrophe of her 'sermon', where she turns from her Italian interlocutors to 'Care cicale inglesi, francesi, tedesche, spagnole, olandesi, ungheresi, scandinave, eccetera eccetera amen' [Dear chatterers all — English, French, Germans, Spaniards, Dutch, Hungarians, Scandinavians, etc., etc., amen] (p. 161), including them in her diatribe.

Fallaci has never been afraid of making enemies, attacking positions, groups, individuals that fall short of her expectations, or betray them, or contradict them. Yet, over the resulting hostility towards Fallaci there has always hung a haze of equivocation. Is it really due to aggressive, overbearing and unreasoning behaviour — an ultimately megalomaniac ego — on her part? Is it due to political differences or differences of ethical judgement? Or is it because Fallaci's uncompromising moral spotlight embarrassingly leaves her targets nowhere to hide, and exposes their undignified evasions or double standards?

These explanations cannot be disentangled, and none of them can be dismissed. There is about Fallaci something of Jesus sweeping the money-changers out of the Temple forecourt, an uncompromising purity or absolutism that will have none of the shifts of daily commerce. Personality and principle are indistinguishable, and leave no room for human inconsistency and mutual tolerance. Fallaci's thesis in *La rabbia e l'orgoglio* is that the war of certain Islamic fundamentalists (Fallaci might say, of Islam itself) against the West has been going on for over twenty years. She claims a privileged vantage point to know this, but she is not exempt from charges of prejudice or of equating very specific struggles with a world-wide *jihad* by Islam as a whole.

The autobiographical investment and the autobiographical deployment everywhere visible in *La rabbia e l'orgoglio* is everywhere visibly in the service of what Fallaci conceives to be a libertarian, ethical and humanitarian mission. Her persona is inseparable from her mission. Whereas autobiography is generally taken to be the inscription of the achieved wholeness of the individual or a fragmentary inscription of a fragmented self, the autobiographical dimension of this work is of a different kind: the autobiographical persona's integrity subsists in 'silence' and 'exile', to express itself potentially in the new book she is working on — 'il mio bambino' (p. 14) — and in actuality in the 'urlo' which is *La rabbia e l'orgoglio* itself. The autobiographical persona is posited as pre-existing its textual realization, having been strenuously constructed out of a lifetime of preceding experiences stemming from Fallaci's formative adolescent experience of resistance against Fascism and Nazism.[14]

The reactions in Italy to Fallaci's outburst have been varied. Politicians have evaded the issue raised by Fallaci (of an inevitable confrontation between Islam and the Western world) by dismissing that outburst as over-emotional. Cultural and intellectual figures from Umberto Eco and Dacia Maraini to Dario Fo, Franca Rame, Jacopo Fo and Tiziano Terzani have taken various stands more or less effectively refuting her arguments.[15] The singer Jovanotti staged a peace concert in opposition to her war-cry and held an internet poll which saw the respondents almost exactly divided between Fallaci and Jovanotti.[16] The degree and kind of attention that should be given in the Western world to Fallaci's war-cry is a matter of opinion and judgement, but also responsibility. *La rabbia e l'orgoglio* has all the air of a self-fulfilling prophecy, and all who care about the future of humanity on this planet must be concerned to do everything possible to prevent that prophecy of all-out civilizational conflict from being realized. This means that we in the West as potential interlocutors of Fallaci's text must take it seriously to the extent of considering it also from the point of view of potential non-'Western' interlocutors, and specifically of Muslims, breaking down as far as possible that Muslim-'Western' divide.

It has never been possible to restrict communication to its intended audience, and less than ever is it possible in our age of mass communication. Fallaci's Italian text was immediately accessible to Muslims in Italy or with knowledge of Italian, who are fairly numerous. Its translation into other major European and world languages has already made it very widely accessible. In any case, Fallaci includes Muslims among her intended interlocutors, as we have already seen: 'Guerra avete voluto, guerra volete? Per quel che mi riguarda, che guerra sia. Fino all'ultimo fiato' [Is it war you wanted, is it war you want? As far as I'm concerned, let it be war. To the last gasp] (p. 35). To declare war against Islam is the best way to encourage Muslims to make common cause against you. It is a point that was quickly made by Chalmers Johnson in the wake of the horror of September 11th, and quickly taken up by Tiziano Terzani, that one of the main aims of those terrorist attacks was to provoke retaliation against the Islamic world and thus further mobilize it against the West.[17] One of the potential interlocutors of *La rabbia e l'orgoglio*, whether directly addressed by Fallaci or not, whether intended by her or not, is Usama Bin Laden himself, or followers of his. He or they can only read with satisfaction Fallaci's graphic description of the horrific annihilation of the Twin Towers (like a re-run of the video recordings of the event). He or they must read with even more satisfaction Fallaci's vituperation of those across the world whom she accuses of having exulted over the mayhem. And their satisfaction must reach a peak when she vituperates

Islam as such and Muslims in general, including Bin Laden himself, in the most offensive language, and champions the superiority of Western civilization over what she sees as the nullity, or worse, of Islam. *La rabbia e l'orgoglio*, reacting to the message of September 11th, does Bin Laden's work for him.

Theatricalization makes for formidably powerful and potentially infectious rhetoric. In a world of global communication, it defies all controls, like a nuclear chain reaction. Everyone is a potential interlocutor. If the chain reaction unleashed by Fallaci's *La rabbia e l'orgoglio* does not endlessly proliferate, its publication might serve an unintended saving purpose. It might help arouse world society not to all-out civilizational war but, on the contrary, to the need for fuller mutual respect between radically diverse groups. The world is full of fundamentalisms — monotheistic, polytheistic or atheistic, including humanism and the divine right of capitalism. Islam in its several variants must decide whether it is a religion for humanity as a whole to be freely chosen by reason and conscience or whether it is to be a divisive religion attempting to impose itself by force through terror and carnage. Non-Muslims must learn to understand Islam better and seek a universalism that will include all with equal dignity. We in the humanities cannot seek detachment from these issues, if our commitment is really to humanity. We Italianists need to review the presence of Islam as Other in Italian culture and history, sometimes in open antagonism, at other times as a silence and an absence, often as an inadequately acknowledged interlocutor, and now that Islam is an important presence in Italian society we should also pay attention to the human and cultural consequences of this. If Fallaci, albeit unintentionally, leads us to this perception, perhaps we should be grateful to her.

Notes to Chapter 12

1. See Jonathan Culler, 'Apostrophe', in *The Pursuit of Signs: Semiotics, Literature, Deconstruction* (London and Henley: Routledge & Kegan Paul, 1981), pp. 135–54; and Barbara Johnson, 'Apostrophe, animation and abortion', *Diacritics*, 16:1 (1986), 29–47, repr. in *Feminisms: An Anthology of Literary Theory and Criticism,* ed. by Robyn R. Warhol and D. P. Herndl (New Brunswick, NJ: Rutgers University Press, 1991), pp. 630–43.
2. For some discussion and further references on this issue, see J. Gatt-Rutter, *Oriana Fallaci: The Rhetoric of Freedom* (Oxford: Berg, 1996), pp. 65–70, 104–05, 109–10, 124–29, 141, 154; and 'Fact and Fallaci in Literary-Land', in *Novel Turns Towards 2000: Critical Perspectives on Contemporary Narrative Writing from Western Europe,* ed. by J. Gatt-Rutter (Melbourne: Voz Hispánica, 2000), pp. 23–34.
3. See Brian Richardson, 'The Poetics and Politics of Second Person Narrative', *Genre*, 24.3 (Fall, 1991), 309–30; Monika Fludernik, 'Introduction: second-person narrative and related issues', *Style*, 28.3 (Fall 1994), 281–311; 'Second-person narrative as a test-case for narratology: the limits of realism', *ibid.*, 445–82; and 'Second-person narrative: a bibliography,' *Style*, 28.4 (Winter 1994), 525–78. Fallaci's *Un uomo* (1979) is discussed by Fludernik both in her 'Introduction' (p. 294), and also in her 'Second-person narrative as a test-case for narratology' (pp. 450–51). See also Giovanna Rosa, 'Il nome di Oriana', in *Pubblico 1982 — Produzione letteraria e mercato culturale*, ed. by V. Spinazzola (Milan: Milano Libri, 1982), pp. 57–80; repr. in *Il successo letterario*, ed. by V. Spinazzola (Milan: Unicopli, 1985); and J. Gatt-Rutter, 'Narrative "You" and "I" in the opening of Oriana Fallaci's *Un uomo*', in *Essays in Modern Italian and French Literature: In remembrance of Tom O'Neill,* ed. by A. Hurst and T. Pagliaro, special issue of *Spunti e Ricerche* (1994), pp. 50–59.

4. A distinction between open-ended 'dialogic' and closed 'dialectical' structures of discourse is pursued along Bakhtinian lines in Don Bialostosky, 'Dialogic Criticism', in *Contemporary Literary Theory*, ed. by G. Douglas Atkins and Laura Morrow (Amherst, Mass: The University of Massachusetts Press; London: Macmillan, 1989), pp. 216–28 (esp. pp. 218–21).
5. Oriana Fallaci, *La rabbia e l'orgoglio* (Milan: Rizzoli, 2001). Quotations are drawn from this volume and page references to it will be shown in my text. Of the many differences (mostly passages included in the volume but omitted in the article) between the volume and the shorter text published in the *Corriere della sera*, I will refer only to those relevant to the argument of this essay. The text of the *Corriere* article can be found on the web at:*http://www.corriere.it/speciali/fallaci/fallaci1.shtml>*. Fallaci translated an amended version of the volume into her own English as, *The Rage and the Pride* (New York: Rizzoli, 2002). As this version differs from the original and addresses a mainly US audience in Fallaci's own peculiar English, I have throughout translated quotations directly from her original Italian text. Fallaci has followed up *La rabbia e l'orgoglio* with *La forza della ragione* [*The Force of Reason*] (Milan: Rizzoli, 2004), on the theme of 'Eurabia'. In the same year there appeared her brief, and more directly autobiographical *Oriana Fallaci intervista Oriana Fallaci* (Milan: Rizzoli, 2004), which was amplified as *Oriana Fallaci intervista se stessa. L'Apocalisse* (Milan: Rizzoli, 2005). *La rabbia e l'orgoglio*, *La forza della ragione* and *Oriana Fallaci intervista se stessa. L'Apocalisse* were brought out together in a single volume as *La Trilogia* in 2004 (Milan: Rizzoli).
6. This appears on p. 51 of the published volume.
7. Cf. note 4 above.
8. Samuel P. Huntington first announced his hypothesis interrogatively in the article 'The Clash of Civilizations?' in *Foreign Affairs*, 72.3 (Summer 1993), 22–49, and developed it affirmatively in *The Clash of Civilizations and the Remaking of World Order* (New York: Simon & Schuster, 1996).
9. Bikhu Parekh, *Rethinking Multiculturalism: Cultural Diversity and Political Theory* (London: Macmillan; Cambridge, Mass: Harvard University Press, 2000), pp. 307–12.
10. *Il Giorno* web-site, 17/06/02: <http//ilgiorno.quotidiano.net/>.
11. Oriana Fallaci, *Intervista con la storia* (Milan: Rizzoli, 1974; extended and revised 1977); a different selection translated by John Shepley as *Interview with History* (London: Michael Joseph, 1976).
12. Other works by Fallaci particularly relevant in this context are: *Se il sole muore* (Milan: Rizzoli, 1965); trans. by Pamela Swinglehurst as, *If the Sun Dies* (London and New York: Athenaeum, 1966); *Niente e così sia* (Milan: Rizzoli, 1969); trans. by Isabel Quigley as *Nothing and Amen* (London: Michael Joseph, 1972) and *Nothing and So Be It* (New York: Doubleday, 1972); *Lettera a un bambino mai nato* (Milan: Rizzoli, 1975, revd. 1994); audio recording 'Oriana Fallaci legge *Lettera a un bambino mai nato*' (Milan: Rizzoli, 1993); trans. by John Shepley as *Letter to a Child Never Born* (London: Arlington Books, 1975; and New York: Simon and Schuster, 1976; revised translation London: Hamlyn, 1982); *Un uomo* (Milan: Rizzoli, 1979); trans. by William Weaver as *A Man* (New York: Simon and Schuster, 1980; London: Arrow Books, 1981); *InsciAllah* (Milan: RCS Rizzoli, 1990); trans. by Oriana Fallaci from a translation by James Marcus as *InshAllah* (New York: Doubleday, 1992; London: Chatto & Windus, 1992).
13. Cf. Giorgio Torelli, 'La "strega di Piazza Carlo Erba" ha messo nel sacco i peccati di Hollywood', *Candido*, 32–35 (1961). (Precise details unknown. A cutting of this review of Fallaci's *I sette peccati di Hollywood* [*Hollywood's Seven Deadly Sins*] is held in the Fallaci Collection of the Mugar Library in Boston, Mass.)
14. The rhetorical nature of Fallaci's return to silence at the end of *La rabbia e l'orgoglio* became clear in 2004 with the publication of both a sequel, *La forza della ragione*, and her autobiographical testimonial in which she 'interviews' herself, appending an 'Apocalypse'. See note 5 above.
15. Under the title 'La terrorista Oriana Fallaci', various of these ripostes were posted on the web at <www.orianafallaci.6go.net>. The one by Dario Fo, Franca Rame and Jacopo Fo is entitled 'Dai una possibilità alla pace'. See Umberto Eco, 'Le guerre sante passione e ragione', *La Repubblica* (5 October, 2001). Dacia Maraini's 'letter' in response to Fallaci's appeared in the *Corriere della sera* (5 October, 2001). Tiziano Terzani's interventions and reflections have been collected in his volume, *Lettere contro la guerra* (Milan: Longanesi, 2002). See also J. Gatt-Rutter,

'Civilization under siege? September 11, Oriana Fallaci, Islam, and us', *Melbourne Journal of Politics*, 30 (2005–06), pp. 98–117.
16. 'Jovanotti contro Oriana Fallaci' (1094 people responded to the poll): <http://zapping.35mm.it/magazine/sondaggi.xtml?id=212>
17. Terzani, pp. 43–44; Chalmers Johnson, 'Blowback. U.S. actions abroad have repeatedly led to unintended, indefensible consequences', *The Nation* (15 October, 2001), 13–15. On p. 14, Johnson remarks: 'In fact, mindless bombing is surely one of the responses their grisly strategy hopes to elicit.'

BIBLIOGRAPHY OF PUBLICATIONS BY JOHN WOODHOUSE

❖

Books, Editions and Edited Books

1968　*Italo Calvino: A Reappraisal and an Appreciation of the Trilogy* (Hull: University Publications), 96 pp.

1970　Italo Calvino, *Il barone rampante*, ed. with intro. and notes (Manchester: Manchester University Press), xxvi + 289 pp.

1971　Vincenzio Borghini, *Scritti inediti o rari sulla lingua*, ed. with intro. and notes (Bologna: Commissione per i Testi di Lingua), lxxxix + 354 pp.

1974　Vincenzio Borghini, *Storia della nobiltà fiorentina*, ed. with intro. and notes (Pisa: Marlin/Centro Nazionale delle Ricerche), liii + 378 pp.

1978　*Baldesar Castiglione: A Reassessment of the 'Courtier'* (Edinburgh: Edinburgh University Press), xi + 217 pp.

1978　Gabriele D'Annunzio, *Alcyone*, ed. with intro. and notes (Manchester: Manchester University Press), 164 pp.

1983　Gabriele Rossetti, *Lettere familiari*, ed. by P. R. Horne & J. R. Woodhouse (Vasto: Comitato per il bicentenario), xxxvi + 204 pp.

1988　Co-editor, *The Languages of Literature in Renaissance Italy: Essays presented to Cecil Grayson* (Oxford: Clarendon Press), xii + 279 pp.

1988　Gabriele Rossetti, *Carteggi*, vol. II, ed. by P. R. Horne, T. R. Toscano, & J. R. Woodhouse (Naples: Loffredo), xxxix + 250 pp.

1991　*From Castiglione to Chesterfield: The Decline in the Courtier's Manual,* Inaugural Lecture for the Fiat-Serena Chair (Oxford: Clarendon Press), 18 pp.

1995　Gabriele Rossetti, *Carteggi*, vol. III, ed. by P. R. Horne, J. R. Woodhouse & Alfonso Di Caprio (Naples: Loffredo), xxxv + 782 pp.

1996　Gabriele Rossetti, *Carteggi*, vol. IV, ed. by P. R. Horne, J. R. Woodhouse & Alfonso Di Caprio (Naples: Loffredo), xl + 548 pp.

1997　*Dante and Governance*, ed. by J. R. Woodhouse (Oxford: Clarendon Press), 179 pp.

1998　*Gabriele D'Annunzio: Defiant Archangel* (Oxford: Clarendon Press), xv + 406 pp.

1999　*Gabriele D'Annunzio: Arcangelo ribelle* (Rome: Carrocci) (Premio Dannunziano 2000)

2001　*D'Annunzio e le Isole Britanniche*, ed. by Dante Marianacci & John Woodhouse (Edinburgh: Quaderni dell'Istituto Italiano), 107 pp.

2001　Gabriele Rossetti, *Carteggi*, vol. V, ed. by P. R. Horne, J. R. Woodhouse & Alfonso Di Caprio (Naples: Loffredo), xlii + 557 pp.

2003　*Gabriele D'Annunzio tra Italia e Inghilterra* (Pescara: Ediars), 185 pp.

2004　*Il Generale e il Comandante: Ceccherini e D'Annunzio a Fiume* (Bologna: Gedit), 336 pp.

2006　Gabriele Rossetti, *Carteggi*, vol VI, ed. by P. R. Horne, J. R. Woodhouse & Alfonso Di Caprio (Naples: Loffredo), lx + 435 pp.

Articles, Chapters in Books, Reviews

1966 'Ottocento', *The Year's Work in Modern Language Studies*, 27 (1965), MHRA, pp. 342–50.

1967 'Ottocento', *The Year's Work in Modern Language Studies*, 28 (1966), MHRA, pp.387–96.

1967 'Vincenzio Borghini and the Continuity of the Tuscan Linguistic Tradition', *Italian Studies*, 12, 26–42.

1968 'Italo Calvino and the rediscovery of a Genre', *Italian Quarterly*, 12, 45–66.

1970 'Fantasy, Alienation and the *Racconti* of Italo Calvino', *Forum for Modern Language Studies*, 6, 399–412.

1970 '*La testimonianza di Travale*, ovvero di un mangiatore di pane medievale', *Lingua Nostra*, 21, 73–75.

1970 '*Carafulleria*', *Lingua Nostra*, 31, 110–11.

1971 'Some Humanist techniques of Vincenzio Borghini', *Italian Quarterly*, 15:58–59, 59–86.

1971 'Vincenzio Borghini's theory of the decay of Tuscan', *Studi secenteschi*, 11, 101–15.

1971 'Donne contigiate o *gonne* contigiate', *Lingua Nostra*, 32, 111–12.

1972 'Per un'edizione dei *Pensieri e Annotazioni* di Vincenzio Borghini', *Lingua Nostra*, 33, 39–45.

1972 'La glottologia vitale e la vita glottologica di Vincenzio Borghini', *Lingua nostra*, 33, 114–20.

1973 'Per una *Storia della nobiltà fiorentina* finora inedita', *Studi secenteschi*, 14, 3–12.

1973 'Vincenzio Borghini e la rassettatura del *Decameron* del 1573, un documento inedito', *Studi sul Boccaccio*, 7, 303–15.

1973 'Vincenzio Borghini, Lessicologo', *Lingua Nostra*, 34, 46–54.

1975 Italo Calvino, 'Il bosco sull'autostrada', translated with John Mathias: *Y Coedwig ar y Draffordd* in *Storiau tramor*, ed. by B. Jones (Llandysul: Gwasg Gomer), pp. 28–31 (Welsh Arts Council Prize).

1978 'Conversazione e conservazione: un aspetto del purismo linguistico di Vincenzio Borghini', in *Essays presented to Myron P. Gilmore*, ed. by Sergio Bertelli, 2 vols (Florence: La Nuova Italia), I, 347–61.

1979 'D'Annunzio giovane e il verismo: qualche giudizio e pregiudizio inglese', in *D'Annunzio giovane e il verismo: Atti del convegno*, ed. by Edoardo Tiboni & Luigia Abrugiati (Pescara: Centro Studi Dannunziani), pp. 140–51.

1979 'Baldesar Castiglione: Book IV of the *Cortegiano*, a pragmatic approach', *Modern Language Review*, 74, 62–68.

1980 'The Fascist era and beyond', Chapter 16 in J. H. Whitfield, *Short History of Italian Literature* (Manchester: Manchester University Press), pp. 289–321.

1980 'Rampant non-conformity: an orthodox guide to Italo Calvino', *Journal of the Association of Teachers of Italian*, 29, 23–29.

1980 'Impronte shelleyane sul paesaggio dannunziano', in *Natura e arte nel paesaggio dannunziano: Atti del convegno*, ed. by Luigia Abrugiati (Pescara: Centro Studi Dannunziani), pp. 67–81.

1982 'La cortegiania di Niccolò Strozzi, con il testo inedito dei suoi *Avvertimenti necessari per i cortigiani*', *Studi secenteschi*, 23, 141–93.

1982 'Dante Gabriel Rossetti, D'Annunzio e il preraffaellismo', *Rassegna Dannunziana*, 1:2, 1–12.

1982 '*Il trionfo della morte*: traduzioni e reazioni anglosassoni', in *Il trionfo della morte: Atti del convegno*, ed. by Edoardo Tiboni (Pescara: Centro Studi Dannunziani), pp. 239–58.

1982 'Per il carteggio inedito di Gabriele Rossetti a Charles Lyell', *Oggi e Domani*, Anno X, nos. 1, 2, 3 and 5 (4 items, pp. 25)

1983 'Gabriele Rossetti, esule fra gli Inglesi', *Oggi e Domani*, 11:4, 5–11.

1983 'Gabriele Rossetti and Charles Lyell, new light on an old friendship', (with Philip Horne), *Italian Studies*, 38, 70–86.

1983 'Canto novo e i nuovi rimatori inglesi', in *Canto novo nel centenario della publicazione: Atti del convegno*, ed. by Edoardo Tiboni (Pescara: Centro Studi Dannunziani), pp. 158–77.

1983 'La virtù vinta dall'inganno: gli *Avvertimenti aulici di Niccolò di Tommaso Strozzi*', *Atti dell'Accademia dell'Arcadia*, Serie 3a, 8:1, 85–103.

1984 'Dante Gabriel Rossetti, D'Annunzio e il preraffaellismo', in *I Rossetti tra Italia e Inghilterra: Manifestazioni rossettiane 1982–3: Atti del convegno*, ed. by Gianni Oliva (Rome: Bulzoni), pp. 353–72.

1984 'D. G. Rossetti, traduttore della *Vita nova*', in *Dante Gabriele Rossetti*, ed. by Corrado Gizzi (Milan: Mazzotta), pp. 69–74.

1984 'Samuel Johnson and the *Accademia della Crusca*, a conjunction of anniversaries', *Notes and Queries*, n.s. 32:230, 3–6.

1984 'The Reluctant Academicals: linguistic individualism in England after the *Crusca*', in *'Il più bel fiore': The Emergence of Linguistic National Consciousness in Renaissance Europe*, ed. by Fredi Chiappelli (Florence and Los Angeles: La Crusca), pp. 175–84.

1984–1994 Italian Editor of *Modern Language Review*, vols 79–89.

1985 '*La figlia di Iorio*: vent'anni di critica inglese e la traduzione singolare di W. H. Woodward del 1926', in *La figlia di Iorio: Atti del convegno*, ed. by Edoardo Tiboni (Pescara: Centro Studi Dannunziani), pp. 275–88.

1985 'Gabriele D'Annunzio's election victory of 1897 — new documents, new perspectives', *Italian Studies*, 40, 63–84.

1987 'Gabriele D'Annunzio's reputation and critical fortune in Britain', *Annali d'Italianistica*, 5, 245–58.

1987 'Curiouser and spuriouser: two English influences on Gabriele D'Annunzio', *Italian Studies*, 42, 69–80.

1987 'La fortuna inglese della *Fiaccola sotto il moggio*', in *La fiaccola sotto il moggio: Atti del convegno*, ed. by Edoardo Tiboni (Pescara: Centro Studi Dannunziani), pp. 219–34.

1988 'Attila's ashes and Charlemagne's chivalry: a preliminary view by Vincenzio Borghini', in *Renaissance and Other Studies. Essays Presented to Peter M. Brown*, ed. by Eileen A. Millar (Glasgow: Glasgow University Press), pp. 175–91.

1988 'Straws and Pearls: Borghini's defence of Dante's Language', in *The Languages of Literature in Renaissance Italy: Essays Presented to Cecil Grayson*, pp. 223–41.

1988 'Vincenzio Borghini's view of Charlemagne's Empire: a study with unpublished texts', *Viator*, 19, 355–75.

1988 'Di certi *Avvertimenti* inediti di Paolo Giordano Orsini', *Studi secenteschi*, 29, 81–94.

1988 'Preraffaellite truccate, le donne dipinte dal D'Annunzio', *Atti del Convegno internazionale dell'AISLLI, Toronto 1985* (Florence: Olschki), pp. 929–39.

1989 'From Italo Calvino to Tonio Cavilla: the first twenty years', in *Calvino Revisited*, ed. by Franco Ricci (Toronto: Toronto University Press), pp. 33–50.

1989 'Victorian verecundity: D'Annunzio's prudish public', in *Moving in Measure: Essays for Brian Moloney*, ed. by Judith Bryce & Doug Thompson (Hull: Hull University Press), pp. 107–21.

1990 'Conflitti e consolazioni in Gabriele Rossetti', in *L'esilio romantico. Forme di un conflitto* (proceedings of the Keats-Shelley memorial conference), ed. by Joseph Cheyne & Lilla Maria Crusafulli Jones (Rome: Adriatica), pp. 245–64.

1990 'Gabriele D'Annunzio e la cultura anglosassone', in *Gabriele D'Annunzio a cinquant'anni dalla morte: Atti del convegno*, ed. by Edoardo Tiboni, 2 vols (Pescara: Centro Studi Dannunziani), II, 627–46.

1991 'La morte del *vir perfectus* e la nascita dello snob', in *L'Europa delle corti alla fine dell'Ancien Régime: Atti del convegno*, ed. by Cesare Mozzarelli (Rome: Bulzoni), pp. 279–306.

1991 'D'Annunzio a Fiume: testimonianze inglesi inedite o rare', in *L'Italia contemporanea: saggi per onorare Paolo Alatri*, ed. by C. Carli & P. Melograni (Naples: Edizioni Scientifiche Italiane), II, 151–66.

1991 'D'Annunzio tra Italia e Inghilterra', in *D'Annunzio Europeo*, ed. by Pietro Gibellini (Rome: Lucarini), pp. 241–65.

1991 'OXPROD: Il progetto Oxford per la diversificazione delle lingue straniere', *Lingua e letteratura italiana nel mondo oggi: Atti del convegno internazionale dell'AISLLI, Perugia,* ed. by Ignazio Baldelli & Bianca Maria Da Rif, 2 vols (Florence: Olschki), II, 711–22.

1992 'Baldesar Castiglione tra idealismo e realtà', in *Traités de savoir-vivre italiens: Travaux*, ed. by Alain Montandon (Clermond Ferrand: Presses Universitaires Blaise Pascal), pp. 213–24.

1993 'Creative plagiarism: D'Annunzio's varied sources', Chapter 16 in *The Italian Lyric Tradition: Essays for F.J. Jones*, ed. by Gino Bedani, Remo Catani and Monica Slowikowska (Cardiff: University of Wales Press), pp. 91–107.

1993 'Insouciance and insincerity: courtly virtue after Castiglione', in *The Cultural Heritage of the Italian Renaissance: Essays for T. G. Griffith*, ed. by Clive Griffiths & Robert Hastings (Lampeter: Edwin Mellen), pp. 176–95.

1993 Obituary of Alphonse Sammut, *Journal of Anglo-Italian Studies*, 3, ix-x.

1994 'The tradition of Della Casa's *Galateo* in English', in *The Crisis of Courtesy*, ed. by Jacques Carré (Leiden: Brill), pp. 11–26.

1994 'The Englishing of D'Annunzio, or Thomas Bowdler Rides Again', *Journal of Anglo-Italian Studies*, 3, 153–68.

1994 'Honourable dissimulation: some Italian advice for the Renaissance diplomat', *Proceedings of the British Academy*, 84, 25–50.

1994 'Italian Monolingual Dictionaries', in *The Encyclopedia of Language and Linguistics*, ed. R. E. Asher, 10 vols (Oxford: Pergamon), II, 919–92.

1995 'Lord Byron e la Grecia: un precursore illustre di Gabriele D'Annunzio', in *Verso l'Ellade: Atti del convegno*, ed. by Edoardo Tiboni (Pescara: Ediars), pp. 221–34.

1995 'Vincenzio Borghini, Michele Barbi e la *Nuova filologia*', *Convegno della Società Dantesca (1888–1988)*, ed. by Francesco Mazzoni (Milan-Naples: Ricciardi), pp. 191–206.

1995 'Vincenzio Borghini and the Foundation of the *Accademia della Crusca*', in *Italian Academies of the Sixteenth Century*, Colloquia of the Warburg Institute, ed. by David Chambers & François Quiviger (London: Warburg Institute), pp. 165–73.

1995 'From Castiglione to Careertrack', *Rivista di Letterature moderne e comparate*, 48, 1–18.

1996 'D'Annunzio e la prima guerra attraverso occhi inglesi', in *D'Annunzio e la prima guerra*, ed. by Francesco Perfetti (Genoa: Fondazione del Vittoriale), pp. 179–90.

1996 Obituary of J. H. Whitfield in *Renaissance Studies*, 10, 122–25.

1996 'Caveat lector: D'Annunzio's autobiographical prestidigitation' (review article), *Modern Language Review*, 91, 610–18.

1997 'La Regina Victoria, Samuel Butler e il Grand Tour', in *Storia di Terre, Storia di Lago: Atti del convegno*, ed. by Luigi Polo Fitz (Novara: Istituto per la Storia del Risorgimento), pp. 183–203.

1997 'Dante and Governance, contents and contexts', in *Dante and Governance*, pp. 1–11.

1998 'D'Annunzio and Yeats', *Journal of Anglo-Italian Studies*, 5, 212–30.

1998 'Per un'analisi della rottura tra D'Annunzio e il Generale Ceccherini, con un carteggio inedito', *Rassegna dannunziana*, 15, 1–10.

1998–2000 Various obituaries of Cecil Grayson in the *Times*; *Italian Studies*, 54, 1999, 1–4; *Annual Report of the Dante Society of America*, 116, 277–81, *Proceedings of the British Academy*, 105, 460–70, *Bibliofilia*, 102, 237–40.

1999 'D'Annunzio e l'impresa fiumana: reazioni britanniche, con uno studio delle carte diplomatiche inedite del *Foreign Office*', *Rassegna Dannunziana*, 18:38, 27–34.

2000 'Towards a revival of Borghini Scholarship', (review article) *Modern Language Review*, 95, 85–91.

2000 'The Rise and Fall of the Renaissance Gentleman: Castiglione and the Courtesy Books', in *The Rise and Fall of the Renaissance Gentleman*, ed. by Dante Marianacci (Edinburgh: Quaderni dell'Istituto Italiano), pp. 15–27.

2000 'Tradurre o tradire l'*Alcyone*: i problemi inerenti', in *Da Foscarina a Ermione: Alcyone: prodromi, officina, poesia, fortuna: Atti del convegno*, ed. by Edoardo Tiboni (Pescara: Ediars), pp. 237–52.

2000 'D. G. Rossetti's translation and illustration of the *Vita nova*', in *Britain and Italy: From Romanticism to Modernism. Essays for Peter Brand*, ed. by Martin McLaughlin (Oxford: Legenda), pp. 67–86.

2000 *Introduction* to Baldesar Castiglione, *The Book of the Courtier*, translated with notes by Leonard Ekstein Opdyke (Chatham: Wordsworth Books), pp. ix-xxv.

2001 'Dall'Alberti al Castiglione: ammonimenti pratici di cortesia, di comportamento e di arrivismo', in *Leon Battista Alberti e il Quattrocento: Atti del convegno*, ed. by Luca Chiavoni (Florence: Olschki), pp. 193–210.

2001 'L'avventura fiumana', in *Le molte vite dell'Immaginifico. Biografia, mitografia e aneddotica: Atti del convegno*, ed. by Edoardo Tiboni (Pescara: Ediars), pp. 173–87.

2001 'The Rossetti siblings in the correspondence of their father', *Journal of Anglo-Italian Studies*, 6, 303–20.

2001 'The reputation of Gabriele D'Annunzio in the British Isles', in *D'Annunzio e le Isole Britanniche*, ed. by Dante Marianacci & John Woodhouse (Edinburgh: Quaderni dell'Istituto Italiano, 2001), pp. 9–17

2002 '*Il gran Pan non è morto*: the vitality of D'Annunzio's irrepressible critics', (review article), *Modern Language Review*, 97, 850–62.

2002 'Literature 1900–1944', in *Liberal and Fascist Italy*, ed. by Adrian Lyttleton (Oxford: Oxford University Press), pp. 216–32.

2002 'Tra glottologia e genealogia: lo storicismo civico-patriottico di Vincenzio Borghini', in *L'Accademia della Crusca per Giovanni Nencioni*, ed. by Domenico De Martino (Florence: Le Lettere), pp. 131–41.

2002 Sixteen miscellaneous entries in *The Oxford Companion to Italian Literature*, ed. by Peter Hainsworth & David Robey (Oxford: Oxford University Press).

2003 'Dal *De curialium miseriis* al *Libro del cortegiano* e oltre', in *Il sogno di Pio II e il viaggio da Roma a Mantova: Atti del convegno*, ed. by Arturo Calzona et al. (Florence: Olschki), pp. 423–41.

2004 'La dinastia rossettiana a Londra', in *Gabriele Rossetti a 150 anni dalla morte: Atti del convegno*, ed. by Gianni Oliva (Naples: Loffredo), pp. 85–105.
2004 'L'assegnazione al Poeta nel 1917 della *Military Cross*', *Rassegna Dannunziana*, 22:45, 49–51.
2004 'Qualche ricordo tra Firenze e Bologna', in *Per i cento anni di un Maestro: scritti in onore di Raffaele Spongano*, ed. by Emilio Pasquini & Vittorio Roda (Bologna: Bonomia Press), pp. 161–63.
2004 Entries on 'Arthur Serena' and 'Cecil Grayson', in the *Oxford Dictionary of National Biography*, ed. H. C. G. Matthew, 60 vols (Oxford: Oxford University Press)
2005 'Teofilo Folengo, buongustaio compassionevole', in *Da Dante a Montale: Studi in onore di Emilio Pasquini*, ed. by Gian Mario Anselmi et al. (Bologna: Gedit), p. 419–29.
2005 'D'Annunzio e i suoi corrispondenti anglofoni nell'Archivio del Vittoriale', in *D'Annunzio epistolografo: Atti del convegno*, ed. by Edoardo Tiboni (Pescara: Ediars), pp. 424–33.
2005 'I valori sempiterni dell'opera di Francesco Petrarca', in *Petrarca e la Lombardia*, ed. by Giuseppe Frasso, Giuseppe Velli & Maurizio Vitale (Roma-Padova: Antenore), pp. 1–12.
2005 'Giacomo Leoni, la traduzione del *De re aedificatoria*, e influssi albertiani sull'architettura inglese del Settecento', in *Leon Battista Alberti tra scienze e lettere: Atti del convegno*, ed. by Alberto Beniscelli & Francesco Furlan (Genoa: Accademia Ligure di Scienze e Lettere), pp. 195–216.
2006 'Dannunzio's Theatre', in *A History of Italian Theatre*, ed. by Joseph Farrell and Paolo Puppa (Cambridge: Cambridge University Press), pp. 323–38.
2006 'La dimensione umana del *De re aedificatoria*: Dall'architrave al vaso da notte', in *Leon Battista Alberti teorico delle arti e gli impegni civili del 'De Re Aedificatoria'*, ed. by Paolo Francesco Flore (Florence: Olschki, 2006), pp. 403–17

Various reviews not listed, in *Italian Studies, Journal of the Royal Society of Arts, Lettere italiane, Medium Aevum, Modern Language Review, Notes and Queries, Studi e Problemi di Storia Letteraria, Times Literary Supplement*.

INDEX

❖

Abba, Giuseppe Cesare 11
Abruzzo 3, 55–77
Accademia d'Italia, Reale 114, 115, 131 n.9
Ackroyd, Peter 29, 36 n.24
Adria, L' 99
Aeschylus 121
Albanese, Guido 55
Alfieri, Vittorio 1, 11
Allen, Woody 33, 172
Amerighi, Talía 41
Angier, Carole 23–36
Anissimov, Myriam 34 n.1
anni di piombo 5, 170, 174
Antongini, Tom 11, 114
Arafat, Yasser 190, 191, 196
Aretino, Pietro 11
Ariosto, Ludovico 11, 123
Artieri, Giovanni 133, 139, 141
Asor Rosa, Alberto 155
Augustine, St 190

Bacon, Roger 172, 184 n.29, 210 n.52
Baiardo, battle of 151, 158, 160–62, 164
Baldacci, Luigi 121
Balzac, Honoré de 107
Barbella, Costantino 59, 64, 65, 69, 71
Barcelona 136
Barenghi, Mario 149, 154, 160
Barrès, Maurice 116
Barthes, Roland 97
Barzilai, Salvatore 102, 110 n.18
Barzini, Emma 133, 136, 143 n.5
Barzini, Luigi 133, 139, 143 n.2
Bassani, Giorgio 154
Bassich, Mario 100, 101
Baudelaire, Charles 97, 105
Belforte, Francesco 135, 144 n.18
Bellis family 91
Benco, Silvio 102, 110 n.28
Benda, Julien 25
Benedetti, Achille 133, 136, 140
Benedetti, Carla 167 n.40
Berlusconi, Silvio 197
Bhutto, Ali 190
Biagi, Guido 42, 45
Bianchini, Luisa 81, 92
Bin Laden, Usama 194, 195, 196, 199, 200, 201, 202

Bishop, Elizabeth 18
Blair, Anthony 197
Blumenthal, Liuba 17
Boccaccio, Giovanni 10, 63, 126
Boccardi, Alberto 100
Boccioni, Umberto 123
Bontempelli, Massimo 4, 5, 114–32
Borgese, Giuseppe Antonio 39
Boswell, James 11, 28
Bottai, Giuseppe 20, 115, 117, 119, 129, 131 n.16, 166 n.23
Botteghe oscure 156
Bourdieu, Pierre 97
Brandeis, Irma 17–18
Briganti, Alessandra 99
Brigate rosse 179
Broglio, Mario 132 n.30
Browning, Robert 39, 41
Buontalenti, Bernardo 85

Calvino, Italo, 4, 5, 6, 14, 21, 35, 148–67
Calvino, Mario (father) 152, 149–64
Calvino, Evelina (Eva) Mameli (mother) 155–57, 159, 163
Camon, Ferdinando 161, 164, 166 n.29
Campbell, Anne 88
Campbell, John 88
Campbell, Marion 88, 89
Campo, Cristina 20
Capa, Robert 135
Caprin, Giuseppe 100–03
Capuana, Luigi 38, 121
Caramanico dei Conti d'Aquino, Princess 41
Caramelli, Ermengarda 42
Cardarelli, Vincenzo 131 n.10
Carducci, Giosuè 38, 41, 42, 44, 50, 51, 99, 107, 121, 124–26
Carlyle, Thomas, 38, 45, 46, 50
Carney, W.P. 134
Carrà, Carlo 126, 127
Casanova, Giacomo 11
Casaubon, Isaac 170–86
Cascella, Basilio 65
Casini, Tommaso 126
Cauda, Giovanni 105
Cellini, Benvenuto 1, 11
Cesari, Giulio 102, 103, 108

Champollion, Jean-François 181
Cherbuliez, Victor 107
Chesterton, G. K. 178
Chiarini, Giuseppe 41
Christian Democrats 179
Cianca, Alberto 194
Cicognani, Bruno 40, 42, 45
Cima, Annalisa 17
Cocteau, Jean 25
Colautti, Arturo 11 n.17
Coleridge, Samuel Taylor 25
Communism / communists 4, 13, 134–42, 148, 152, 175, 199
Comte, Auguste 101
Conrad, Joseph 25, 35 n.12, 163–64, 167 n.43
Contini, Gianfranco 17, 18, 159
Convito, Il (periodical) 47, 101
Corpo Truppe Volontarie (CTV) 139–43
Corpus Hermeticum 172
Corriere della sera 133–34, 188, 191, 203
Corti, Maria 14, 21 n.12
Cossu, Duilio 166
Coverdale, John F. 143 nn. 2 & 13
Croce, Benedetto 19, 35 n.11, 39, 42, 47, 125–26, 128, 148
Cronaca Bizantina 38, 41, 66, 99, 101, 110 n.17
Cross, Donatella 60
Crusades 170, 197
Culler, Jonathan 189

D'Ancona, Alessandro 126
D'Annunzio, Gabriele 1, 3–6, 10, 11, 38–53, 55–77, 99, 101, 109 n.12, 110 n.17, 114–32
Dalai Lama 190
Dante 2, 10, 11, 16, 25, 52 n.34, 99, 116, 118, 168
Darwin, Charles 4, 25, 101, 106
Daudet, Alphonse 105, 106, 112 n.62
De Amicis, Edmondo 38, 99
De Bortoli, Ferruccio 188, 192–93
Decadence 2, 4, 46–50, 71, 125
De Cecco, Paolo 65, 70
Dee, John 175, 185 n.31
De Franceschi, Camillo 102
De' Giorgi, Elsa 14, 21 n.13
Degli Uberti, Anna 17
Del Lungo, Isidoro 42
De Nardis, Camillo 70
De Sanctis, Alessandro 99
De Stefano, Cristina 20
Dictionary of National Biography 1
Divisionism 81
Domenica del Fracassa 41
Domenica letteraria 38, 110 n.17
Don Chisciotte (periodical) 99
Donzelli, Ferdinando 81, 87
Dostoevsky, Fyodor 25
Duprè, Giovanni 69

Duse, Eleonora 42, 131 n.23

Eco del popolo 110 n.18
Eco, Umberto 5, 168–87, 201, 203 n.15
Einaudi (publisher) 25, 26, 149
Eliot, T.S. 29
Espresso, L' 169, 173, 185 n.33
Ethiopia, conquest of 133, 139, 143 nn. 1 & 15, 179

Fabre, Jean Henri 25
Falange, the 138–39
Fallaci, Oriana 5, 188–204
Falqui, Enrico 124
Fanfulla della Domenica 38, 41, 110 n.17
Fascism 4, 9, 11, 13, 14, 16, 17, 19–20, 21 n.20, 22, 28, 113–15, 117, 119, 129, 130 n.6, 131 n.8, 131–45, 150, 156, 161, 163, 166, 175, 179, 180, 187, 190, 194, 201
Fassino, Piero 25, 35 n.11
Ferdinand I of Tuscany 85
Ferrari, Paolo 104
Ferretti, Gian Carlo 159
Fink, Guido 154
First World War 16, 19, 39, 100, 133
Flamini, Francesco 126
Flaubert, Gustave 97, 106
Florence 12, 14, 16, 19, 20, 38, 40–42, 44, 47, 61, 63, 79, 87, 109 n.9, 110 n.20, 171, 184 n.14
Fo, Dario 201, 203 n.15
Fo, Jacopo 201, 203 n.15
Fogazzaro, Antonio 11, 38, 49, 54 n.69, 101, 105
Follett, Ken 196
Forgacs, David 47
Forte, Riccardo 133
Fortini, Franco 15, 21 n.20, 166 n.32
Foscolo, Ugo 11
Fracci, Carla 17
Franco, General Francisco 134–42
Freemasons 172, 178
Freud, Sigmund 27
Futurism 4, 118–32

Gabinetto Vieusseux 16–19
Gadda, Carlo Emilio 11–14, 20, 114, 130 n.2
Galli, Dina 125
Galli, Lina 101–02
Garibaldi, Giuseppe 11, 115, 131 n.10
Garibaldino, Il, 143 n.3
Garosci, Aldo 194
Gasperi, Jolanda 25
Gatto, Alfonso 150
Gatt-Rutter, John 101, 103
Gayre, Reinold 88
Gazzetta del popolo, La 133
Gelli, Lucio 183
Gentilli, Alberto 102
Ghiglia, Oscar 79
Gide, André 25

Ginzburg, Natalia 20
Giubbe Rosse 127
Giustizia e libertà 13
Goldoni, Carlo 11, 104
Gravina, Maria 65
Grita, Salvatore 107
Guadalajara 139, 140, 142
Guarnieri, Silvio 14, 19
Guglielminetti, Marziano 51 n.11

Hamilton, Ian 29
Hardouin di Gallese, Maria 65
Harry Potter 196
Hemingway, Ernest 135
Hendrefigillt 72–95
Hérelle, Georges 65
Hermeticism 12, 117
Hitler, Adolf 20
Holmes, Richard 29–30
Holroyd, Michael 30, 35 n.9, 36 n.23
Homer 25, 56
Humanism 10, 11, 109 n.9, 202
Huntington, Samuel 192
Huxley, Aldous 25

Ibsen, Henrik 121, 131 n.23
Indipendente, L' 3, 98–108
irredentismo 100, 102
Isella, Dante 17

Johnson, Barbara 189
Johnson, Chalmers 201
Johnson, Samuel 28, 207
Jovanotti 201
Joyce, James 97, 98, 108, 193
Jurettig, Enrico 100

Kabbalah, the 170, 172, 176
Kilberry 88
Kircher, Athanasius 172, 176, 181–82, 185 n.31, 187 n.61
Knockbuy 88
Koestler, Arthur 137

Lacerba 128
Leconte de Lisle, Charles-Marie 105–06
Legionario, Il 133
Leoni, Barbara 3, 65–67, 72
Leopardi, Giacomo 10, 11, 18, 114, 123, 132 n.31, 167 n.38
Levi, Carlo 155–56
Levi, Lucia 28, 30
Levi, Michele 25
Levi, Primo 2, 5, 20, 23–36
Licata, Glauco 134, 145 n.49
Lilli, Laura 143 n.1
Lilli, Virgilio 133–42
Livorno (Leghorn) 3, 79–96

Lloyd Cricchio, Margaret 82, 86, 87, 94 n.23, 95 n.25
Lloyd family 79–96
Lloyd, Llewelyn 3, 79–96
Lodi, Luigi 71, 110 n.17
Lombroso, Cesare 101
London, Jack 25
Longanesi, Leo 16, 133
Lull, Ramon 172, 182

Macchiaioli 3, 79
Machiavelli, Niccolò 11, 111 n.48
Madrid 133–36, 140
Maier, Bruno 104
Malaparte, Curzio 120, 131 n.19
Manzoni, Alessandro 25, 35 n.21, 136
Maraini, Dacia 201, 203 n.15
Marcenaro, Giuseppe 17, 18
Marinetti, F. T. 4, 118–20, 122–23, 127–30
Marino, Giovambattista 67
Markus, Dora 17
Martini, Fernando 41, 42, 44
Marxism and Marxists 136, 137, 173, 174
Marzocco, Il 42, 101
Massai, Mario 133
Matcovich, Enrico 100
Mayer, Susan 89, 90, 95 n.36
Mazzini, Giuseppe 44, 45, 105 n.15
Medici, Francesca de' 85
Messina, Bianca 19
Messina, Francesco 19
Micheli, Guglielmo 93
Michetti, Francesco Paolo 3, 58, 64–73
Michetti, Giorgio 70
Michetti, Nunziata 65
Milan 16, 110 n.20, 127, 128
Milanini, Claudio 151, 156, 165 n.11
Modigliani, Amedeo 79
Moloney, Brian 103, 105, 106
Momigliano, Arnaldo 115
Montale, Eugenio 2, 5, 11–22, 108 n.2
Montanelli, Indro 145 n.49
Montano, Ettore 70
Montello, Il 129
Morelli, Domenico 66
Moro, Aldo 179
Mortari, Curzio 133
Mussolini, Benito 1, 9, 13, 121, 133, 134, 138, 141, 143 n.2, 150

Naples 41, 63, 64, 69, 101, 140
Napolitano, Gian Gaspare 133
Nardi, Isabella 40, 43–46
Nardi, Piero 11
Nascimbeni, Giulio 16–17, 19
Naturalism 46, 66, 191, 103, 106–07, 112 n.62
Nencioni, Enrico 3, 5, 38–54, 56
neorealism 158

Nerval, Gérard de 29, 30
Nicoli, Paola 17
Nietzsche, Friedrich 25, 101, 131
Nissim, Luciana 25
Nordau, Max 101, 105
Nuova Antologia 38, 41, 42
Nuovo Tergesteo, Il 100, 109 n.15

Oberdan, Guglielmo 100, 102
Ockham, William of 181
Ohnet, Georges 103
Ojetti, Ugo 80
Omnibus 133
Orcagna, Andrea 72
Orel, Silvana Monti 98, 99
Orwell, George 135

P2: 186 n.54
Palazzo Pitti 48, 79
Palizzi, Filippo 66
Panagoulis, Alekos 189
Pannilini, Count Augusto Gori De 41
Panzini, Alfredo 131 n.18, 132 n.36
Papi, Laura 17
Papini, Giovanni 123, 127–29
Papini, Roberto 81
Paradosso, Il 149, 156, 164
Pascarella, Cesare 99
Pascoli, Giovanni 110 n.18, 120, 121
Pasolini, Pier Paolo 15, 179
Pater, Walter 38, 45, 71
Pavese, Cesare 12
Pellico, Silvio 11
Penna, Sandro 18, 19
Pentich, Graziana 150, 164
Pepe, Vittorio 70
Pepys, Samuel 11
Perec, Georges 26
Pergolesi, Giovanni Battista 115
Pescara 55–77, 114–17, 119, 125–26
Pescio Bottino, Gemma 148–49, 165
Petrarch 1, 6, 10, 11, 14, 16
Pettinato, Concetto 133
Pintor, Giaime 19
Piovene, Guido 4, 5, 133, 136–39, 141, 144 n.29
Pirandello, Luigi 28, 114, 121–22, 130, 131 nn.18 & 36
Placci, Carlo 40, 42, 43, 52 nn. 33 & 34
Poggiali, Ciro 133
Popolo d'Italia, Il 121, 133
positivism 11, 46, 191, 176
Postel, Guillaume 172, 182
Pratolini, Vasco 13
Praz, Mario 39, 47
Pre-Raphaelites 3, 47
Primoli, Joseph-Napoléon 41–43, 52 n.33

Quilici, Nello 133, 135

Radcliffe, Ann 63
Rame, Franca 201, 203 n.15
realism 11, 46, 98, 108 n.6, 164
Rebay, Luciano 17
Renaissance 6, 10, 11, 41, 124, 171, 175
Renan, Ernest 101, 104
Renier, Rodolfo 126
Resistance 13, 35 n.11, 150, 155, 164, 175, 186 n.42, 189, 190, 201
Revelli, Nuto 25
Rodocanachi, Lucia 17
Roero, Percivalle 166 n.20
Romagnoli, Ettore 126
Rome 10, 12, 13, 41–44, 64, 65, 67, 79, 101, 110 n.18, 117, 136, 139, 141, 144 n.42
Rosicrucians 172, 176, 182, 184 n.26
Rossetti, Dante Gabriel 38, 47
Rossetti, Domenico 98, 109 n.9
Rossetti, Gabriele 1
Rossi, Cesare 102
Rossi, Ernesto 100
Rossi, Esterina 17
Rossi, Paolo 176
Roth, Philip 33
Ruinas, Stanis 133, 137, 139–41, 144 n.42
Rushdie, Salmon 195
Russolo, Luigi 128

Saba, Umberto 25
Salinger, J. D. 29
Salmoni, Alberto 28
Salvemini, Gaetano 194
Salvini, Tommaso 42
Sandri, Sandro 133, 138, 143 n.3
Sartorio, Giulio Aristide 65
Savinio, Alberto 122, 131 n.8, 132 n.27
Scarfoglio, Edoardo 65, 99, 101, 104, 107, 109 n.12
Scarlatti, Alessandro 115
Schopenhauer, Arthur 103, 104
Sciascia, Leonardo 35 n.10, 135, 142, 179
Second World War 4, 13, 141, 175
Segala, Renzo 133, 134, 136, 138–40, 145 n.50
Serao, Matilde 38, 41, 42, 65, 99, 110 n.19
Serri, Mirella 19
Servadio, Gaia 25
Settembrini, Luigi 11
Seymour, David 135
Shakespeare, William 103, 106
Shaw, George Bernard 101
Shelley, Mary 38
Shelley, Percy Bysshe 29, 190
Sicily 142
Singer, Chichita 166
Slataper, Scipio 98, 104, 109 nn.9 & 10
Società di Minerva 98
Soffici, Ardengo 123, 128
Sogliani, Ugo 100

Sommaruga, Angelo 99
Sorrentino, Lamberto 133, 135–36, 144 n.29
Spanish Civil War 4, 133–45
Spaziani, Maria Luisa 17
Spencer, Alessandro Gomez 143 n.5
Spencer, Herbert 101
Spurling, Hilary 23, 35 n.9
Stampa, La 133
Starace, Achille 166
Stephens, Pernbrook 134
Stevenson, Robert Louis 29
Stoppard, Tom 30
Strachey, Lytton 28
Strowel, Marie-Pierre 39
Stuparich, Giani 104
Svevo, Italo 3, 4, 5, 97–112
Swinburne, Algernon 38, 39, 47, 52 n.34

Tanzi, Drusilla 17
Templars 175, 179, 180
Tennyson, Alfred, Lord 38, 39
Terracini, Benvenuto 159
Terzani, Tiziano 201, 203 n.15
Thackeray, William Makepeace 40, 50, 51 n.15
Thomson, Ian 23–35
Tibullus 25
Tolazzi, Gerti 17
Tomaselli, Cesco 133
Tosti, Francesco Paolo 64, 65, 69–71
Tribuna, La 48, 67
Triester Zeitung 99
Trilussa 99, 125, 132 n.38
Trithemius 172, 180, 181
Turgenev, Ivan 101

Uffizi 79
Ungaretti, Giuseppe 6 n.4, 9, 11–15, 20, 114

Unification 2, 44, 50, 64

Valladolid 133, 139, 140
Vallecchi, Attilio 121
Valori plastici 132 n.30
Vamba 99
Vasari, Giorgio 11
Vassallo, Luigi Arnaldo 110 n.17
Veneziani, Livia 101, 102
Venice 115
Venturi, Marcello 163
Verga, Giovanni 106, 114, 115, 117, 121, 130
Veruda, Umberto 102, 103
Vico, Giambattista 1, 11
Villari, Paolo 42
Vita nuova (periodical) 52 n.40, 101
Vittorini, Elio 12, 13, 120, 154
Voce, La 109 n.9, 126
Volta, Alessandro 133, 137–38, 144 n.23
Vraie Italie, La 123

Wagner, Richard 101
Weimar Conference 19
Wells, H.G. 25
Whellens, Arthur 86, 87, 91, 95 n.25
Wojtyla, Pope (John Paul II), 197
Wollstonecraft, Mary 29
Woodhouse, John 1, 2, 5, 10, 55, 148, 149, 156, 164, 165, 168

Zampa, Giorgio 17, 18
Zampieri, Riccardo 100–02
Zamponi, Simonetta Falasca 143 n.15
Zehetmayr, J. W. Ll. 84, 86
Zoccolanti, gli 64
Zola, Émile 4, 56, 103–07, 111 n.39
Zucconi, Giselda 70